GREENING PAUL

GREENING PAUL

Rereading the Apostle in a Time of Ecological Crisis

David G. Horrell, Cherryl Hunt,
and Christopher Southgate

BAYLOR UNIVERSITY PRESS

Cover Design by Jeremy Reiss

Library of Congress Cataloging-in-Publication Data

Horrell, David G.
Greening Paul : rereading the apostle in a time of ecological crisis / David
G. Horrell, Cherryl Hunt, and Christopher Southgate.
p. cm.
Includes bibliographical references and index.
ISBN 978-1-60258-290-3 (pbk. : alk. paper)
1. Bible. N.T. Epistles of Paul--Criticism, interpretation, etc. 2. Nature
in the Bible. 3. Ecotheology. I. Hunt, Cherryl. II. Southgate, Christopher,
1953- III. Title.
BS2650.52.H68 2010
261.8'8--dc22
2010000790

Printed in the United States of America on acid-free paper.

CONTENTS

PREFACE

This book is among the outputs from a collaborative research project at the University of Exeter, UK, on "Uses of the Bible in Environmental Ethics" (for details and other publications, see http://huss.ex.ac .uk/theology/research/projects/uses). The project has sought to foster collaboration and interaction between biblical scholars and theologians, and this intention is embodied in this work, which reflects our diverse training, experience, and perspectives in the areas of biblical studies, science, and theology.

The project was funded by the Arts and Humanities Research Council of the UK, and it is our very pleasant duty first to thank the Council for their generous support (Grant no. AH D001188/1). The AHRC "provides funding from the government to support research and postgraduate study in the arts and humanities, from archaeology and English literature to design and dance. Only applications of the highest quality and excellence are funded, and the range of research supported by this investment of public funds not only provides social and cultural benefits but also contributes to the economic success of the UK" (www .ahrc.ac.uk).

We would also like to thank the other members of the project team —Francesca Stavrakopoulou, Dominic Coad, and Jonathan Morgan—

for many stimulating and helpful conversations, and also the members of our advisory board (in various capacities and at various times) — Edward Adams, John Barton, Stephen Barton, Esther Reed, and John Rogerson — for very valuable support and advice. We are particularly grateful to two international visitors, Ernst Conradie and Harry Maier, who each spent a month at Exeter as a Visiting Professor and whose insights and suggestions have greatly stimulated and enriched our work. We are also indebted to many others too numerous to name, both colleagues at Exeter and visitors to the project seminar; we would also like to thank all those who have offered comments and questions on the occasions when we have presented material related to this book at conferences and seminars.

We have incorporated into this book two of our previously published coauthored essays. In chapters 1 and 2 we have used (and expanded) our material in "Appeals to the Bible in Ecotheology and Environmental Ethics: A Typology of Hermeneutical Stances," SCE 21 (2008): 219–38. In chapter 4 we have similarly utilized "An Environmental Mantra? Ecological Interest in Romans 8.19-23 and a Modest Proposal for Its Narrative Interpretation," JTS 59 (2008): 546–79. We are grateful to the editors and publishers of both essays for their permission to reuse that material here. We have also drawn in various places on some of our previous individual publications. These are indicated in the notes and listed in the final bibliography. However, we particularly note our gratitude to Westminster John Knox Press for permission to draw on sections of Christopher Southgate's The Groaning of Creation: God, Evolution, and the Problem of Evil (Louisville, Ky.: Westminster John Knox, 2008), and to SCM Press for permission to reproduce parts of the argument of his "The New Days of Noah: Assisted Migration as an Ethical Imperative in an Era of Climate Change," published in Creaturely Theology, edited by Celia Deane-Drummond and David Clough (London: SCM Press, 2009), 249–65. Abbreviations follow SBL style.

We have worked together over the last three years on the material that here reaches published form, and every section of the book has passed through each of our hands (or rather, our computers) several times. Although we could each point to sections where an individual voice is most apparent, our thoroughly collaborative approach means that our individual contributions have been tightly woven together, sometimes after considerable debate and disagreement! This means, we hope, that this book is more than the sum of its parts, more, for sure, than any one of us could have produced alone. It also means that while we together affirm the arguments of the book as a whole, none of us would fully affirm, at least not with equal enthusiasm, all of the arguments proposed at every point. We hope it is not inappropriate here to express our gratitude to one another for our working together—and in such a way that friendships remain!

Last, but by no means least, we would like to express our individual thanks to those whose very particular love and support so enrich and empower our lives: Caroline, Emily, and Cate Horrell, Richmond Hunt, Iris and Kenneth Mills, Sandy Southgate, and Jac and Jane Copeland.

Exeter, August 2009

INTRODUCTION

In recent years environmental issues have come to the center of political and ethical debate. There are many such issues that call for our concern, from pollution and waste disposal to deforestation and species loss. The most prominent of all is undoubtedly global warming. The increasingly clear scientific evidence for anthropogenic global warming, and the alarming range of predictions as to its likely future impacts—not to mention the present impacts already evident around the world—make this issue among the most crucial (and difficult) long-term challenges facing the global community.[1] The change in American leadership from President Bush to President Obama has dramatically shifted the United States stance on this subject, and those who deny that climate change is a significant threat, or who question whether it is being exacerbated by human action, are increasingly the contemporary equivalent of "flat-earthers."

Questions about the environment, or about ecology—a preferable term in many ways, since it suggests the sense that we are talking about the communities of living things in which we find our home (*oikos*), rather than about things that happen to surround us (our *environs*)—

are therefore among the issues that call for attention from theologians and ethicists. But Christian theologians and biblical scholars have also been provoked into consideration of this topic by the critical questions that have been raised about the legacy and impact of the biblical and theological tradition, as we discuss in chapter 1. Is it the case that the biblical tradition inculcates an anthropocentric worldview, in which humanity is given license to exploit the earth for human benefit? Does biblical eschatology imply that the earth is of only passing significance for the elect who will be redeemed in heaven?

There has been considerable work done to explore, from a variety of stances, what the meaning and implications of various biblical texts are, and the ways in which they might contribute positively to a theological and ethical response to the contemporary ecological crisis.[2] Indeed, fresh engagement with biblical texts in the light of new and pressing issues, in ever-changing contexts, has always characterized the way the Christian tradition responds to such challenges.

Yet to date, despite frequent (often rather passing) appeals to certain favorite texts in the Pauline letters in support of the ecological agenda, there has been no thorough, wide-ranging attempt to read Paul from an ecological perspective. While such engagement can and should be fruitfully undertaken with the whole range of biblical texts,[3] there are good reasons to attempt this task with the Pauline letters. Paul's crucial and central role in the making of Christian theology has long been recognized, and it is famously expressed in the provocative claim that he is the "real" or "second" founder of Christianity.[4] While Christians will always insist that Jesus Christ is the founder of Christianity and the center of the New Testament's message, it is clear that Paul's letters provide not only the earliest Christian writings but also the crucial early reflections on the meaning and significance of the "Christ-event." It is Paul, above all, who is responsible for first articulating a gospel focused on the death and resurrection of Christ, an offer of salvation to all who have faith in him. Especially in the Protestant tradition, that essentially Pauline gospel of justification by faith in Christ has profoundly influenced the content and character of Christian theology. And just as there are critical and difficult questions to be faced concerning the ecological implications of other biblical texts, so too there are in regard to Paul: Does the Pauline tradition essentially and unavoidably set out a gospel focused more or less exclusively on the redemption of human beings, with an ethic correspondingly focused only on inter-human (or intra-ecclesial) relationships? Or can the Pauline letters offer resources for an ecological theology and ethics, for a Christian tradition reshaped and rearticulated in light of the ecological challenges that face us today?

That last question is, in a nutshell, the issue we address in this book. We do so, it is important to note, through an engagement with the Pauline corpus as a whole, rather than only with those letters generally deemed authentic. Each of the Pauline letters, whether or not written by the apostle, forms part of the canon of Scripture and thus stands to shape and inform Christian theology and ethics. This stance does not mean, however, that we ignore questions of authorship entirely or that we read the Pauline corpus as an easily harmonized whole. Indeed, we take care to distinguish the particular perspectives of different letters, notably in our readings of Romans 8 and Colossians 1 in chapters 4 and 5. Yet this care in distinguishing the different perspectives of each letter is equally important whether or not Paul is their author.

We begin, however, with a broader focus. The opening chapter constitutes a classificatory survey of the kinds of engagement with the Bible in general found in ecotheological writing—and in writing that opposes the contemporary environmental agenda. This survey is, we trust, valuable in itself both as an overview of a field of increasing importance, and as an attempt to elucidate the different approaches and assumptions at work in the various kinds of appeals to the Bible made in relation to this topic.

In chapter 2 we move to a critical analysis of these various approaches, an analysis that, drawing on the work of Ernst Conradie, leads to an argument for a particular stance toward the use of the Bible in ecotheological and ethical work. This stance falls somewhere between approaches that—to put it briefly and simply—claim to be presenting what the Bible really says and those that subject the Bible to critical evaluation according to a contemporary set of ethical values.

The position we outline here is crucial to the remainder of the book. We adopt a self-consciously constructive and creative approach, recognizing that we are reading Paul in the light of our own context and priorities, *making* new meaning from the texts, but seeking to do so in a way that is in demonstrable continuity with the Pauline material and is thus potentially persuasive as a faithful form of Christian theology.

A further aspect of our methodology is set out in chapter 3, where we outline the turn to narrative in general, and in Pauline studies in particular, and set out a classification of narrative types that informs our subsequent studies. This narrative methodology is important not only because some form of cosmological narrative is, we argue, at least implicitly present in all forms of ecotheology, but also because it enables us to explore Pauline texts fruitfully and allows those texts to contribute constructively to the formulation of a Pauline ecotheology.

The second main section of the book is devoted to the two Pauline texts most frequently cited in ecotheological discussion: Romans 8:19-23 and Colossians 1:15-20. In chapters 4 and 5 we deal respectively with these two texts, surveying the ways in which their ecological interpretation has emerged and employing a narrative approach in order to outline the "story of creation" that is implied in each case. In chapter 6 we then compare the two texts and their stories of creation. While we argue that these texts can indeed contribute a great deal to a contemporary ecotheology, we also suggest that many ecotheological appeals to these favorite passages pass too quickly over their difficulties, or too easily assume that they sufficiently indicate environmental-ethical responsibilities. One of the implications of adopting a consciously constructive stance toward interpretation is that we acknowledge fully that we are moving beyond what Paul (or other authors) "intended" and beyond what was conceivable or relevant in a first-century context. Picking up the methodological perspectives outlined in chapters 2 and 3, we draw on the material from Romans 8 and Colossians 1, interpreting it in ways informed and shaped by contemporary science and theology, and outline a hermeneutical "lens," one that both emerges from, and goes on to shape, our reading of the Pauline letters.

The final section of the book presents an outline of Pauline theology and ethics, seen through and shaped by this lens. In other words, having begun with the texts in the Pauline corpus that have (rightly) been recognized as of particular ecological relevance, we here proceed to an ecologically motivated rereading of Paul's letters more generally — a task that has not previously been attempted — in order to see to what extent the wider resources of Pauline theology and ethics might be fruitfully engaged in an ecotheological direction. In chapter 7, after briefly surveying the various attempts to identify a central theme in Pauline theology, we propose that a participatory perspective, with the theme of reconciliation at its heart, offers the most potential for an ecological rereading of Pauline theology. We argue that there is scope for extending the notion of participation to include all things, and not just the elect from humanity. Paul's letters offer glimpses of a "story of creation" that implies the goodness and ultimate redemption of all things: cosmic reconciliation can stand at the center of an ecological Pauline theology, and such a theology will be profoundly and inescapably eschatological — a point that highlights the importance of our narrative approach. We compare our Pauline ecotheological narrative with other contemporary ecotheological narratives, narratives that are often only implicit, and argue for the positive value of the Pauline model to contemporary Christian ecotheology.

In chapter 8 we turn to Paul's ethics, taking our point of departure from the proposal that two moral norms encapsulate the heart of Pauline ethics: other-regard and corporate solidarity. We argue that in relation to both of these themes there is clear potential to develop Pauline ethics in an ecological direction, recognizing that this entails going beyond what the texts themselves explicitly state or envisage. Other-regard, we propose, can legitimately be broadened to encompass the nonhuman community; and the particular pattern of other-regard to which humans are called can be described as a form of ethical kenosis. Corporate solidarity can also be developed, with good Pauline warrant, to encompass "all things"; and the notion of reconciliation, cast in a way that is scientifically as well as theologically cogent, can inform our ethical reflection on ecological issues. We also maintain, drawing on our earlier construals of a Pauline ecotheological narrative, that a Pauline ecological ethics must be eschatological. We thus place ourselves at a particular point in the story of God's liberation and redemption of the cosmos.

Included in this final chapter are reflections on possible concrete applications of this ethical perspective to specific issues in environmental ethics. In particular, we discuss the case for Christian vegetarianism and for action to reduce species extinction. Nonetheless, it is important to stress that this is not primarily a work of ethics, or even of theological ethics, but rather a work that establishes the hermeneutical groundwork for theological ethics, with some tentative pointers in the latter direction. As such, this book is intended to build strong connections between biblical studies and theological ethics, and to offer an example of the ways in which the biblical texts may be read and appropriated from a theologically, ethically, and scientifically informed perspective. And as we stress throughout this work, what this requires is an acknowledgment that interpretation is a constructive, creative task in which meaning is made in the interplay between the reader and her context and the texts in their ancient context.

This last comment also indicates our awareness that we read from a particular context, and that this inevitably and rightly shapes our interpretation. It is only proper to acknowledge, then, our own reading context, the "place" from which we interpret, even if we are only partly conscious of the extent to which that location shapes our reading.[5] We are white, British academics, shaped by the Protestant tradition, two of whom have a background in science, and whose perspective on the biblical texts is therefore strongly shaped by the findings of contemporary science with regard to subjects such as evolution and ecology. We have tried to take a fully international and ecumenical perspective, but we are doubtless shaped by our context in which, for example, arguments concerning creation versus evolution, or debates over various construals of Christian eschatology, are far less prevalent than they are in some parts of the United States. Yet we would also claim that our reading is more than simply a reading from a particular location. It is unavoidably that, of course, but we retain the hope that such located readings can communicate across a diversity of contexts and can, potentially, be found *persuasive* not only by those who (broadly) share our context, but also by those who do not. No doubt there will and should be many different perspectives on our current environmental challenges, perspectives whose priorities are shaped by the social location of their proponents. But there is a sense in which this is a global crisis, one that, as our political leaders frequently say, requires global solutions. For this reason it calls for a global discussion in which those from all locations speak and listen as we seek to discern a way ahead. To explore the ways in which a rereading of the Pauline letters might inform an ecological Christian theology and ethics is, needless to say, only a small part of what is needed in such a global conversation, but insofar as it may help to equip Christians to reshape their own perspective on our environmental crisis, it is, we hope, a task worth undertaking.

PART I

Toward an Ecotheological Hermeneutic

Chapter 1

A SURVEY OF ECOTHEOLOGICAL APPROACHES

1.1 INTRODUCTION

Our first task is to survey and seek to classify the kinds of appeal to the Bible that are made in the context of theological discussions of ecology and the environment. This opening chapter thus serves in part as a survey of an important and expanding field, and, more significantly, as an attempt to probe critically the hermeneutical modes in which interpreters operate, with a view to articulating a cogent stance for an ecological hermeneutic that will itself be both cogent and fruitful. In this first part of the book, then, our focus will be broad, our aim being to develop, through critical survey and methodological discussion, a framework for our ecological engagement with the Pauline writings. This more focused engagement with Paul will be the subject of the subsequent sections of the book.

In classifying uses of the Bible according to the type of hermeneutic they represent, we shall also make comparisons with the kinds of treatment of the Bible found in feminist theologies. The value of the comparison is not merely illustrative. In part it indicates the broad similarities between these two approaches to biblical interpretation, and reflects too the fact that they share common agendas and concerns (most evidently in ecofeminism). More significantly, it reflects our conclusion that in both forms of criticism—their important differences notwithstanding—there is a broadly similar relationship between contemporary theological and ethical commitments on the one hand and the biblical texts on the other.

A number of qualifications and caveats should be stressed at the outset. First, it should be noted that the classification we develop below is, inevitably, an oversimplification. Like any typology, it simplifies in order to categorize, in the conviction that important differences of approach can thus be highlighted. Second, it should be signaled in advance that the stances represented in our initial typology are, in fact, problematized in the following chapter, where a critical evaluation of the range of hermeneutical stances forms a basis for articulating a more cogent approach to developing what we call an ecological hermeneutic. Third, it should be stressed that, in many cases, the approaches we discuss below do not necessarily represent the way in which a given author *always* reads the biblical texts. Rather, the various stances represent different *reading strategies*; authors may consistently adopt one approach over others, or they may employ different strategies, depending, inter alia, on the text in question. Nonetheless, the classification is useful, we believe, in illuminating not only the different kinds of appeal to the Bible that are made, but also the different commitments that underpin these appeals.

Discussion of the impact of the biblical texts and the Christian tradition on contemporary environmental attitudes and practices has been hugely influenced by Lynn White Jr.'s now classic article on "The Historical Roots of Our Ecologic Crisis."[1] White is, apparently, "the most cited author in the field of the ecotheological discussion," whose short article has generated a host of responses from theologians and biblical scholars.[2] White argues that "[e]specially in its Western form, Christianity is the most anthropocentric religion the world has seen."[3] Sweeping aside other ancient mythologies, with their cyclical views of time and their animistic sacralization of nature, Christianity "not only established a dualism of man and nature but also insisted that it is God's will that man exploit nature for his proper ends." Thus, "Christianity made it possible to exploit nature in a mood of indifference to the feelings of natural objects."[4] White concludes that the active conquest of nature that characterizes the modern technological project, and which has led to the "ecologic crisis," has in large part been made possible by the dominance in the West of this Christian worldview. Christianity therefore "bears a huge burden of guilt."[5] White does not, however, dismiss the Christian tradition out of hand; he appeals to the figure of St. Francis as a positive model, a potential "patron saint for ecologists."[6] Also important is White's insistence that religious worldviews are of profound importance in shaping our actions; he does not see salvation in secularism:

> What people do about their ecology depends on what they think about themselves in relation to things around them. Human ecology is deeply conditioned by beliefs about our nature and destiny—that is, by religion . . . More science and more technology are not going to get us out of the present ecologic crisis until we find a new religion, or rethink our old one.[7]

White does not explicitly cite biblical texts, giving only an overview of the biblical creation story.[8] Discussing the making of humanity in God's image, he concludes that in the Christian tradition "[m]an shares, in great measure, God's transcendence of nature."[9] The rest of his arguments concentrate much more on the historic development of Christian thought and early science during his own period of specialism, the medieval era. Nonetheless, in seeking to refute White's claims, biblical scholars and theologians have often felt the need to engage with problematic biblical texts, focusing not only on the Genesis description of humans as in the image and likeness of God, but also on their mandate to subdue and rule the Earth (Gen 1:26, 28).[10]

While White's critique has led to a focus on the meaning and impact of the Bible's creation stories, questions have also been raised about the impact of biblical eschatology.[11] A number of biblical texts appear to present images of cosmic destruction, depicting what will happen on "the day of the Lord," the coming day of God's judgment and salvation (e.g., Joel 1:15; Amos 5:18-20; 1 Thess 5:2). Some texts suggest that catastrophes on the Earth must precede this final day of salvation (e.g., Mark 13:8, 24-25); others depict Christians' being "caught up" to meet the returning Lord in the air (1 Thess 4:16-17). Such texts, along with the enigmatic apocalyptic scenarios depicted in the book of Revelation, have, of course, shaped the development of contemporary Christian eschatologies. The critical question is whether such eschatological views, explicitly or implicitly, foster a view of the Earth as merely a temporary and soon-to-be destroyed home for humans, from which the elect will be rescued.[12] Second Peter 3:10-13 is widely recognized as the most problematic text from this point of view, since it not only depicts a coming day of cosmic conflagration, but also urges believers to act in such a way as to "hasten" the coming of that day.[13] The implication would be that preserving the Earth is hardly a priority, and may even represent opposition to the progress of God's eschatological purposes.

As Ernst Conradie notes, many biblical contributions to ecological theology have been "deliberately aimed at defending Christianity against the accusations of Lynn White."[14] Considerable energy has also been expended in attempts to demonstrate that the various eschatological texts do not undermine or contradict Christian efforts to care for the environment, and that the Bible's eschatological visions do not imply a devaluation of the current created order. The positive counterpart to this defensive response has been the effort on the part of various scholars to demonstrate "that the Bible can indeed offer profound ecological wisdom but that this has all too often remained hidden or implicit."[15] Taken together, both these responses represent our first category of uses of the Bible, one that, following Francis Watson, we shall term a strategy of "recovery."[16] We now discuss this in more detail.

1.2 READINGS OF RECOVERY
Rescuing the Bible from Misinterpretation and Recovering Its Ecological Wisdom

Focusing on the Pauline reception of Genesis 1–3 and feminist readings of these texts, Watson outlines two modes of biblical interpretation, recovery and resistance. For each approach he points out an analogy between the reading strategy and a biblical myth. "The Genesis myth corresponds to the revisionary reading that seeks to rescue the text from what is taken to be a history of misreading"—a reading of recovery.[17] In other words, the pattern of the Genesis story is one of a pristine beginning, of a good and positive place, which is lost and obscured through the disobedience that follows its initial creation. Similarly, readings of recovery reflect a conviction that the biblical text is "good," not itself the problem; the problems and distortions arise through the acts of later interpreters, who obscure and distort the positive meaning of the original. Such an approach is comparable with what Conradie, following Paul Santmire, describes as an "apologetic" approach to the relation of the Christian tradition to environmental issues: biblical resources provide a positive basis for an environmental ethic. In the context of feminist theology, such strategies have been termed "retrieval."[18] Put simply, the approach here is to argue that the biblical texts, rightly interpreted, can and do resonate with and support the reader's ethical perspective, be it feminist or environmentalist: positive resources to support such agendas can be derived from the text. The problems lie not so much in the texts themselves but in the traditions of their interpretation—which may be labeled, and criticized, as androcentric or anthropocentric, respectively.

Thus, a feminist strategy of recovery will be concerned to show, inter alia, how and where the biblical texts affirm the equality of women and men—as in Elisabeth Schüssler Fiorenza's reconstruction of earliest Christianity as a "discipleship of equals"[19]—or reveal the active participation of women in mission and leadership.[20] This equality and participation have, it is argued, too long been concealed owing to the androcentric bias and presuppositions of the "malestream" of interpretation: classic examples are found in the standard treatments of texts like Romans 16:7 (where Junia has until recently been misrepresented as a man named Junias) and 1 Corinthians 11:10 (where the woman's authority has long been misconstrued as her submission under authority).[21] It should be stressed here that most feminist exegetes do not work exclusively in the mode of "recovery," or "retrieval."[22] Suspicion, or resistance, is also an important reading strategy (on which see below). Nonetheless, the strategy of recovery represents one feminist mode for reading the Bible, and one that is particularly prominent—

for reasons we shall explore below—in what one might label evangelical feminist treatments.[23]

In relation to environmental issues, and specifically the charges Lynn White levels at Christianity, an ecotheological reading of recovery will be concerned to show, inter alia, that the biblical texts *can* be a significant source of ecological wisdom—that they do *not* sanction an exploitative form of human dominion over the Earth, *do* inculcate a sense of the goodness of the whole created order, and *do* convey a picture of redemption as encompassing "all things" and not only human beings. Such a claim is now embodied in *The Green Bible*, where the highlighting (in green!) of texts that refer to the Earth is intended to reveal the "clear" message of the Bible, that "[w]e are called to care for all God has made."[24] Let us consider some specific examples of such a strategy of recovery.

First, there are treatments of Genesis 1:28 which seek to redeem the text from being implicated in generating the attitudes and practices White criticizes so sharply. Norbert Lohfink, for example, though surprisingly without any reference to White, argues that the "blessing" of Genesis 1:28 refers to the divine plan for each nation to "take possession of their own regions,"[25] and for humans to domesticate animals in a way that establishes a form of peaceful coexistence,[26] such that it is inappropriate to use this text "to legitimate what humanity has inaugurated in modern times . . . The Jewish-Christian doctrine of humanity . . . regards human beings very highly, but it would never designate them as absolute rulers of the universe."[27] A sophisticated treatment of the same issues, this time explicitly in response to White's charges, is found in Richard Bauckham's essay on "Human Authority in Creation." Bauckham argues that

> the dominant theological tradition before the modern period did articulate a strongly anthropocentric view of the human dominion, largely as a result of imposing on the biblical texts understandings of the human relationship to nature that were of Greek, rather than biblical, origin. However, the facts that the dominion was understood as a static fact, not a mandate for extension, and the world was understood as created

ready and adapted to human use, not requiring large-scale technological modification, distinguish this view sharply from the interpretation of the dominion that accompanied the rise of the modern project of technological domination of nature . . . the medieval view was not itself sufficient to authorise that project.[28]

Thus Bauckham concludes that it was only with the Renaissance, and the separation of these anthropocentric ideas from their broader context in a theocentric worldview, that the notion of human dominion came to acquire a new significance.[29] This notion was developed in Francis Bacon's "vision of scientific progress . . . as the implementation of the God-given human dominion over nature, which Bacon himself presents as the meaning of Genesis 1:28."[30] Dominion came to be seen as a "historical task,"[31] with humans charged to "play the role of God in relation to the world."[32] Thus, according to Bauckham, "[t]he attitudes that have led to the contemporary ecological crisis can be traced back to this source, *but no further.*"[33] In essence, the claim here is that the problem lies not with the biblical text but only with the ways it was misinterpreted, first through the lens of essentially nonbiblical Greek ideas and then much later in the context of Renaissance views of human possibilities and progress. Indeed, Bauckham suggests, biblical themes such as the placing of humanity *within* the community of creation, and the praise of God by all creation, offer the basis for a positive environmental ethic and a theological framework within which dominion can be much more positively interpreted.[34]

A further highly influential attempt to recover from such biblical texts as Genesis 1:28 a message compatible with, and of positive value to, the ecological agenda is the reinterpretation of the notion of human dominion through the lens of a model of stewardship. For very many readers, particularly those writing from an evangelical stance, the language of rule and dominion can be reliably read as a mandate for a stewardship model of humans' care of the Earth, linked specifically with texts such as Genesis 2:15 and more generally with what is taken as a biblical picture of divine and kingly rule. Indeed, this model serves as a central plank in many attempts to construct a biblical environmental ethic.[35] Yet not only are there questions to be raised about the ethical value of the model itself, it may also be questioned whether it is such a "biblical" image as its proponents claim, particularly in terms of the relationship of humans to creation.[36]

There is a further "apologetic" strategy for redeeming Genesis 1:28 from White's accusations; this is found in efforts to retrieve a positive sense of the relationship between humanity and the rest of creation outlined there by highlighting the repeated declarations earlier in Genesis 1, that creation is valuable, is "good" in God's sight even before humans appear (vv. 10, 12, 18, 21, 25).[37] These texts are thus being "recovered" to affirm the value of nonhuman creation, thereby counteracting any strain of a human-nature dualism that denigrates creation.

As a second major example of environmentally focused readings of recovery, there are attempts to show how the figure of Jesus in the New Testament can offer a positive role model for ecotheology.[38] Probably the favorite Gospel texts for "green" theologians are the well-known verses where Jesus refers to God's care for birds and flowers (Matt 6:25-34//Luke 12:22-31; cf. also Matt 10:29). These are taken to indicate a harmony with and sensitivity toward nonhuman creation on the part of Jesus.[39] Mention is also often made of the extent to which Jesus' parables employ imagery of the natural world and agriculture.[40]

Adrian Leske develops these ideas through a study of Matthew 6:25-34. He locates this text within the tradition of prophetic vision of the coming renewal of creation, and suggests that Jesus is here reminding people "to live now as the restored covenant people."[41] The imagery of food, drink, and clothing relates to the anticipated celebration of the kingdom of God, often pictured in terms of a banquet. So the message is that "[t]he time of restoration has come."[42] This transformation is not only for humans, but encompasses the whole creation. In terms of ecological principles and practices, the text indicates that

> [a]ll beings have value, even the most insignificant like the birds of the air or the grasses of the field. Jesus calls on his followers to learn from nature around them, to listen to the voice of God's created world. This . . . implies a kinship with other members of Earth community . . .

[i]t also implies that every aspect of the Earth community—be it human, animal, or plant life—has its purpose in God's design, and thus is of intrinsic worth . . . this principle of interconnectedness . . . is an underlying theme in Jesus' saying on anxiety in Mt. 6:25-34 . . . Considering the prophetic background to these verses, the further implication is that members of the kingdom of God are called to share in the renewal process of all of creation and thus to do the will of their Father in heaven (Mt. 7:21). Ecojustice is an integral part of the will of the Creator.[43]

Equally positive about Jesus as a proto-environmentalist is Sean McDonagh, who writes that

[a] Christian theology of creation has much to learn from the attitude of respect which Jesus displayed towards the natural world . . . Jesus shows an intimacy and familiarity with a variety of God's creatures and the processes of nature. He is not driven by an urge to dominate and control the world of nature. Rather he displays an appreciative and contemplative attitude towards creation . . . The gospels tell us that nature played an important role in Jesus' life.[44]

He spent "formative" time "in the desert," "regularly returned to the hills to pray" and "regularly interspersed" his teaching "with references to the lilies of the fields . . . the birds of the air . . . and the lair of foxes."[45]

McDonagh goes on, as do many others, to point to specific Pauline texts as indications of a New Testament vision in which all creation is caught up in the redeeming and reconciling work of God. He sees the key texts as being Romans 8:18-25, Colossians 1:15-20, and Ephesians 1:10, which together proclaim the cosmic scope of God's saving work in Christ.[46] Again, interpretations pursuing this strategy may well point to the anthropocentric bias of previous interpreters as, for example, in interpretations of the Colossian hymn that (despite its apparently cosmic focus on τὰ πάντα) see its scope as (only) the church, or humanity in general (see chap. 5 below).

A third example of recovery is found in attempts to grapple with those eschatological texts that might be taken to imply that caring for the present world is an irrelevant distraction for Christians, since God has promised to bring an end to the current cosmos and bring about a new creation (a promise whose fulfillment Christians should eagerly anticipate). As we mentioned above, texts like Mark 13:24-31, Hebrews 12:25-29, 2 Peter 3:5-13, and Revelation 6:12-17, are those which most clearly call for a reading of "recovery" in view of the difficulties they raise. So, for example, in an essay on "New Testament teaching on the environment," Ernest Lucas seeks to address the apparent difficulties of 2 Peter 3. First, he notes that the most likely reading of 3:10 is not that the Earth will be "burned up," as some manuscripts and English translations have it, but that it will be "found," or exposed for judgment (cf. NRSV, ESV). Second, he argues that the term "elements" (στοιχεῖα) in 3:10 refers not to the physical universe, but to spiritual powers or heavenly beings. More generally, he argues that the author is probably using "figurative" language about cosmic events: "Hence we should be wary of reading it as a literal account of the end of the physical cosmos." The primary focus is on God's judgment, for which the metaphor of fire is used in the Old Testament. And since the author uses the Greek word καινός (new in quality) rather than νέος (new in the sense of previously nonexistent), Lucas argues that "although 2 Peter 3 is speaking of a radical transformation of the heaven and the earth, it is a renewal through transformation, not a total destruction of the old and its replacement by something quite different." Thus, he argues, "[i]t is certainly not a basis for arguing against Christian concern for, and involvement in, ecological issues."[47] A similar defense of 2 Peter 3 is mounted by Steven Bouma-Prediger. In conclusion he asserts, stressing similar points, that "the text rightly rendered speaks of a basic continuity rather than discontinuity of this world with the next . . . Biblical eschatology affirms the redemption and restoration of creation."[48] Indeed, the thrust of most defensive or "recovery"-like interpretations of the eschatological texts has been to stress that the biblical picture is not one of destruction and replacement but rather one of transformation and significant continuity.[49] As we shall see, even if this claim is correct (and it is open to very serious doubt, as we note in chap. 2 below), it does not so easily overcome the difficulties that the eschatological promises present for any attempt to validate an ethical mandate to preserve the Earth.

All of these ecological readings of recovery, in their various ways, are concerned to show that the biblical texts do have positive resources to offer to the ecological agenda, and that the regrettably anthropocentric and anti-ecological ideas that have fueled or colluded with exploitation of the environment stem from a history of skewed interpretation, rather than from the texts themselves. Just as feminist writers have drawn attention to the androcentrism of commentators and translators, and have sought to recover the texts from such misreading, so ecotheological writers have sought to identify the extent to which anthropocentric presumptions have affected the interpretation of the Bible, and have made attempts to recover the texts' ecological potential.

1.3 RESISTANCE TYPE A
Resisting the Bible in the Interests of Ecology

Differing fundamentally from readings of recovery are what Watson labels readings of resistance. In this case, it is the Exodus myth, rather than the story of beginnings in Genesis, which for Watson illustrates the mode of interpretation: instead of an attempt to return to a positive and valuable "origin," masked beneath subsequent layers of distortion, here the original itself is seen as the locus and cause of oppression which must be exposed as such and resisted.[50] Here the approach is not one of rediscovering the positive value of texts hidden beneath a history of misinterpretation but of facing, resisting, and escaping intrinsically negative texts. In the context of feminist hermeneutics, Fiorenza describes such an approach as an exercise of "suspicion,"[51] while Santmire uses the label "reconstructionist" for this sort of approach to engaging the Christian tradition with environmental issues: the biblical and theological tradition is considered so problematic that "a new edifice of thought must be built, from the ground up, with new foundations and new categories."[52]

In relation to feminist concerns, readings of resistance are concerned to highlight the misogynism and patriarchy explicit or implicit within the texts, and to expose the negative impact, real or potential, of these "texts of terror" upon women past and present. Resistant readings insist, sometimes in explicit opposition to apologetic attempts to claim biblical texts as supportive of feminist concerns, that certain texts and traditions are irredeemably patriarchal and resist feminist retrieval. Mary Daly and Daphne Hampson are well known for making this claim in relation to the Christian tradition as a whole.[53] Many studies, however, highlight the need for a resistant stance toward certain texts, without that implying any overall rejection of, or even resistance against, the tradition as a whole. As with a stance of "recovery," so too with "resistance" we are talking about one interpretative strategy that may be adopted by interpreters, *not*, in many cases, a consistent and constant interpretative position. Rather, as we shall see later, we are dealing with a reading stance that, on the basis of certain hermeneutical keys, leads to resistance in some instances, and not in others, often in the context of a broader attempt to "recover" the authentic and liberating word of God from the texts. Resistance (or suspicion) and recovery (or retrieval) are frequently seen, and practiced, as two essential aspects of the interpretative task. Here one might mention as examples Phyllis Trible's *Texts of Terror*, which explores the violent and damaging portrayals of women in some Hebrew Bible stories,[54] or Kathleen Corley's reading of 1 Peter. Corley insists that 1 Peter's call to follow in the footsteps of Christ in enduring suffering without complaint (cf. 1 Pet 2:18–3:6)

> merely perpetuates a cycle of victimization, violence, and abuse in domestic situations . . . [T]he myth of Jesus as "Suffering Servant" should not be made into a model for Christian life, particularly for Christian women . . . Of all Christian Testament texts, the message of 1 Peter is the most harmful in the context of women's lives. Its particular message of the suffering Christ as a model for Christian living leads to precisely the kinds of abuses that feminists fear . . . The basic message of 1 Peter does not reflect God's liberating Word.[55]

In relation to environmental issues, readings of resistance explicitly or implicitly side with Lynn White's critique of Christian anthropocentrism in their interpretation of specific biblical texts. Some, paralleling Daly and Hampson, conclude that a "turning to the Earth, as the one true dwelling place for human beings and all other living beings, must free itself from the Christian tradition,"[56] while others are more focused in their critique of specific biblical passages. Certain texts are seen as culpable in terms of generating damaging forms of anthropocentrism, or supporting views of the world as a resource for human exploitation, or as a material realm soon to pass away and thus expendable. From the perspective of commitment to certain ecological, or "ecojustice," principles, such texts must therefore be resisted and opposed. Again, as with comparable feminist readings, this may be done in deliberate opposition to studies that claim that the texts are really ecofriendly.

Some examples of this kind of approach may be found in the five-volume Earth Bible series. Fundamental to the studies produced by the Earth Bible team is a set of six ecojustice principles:

The principle of intrinsic worth: The universe, Earth and all its components, have intrinsic worth/value.

The principle of interconnectedness: Earth is a community of interconnected living things that are mutually dependent on each other for life and survival.

The principle of voice: Earth is a subject capable of raising its voice in celebration and against injustice.

The principle of purpose: The universe, Earth and all its components, are part of a dynamic cosmic design within which each piece has a place in the overall goal of that design.

The principle of mutual custodianship: Earth is a balanced and diverse domain where responsible custodians can function as partners, rather than rulers, to sustain a balanced and diverse Earth community.

The principle of resistance: Earth and its components not only suffer from injustices at the hands of humans, but actively resist them in the struggle for justice.[57]

In a way analogous to the functioning of feminist convictions, these principles effectively form an ethical standard against which the biblical texts are measured: the key task is to discern whether "the text is consistent, or in conflict, with whichever of the six ecojustice principles may be considered relevant" in any particular case.[58] Where the texts cohere with the principles, they may be fruitfully and positively read; where they do not, exposing and resisting may be more appropriate interpretative strategies. We noted above, for example, how problematic eschatological writings can be in relation to ecotheology. Thus, in investigating New Testament visions of the "End," Keith Dyer candidly notes "a huge problem for ecotheology in those texts that resist retrieval and advocate our . . . 'earnestly desiring' such an end" (cf. 2 Pet 3:12). The question for Dyer is to determine "[w]hich texts can be retrieved and which still resist" any attempt at positive ecological reading.[59] The volumes of the Earth Bible series therefore contain examples of readings of recovery and of resistance, depending on the texts in view—and, of course, on the stance and perspective of the reader.

Gene McAfee, for example, reads the story of Abraham in Genesis and finds it "frequently at odds with principles of ecojustice."[60] He also points out the forms of patriarchy inherent in the text. Howard Wallace is unconvinced by attempts to recover a positive reading of Genesis 1:28: "The roots of any modern ecological problems to which an emphasis on Genesis 1:28 and human domination of creation has contributed, would thus seem to be embedded in the biblical text itself and its own internal means of interpretation."[61] Keith Carley reads Psalm 8 as "an apology for human domination"—as a text which does not take account of the interests of the Earth and thus does not conform to the ecojustice principles.[62] The model of domination which the psalm presents and legitimates—"a classic expression," Carley suggests, "of the dominating male ego"—has been a cause of suffering for too long, and needs to be rejected.[63] Norman Habel, main editor of the series, and evidently concerned to confront the naive assumption evident in many works on ecotheology "that the Bible is environmentally friendly,"[64] poses a series of questions about John 1 and its attitude to Earth.[65] For Habel, "the text of John 1 seems to devalue the domain of Earth—the material world below—over against heaven, the spiritual world above."[66] Insofar as it does so, it does not reflect the ecojustice principles, and so must be subjected to "a hermeneutic of suspicion."[67] Habel offers a similarly critical reading of Genesis 1:26-31, insisting that "[t]he verb *kabash* ('to subdue') not only confirms the status of humans as having power over

Earth; it also points to harsh control . . . The orientation of the human story (Gen 1:26–28) is overtly hierarchical: humans are authorized to rule other creatures and to subdue Earth."[68]

In the Earth Bible project, then, we see first and foremost a clear commitment to ecojustice principles, worked out, we are told, "in dialogue with ecologists" but deliberately not formulated using biblical or theological terms, so as "to facilitate dialogue with biologists, ecologists, other religions traditions . . . and scientists."[69] The biblical texts are then read against the backdrop of these principles, and found to warrant positive recovery or negative resistance according to whether, and how, in their readers' view, they cohere with these principles. Indeed, it should be stressed that the Earth Bible project entails an approach which combines suspicion/resistance and recovery, though some essays (depending, of course, on the texts in view and on the author's perspective) offer a more "recovery"-oriented reading while others present a more consistently critical, resistant stance.[70] Both in feminist theology and in ecological hermeneutics, this stance of ethical resistance — a stance which exposes the problems and dangers of certain biblical texts — is well established in scholarly circles. Less evident in academic scholarship, but worthy of attention for its popular impact, is a different kind of resistance to which we turn next.

1.4 RESISTANCE TYPE B
Resisting the Ecologists in the Name of the Bible

Exactly the opposite approach to the one explored above is found in works that oppose the contemporary agenda, be it feminist or environmentalist, because of a conviction that such an agenda runs counter to the Bible. In these cases, it is the Bible — as interpreted, of course, by a particular community of readers — that is perceived as the final and non-negotiable locus of authority. Such anti-feminist or anti-environmentalist readings generally gain little attention in academic circles, where broadly liberal values and approaches informed by the tradition of biblical criticism tend to be dominant. But these readings warrant our attention because they are of considerable popular influence, especially in some evangelical and fundamentalist circles, notably in the United States.

In relation to the feminist agenda, this kind of resistance is represented in studies which insist that the biblical teaching does support male
headship and/or leadership, and that to sustain loyalty to the Bible and
avoid mere cultural conformity, the church should also adhere to such
views and their correlative practices. Examples of such a position can
be found in both evangelical Protestant and conservative Catholic circles. Wayne Grudem, for example, in his widely used *Systematic Theology*,
claims that although the Bible supports the equal dignity and value of
men and women, it also teaches that there are differences between them
in roles and authority (1 Cor 11:3), differences that reflect, amongst
other things, creational distinctions (Gen 2:7, 18-23) and the events of
the fall (1 Tim 2:13). This results in a clear expectation that, in Christian
marriage, a wife should be subject to her husband's authority, albeit
with an expectation of considerate loving care on the husband's part
(Eph 5:22-33; Col 3:18-19; Titus 2:5; 1 Pet 3:1-7).[71] John Paul II, while
emphasizing the mutuality of man and woman in marriage, also speaks
of women having specific vocations determined by their "genius"; such
a vocation cannot include a calling to priesthood because, in the biblical
accounts of the institution of the Eucharist, Christ's only companions
are his male apostles.[72] The same argument is used by Manfred Hauke,
who also uses the biblical texts (Gen 3:16; 1 Cor 11:3-10 and the household codes of Colossians and Ephesians amongst others) to support the
subordination (though not inferiority) of women to men.[73]

In relation to environmental issues, there are some arguments
that explicitly oppose the ecological agenda, and others that do so less
directly. Examples of the former include, from fundamentalist circles,
the books of Constance Cumbey and Dave Hunt, both of which view
"any attempt at environmental stewardship—even any use of terms
like 'ecological' and 'holistic'—as part of the [New Age] plot."[74] For
Cumbey and Hunt, any Christian talk of global awareness is evidence of
New Age influence, which is itself seen as a mask for a developing form
of satanic tyranny.[75] It should be noted, however, that, despite some
sharp criticism of evangelical Christianity's anti-ecological stance,[76] so
far as we have been able to ascertain, there are few examples of academic publications that directly criticize the practice of environmental

care.[77] When environmentalism is attacked, it is usually because it is seen as one facet of a broader target of criticism, such as the New Age movement—a key focus for evangelical anxieties in the 1980s—or theological or political liberalism, or as a distraction from the more important task of evangelism with a view to humans' finding salvation. Some Internet commentators, for example, cite texts like 2 Peter 3:10-13 as biblical proof that there is a fiery judgment coming, and that avoiding this through personal conversion is the real priority.[78] More significant to assess, therefore, is the impact of doctrines—especially eschatological doctrines—that might have a direct or indirect effect on environmental attitudes and practices.

In terms of a "biblical" reading that has less direct, but nonetheless significant, ecological implications, we should consider the broader connections between the views expressed by Cumbey, Hunt, and others, and the popular and highly influential reading of biblical eschatology known as dispensational premillennialism.[79] This form of eschatological expectation has been popularized in books such as Hal Lindsey's *The Late, Great Planet Earth* and more recently in the series of novels by Tim LaHaye and Jerry Jenkins.[80] On this view, history is divided into various phases, or divine dispensations, and will culminate in a great tribulation, a battle between good and evil (Armageddon), and a millennial reign of Christ on the Earth. Prior to the tribulation, however, Christians will be raptured from the Earth. While this eschatology is probably not of major significance in British and continental European Christianity, its influence in the United States is greater.[81] It has a significant if indirect impact on the environmental agenda to the extent that it fosters a view of natural disasters and signs of earthly decay as indicators of the imminent end, and as such to be welcomed. It also focuses Christian hope on the rescuing of the elect from a doomed Earth, rather than (say) on the liberation and renewal of all creation.[82] Working to preserve the natural environment is not only pointless, it is working against God's purposes (and thus for Satan's), since the destruction of the physical elements of the cosmos must happen before the End.[83] After the end of the cold war, in the United States, a "few evangelicals tried to harmonize premillennialism with an ethic of environmental activism, but the task was a difficult one."[84] Indeed, there are clearly still some evangelicals who maintain that the call to care for the Earth is a distraction from the real priorities of evangelism (see n. 78 above).

Remembering the caveats expressed at the beginning, we again have to beware of oversimplifications. In recent years, the perceived threat from the so-called New Age movement has seemed to wane in the minds of evangelicals. Also, the urgency of the environmental crisis has reached the public consciousness to a greater degree, emptying something of the appeal from the arguments of Cumbey and Hunt and bringing a wider acceptance of the need for Christian responsibility toward nonhuman creation. Thus we find a self-described premillennialist such as Tony Campolo seeking to engender the Christian practice of care for creation, while at the same time avoiding the perceived dangers of nature-worship. The book's title expresses these aims well: *How to Rescue the Earth without Worshipping Nature: A Christian's Call to Save Creation.*[85]

Nonetheless, other voices from the evangelical camp, while advocating Christian responsibility for the environment, are wary of tendencies to downplay the primacy of humanity within creation; they therefore dispute some apologetic approaches to the text. E. Calvin Beisner has offered a forceful critique of evangelical environmentalism from an evangelical perspective. Beisner does not deny the importance of caring for the creation, and agrees that humanity has a responsibility to exercise stewardship. But he disputes much of the evidence used to suggest that there is an environmental crisis, including that concerning the impact of global warming.[86] The environment, he insists, "is improving, not deteriorating."[87] Beisner notes that environmental devastation is often portrayed by the Bible as being caused by God, suggesting that the story of the withered fig tree might be construed as teaching us that "nature really should be expected to meet man's needs," and that wilderness is a negative image showing the effects of man no longer having dominion.[88] This interpretation is accompanied by an optimism regarding human technological progress, "stemming from the application of the Christian worldview," which Beisner sees as "a foretaste of the restoration of the cursed creation foretold by Paul and entailed by the Incarnation, death, and resurrection of Christ."[89] Beisner argues that humanity's God-given task is to turn the Earth from wilderness into garden, increasing its bounty and productivity, thus reversing the effects of fall and curse. He favors unfettered economic development as the best means by which developing (as well as developed) countries can increase their wealth and improve their environments. And he does not see any need for those in the richest countries, like the United States, to reduce their levels of consumption. Moreover, contrary to those environmentalists who see the size of the human population as a threat, "biblical Christians," Beisner argues, can be confident that

> continued population growth will result not in the depletion but in the increased abundance of resources, and not in increased pollution of the earth but in its increased cleansing and transformation from wilderness to garden, "from its bondage to decay . . . into the glorious freedom of the children of God" (Rom. 8:21).[90]

Beisner's angle on the Bible's teaching with regard to the environment well illustrates the argument of Harry Maier, surveying historical and contemporary debates among evangelicals and fundamentalists: that despite the general trend toward a "greening" of American fundamentalism, there is still a significant debate within these circles, with some opposed to this move.[91]

It would perhaps be easy for us, writing in Britain and in an academic context, to dismiss the views outlined in this section as those of a religious minority, whose form of biblical interpretation hardly warrants serious consideration.[92] However, it is worth pausing to consider the possible impact of this perspective, via its influence on the evangelical Right, on United States foreign and environmental policy.[93] It is disturbing to read, for example, how Hal Lindsey depicts both Communist and Arab countries as the key axes of satanic opposition to God's righteous ones.[94] With the end of the cold war that dominated the political terrain until the late 1980s, it is striking how the Islamic world has come into focus as the new and uncontested axis of evil.[95] More specifically on environmental matters, there is at least anecdotal evidence that expectation of an imminent parousia has, at times, shaped policy on the exploitation of natural resources.[96] James Watt, Ronald Reagan's secretary of the interior, "questioned at his confirmation hearing about preserving the environment for future generations, forthrightly replied, 'I do not know how many future generations we can count on before the Lord returns.'"[97] Despite Watt's statement being frequently quoted to suggest that he did not see preservation of resources as an issue, it is important to note that his statement continues, "whatever it is we have to manage with a skill to leave the resources needed for future generations."[98] Nonetheless, at the very least, the idea of the Lord's (possibly imminent) return is here linked with consideration about stewardship of natural resources. We may plausibly consider that a combination of theological tendencies and convictions—the idea of Christ's imminent return, or of a "rapture" of Christians from the Earth, a focus on the conversion and salvation of (human) individuals, and so on—can easily lead to a view in which the rest of creation is, at best, of secondary importance, or at worst, a mere stage for the outworking of the drama of human salvation, destined to be destroyed as the end times approach.

There is an interesting analogy here with the creationist movement, which is also strong in the same church circles that have promoted an implicitly anti-environmentalist stance in the politics of the United States. In that movement evolutionary views are resisted as being contrary to biblical teaching (as understood within that tradition)—both as to the character of the creation and as to humans' unique place in it—and also in some cases as being associated with a materialist metaphysic and an un-Christian ethic.[99] Ecological science may be resisted for the same combination of reasons: as offering an unbiblical cosmology and anthropology, being intrinsically anti-monotheistic, and as promoting an ethic contrary to the "American way."[100]

1.5 PRELIMINARY COMPARISON
Toward a Critical Assessment

While there are clearly all kinds of differences between the two types of "resistance," one notable similarity is that, in certain respects, they *agree* on what certain biblical texts *say and mean*: the texts *do* teach women's subordination to men, or creation's subordination to humanity; they do not teach equality of roles between the sexes, nor a responsibility to preserve the whole of creation. The basic disagreement concerns whether one should therefore resist the Bible, given a commitment to feminist or ecological values, or resist those ("secular," "liberal") values, given a commitment to the authority of the Bible. To this extent at least, the differences have to do not so much with what the text is interpreted as saying, but with the contemporary stance and ethical commitments of the readers, and their conviction as to where the locus of authority lies—or, perhaps better, the way in which they construe biblical authority within a particular model of biblical hermeneutics. The three modes of biblical interpretation discussed so far may be visualized and compared in tabular form:

Strong view of biblical authority	Resistance Type B: Commitment to biblical authority is taken to imply rejection of the ecological agenda	Recovery The Bible, rightly read, supports the "green" agenda
	(No strong motive to engage in biblical interpretation on this subject)	Resistance Type A: Commitment to ecological principles requires critical resistance of (some) biblical texts
		Strong commitment to ecological values

Naturally such a table simplifies crudely what is in reality a range of readings and reading strategies, just as the categories as a whole segregate the mixture of modes and strategies in many feminist and ecological readings of the Bible. But as with Weberian ideal-types, which never fully correspond with the more messy empirical realities, so these categories too can be valuable for analytical purposes, for helping us to see what is going on in different types of reading. A reading of recovery, particularly if pursued consistently as an overall approach to the Bible, reflects a strong commitment to both biblical authority (construed in a certain way, of course) and to ecological (or feminist) values. The two types of resistance we have labeled A and B reflect a primary commitment to one axis: to the Bible, in the case of the fundamentalists; to the principles of ecojustice, in the case of the Earth Bible project.

This preliminary analysis and comparison highlights, then, how different interpretations of the Bible, despite their being explicitly focused, often, on exegetical or historical arguments, are shaped by differing views of biblical authority and contemporary ethical commitments. Indeed, sometimes a particular view of biblical authority, combined with a particular contemporary ethical commitment, *requires* a certain kind of reading of the Bible, in order to remain internally consistent: an evangelical committed to a "high" doctrine of Scripture, but also convinced of the moral imperative to care for the environment, *must* develop some form of a reading of recovery, or else one or other of the convictions has to give. Yet, as we shall see in the following chapter, there are difficulties with each of these approaches to interpretation, and highlighting these difficulties can help us to articulate a more adequate basis for an ecological engagement with the Bible, and with Paul in particular. Having completed this classificatory and analytical survey, then, we proceed to a critical analysis which lays the foundations for an ecological hermeneutic.

Chapter 2

THE ROLE OF HERMENEUTICAL LENSES FOR AN ECOTHEOLOGY

In the previous chapter, we surveyed the kinds of engagement with the Bible that have emerged in relation to ecological and environmental issues, classifying these into readings of recovery (which seek to show that positive support for environmental care can be found in the Bible), readings of Resistance Type A (which resist and oppose biblical texts deemed to run counter to ecojustice principles or to denigrate the Earth), and readings of Resistance Type B (which resist the contemporary environmental agenda because of a conviction that these run counter to what the Bible teaches). There are, however, problems with each of the three strategies, and the identification of these problems can help us articulate a more adequate hermeneutical model. This is the task of the present chapter.

2.1 READINGS OF RECOVERY

Readings of recovery often involve strained and unconvincing attempts to show that a text supports and promotes the values for which the contemporary author is arguing. A number of the attempts to present an ecofriendly Jesus, for example, cited above, as with attempts to present a proto-feminist Jesus, seem to engage in rather unconvincing special pleading, and invite the criticism so long ago articulated by Albert Schweitzer in his devastating critique of previous attempts to write a life of Jesus: that in drawing their portraits of Jesus, these authors have in fact given a portrait of their own theological and ethical convictions. As Schweitzer put it, "each individual created Jesus in accordance with his own character."[1] Moreover, and this is a point to which we shall return, readings of recovery (and other readings too) can fail to take adequate account of the extent to which the texts are, unavoidably and necessarily, open to a range of different, plausible readings.[2] Competing readings of Genesis 1:26-28, for instance—as a mandate for human domination, or a call to responsible stewardship?—are often presented as arguments about the "real" meaning of the text. James Barr, for example, criticizes White, arguing that the Hebrew words are not as "strong" as has often been suggested, and that the biblical foundations of the doctrine of creation "would tend . . . away from a licence to exploit and towards a duty to respect and to protect."[3] Richard Bauckham's argument that the ideology of technocratic and aggressive human domination of nature can be traced back to the Renaissance "and no further" is a sophisticated example of an attempt to show that the text itself does not mandate such a project.[4] Yet the text in Genesis 1:28, as with any other textual example, can sustain a variety of readings, readings which, of course, arise from and are shaped by changing historical circumstances and specific readerly locations. As Peter Harrison insists, noting how the critical and historically focused responses of Barr fail to meet their target, the Lynn White thesis is not about the original, historical meaning of the text but about the history of interpretation, about what the text has been taken to mean.[5] Indeed, what readings of recovery can all too easily present as a rediscovery of the "real" meaning of the text, rescued from its pernicious "misinterpreters," is in fact an argument for a *better way of reading the text*, an argument that takes its place in the competitive arena of various possible readings; and the range of readings is itself always developing in new and changing contexts. What this redescription then implies, of course, is that we need to articulate (and argue about) the grounds on which we determine what constitutes "better" and "worse" readings.

A similar point could be made about the attempts to show that eschatological texts do not undermine a Christian call for environmental concern. Unlike those who are happy to employ both resistance and recovery—for whom certain texts, like Genesis 1:26-28 and 2 Peter 3:10-13, may be resisted and subjected to criticism—those committed to both a high view of Scripture and to environmental action have to try to show that such texts are not as problematic as sometimes thought. Yet as we have already noted in the previous chapter, there are both exegetical/historical and theological/ethical questions to raise. In terms of the exegetical/historical arguments that these texts imply a continuity between new and old creation, or use cosmic imagery to depict dramatic change on the sociopolitical plane,[6] Edward Adams' recent, thorough treatment makes it difficult to deny that at least some of the depictions of cosmic collapse in the New Testament (notably in Mark 13:21-27 [and parallels]; Heb 12:25-29; 2 Pet 3:5-13; Rev 6:12-17) do indeed envisage a destruction and re-creation of the cosmos.[7] Adams stresses that, given the range of conceivable cosmologies at the time, complete annihilation was not something that was envisaged. But he equally shows how the cosmic catastrophe texts do seem to have in view a real dismantling of the cosmos, a destruction or dissolution of the present world, followed by its re-creation or reconstitution in a radically new form. Moreover, even if some scenario of continuity with transformation is in view, as is most frequently argued by those seeking to rescue these eschatological texts from anti-environmental implications, this does not necessarily mandate any program of care for the present world. For God is very clearly the one who will bring about this new creation, and, in the process, will restore or remove whatever corruption and wickedness characterizes the present cosmos. Furthermore, this new creation, however much it is brought about by the transformation of the old, is depicted as being so radically different from the world of our experience and knowledge that no human action can bring it about.

In short, the key problem with a reading of recovery, when consistently pursued, is that it must seek to show that no text in the Bible truly undermines a commitment to environmental care, or, put positively, that the Bible as a whole can and does teach the importance of human concern for the Earth. The more this is presented as what the (whole) Bible "teaches," the more problematic it becomes.[8] The claim that stewardship, for example, constitutes "the Bible's picture of the intended relationship of God, humanity, and the created world,"[9] fails to acknowledge the extent to which this is a doctrinal construction, prioritizing a certain reading of humanity's role in the creation stories (e.g., Gen 2:15), construing "dominion" to mean stewardly responsibility (Gen 1:26-28), and generally applying a model of divine and kingly oversight to the human-nature relationship. In contrast to this claim, John Reumann notes how little steward(ship) terminology is used in the Bible, stating that "[t]here are virtually no Old Testament roots for what the New Testament and Church Fathers did with the *oikonomia* theme" and "[i]t cannot be claimed that *oikonomia* constitutes a major New Testament theme." Moreover, where this imagery does occur, it does not relate to human responsibility for nonhuman creation.[10] In other words, nowhere does the Bible *say* that humans are appointed stewards of creation.[11] This recovery approach therefore runs into difficulties in having to argue for what turn out to be exegetically implausible or fragile positions, at least in regard to certain "difficult" texts, and in trying to claim that environmental ethical action is directly anticipated and mandated in the Bible.

2.2 READINGS OF RESISTANCE TYPE B

Fundamentalist and evangelical readings of resistance ("Type B") can likewise be criticized for cloaking a particular and selective construal of the biblical message behind the claim to be presenting simply "what the Bible says." The key difference here is that what the Bible says is not seen as ecofriendly (or women-friendly, etc.), but the opposite. The stress in contemporary biblical studies on the diversity of theological and ideological perspectives represented in the biblical books of course runs directly (and deliberately?) against any such harmonizing appeals to "the" (singular) message of the Bible. But it does not require a very profound engagement with contemporary biblical studies to see how readings of resistance of the type we have surveyed involve both a very particular construal of the meaning of selected biblical texts and a prioritization of certain texts which serve, in effect, as a canon within the canon—the rule which determines the reading of the rest. What may be presented as "biblical teaching," or "what the Bible says," is rather a particular construal of certain biblical texts, prioritized over other biblical texts, and read in the light of a particular understanding of the reader's contemporary context. Yet it should also be acknowledged that the kind of anti-ecological interpretation of the Bible that this stance represents cannot be shown to be false or misguided through exegesis alone. The reading that sees passages speaking of cosmic catastrophe as anticipating some kind of total and literal cosmic collapse, and a replacement of the current world with "a new heavens and a new earth" (2 Pet 3:13), and sees the associated Christian responsibility as evangelism, is no less plausible a reading (and perhaps a more plausible reading) than that which stresses a continuity between the old and new creation in a bid to encourage and support Christian environmentalism. What this means is that the contest over differing approaches to the Bible and environmental ethics cannot be fought simply at the level of biblical exegesis, but equally requires an engagement with hermeneutical, theological, and ethical questions. Indeed, one issue these fundamentalist readings do raise, resistant as they are to the contemporary liberal agenda in environmental ethics, is the issue of how Christians can avoid having their commitments determined by broader ("secular") social trends and can retain a perspective from which to gain critical purchase on the world as it is.[12]

2.3 READINGS OF RESISTANCE TYPE A

The other type of resistance ("Type A") faces a different kind of criticism. By making clear and explicit its contemporary ethical convictions, and measuring the biblical texts against these, it eschews any claim that the Bible as a whole supports these convictions, and opposes—deliberately and explicitly—any naive reading of recovery that promotes the Bible as an ecofriendly (or women-friendly) text. In the Earth Bible project, for example, the Bible is granted no explicit authoritative status. Authority effectively lies with the ecojustice principles, principles which are not presented as emerging from the biblical or Christian tradition. Francis Watson, interestingly, traces this type of modern approach back to Kant's attempt, in *Religion within the Limits of Reason Alone* (1793), to offer an account of how the truths embodied in biblical and Christian doctrine can be independently discerned by "reason." Watson comments:

> Kant's work is the forerunner of all more recent attempts to interpret scripture on the basis of an ethical-political criterion that is already known independently of the texts. Scripture can only say what the criterion allows it to say [or, we might add, is criticized and resisted where it does not say this], and what it is allowed to say is only what we can already say to ourselves even without scripture. The textual embodiment of the criterion is of only limited usefulness, for the particularity of biblical narrative is an imperfect and potentially misleading vehicle for the universal truths of reason or for the various contemporary projects of liberation.[13]

By so clearly making a set of contemporary values the court of appeal, the canon against which various biblical texts are tested—as in the Earth Bible's ecojustice principles, where the principles are deliberately formulated so as *not* to show any connection with, or derivation from, the biblical and theological tradition—such approaches make no attempt to show how these values can emerge (or indeed have emerged) from a (particular) reading of the tradition, and thus, crucially, severely limit their ability to be *persuasive* for those within that tradition. It seems, in this approach, that the Bible is pretty much dispensable. While formulating the ecojustice principles in a nonreligious way may facilitate dialogue with those outside the Christian tradition (see above), it is unclear why anyone with no connection with the Christian tradition should be particularly interested in whether, and where, the Christian Bible conforms to or differs from any one of the six principles (cf. the lower left quadrant in the table in §1.5 above).[14] Conversely, to be potentially persuasive as an attempt to reshape Christian ethics, an ecological reading of the Bible would need to demonstrate that it offers an authentic appropriation of the Christian tradition. That claim, of course, begs a whole series of further questions, which cannot be fully addressed here. But we may at least begin to grapple with the issue of formulating an ecological hermeneutic by suggesting a further category which may prove a more fruitful and cogent way forward.

2.4 REVISION, REFORMATION, RECONFIGURATION
Toward an Ecological Hermeneutic

The crucial question that follows from the above is how to name and to explicate the kind of hermeneutic which is somehow positioned between recovery and resistance, which does not naively present itself as a recovery of ecological wisdom from the Bible ("Recovery"), nor distance itself from the Christian tradition through a prior and determinative commitment to ecojustice principles (Resistance Type A), nor distance itself from contemporary ethical challenges and the contribution of science to understanding those challenges through a reactionary claim to allegiance to the Bible (Resistance Type B). Paul Santmire's categories to label the various approaches to the relationship between ecological theology and the Christian tradition provide one way to begin to articulate such a hermeneutic. Having discussed "reconstructionists" (those who reject the classical Christian tradition as offering no viable resources for ecological theology) and "apologists" (those who defend the positive ecological implications of the tradition, rightly interpreted) — two categories which broadly correlate with "Resistance (Type A)" and "Recovery" respectively — Santmire describes a third approach in the construction of ecological theology which he labels that of the "revisionists."[15] These revisionists, among whom Santmire includes himself,

> have worked mainly within the milieu of classical Christian thought . . . Since, moreover, the Old and New Testaments are the font of the classical theological tradition in the West, and since these scriptures are taken as the chief norm for all teachers and teachings (*norma normans*) by the tradition itself, the revisionists, as a matter of course, also have given the highest priority to biblical interpretation. At the same time, however, the dynamics of the classical tradition, thus understood, constantly call forth a *re-forming* of the tradition itself, as that term itself has historically suggested.[16]

Similarly, James Nash speaks of employing a "reasonably and modestly reformed Christian theology" to provide "an ultimate, sustaining foundation for ecological integrity."[17]

One obvious advantage of this approach, whether we call it "revisionism," "reformation," or something else, is that it is actually a more honest denotation of what fundamentalist and evangelical readings, whether of recovery or of resistance, really are. As we mentioned above, any attempt to recover a "biblical perspective," to promote a "biblical view," involves not only the prioritizing of certain texts over others but also the interpretation of those texts in the light of contemporary issues and concerns, a process which is ever ongoing. Indeed, one problem with readings of recovery of the sort surveyed above is that they tend to imply that one can leap from biblical exegesis to contemporary theology and ethics. For example, an attempt to read ecological values directly from Jesus' attitude to birds and flowers may not do justice either to the gap that separates the biblical texts from our own world and its concerns or to the work that therefore needs to be done in order for the ancient texts to contribute creatively to an adequate contemporary response.[18] The claim to be promoting simply "what the Bible says" is a pernicious one, which masks the agency of the interpreter; while the claim to be drawing on the tradition and re-forming it in the light of contemporary demands makes the contemporary reader's agency visible and thus invites, rather than excludes, critical evaluation and contestation.[19] The concept of "stewardship," discussed above, is again a telling example. Rather than regarding it as a biblical image, or a biblical "basis" for Christian environmentalism, it is more helpful to consider it, in Conradie's terms, as a doctrinal or heuristic key.[20] Such keys, Conradie suggests, "are not directly derived from either the Biblical texts or the contemporary world but are precisely the product of previous attempts to construct a relationship between text, tradition and context." As such, they have a "double function . . . They provide a key to unlock the meaning of *both* the contemporary context *and* the Biblical texts and simultaneously enable the interpreter to establish a *link* between text and contemporary context."[21]

In other words, what Conradie's model of the process of biblical interpretation highlights is that meaning is made in the encounter between the text (and its ancient context) and the reader (and their contemporary context). Doctrinal "keys" represent the kind of central idea or motif that emerges from a reading of the text in a particular situation with particular pressing priorities. So, in the context of medieval Catholicism and his own sense of a guilty conscience, Martin Luther discovered in his reading of Paul a central doctrinal idea—justification by faith—that then became a key to reading and interpreting the biblical tradition, developing a doctrinal and theological tradition that, at the same time, brought certain parts of the biblical canon into central focus (Romans and Galatians in particular) and marginalized others (such as the letter of James). Just as justification by faith is the central doctrinal key in the Lutheran tradition, so, more recently, keys such as "liberation" have become central to liberationist and feminist readings of the Bible. Stewardship, similarly, is a doctrinal key, albeit a less comprehensive one, that functions as a way to interpret the meaning of crucial texts such as Genesis 1:26-28 and that, by drawing out one key image, serves to "interpret" the biblical tradition in a way that is relevant and creative for the current situation.

Any key will, Conradie insists, inevitably "distort" both text and context, perhaps ideologically—that is, in legitimating and concealing the interests of dominant social groups.[22] Doctrinal keys should thus be subject to a hermeneutic of suspicion.[23] But precisely by identifying them as doctrinal or hermeneutical keys—rather than as simply what the Bible "says"—this critical suspicion is invited.

Conradie's term "key" is a particularly interesting one. The most obvious connotation would be that it is a hermeneutic device which "unlocks" the text, allowing its meaning, even its real nature, to be revealed. A fascinating subsidiary connotation is that of a musical key which sets the "tenor" in which the text is to be re-performed by the interpreter.[24] In more recent work he has used the term "doctrinal construct," thus stressing the idea that this is something *made* in the process of reading and interpreting the text.[25] Interpretation requires that some point of similarity or analogy be found between the text and our (different) situation. "However," Conradie writes, in a recent article, "since such similarities are not always evident, we often have to construct such a similarity, to *make* them similar. This is also suggested by the root of the word 'identify'—from the Latin *idem* (same) and *facere* (to make)."[26]

While sympathetic to the connotation of a key as something like a musical key, and finding important the point stressed by the notion of a construct—namely, that this is a process of finding and *making* meaning and significance—we would suggest that the image of a hermeneutical *lens* can perhaps more helpfully capture the most important aspects of this idea. A lens—which is, of course, itself something *made*, constructed—shapes and configures what we see, bringing aspects of the object being examined into particular focus (though it may blur or otherwise distort others). And a lens can be two-way: just as a pair of glasses changes how the wearer sees those in front of her, so too the glasses change the way the wearer's eyes appear to others. A doctrinal or hermeneutical lens, then, not only shapes our view of the biblical text, but also determines how we and our context are viewed, and which aspects of our own context the biblical text relates to.

Conradie also shows how the six ecojustice principles of the Earth Bible Project function as doctrinal keys and could indeed be rearticulated as a "small dogmatics."[27] For example, "[t]he first two principles on the intrinsic worth (instead of the utilitarian value) of all matter and on interconnectedness form an incipient doctrine of creation. The emphasis on the earth community and a kinship between all creatures could also be read as a revised and more inclusive ecclesiology," and so on.[28] While Conradie is well aware of the possible objections to this reinterpretation of the principles—it would be "a form of colonisation and conquest and would not recognize the resistance against doctrinal interference in biblical exegesis"[29]—there are clear strengths in his approach.

Importantly, Conradie's approach provides a way by which one can see how the ecojustice principles exhibit points of connection with, and in part (though by no means exclusively) emerge from the biblical and Christian tradition, while at the same time functioning as a critical guide to the reading of that tradition.

Another benefit of this approach is that it prevents the contemporary ethical "canon" from seeming—as it did in the section on resistance (Type A) above—to appear *de novo*, without explicit connection with the tradition it simultaneously serves to criticize, and yet claiming to exercise an ethical authority over that tradition.[30] Indeed, this approach enables us to describe readings of resistance ("against" the Bible) differently. They are not, despite their depiction as such by opponents, and except in the cases where the tradition as a whole is rejected, attempts to overthrow the tradition, to reject it in toto, nor even to subject it merely to "assessment" against a contemporary ethical canon. What they are is attempts to (re)read the tradition from a particular perspective, a perspective that, *on theological and ethical grounds*, discerns where and how the word of "good news" is to be found. This is an approach with good historical pedigree, from Augustine's insistence that the only valid understanding of the Scriptures is that which serves to build up the double love of God and neighbor,[31] to Luther's focus on justification by faith as the heart of Scripture and the gospel, and so on.[32]

It seems to us that a kind of acknowledged circularity is necessarily intrinsic to a fruitful hermeneutic: *hermeneutical lenses are at one and the same time products of the tradition and the means for its critical rereading and reconfiguration.* Equally crucial, however, is the impact of the relevant contemporary context in generating the particular priorities which shape the formulation of hermeneutical lenses. Again one could list all kinds of examples, from Luther's frustration with the system of medieval Catholicism, to liberation theology's emergence from the context of poverty and oppression in Latin America, or feminist theology's emergence amidst a radical social reassessment of patterns of relationship between men and women. In the current context, with a growing awareness of the magnitude of the ecological challenges facing us, a further reconfiguration of the tradition through a newly focused biblical hermeneutic is surely timely.

An initial requirement for an ecological hermeneutic, again on a parallel with feminist theology, would be that it articulates the particular hermeneutical lenses that can enable a positive, creative, yet also critical rereading of the tradition. Thus it can and must be a hermeneutic that practices both "recovery" and "resistance," or "retrieval" and "suspicion."

At the same time, however, such a hermeneutic will not pretend that reading biblical texts can *suffice* for formulating a contemporary ethic, nor will it pretend that its hermeneutical lenses emerge solely from the texts, nor even the tradition, alone. This latter is an important point, since it implies the conviction that an adequate ecological hermeneutic must be one forged in dialogue with (inter alia) scientific understandings of the world, just as feminist and liberationist hermeneutics use the tools of social-scientific and political analysis. Defending a model of the theological enterprise which requires dialogue with, and appreciation of, the findings of modern science, as opposed to polemical isolation from such claims, would take us far beyond the scope of this book.[33] However, engagement with multiple perspectives has always been the way the tradition has operated. There must therefore be some methodological criteria by which to judge the appropriateness of a hermeneutic that draws on a range of disciplines and "data."

In this regard it is interesting to consider the criteria offered by Ian Barbour, first for evaluating models in science, and then models in religion.[34] Barbour regards the "four criteria for assessing theories in normal scientific research" as being: agreement with data (noting that theories are always underdetermined by data), coherence (consistency with other accepted theories, and ideally conceptual interconnection with those theories), scope (also, comprehensiveness or generality), and fertility (is the theory fruitful for generating new hypotheses and suggesting new experiments?).[35] We note that creation science, viewed as science, massively fails the first, second, and fourth criteria. Creation science would therefore be an example of a discipline that would be inappropriate as a conversation partner for an ecotheological hermeneutic.[36]

Interestingly, Barbour proposes that the same four criteria can be used by a "paradigm community" working within the framework of a religion. Here the "data" are the experience of that community expressed in "individual religious experience and communal story and ritual."[37] In a Scripture-based religion such as Christianity, we presume Barbour would see reflection on Scripture as a key component of that element of "data" he calls "communal story," as well of course as a central element of most ritual practice. "Coherence" he sees in terms of consistency with other accepted beliefs, leading to intersubjective continuity of tradition. "Scope" is here taken to include the application of the theological method in question to "other kinds of human experience beyond the primary data . . . In a scientific age, [beliefs] must also at least be consistent with the findings of science."[38] "Fertility" Barbour sees in terms both of personal transformation and applications to key ethical issues of our day, and he names environmental destruction as an example of the same. While one might cavil at the almost scientistic tone of Barbour's approach to the scope of a particular theology,[39] we would hold that a biblical-literalist methodology would fail not only this criterion, but elements of each of the others, so that too would not be a satisfactory way of approaching Pauline texts ecotheologically.

More positively, we suggest that Barbour's criteria give some useful pointers concerning the aims of our own reading of Paul, developed in the chapters that follow: a constructive and theologically engaged reading will need to be based on the "data" of the Pauline correspondence and its exegesis, to make coherent sense of Pauline theology and ethics as a whole, to be informed by science and other relevant contemporary sources of insight and knowledge, and to generate a fruitful response to contemporary environmental issues in terms of suggested attitudes and behaviors.

Stanley Hauerwas and David Burrell, operating within a narratival approach to theology, also pose the question: By what criteria is a narrative valuable?[40] This question will be of particular importance to us as we develop our own hermeneutical approach, which involves a search for the implicit narratives behind key Pauline texts (see chaps. 4–6) and behind contemporary ecotheologies (chap. 7).

Hauerwas and Burrell ask themselves what effect any narrative may have on those who decide to adopt it. They claim that any story that is adopted will have to display: (1) power to release us from destructive alternatives; (2) ways of seeing through current distortions; (3) room to keep us from having to resort to violence; and (4) a sense for the tragic—how meaning transcends power. These are criteria much more concerned with the moral effects of narrative than with critical-realist claims made by theories, as in Barbour's work. However, it is interesting to see the link between Hauerwas and Burrell's second criterion and Barbour's concern for agreement with data, coherence, and scope; and also between their other criteria and Barbour's concern that theological theorizing might be fertile in terms of great ethical issues of our time, a concern which is at the heart of our current study.[41]

2.5 CONCLUSION

Having surveyed and classified the kinds of appeal to the Bible made in the context of contemporary environmental debate, we have proceeded to a critical analysis of these approaches. To label these approaches as modes of recovery or resistance can be helpful, we believe, in uncovering the stance adopted toward the biblical text and toward contemporary ethical commitments, particularly since these kinds of orientations and motivations often remain implicit in scholarship. We have then argued for an approach that falls somewhere in between, and thus also avoids the weaknesses of, on the one hand, claiming simply to be recovering or reproducing what the text really says, and on the other hand, opposing the text on the basis of a contemporary commitment, without showing how that hermeneutical position can be generated and sustained with the resources of text and tradition. We have given examples of these polar opposites: the stewardship approach commonly espoused by evangelicals on the one hand, which claims to recover a positive environmental message taught by the Bible, and the Earth Bible approach on the other, which uses a set of ecojustice principles as a form of canon for critical assessment of the Bible.

We have also sought to show how a form of "revisionist" hermeneutic is most cogent, at least for an approach that wishes to remain in positive contact with the Christian tradition, since it avoids the pitfalls of either approach outlined above. Conradie's notion of doctrinal constructs, or, as we prefer to label them, hermeneutical lenses, provides a valuable way forward here, for it grasps and expresses the way in which biblical interpretation is inevitably a constructive process. The engagement between ancient text and modern context is one in which similarities are *made* by bringing certain motifs, ideas, or themes to the center, in a way that unavoidably "distorts" the text, making of it something new, prioritizing some aspects of it and interpreting them in a particular way, and marginalizing or ignoring others. The task that this approach suggests is to articulate what kind of hermeneutical lens(es) might emerge from a (re)reading of the biblical texts in our contemporary situation and might appropriately resource an ecological theology. The kinds of criteria outlined by Barbour, and by Hauerwas and Burrell, offer valuable guidance on what a successful attempt at this task might look like. This is clearly a task that calls for nothing less than a new engagement with the whole of the biblical tradition, the kind of comprehensive study attempted by the ongoing Earth Bible project.[42] But in the subsequent parts of this book we attempt a more limited task: a new engagement with Paul. Before we proceed to the Pauline texts, however, there is a further aspect of our methodology to discuss.

Chapter 3

A NARRATIVE ECOTHEOLOGY?

Along with an approach informed by Conradie's notion of doctrinal constructs, which we have developed in terms of a hermeneutical lens, another key aspect of our methodology is narrative analysis. This kind of analysis, we shall argue, opens up a particularly fruitful perspective on key Pauline texts, and enables those texts to contribute to contemporary ecotheological formulation. In the present chapter, we first outline the turn to narrative in recent decades, before setting out a typology of narratives that will inform the exegetical investigations in the chapters to follow.

3.1 THE IMPORTANCE OF A TURN TO NARRATIVE

In the early 1980s a number of significant works signaled a major (re)turn to narrative as a fundamentally important theological and philosophical category. In the wake of the Enlightenment, some came to view story, or myth, as a pre-critical, unscientific mode of thought that could be superseded by an approach which drew out principles or ideas in their own right. On this view the narrative framework is a mythological husk which can (and must) be discarded. Rudolf

Bultmann's program for the demythologization of the New Testament's message is a clear example of such an approach.[1] But the subsequent critique of foundationalism, and specifically of the idea that there can be tradition-independent statements of rational or universal principles, has been part of the wider intellectual scene within which narrative has been rediscovered. In 1981, for example, George Stroup published *The Promise of Narrative Theology*, in which he argued for the fundamental importance of narrative to theology.[2] Also in 1981, Alasdair MacIntyre published his enormously influential *After Virtue*, in which he argued that the inability of modern Western ethics to produce anything more than continual disagreement about various quandaries reflected the collapse of its narrative foundations.[3] Drawing especially on Aristotle and Augustine, and their synthesis in Thomas Aquinas, MacIntyre argued that it is only within a particular tradition, which is narratively constituted, that we can cultivate the kinds of virtues that are the basis for the moral life. MacIntyre's approach has been highly influential, not least on Stanley Hauerwas, one of the foremost contemporary theological ethicists, for whom narrative is fundamentally important in terms of forming identity, community, character, and conduct.[4]

Now, in the context of postmodernity, it is frequently asserted that every mode of thought is essentially a narrative, a particular story about the way the world is.[5] John Milbank, for example, sees capitalism, Marxism, and so on, as competing narratives seeking to outnarrate one another. Christianity, likewise, is a competing narrative that can be convincing insofar as it can "*persuade* people—for reasons of 'literary taste'—that [it] offers a much better story."[6] Likewise, Hauerwas sees the Christian narrative as in conflict with the "liberalism" of the West, which promotes its own particular story about the world: "The story that liberalism teaches us is that we have no story, and as a result we fail to notice how deeply that story determines our lives."[7] Narrative, it seems, is a fundamental category that can be used to describe all, or virtually all, modes of knowledge and being in the world.

3.2 NARRATIVE IN PAULINE STUDIES

The turn to narrative in Pauline studies also took place in the early 1980s, with the publication in 1983 of Richard Hays' highly influential study, *The Faith of Jesus Christ: The Narrative Substructure of Galatians 3:1–4:11.*[8] Using literary tools derived from the work of A. J. Greimas,[9] Hays sought to determine the "narrative substructure"—the story of Christ—on which a clearly nonnarrative text is dependent.[10] This kind of narrative approach has since been developed in studies of the New Testament and specifically of Paul by N. T. Wright, Ben Witherington III, and James Dunn, among others.[11] Douglas A. Campbell, calling the story of Jesus and its connection to other stories "an *irreducible* element in Paul's soteriology,"[12] notes the following features suggestive of narrative: a personal dimension conveyed largely by the activity of personal actors who perform actions and to whom events happen, and actions and events unfolding in a timeline, creating a "plot," with this plot often having a problem-solution structure.[13]

It is interesting to note how the history and development of this kind of approach to Paul reflects the changing circumstances and perceptions of Paul's modern interpreters. Hays, for example, often looks back favorably to the salvation-historical reading of Paul represented by Oscar Cullmann, a reading that saw an ongoing story of salvation underpinning Pauline theology. Indeed, there are parallels between the modern debate over the shape of Pauline theology and the older debate (involving especially Bultmann, Cullmann and Ernst Käsemann) concerning *Heilsgeschichte* in Paul.[14] Yet one of the reasons Käsemann reacted so vigorously against Cullmann's salvation-historical, narrative-type reading was because of its pernicious appropriation in Nazi ideology. Käsemann was concerned to oppose "a conception of salvation history which broke in on us in secularized and political form with the Third Reich and its ideology." "Our experience," he writes, "has made a theology of history suspect for us from the very outset."[15] While we would do well to remain sensitive to the problems of a certain conception of *Heilsgeschichte*, with its notions of linear progress and human (over)optimism, the contemporary development of a narrative approach seems to fit well with movements in contemporary theology and philosophy, and can be developed in ways that avoid the problems Käsemann so vigorously opposed. Recent interpreters, though, continue to disagree about whether Paul's theology is best grasped through a narrative approach, or whether this fails properly to appreciate his apocalyptic depiction of a vertical "interruption," the punctiliar moment of the Christ-event.[16]

In our view, there is much to be said in favor of a narrative approach to Paul. Concern to emphasize the radical intervention that the Christ-event represents and to avoid the problems with a story of gradual development should not lead us to ignore the extent to which there is a story of God's saving purposes told by Paul.

Certainly, Paul uses the language of demolition and renewal, particularly in Galatians. But Paul also speaks of the Christ-event as the culmination of a story which he roots in time and in the Scriptures, which remain for him a divinely given source of instruction (Rom 15:4). One need not rehearse all the elements of that story, from Adam's creation and "fall," through the promise to Abraham and the coming of the law through Moses, and so on. It is sufficient to note how hard those who deny this must work (exegetically) to downplay this sense of a story in Paul. J. Louis Martyn, for example, describes Paul's interpretation of God's promise to Abraham's seed (Gal 3:16) as being "as polemically *punctiliar* as it is polemically *singular* . . . The distinction between linear and punctiliar is . . . a distinction drawn by Paul himself. In Galatians 3:16 he denies the Teachers' linear, redemptive-historical picture of a covenantal people, affirming instead the punctiliar portrait of the covenantal person, Christ."[17] Even Galatians 4:4, Martyn insists, despite its clear setting of the coming of Christ in the context of time (ὅτε δὲ ἦλθεν τὸ πλήρωμα τοῦ χρόνου) does not refer "to a point that lies at the end of a line." On the contrary, "Paul does not think of a gradual maturation, but rather of a punctiliar liberation, enacted by God in his own sovereign time."[18] But, as so often tends to happen, the alternative Martyn wishes to refute is painted in terms that make it easier to deny. Paul does not have to think of this story as a simple "line," nor that it reflects a process of "gradual maturation," in order to see the coming of Christ as something that is to be comprehended within the context of a history of God's dealings with Israel and the world, a history in which (viewed from the perspective of the Christ-event) there are some moments, some points, of especial significance, as in the announcement of the promise of blessing to Abraham's seed (cf. Gen 12:3; 13:15; 17:8-9). This story is not simply linear, or steadily progressive: it is punctuated by key moments of which the coming of Christ is *the* definitive, climactic moment, which shows that the story is in its final chapter. But it is a story nonetheless. Similarly, Campbell concludes that

> at the heart of [Paul's] gospel and its claimed transformations of Christians, whether Jew or non-Jewish Greek, is an interplay between personal actors: the Father, his Son, and their Spirit . . . it would seem that a degree of narrative explanation is *essential* and hence *unavoidable* if an accurate account of Paul's thinking at these points is to be given; narrative is far more than a merely useful methodological perspective.[19]

Accepting that an implicit narrative (or narratives) can be discerned within Paul's writings, we will proceed to explore the form and content of the specifically cosmological narratives which underlie our key passages and also, subsequently, compare these with the narratives that implicitly underpin contemporary ecotheologies. The Pauline texts in which we are most interested are, for obvious reasons, those in which some form of cosmological narrative is apparent—some kind of story of the past, present, and future of the whole cosmos, the "creation." Ecotheologies, in general, are for the same reasons inevitably informed by some kind of cosmological narrative (see below and §7.8 for examples).

Michael Toolan outlines some typical characteristics of narratives: (1) a degree of fabrication, indeed prefabrication (though perhaps the term "constructedness" would be more helpful in thinking, as we shall be in the present work, of cosmological narratives underpinning ecotheologies); (2) trajectory—having a beginning, middle, and end (this is a particular characteristic of cosmologies, at least those at all influenced by either the biblical or yet the scientific imagination); (3) a teller, however hidden, who is moreover at some remove from the action, probably spatially and definitely temporally. Toolan concludes that "a minimalist definition of narrative might be: a perceived sequence of non-randomly connected events."[20]

Indeed, all ecologically concerned theology can be understood in narrative terms, because such theology's concern for the created world must be grounded in some cosmology or other. And every cosmology can be understood in chronological terms as a narrative of the unfolding of the creation from the distant past, through the present, and into the future. This is very evidently true of scientific cosmologies framed since the discovery of the vast age of the universe and the evolution of earth's biosphere over great spans of time. It is no less the case when Paul's few mentions of the nonhuman creation are read in an effort to infer the underlying cosmology reflected in those passages, and to relate it to contemporary scientific understandings and ecological questions. And (to return for a moment to Campbell's criteria for interpretation in terms of narrative) a Christian theological cosmology is always a narrative about the activity of a personal God relating to creation on an unfolding timeline, activity that by virtue of reflecting the divine purposes must constitute at some level a "plot."

So, while Käsemann found it necessary to argue against an essentially narrative reading of Paul at a particular place in time, we would argue that a narrative approach to Paul is particularly helpful now in bringing the apostle's theology into engagement with contemporary environmental issues, given the various kinds of cosmological narratives that inevitably underpin construals of "the environment" and its possible futures.

3.3 NARRATIVE TYPES

It will be helpful, therefore, to give attention to the different genres into which narratives characteristically fall. For this purpose we use the categories developed by Northrop Frye, and later applied by James F. Hopewell to the study of the narratives by which Christian individuals and congregations live.[21] This will both help us to clarify the nature of the stories to which the texts refer—neither in the case of Romans 8:19-23, nor in Colossians 1:15-20, the two key texts on which we focus in Part II, is the overarching narrative to which the writer appeals altogether clear—and will also suggest a way of testing contemporary ecotheological formulations for their fidelity to the Pauline narrative(s) we discern in these texts. (For more on this method see chap. 7.)

It is often said that there are only a few "plots" in all literature. Christopher Booker in a recent study identified seven.[22] Frye's contribution was to show that there were four basic narrative categories, "broader than or logically prior to, the ordinary literary genres . . . the romantic, the tragic, the comic, and the ironic or satiric."[23] To explicate these, we draw here on Hopewell's helpful summaries.

First, the category of the comic story. Comic stories move from problem to solution. Apparent difficulties are resolved by a deeper wisdom. As Hopewell puts it, "Comedy projects a world that ultimately integrates its seemingly antithetical elements . . . Comedies end in unions—pacts, embraces, marriages—that symbolize the ultimately trustworthy working of the world."[24] The most famous comedy in Christian literature is that of Dante; perhaps the most chilling and mysterious is the story of the (near) sacrifice of Isaac (Genesis 22).

The second of Frye's categories that Hopewell examines is that of romantic stories. These involve a quest for a desirable object: "The hero or heroine leaves familiar surroundings and embarks on a dangerous journey in which strange things happen but a priceless reward is gained."[25] This category of story lacks the clarity of the comic. Hopewell notes that "[t]he world instead gives paradoxical signals: souls are eternally damned in it, yet God does not fail those who trust in him."[26] This world "is fundamentally equivocal and dangerous, challenging the believer to seek its blessings amid the perils of evil forces and events. God's steady providence . . . accompanies the self who launches out toward God in an exciting, romantic adventure."[27] Frye holds that

[t]here are thus two concentric quest-myths in the Bible, a Genesis-apocalyptic myth and an Exodus-millennium myth. In the former Adam is cast out of Eden, loses the river of life and the tree of life, and wanders in the labyrinth of human history until he is restored to his original state by the Messiah. In the latter Israel is cast out

of his inheritance and wanders in the labyrinths of Egyptian and Babylonian captivity until he is restored to his original state in the Promised Land.[28]

Milton reflected on the former quest in his romantic (in Frye's terms) cycle *Paradise Lost* and *Paradise Regained*; an example of a modern Christian romance would be C. S. Lewis' science-fiction trilogy, *Out of the Silent Planet, Perelandra*, and *That Hideous Strength*.

The next of Frye's categories considered by Hopewell is tragedy, which "portrays the decay of life and the necessary sacrifice of the self before resolution occurs. The self in tragedy, as in romance, is heroic, but unlike the romantic hero, the tragic hero submits to a harshly authentic world . . . The divine is revealed largely as the eternal law or word made plain only to the self subject to it."[29] Hopewell goes on, "When portrayed as a tragic hero, Christ accepts the cross, with the intervention of neither romantic miracle nor comic gnosis. Those who follow the way of Christ live their lives tragically in the shadow of the cross. They suffer; they die to self and gain justification only beyond, and through, Christ's death and their own."[30] The story of Adam in Genesis, taken by itself, is a kind of tragedy; it reveals what Frye calls "an epiphany of law, of that which is and must be."[31] Christ as tragic hero is seen most clearly in the story of Gethsemane.

The last category to consider is the ironic, which for Frye also includes the satiric. Ironic stories challenge heroic and purposive interpretations of the world: "Miracles do not happen; patterns lose their design; life is unjust, not justified by transcendent forces . . . In an ironic setting one is freed only as one accepts the arbitrary working of life and reaches out to a humanity in common plight."[32] Hopewell continues: "It is by repudiating situations in which spirit power is said to dwell miraculously that true human stature emerges."[33] The twentieth century produced great examples of irony in Orwell's *1984* and the work of Kafka; as Frye points out, the irony is at its most telling, most "militant," when religious motifs themselves are parodied.[34] But the Bible operates also in the ironic mode, most famously in Ecclesiastes. And the story of Job, shorn of its final chapter, is an ironic tale. Frye comments that "[b]y justifying himself as a victim of God, Job tries to make himself into a tragic Promethean figure, but he does not succeed."[35]

It follows from the above analysis that narratives cannot have simultaneously a comic and a tragic shape, or simultaneously a romantic and an ironic shape. Difficulties cannot be both illusory and canonically inexorable. Quests cannot be at the same time supernaturally authenticated and futile.[36] However, "neighboring" pairs of genres, where such polar oppositions do not exist, can be blended, as in romantic comedies, or tragedies with a strongly ironic component. Later in the book we shall see that contemporary ecotheologies, viewed in terms of their underlying cosmological narratives, may fall into very different, indeed radically opposed, genres (see §7.8). As Hopewell saw, those who understand the world in ways that are opposite in terms of genre will find it very difficult to share their insights with one another.[37]

3.4 CONCLUSION
A Narrative Framework for Interpretation

The preceding material will have given some indication as to the ways in which a narrative approach will inform our investigation. First, we shall seek to consider the implied narrative substructure(s) of key Pauline texts, especially insofar as this depicts a story of the past, present, and future of creation. Second, we shall seek to consider what kind of narrative(s) these key Pauline texts seem to present, to ask what is their characteristic shape in terms of the categories Frye sets out, and consider whether this shape should be normative for an ecotheology. In both cases there is, of course, an obvious question to consider; that is, whether these various Pauline texts present a coherent single story of creation, or whether they rely on different, and perhaps incompatible, narratives. Since we include Colossians in our detailed consideration of texts, despite the suspicion that it may be deutero-Pauline, this will be an especially pertinent question.

Before we proceed to the Pauline texts, it is worth noting some broader reasons why the narrative approach may prove valuable in a study such as this. If it is true, as some recent writers imply, that all convictions about the world derive from some kind of story or tradition, recounted in a community and reflected in that community's practices, then exploring the narrative structure of Pauline thought is important in various ways. First, in opposition to a certain kind of cerebral Christianity, it shows that Pauline thought cannot be conveyed as a series of propositions to be "believed" but only as a story which is "lived," retold, and embodied in the practices of the community which celebrates that story.[38] As such, the narrative approach highlights an inextricable connection between what are generally referred to as Paul's "theology" and his "ethics." As philosophers and theologians like MacIntyre and Hauerwas have insisted, narratives form communities and inculcate certain patterns of practice, the reflection on which constitutes the discipline of ethics. Second, it shows that Pauline ethics, and Christian ethics more generally, is not a set of principles or judgments on issues, such as could easily be abstracted from the story and its community and recommended or implemented in wider public policy. Rather, Pauline ethics is firmly grounded in a character-forming narrative which has its essential basis in the Christian community and its corporate life.[39] Exploring the narrative structure of Paul's story/stories of creation is an important step in moving toward a discussion of the kind of practices that such narrative(s) might generate and sustain: ecotheology and ecoethics are here tightly interconnected. Third, if other modes of thought are also deemed to have an essentially narrative, tradition-dependent basis, this implies that they too will be linked with specific communities and modes of practice, though this may be obscured or denied when those communities see themselves only as engaged in a search for rational truths, such as perhaps in the case of science. It also implies that such narratives may shape identity, values, and practice, even if they claim only to relate to a specific "area" of life. Moreover, if all modes of thought are regarded as story-based, then Paul's story is competing on a somewhat more level playing field than might have once been thought. Instead of a mythological, ancient story being contrasted with the rational truths of science or economics, we see instead—if we follow Milbank and others—competing narratives about the world. We may then ask about how Paul's story and these other stories construct a sense of identity and shape human action. Capitalism's increasingly globalized story, for example, describes human beings as customers and producers and increasingly narrates their relationships in market terms; it tends to depict human interaction with the nonhuman world in terms of resources, prices, market value; it has a very particular understanding of "freedom." Ecotheologies, and other modes of environmental engagement, also reflect particular narratives about the world. Exploring and narrating the Pauline story can be a means to articulate a counter-narrative, a challenge to dominant economic and cultural narratives, a means to envisage communities in which a different story constructs a different sense of identity and undergirds different patterns of practice. In a world conscious of the power of stories to form identity, values, and practice, the rediscovery of Paul's gospel story *as story* is of critical value. Indeed, our overall argument will be that a narratively focused engagement with the Pauline texts—and, *mutatis mutandis*, with other biblical texts, too—enables a theologically and ethically fruitful ecological reading to be developed. In the next section of this book, we proceed to the task of developing that reading, focused first on the two texts that have loomed largest in ecological engagement with Paul: Romans 8:19-23 and Colossians 1:15-20.

PART II

The Ecotheological "Mantra"–Texts

Chapter 4

THE GROANING AND LIBERATION
OF CREATION (ROMANS 8:19-23)

4.1 INTRODUCTION

In the opening section of this book we have offered a critical and classificatory survey of the kinds of appeal to the Bible that have been made
in ecotheological discussion, and set out, in broad terms, the methods
that will inform our study of the Pauline material. The key aspects
of those methods are, in the first place, a concern to employ a kind of
"revisionist" approach in our engagement with the biblical texts—a
stance that avoids either claiming that a positive message of creation
care can be found consistently in (or "recovered" from) the Bible, carefully read, or on the other hand measuring the Bible critically against
a set of ethical standards established independently of the biblical and
Christian tradition. Instead we seek to acknowledge that an ecotheological engagement with the Bible will require critical and constructive work, in which certain hermeneutical lenses may emerge through
the reading of biblical texts in light of our contemporary context and
its demands, and may then shape a new appropriation of the biblical
tradition (see chap. 2 above). The second aspect of our method is the
application of a form of narrative analysis, an approach which, we have

suggested, may be valuable both in exegetical analysis and in contemporary application, enabling us to construct a "story of creation" from the Pauline literature. That story may then be able to offer us both a "cast of characters" to be considered in a contemporary ecotheology and ethics and also a normative shape (see chap. 3 above).

In turning to the Pauline literature specifically, our first task is to consider those texts that have already been found to be of most relevance and use to the ecological agenda. There are two obvious candidates from among the Pauline letters: Romans 8:19-23 and Colossians 1:15-20. These two texts have very frequently been cited and employed in ecotheological discussion.[1] Indeed, referring to Romans 8:19-23 in particular, John Bolt notes that this text seems to have become "little more than a mantra for Christian environmentalism."[2] As we shall see, there is good reason for the focus on these two texts from Romans and Colossians since, we shall argue, they are very good candidates to form the basis for the construction of a Pauline hermeneutical lens, through which an ecological engagement with the Pauline tradition more broadly can proceed. Nonetheless, despite the frequent appeals to these texts in ecotheological writing, we shall also argue, in chapter 6, that their contribution to ecological theology and ethics is less obvious, and more problematic, than generally assumed. This only goes to highlight, once again, the importance of a critical and constructive engagement, in contrast to the often implicit stance that straightforward appeal to what the Bible "says" is sufficient. We turn first to Romans 8. This chapter forms a climax to the argument Paul has developed in the opening chapters of Romans, moving from the depiction of humanity's universal imprisonment under sin (1:18–3:20), through the justification and new life made possible through Christ, in whose death and new life Christians participate through baptism (3:21–7:25). The Spirit, which comes to prominence in Romans 8, empowers this new life, enabling believers to fulfill "the righteous requirement of the law" (8:4). Despite the suffering that is the current and inevitable experience of those who are in Christ (8:17), the hope and certainty of their salvation cannot be shaken—and it is in the context of this declaration of hope that Paul locates the experience of the Christians in Rome within the wider story of the whole creation.

4.2 THE EMERGENCE OF AN ECOLOGICAL READING OF ROMANS 8:19-23

Despite evidence that some peoples of the ancient world experienced[3] and reflected upon[4] different forms of environmental degradation, few would assert that such issues feature explicitly in Paul's writings, or that the fate of nature, or the relationship between humanity and our planet's ecosystems, were major issues for Paul as they are in much contemporary debate. However, it would be wrong to assume that we are the first generation to find here a positive attitude toward nonhuman elements of creation and their eschatological fate. Indeed, there has been a range of interpretations of this passage throughout Christian history, of which we provide a few illustrative examples.

The subject of these verses, κτίσις, has been translated and understood in various ways.[5] Whether it is translated "creature" or "creation," throughout the history of its interpretation some commentators have assumed that κτίσις refers to the created world at large, with or without some or all of humanity. This has led to expectations that a positive change will be wrought in the natural world at the eschaton. Thus, Irenaeus finds here a reference to the entire "created order" (*Haer.* 5.32), which will "be restored to its pristine state," a condition he sees characterized by super-fecundity (5.33); this will allow the fulfillment of prophecies in both the Hebrew Scriptures and the sayings of Jesus regarding inheritance of the land, the rewards of the Kingdom, and the characteristics of the new Earth. Irenaeus even wonders, alluding to Isaiah 11:7 and 65:25, "what kind of grain must it be whose very straw is suitable food for lions?" (*Haer.* 5.36). Tertullian (*Herm.* 11) and, later, John Chrysostom (*Hom. Rom.* 14) interpret κτίσις in a similar fashion and also make connections with prophecies from the Hebrew Scriptures; Tertullian links this passage with Isaiah 11:6 in a discussion of the eschaton, while Chrysostom claims that the prophesied "perishing" of the heavens and Earth in the Hebrew Scriptures (Ps 102:2-6;

Isa 51:6) is to be seen as a parallel process to that undergone by believers as the "perishable nature puts on the imperishable" (1 Cor 15:53).[6]
Much later, Luther takes κτίσις to refer to created things that have been
made subject to vanity in the form of "man" and will be delivered when
the "old man [is] abolished."[7] Calvin, seeking to encourage believers,
reflects that "even inanimate creatures—even trees and stones—conscious of the emptiness of their present existence, long for the final
day of resurrection, to be released from emptiness with the children
of God" (*Inst.* 3.1.5).[8] Later still, in a famous sermon, "The General
Deliverance," John Wesley is clear that κτίσις refers to all creatures,
and writes of their paradisiacal state prior to the fall of humanity. When
humans made themselves incapable of transmitting the blessings of
God, the flow of blessings stopped and every creature was subjected to
vanity "by the wise permission of God."[9]

At the same time, others adopted a different interpretation of κτίσις.
Because of his belief that souls might be present in other beings,[10] Origen
thought that our passage in Romans might refer to things such as celestial bodies and angelic forces (*Princ.* 3.5.4.116–22; *Comm. Rom.* 7.4). By
contrast, Augustine saw *creatura* (the Vulgate's rendering of κτίσις) as
referring to human spirit, soul, and body (*Exp. quaest. Rom* 53; *Div. quaest.*
83.67; *Fid. symb.* 10[23]). In another permutation, Ambrose sees both
humans and celestial bodies being subject to vanity (*Ep.* 34.4–9), but
finds it possible that angels, and indeed *every* creature, even those free
of the bondage to corruption, might groan on our behalf. However, it
remains unclear what might be included in this category (*Ep.* 34.10–11;
35.1–2). Aquinas follows Ambrose in referring to celestial bodies as the
referent of κτίσις (*ST Suppl. III*, q.91, a.2, ad 6) and finds no grounds
for expecting the renewal of animals, plants, or minerals (*ST Suppl. III*,
q.91, a.5). Around the same time, Bonaventure speaks of "the freedom
of the glory of the sons of God" (Rom 8:21) in the context of "those
who were under the Law" with no reference to nonhuman creatures.[11]
This diversity of interpretation of κτίσις continued into modern scholarship in the twentieth century. An apparent majority[12] prioritize, or
restrict, the referent of κτίσις to what is sometimes infelicitously referred
to as "*sub*-human" creation.[13] However, others see the term as more

inclusive. Karl Barth thinks that Paul "included all creatures, even the nonhuman" while Käsemann sees κτίσις embracing nonhuman creation together with non-Christians.[14] Conversely, some restrict the term to saved humanity: J. Ramsey Michaels considers that κτίσις might be read as "creature" in verses 19-21 but as "creation" in verse 22, and thus suggests that the referent of the earlier verses could be the human body which is awaiting resurrection.[15]

Some, while admitting a nonhuman reference here, make claims that relativize its importance to Paul and give the passage a more heavily anthropocentric focus. So, C. K. Barrett comments that "his main object in mentioning creation is to emphasize the certainty of future salvation for Christians. He is not concerned with creation for its own sake."[16] John Gager claims that, in this passage, the admittedly "cosmic dimension" of the term κτίσις "has been significantly limited to an anthropological category, and its primary reference has become the nonbelieving, human world."[17] Similarly, G. W. H. Lampe insists that, here and elsewhere in the biblical texts "man is in the centre of the picture, and the rest of creation is brought in . . . as a sort of adjunct to man, as the backcloth of the human drama, the setting in which the action of God towards man takes place, and the environment to which man is linked by the nature of his physical body."[18] Still others hedge their bets. According to C. H. Dodd, Paul presumably "shared with many of his contemporaries the belief that, in the Good Time Coming, the material universe would be transfigured into a substance consisting of pure light or glory, thus returning it to its original perfection as created by God . . . What it means, in the realm of logic and fact, it is impossible to say."[19] It is notable that the most human-preoccupied readings of the passage date from the 1950s and 1960s, when the subordination of creation to redemption promulgated by Gerhard von Rad, and Bultmann's existential and anthropocentrising hermeneutic, were prominent influences,[20] and also before ecological concerns pressed onto the agenda.

Writers on ecotheology, by contrast, have cited this passage ever since the field itself emerged in the early 1970s, taking up and stressing the understanding of κτίσις as embracing nonhuman creation.[21] Indeed, it is without doubt one of the most frequently cited texts among those appealing for creation care and Christian environmental concern. Many of these appeals to Romans 8 are quite brief references in general support of envisaging a positive future for the whole of creation,[22] or to encapsulate the environmental crisis ("creation groaning").[23] Others emphasize nature's value to God by using this passage to support their claims for the inclusion of nonhuman creation in God's redemptive project. For example, "An Evangelical Declaration on the Care of Creation" (1994) declares "full good news for all creation which is still waiting 'with eager longing for the revealing of the children of God.'"[24] Citing Romans 8:23, Jürgen Moltmann writes trenchantly, "The vision of cosmic redemption through Christ is therefore not a speculation. It emerges logically from the christology and the anthropology. Without these wider horizons, the God of Jesus Christ would not be the creator of the world, and redemption would become a Gnostic myth hostile to the body and the world."[25] Sean McDonagh appeals to "the classic text of Romans 8:22-24" as a basis for the claim that "[w]ithin the plan of God realized in the resurrection of Christ, humans can help bring about this cosmic redemption."[26] Some writers go further in finding here an expectation that every living creature will eventually be resurrected, a hope that goes back at least as far as Wesley.[27] However, with partial exceptions, none of these writers offers a detailed and hermeneutically developed engagement with biblical texts such as Romans 8, and most fail to deal with the exegetical uncertainties and its context in the letter to the Romans, or to explore in detail its ecotheological implications.[28]

What then of those engaging in detailed exegetical commentary? As would be expected, it is only in works of the past three or four decades that we find ecological concerns explicitly mentioned in connection with this passage. In a paper as early as 1974, Charles Cranfield stressed that this passage takes us beyond treating the environment well merely because we need it; it has "a dignity of its own" and a "right to be treated by us with reverence and sensitivity."[29] It should also be noted that John Gibbs, in his 1971 study of the relationship between creation and redemption in Paul's thought, which included an examination of our passage, linked the whole topic to the ecological crisis.[30] But it is only fairly recently that commentators on Romans, as distinct from ecotheologians in general, have drawn out the relevance of this passage for ecological concerns.[31] For example, Brendan Byrne seeks to find a theological framework for thinking about ecological damage in the allusion he finds in verse 20 to Adam's sin: "[i]t is not fanciful to understand exploitative human pollution of the environment as part of that 'sin' story, along with other evils," and "there is hope that [creation] may also benefit when and where the 'grace' story prevails."[32] Robert Jewett, in the most recent major commentary on Romans, goes further. He clearly reads Paul's comments as expressive of an awareness of human despoliation of the environment: "it seems likely that Paul has in mind the abuse of the natural world by Adam and his descendants."[33] With reference to the revelation of the children of God, Jewett suggests, Paul "assumes that the renewed mind of such groups will be able to discern what God wills for the ecosystem. So the eager longing of the creation awaits the appearance of such transformed persons, knowing that the sources of ecological disorder will be addressed by them in due season."[34]

There have, of course, also been detailed exegetical and historical-critical monographs focused on this text, most recently that of Harry Hahne.[35] However, while these often at least signal the importance of this text to ecological issues, they do not offer any sustained consideration of its ecological implications, nor any extended development of its possible contribution to an ecological theology. The major exception to this general lack of developed engagement between biblical studies and ecological ethics is the work of the Earth Bible Team (2000–2002),[36] whose published volumes include an essay on Romans 8 by Byrne, building on the insights from his commentary, and another by Marie Turner, offering an "ecojustice" reading of Romans 8:18-30 in the light of Wisdom 1–2.[37]

In summary, the emergence of general theological reflection on ecological concerns has, unsurprisingly, mirrored the increasing awareness of negative human impact upon the environment over the past few decades. The changing readings of this passage—traceable, for example, through the work of commentators such as Barrett, Cranfield, and most recently Jewett, as cited above—give a clear indication of the way in which the issues and challenges of the contemporary context shape the questions brought to the text and in turn shape the interpretation of the meaning of the text.

However, the survey above also reveals that while there is, of course, plenty of difference and disagreement over the topic of the passage, this is not necessarily closely tied to the emergence of an ecological perspective. For example, earlier commentators such as Luther can agree with the current consensus that κτίσις refers to creation other than humanity. Irenaeus and Calvin can both envisage a new age in which created beings other than humans enjoy an existence which exceeds current experience and which, in Calvin's case, is non-instrumental—they will be restored even though they will no longer be needed by humankind (*Inst.* 3.25.11).[38] Whereas, as we have seen, a scholar of the 1970s like Barrett can confine the relevance of the passage to human salvation.

What has changed in the last few decades is the significance commentators see in the possible reference to the wider creation, and the interest they show in developing the theme of its freedom. Indeed, just as Romans 9–11 has been rescued from its marginalization as an unimportant excursus under the influence of a contemporary context more attuned to the relevance of Jewish-Christian relations,[39] so Romans 8:19-23 may come to be seen as a (even *the*) theological climax of the letter, under the influence of a context in which the magnitude of the ecological challenge is increasingly a point of public and political consensus.[40] It is also clear, however, that many appeals to this text build a great deal on a rather slim basis, either by assuming that a passing reference to Romans 8 is sufficient by itself, without further hermeneutical analysis and reflection, to undergird a substantial Christian environmental ethic,[41] or by attributing to Paul a too sophisticated and therefore almost certainly anachronistic insight into the causes of ecological disorder and the need to address these.[42] After all, in these few verses Paul gives little guide to any developed view of creation's significance and future destiny. For reasons we shall explore in chapter 6, merely citing this text does not actually get us very far in terms of informing and shaping a Christian environmental ethics. However, in developing a narrative approach to this text we hope to explore the potential of Romans 8 to contribute to an environmental theology, in a way that avoids some of the pitfalls of the ecologically attractive but exegetically superficial or implausible arguments found in some recent appeals to this text.

4.3 A NARRATIVE APPROACH TO ROMANS 8:19-23

We have already set out our reasons for, and approach to, seeking the narrative structure implicit in Paul's theology (see chap. 3). While the applicability of this method to the Pauline letters in general is a matter of some debate, there are two major reasons within this text itself why a narrative approach would seem to offer a fruitful way forward. One is that, like other non-narrative passages in Paul, this seems to be a text which, while itself brief and frustratingly allusive, depends on a certain story about the past, present, and future of creation in God's saving purposes. Creation *"is waiting* with eager longing" (ἀπεκδέχεται), *"was subjected* to futility" (ὑπετάγη), in hope that it *"will be set free"* (ἐλευθερωθήσεται; Rom 8:19-21). Since the account of our subject not only has a beginning, a middle, and an end, but also entails a transformation, this allows us to construct the outlines of a narrative trajectory,[43] while the employment of γάρ and ὅτι indicates causal links between the elements, thus constituting a plot.[44] A second, more specific reason is that the text directly implies that it depends on a shared narrative basis. Paul introduces his comment about creation groaning with the words οἴδαμεν γὰρ ὅτι, "we know that . . ." (v. 22). Most commentators agree that this indicates that Paul is here appealing to knowledge that he can reasonably presume his readers share.[45] So what exactly is it that "we know"? What kind of story of creation forms the narrative substructure of this text?[46]

4.4 THE STORY OF CREATION IN ROMANS 8:19-23

In considering the story of creation that Paul had in mind it will be helpful first to outline the elements of the "plot" and to establish which points are open to debate. The chronological distinctions, it should be noted, while significant to the direction of the plot, are often highly fuzzy, since past-present and present-future are inextricably connected in Paul's presentation here.[47]

Past (with ongoing present reality)

   I.   Paul's use of κτίσις (vv. 19-23) itself implies some past event or act of making/founding/creating, though it remains open to discussion whether the reference is to the whole product of such an event ("the creation," in toto), or to an individual who has been created ("the creature").

  II.   The current, and presumably prior, state of κτίσις, is bondage to decay, (v. 21). The precise sense remains unspecified, and the meaning is dependent in part on the content ascribed to κτίσις.

 III. κτίσις has been subjected to futility, of an unspecified nature, not of its own choice, though the subjector is not named (v. 20). These two facets of creation's existence highlight the negative dimensions of its past and present experience, which are transformed with the resolution of the story.

Present (continuing from the past)

  IV. The whole of κτίσις is personified as having been, and continuing to, "co-groan" in "co-travail" "until now" (v. 22).

   V.   In this, it accompanies, or is accompanied by, the inward groaning of Paul and his audience, defined as those "who have the first fruits of the Spirit" (v. 23).

Future

  VI. κτίσις longs (now) to see the (future) revealing of the "sons of God" (whose identity is debated [v. 19]).

 VII. Those (human) hearers who have the "first fruits of the Spirit" wait for adoption as God's sons, when their bodies will be redeemed (v. 23).

VIII. κτίσις will be, or hopes to be, liberated from bondage to decay and will obtain the freedom of the children of God (v. 21). Here the plot looks forward to a final transformation which resolves and surpasses the negative state of decay and futility.

Clearly this rich and complex text presents many issues for exegetical discussion, far too many to be treated adequately in a single chapter. We shall focus, then, on the points most crucial for establishing what kind of "story of creation" is presumed and reflected here.

I. The κτίσις

Since the term κτίσις itself implies a creative act, that may be taken as the first event in our narrative. Although the act of creation itself is not described here at all, it seems reasonable to assume — not least given Paul's frequent references to Genesis 1-3[48] — that God's creation of the world as depicted in Genesis 1–2 underpins Paul's reference here (cf. Rom 4:17), despite there being no occurrence of the noun κτίσις in LXX Genesis. As discussed above, a number of writers throughout history have assumed that the term here refers to what we would call "nature," even if they differed as to whether or not other entities, human or angelic, were included with it. With few exceptions, the consensus amongst recent writers is that κτίσις refers to nonhuman creation with or without remainder. Perhaps the subsequent association of this term with "decay" (φθορά), with its own connotations of processes of life and death, suggests that Paul has primarily in mind nonhuman *living* things, rather than the inanimate features of the creation. It is clear that the "expectation" and "groaning" of κτίσις does not preclude a global or cosmic point of reference for the subject of our story, since such personification is found in the Hebrew Scriptures of which Paul makes frequent use. (Elements of creation are commonly personified in poetically structured passages of the LXX [e.g., Isa 44:23, 49:13, 55:12-13; Pss 64:13-14, 97:7-9 LXX] and this passage does have a poetic quality about it.)[49] There are, then, good grounds to conclude that this passage is saying something about nonhuman creation, whatever precisely is or is not included in Paul's implicit definition — something it is impossible to determine.

II. The bondage to decay

Creation's enslavement to decay (ἡ δουλεία τῆς φθορᾶς) is mentioned only as that from which creation will be liberated (v. 21). It is therefore difficult to determine what kind of "event" in the story this depicts, and whether it precedes, follows, or is coterminous with its "subjection to futility" (see next section). Significantly, in terms of the narrative dynamics, this depicts the parlous state in which κτίσις now exists, the resolution of which will bring the story to its climactic and glorious conclusion. Although not explicitly stated in the text, it is often assumed that the bondage to decay derives from or is concomitant with the subjection of κτίσις to futility. In other words, bondage to decay specifies what subjection to futility implies.[50] However, this assumption should be questioned, since it gives a somewhat odd construal of the underlying logic of the passage: if "futility" consists in creation's "bondage to decay," then God[51] has subjected creation to decay in hope that it might be freed from decay. In particular, the striking description of the subjection as being done "in hope" suggests that creation's "futility" was, in the divine economy, the *prelude to liberation* from bondage to decay (*not* the bondage to decay *per se*), in other words, part of the solution (in some mysterious way) rather than part of (or merely a symptom of) the problem. On this reading there would be an interesting though partial parallel with the depiction of human rebellion in Romans 1:18-32, where humanity's refusal to know and worship God leads to God's "giving them over" to sinful passions.[52] The refusal to acknowledge God is not *identified* with the enslavement to sinful passions but precedes God's (consequent) act in handing them over, an act which forms a part—if a difficult and enigmatic one—in the economy of salvation: God has consigned all to disobedience, in order to have mercy on all (Rom 11:32; cf. Rom 5:20, Gal 3:19-24). Similarly, creation came under enslavement to decay, and was then(?) (as a consequence?) subjected by God to futility, in hope . . . But this is to jump ahead in our account.

If the reference in verse 19, either partially or in toto, is to mortal creatures, as seems most likely, then this bondage to decay would presumably be, or at least include, a reference to the inevitability of physical death. This verse has thus been widely seen to support the idea that Paul has in mind here the account of the fall, since Adam and Eve were warned that death would be the result of their eating fruit of the forbidden tree (Gen 2:17, 3:19).[53] Paul alludes to this event in Romans 5:12,

14, in the context of human death, so the reference here to φθορά would imply that he sees death in the natural world as another consequence of primeval human disobedience;[54] in this connection, φθορά is sometimes taken as having some kind of moral connotation, such as degradation, as well as related physical implications.[55]

However, the specifically Adamic reference here is less obvious than most commentators take to be the case. Aside from the obvious fact that Adam is nowhere mentioned in Romans 8:19-23 — a point to which we shall return — Paul's language here does not specifically echo the LXX account of Adam and Eve's fall. The curse of Genesis 3 is upon the fruitfulness of the "ground" (Heb: אדמה; LXX: γῆ [Gen 3:17]), which does not appear to represent the entire living (nonhuman) creation, but only a specific part of it, the soil or earth, as the reference to thorns, thistles, and plants in the subsequent verse of Genesis 3 shows. In large part, the change of usage from γῆ to κτίσις is reflective of a linguistic development in Jewish literature of the period,[56] though it is also one that expands and emphasizes the cosmic dimensions of references to the "Earth."[57] Nonetheless, without denying that the action of Adam is, for Paul, a fundamental point from which corruption and death enter the created order, it is worth considering the possibility that — given only a brief and allusive reference to the enslavement of the whole κτίσις to φθορά — what Paul has in view here is a broader allusion to the unfolding story of Genesis 1–11, in which corruption affects all flesh (כל בשר/ πᾶρα σάρξ; note the repeated use of καταφθείρω in Gen 6:12).[58] This would suggest that the φθορά to which Paul alludes is a broader phenomenon than simply a reference to mortality.

III. Subjection to futility

The next event in the implied story is that κτίσις "was subjected to futility" (v. 20), though whether this should be seen as prior to, coterminous with, or following the enslavement to decay is, as we have noted, open to discussion. This phrase, as with the "enslavement to decay" (v. 21), is commonly taken to be a reference to the curse on the ground (Gen 3:17), following Adam and Eve's disobedience;[59] thus "the one who subjected it" is generally — and convincingly, in our view — taken to be a divine passive, even though the cause of creation's subjection may be traceable back to Adam.[60] So, Luther declares that "through man the whole creature becomes vanity, though, to be sure, against its will . . . For created things are good in themselves."[61] And Calvin maintains that creatures "are bearing part of the punishment deserved by man, for whose use they were created" (*Inst.* 2.1.5).[62] Similarly, and much more recently, Hahne argues that Romans 8:19-22 is "consistent with that strand of Jewish apocalyptic writings that emphasize human responsibility for the corruption of the world," and he sees the focus of the passage as being on Adam's sin as the initiation point for ongoing sinfulness.[63] In most Jewish apocalyptic writings creation is not portrayed as sinful or fallen in itself, although its functioning, or rather malfunctioning, sometimes acts as an indicator of malaise.[64] While Romans 8:19-22 does not unpack the symptoms of futility or decay, Hahne suggests that examples given in Jewish apocalyptic writings indicate what Paul may have had in mind: hardship, disease, and death.[65]

However, it is once again worth taking seriously that in Romans 8:19-23 whatever precisely is in Paul's mind as the *reason* for creation's subjection to futility, he makes no explicit mention of any such reason. Paul makes no indisputable reference to Adam (nor to the Watchers,[66] nor to any other specific event in the primal history of Genesis 1–11); nor does he closely echo the fall/curse story of Genesis 3. While it is clear enough, from what Paul says elsewhere (Rom 5:12) that he sees "one man" as the source of sin's entry into the world, and, through sin, death, it should not be assumed that this particular event is equally prominent in the background of Romans 8:19-23, not least given the rather distinctive content of Paul's compressed allusions to the story of κτίσις. In particular, the crucial word ματαιότης evokes no specific allusion to the Genesis stories. Again there is a comparison to be drawn with Romans 1:18-32.[67] While scholars have argued that Adam's story underlies that text too,[68] specific allusions are far from clear. What does appear as the prominent theme is the activity of humanity in general, in turning from worship of God to idolatry and sexual immorality.[69] In other words, just as Romans 8:19-23 paints a general (if highly compact) picture of the futility of κτίσις, so Romans 1:18-32 paints a general (and more extended) picture of the corruption and futility of humanity. One difference is that, while humanity's actions are depicted as knowingly and deliberately done (1:19-21), there is no suggestion of creation's refusal to acknowledge or worship God, simply the declaration that the subjection was *not* willed on the part of κτίσις. Crucially, however, the same root (ματαιο-) is used in both texts (Rom 1:21, 8:20).

As Cranfield notes, the content of the term ματαιότης is subject to various interpretations;[70] it may simply relate to mortality as experienced by every life form,[71] or refer to the misuse of elements of creation as objects of idolatry (linking back to Paul's theme in Romans 1, esp. v. 21).[72] It is significant to note that ματαιότης is a distinctively Jewish/ Christian word, and is used in the LXX only in the Psalms, Proverbs 22:8, and (most extensively) in Ecclesiastes (note esp. 3:19, where the fact that both human and animal share the same fate in death is an indication that τὰ πάντα ματαιότης). This, along with the echoes of the Wisdom of Solomon in Romans 1:18-32 and Paul's citation of Psalm 93:11 [LXX] in 1 Corinthians 3:20, suggests that a Wisdom influence is most likely in Romans 8:20. Paul here indicates, echoing the constant theme of Qoheleth,[73] that the existence of creation (and of humanity) is futile and frustrated, since it is unable to achieve its purpose, or to emerge from the constant cycle of toil, suffering, and death.[74]

What is worth emphasizing is that, whatever Paul sees as the cause of creation's subjection to futility, his focus is only on the fact of that subjection to futility, and on what lies ahead of it in the narrative plot. The one who does the subjecting is God, the implied agent of the (divine) passive ὑπετάγη; this was not something willed by κτίσις itself. But right from the start, according to Paul, this was a subjection (by God) *in hope.*

IV & V. Creation's groaning in travail and the groaning of Paul and other Christians

Moving on into the "present tense" of our narrative, the groaning and travailing of creation has been variously interpreted: as its suffering of decay and death, or related to its frustration at being unable to fulfill its purpose in God's plans in conjunction with a humanity in right relationship with God.[75] The use of language associated with labor pains has often led commentators to see here a reference to the so-called "messianic woes"; the advent of the messiah is linked with an expectation of tribulation for humanity often concomitant with upheavals in the natural world, reaching a climax before the "birth" of the new age.[76]

The text does suggest some sense of eschatological climax in the pregnant phrase ἄχρι τοῦ νῦν, "right up to now" (8:22), and there are clear precedents in Jewish literature for anticipating times of upheaval in creation before the end of this present age, whichever form that end might take (e.g., Isa 24:1, 3-7, 19-20; 1 En. 80.2-8; Jub. 23.18; 1 QH 11.29–36; Sib. Or. 3.673–81).[77] However, Paul does not indicate that the groaning itself is a characteristic only or specifically of the "end of the age" (cf. 1 Cor 10:11). Rather, creation's travail *continues* right up till the present time (in which the eager expectation of redemption is reaching a fever pitch). Thus, this "laboring" of the κτίσις seems to be depicted as an ongoing and contemporary feature of its existence, as might be expected if Paul has in mind the primeval spread of φθορά and the divine subjection of κτίσις to futility.

Again there are parallels in prophetic and intertestamental writings, where, for example, the Earth (γῆ) is depicted as mourning (Isa 24:4; Jer 4:28), speaking (Hos 2:22), or crying out (1 En. 9:2).[78] The specific image of labor pains recalls the depiction in Jewish writings of the Earth as a womb (Job 1:21; see also 4 Ezra 10:6-14; Philo Opif. 13.43; see VII below).[79] Once again Paul uses κτίσις rather than γῆ, reflecting the developing prominence of this term, though this also serves to emphasize the cosmic scope of the narrative drama.[80] The verb στενάζω is also elsewhere used to depict the cries of suffering Israel.[81]

So the groaning of creation is an ongoing characteristic of its current existence, though it has, according to Paul, reached a crucial moment of eschatological expectation. It is clearly a forward-looking anguish. Also striking is Paul's description of creation as *co*-groaning and *co*-travailing (συστενάζει καὶ συνωδίνει). With whom is the creation groaning? Most commentators consider that the use of πᾶσα and the content of the following verse rules out the suggestion that the co-groaning is specifically with believers or the whole of humanity.[82] The meaning, they suggest, is that all creation is groaning together, amongst itself, or "with one accord."[83] However, since creation is here depicted as a singular character (ἡ κτίσις), and since Paul's characteristic use of συν- words generally indicates a clear conjoining of one partner or group with another, this may be questioned.[84] The groaning of Christian believers is described in exactly the same terms (στενάζομεν), and the Spirit is later described as joining with the Christians in their groaning, interceding with groans of its own (στεναγμοῖς). The grammar of verse 23 is awkward, as the textual variants indicate, but the sense may be construed as implying that not only (οὐ μόνον δέ) does creation join in the eschatological groaning, but that, in particular and in addition, "we ourselves" (ἡμεῖς καὶ αὐτοί)[85] groan "in ourselves" (ἐν ἑαυτοῖς), *and* groan specifically in anticipation of adoption as sons—a specific hope for which creation could not groan. Creation's groaning is a co-groaning with Paul and other Christians and the Spirit, a shared travail that also represents a shared hope, though some aspects of that hope are distinctive to the "sons of God,"[86] who are here described as those who have "the first fruits of the Spirit" (Rom 8:23; cf. 2 Cor 1:22, 5:5, where the Spirit is described as a first instalment or ἀρραβών). The common vocabulary used to describe creation, humanity, and the Spirit indicates that somehow they are caught up in the same process, yearning for the same outcome, which the future dimensions of the story will go on to depict.

VI. Creation's eager longing

Our third present event, the waiting-while-craning-its-neck of κτίσις, reinforces the personification of the subject of our narrative, discussed above. The immediate focus of creation's longing is the revelation of the "sons of God" (v. 19). There has been some debate as to the identity of the υἱοὶ τοῦ θεοῦ in this verse, and possible differences in referent between this term and the τέκνα τοῦ θεοῦ of verse 21. Tracing his suggested background to this passage in the flood tradition, Christoffersson notes the use of υἱοὶ τοῦ θεοῦ in Genesis 6:2 to refer to what are also called the Watchers in the Enochic tradition and suggests that "sons of god" here refers to the angels who are expected to accompany Christ at the παρουσία.[87] Υἱοί is used, he suggests, to denote the angels as opposed to the believers, who are referred to as τέκνα. However, since Paul has already used υἱοί to refer to his readers earlier in this part of the letter (Rom 8:14), uses υἱοθεσία to denote what the Christians yearn for, and goes on to apply it to the people of God shortly thereafter (Rom 9:26), we find this argument unconvincing.[88] So, we conclude that κτίσις here is eagerly awaiting the revelation of the Christian believers and that this unveiling is related to their adoption as sons spoken of in verse 23.

VII. The adoption of the υἱοὶ θεοῦ

The way in which Paul talks of adoption in Romans 8 is sometimes cited as an example of the "already-but-not-yet" tension in much of his teaching. Earlier in this chapter he speaks of the believers as *having* the Spirit (v. 9), of the Spirit as living *in* them (v. 11), and leading them (v. 14). They are children (υἱοί) of God (v. 14) who *have received* a spirit of adoption (v. 15), which confirms to them that they *are* children of God (v. 16). Therefore, it is unsurprising that in verse 23 he speaks of his readers as *having* the Spirit as first fruits but, on the face of it, somewhat surprising that he sees himself and believers as groaning as they *wait for* their adoption. However, adoption is specified here as referring to the redemption of their bodies, suggesting a reference to the resurrection (cf. 1 Cor 15:35-54; 2 Cor 5:1-5).[89] This may connect with the language of parturition noted above (IV); in the Hebrew Scriptures, the Earth may be portrayed as a womb, more specifically in the context of its giving birth to the resurrected dead within it (Isa 26:19: "the earth will give birth to those long dead"; cf. also 4 *Ezra* 7:32).[90] There may be in Romans 8 an echo of these texts, wherein the birthpangs of creation relate to the expected "delivery" of the bodies of the resurrected believers. In his most famous and extended discussion of the resurrection, Paul gives a sense of the "order" of events which must take place: first is Christ, who is ἀπαρχή; then those who belong to Christ at his παρουσία (1 Cor 15:23). Then, interestingly, Paul simply skips to "the end," τὸ τέλος, when Christ hands the kingdom to the Father, having destroyed every power that stands in opposition to God (v. 24). He sees the final event in this battle as the defeat of death itself, "the last enemy" (vv. 25-26). While κτίσις is simply absent from the picture here—though note τὰ πάντα in verses 27-28—this text offers some further support for the idea that the bondage to decay, from which Christians and creation will be delivered, is death itself. The connotations of ματαιότης, as we have seen, may include this idea (cf. Eccl 3:19) but also a sense of purposelessness. First Corinthians 15 also supports what seems to be a sequence, presumed here in Romans 8, where the resurrection of the sons of God is the initial event in a series that will eventually encompass all things, the entire κτίσις.

VIII. The liberation of κτίσις

This brings us to the climax of our narrative. While the revelation of the sons of God forms the immediate focus of creation's expectation, this is important not simply in itself, but insofar as it heralds a wider process of eschatological transformation. The hope that always accompanied the creation's subjection to futility was and is the hope that the creation itself will be liberated. Creation, one might say, has a vested interest in its yearning to see the revelation of the sons of God, their liberation and their glory—or, taking τῆς δόξης, with Jewett, as epexegetical, their "liberation consisting of glory."[91]

It would seem reasonable to suppose that Paul here envisages a situation where κτίσις, along with believers, will enjoy freedom from death and decay. These processes "entered in" through Adam, and came to affect the whole created order, which was subjected (by God) to futility, yet they will be abolished in Christ (Rom 5:12; 1 Cor 15:22). Hahne finds parallels with a specific strand of tradition in Jewish apocalyptic, whereby creation as a whole, not just humanity, will be redeemed, specifically by a process of renewal rather than by its destruction and re-creation.[92]

4.5 SUMMARY AND NARRATIVE ANALYSIS

What then can we conclude about the shape of the story of creation, as it appears to be reflected in Paul's brief and allusive discussion? The following would seem to be an appropriate summary.

The nonhuman creation (whatever precisely the scope of that notion) is in "enslavement to decay," a notion that would appear to refer to physical death and more broadly to destruction and decay, perhaps in a moral as well as physical sense. Given what we know of Paul's thought elsewhere, it is likely that the sin of Adam, through which sin and death entered the world, forms the basic and initial cause for the creation's bondage to decay, though we should take seriously—more seriously than most commentators do—the possibility that Paul here alludes to a broader story, namely the spread of wickedness and corruption throughout the created order. This enslaved-to-decay creation has been subjected to futility by God. Also to be noted, though, is the fact that, in the story of creation as he depicts it here, apart from saying that it was not something that creation itself willed, Paul gives no explicit attention to what preceded or occasioned this subjection to futility. Rather, what Paul wants to emphasize here—a theme in keeping with the wider concerns of the chapter—is that creation was subjected *in hope*. In narrative terms, this means that the focus, from the subjection onwards, is entirely *forward*-looking; there is no description of the act of creation, no indication as to what (if anything) preceded its subjection to futility.

The present—and forward-looking—existence of κτίσις is characterized by a co-groaning and a co-travailing. Although this has reached a decisive eschatological moment, it is to be seen as the state of creation's existence since its subjection. Given the way Paul here also describes both the groaning of believers (v. 23) and the groaning with believers of the Spirit (v. 26), it seems most likely that he here depicts the creation as also bound up with humanity and the Spirit in a solidarity of shared groaning, and, similarly, a shared hope.

This hope, for creation, is focused on the moment of the revelation of the sons of God. It is these adopted children, the Christian believers with whom Paul shares his message of hope, who stand at the center of this redemptive process. They await the redemption of their bodies, presumably a reference to their resurrection; and creation hopes—with a certainty that can match the confidence Paul urges on the Christians at Rome—to share in the freedom and glory that this redemption will bring.

In terms of the analysis of narrative and plot the central character in verses 19-22 is κτίσις, whose "name" appears four times in these verses, and whose anticipated transformation from bondage to decay to freedom and glory is the central story. (This is not to deny, of course, that the *reason* Paul introduces this story here is to set the suffering and hope of the Christians at Rome into a wider context, to depict *their* groaning and their hope as part of a cosmic, and not merely local, drama.) In another sense, however, the sons/children of God are leading characters, since it is their liberation on which that of creation depends and onto which the hopes of creation are focused. In terms of the plot, these children of God are crucial for the progression of the story of creation from groaning to freedom. Yet the character most crucial to the progress of the plot is also a character little evident in the explicit wording of the passage: God. We hear of God in this text only as the one to whom the sons/children belong (υἱοὶ/τέκνα τοῦ θεοῦ, vv. 19, 21). But God's actions, hidden within the force of the so-called divine passives, are clearly the crucial motor of the entire plot, as encapsulated *in nuce* within two (passive) verbs: creation *was subjected . . . will be liberated.*

The story of creation, then, is a forward-looking story in which a tragic state is being transformed, with much suffering and struggle, into one of liberation.[93] The reason for the tragic state is not given, nor are its causes analysed; the focus, rather, is on the divine action that leads both humans and nonhuman creation to freedom and glory.

As we shall see in more detail in subsequent chapters, some of Paul's statements about the transformation of identity in Christ stress the "already" of the typically Pauline now/not-yet (e.g., 2 Cor 5:17), but generally it is clear that this is a process, decisively begun yet still to be worked out through suffering and struggle (e.g., Phil 3:10-14; cf. also Col 1:24). Romans 8 is a particularly developed and powerful depiction of this narrative of process, with its insistence that it is only in conformity to the sufferings of Christ that a sharing in his glory and inheritance is attained (8:17), a narrative in which verses 19-23 so enigmatically include the whole of creation as co-groaning.

In terms of Frye's narrative types outlined in chapter 3 above, we suggest that in the Pauline story of struggle and suffering leading to glory there is more than a hint of a romantic (for Hopewell a "charismatic")[94] genre. The "heroes" of this sub-drama in God's great drama of salvation are "the children of God" as they undertake their "quest," longing to be transformed from one degree of glory to another, to come into that full liberty for which the creation as a whole also longs. In this they follow *the* central hero-figure, Christ himself, who, having faithfully accepted the path of suffering and death, has become the firstborn among many siblings (8:29), the firstfruits from the dead (1 Cor 15:20). Jewett has argued that this Pauline narrative may represent a countercultural contrast to a received "comic" narrative (in Frye's terms) of the Augustan Age, in which the crisis of the breakup of the Roman Republic is replaced by an (ultimately illusory) harmonious union of *urbs et orbs* in the person of the Emperor.[95] The central characters of Paul's narrative are very different from the "imperial version"—with the focus being, as we have seen, on God (through the divine passives), and on "the children of God" as suffering but coming into their glory, as opposed to the establishment of the golden age by Augustus (Virgil, *Ecl.* 4.11–41) or the peacemaking victory of Nero "while still in his mother's arms"—a true comic touch this—as recorded by Calpurnius Siculus (*Ecl.* 1.33–99).[96] But what makes the difference between the narratives so emphatic is *the difference in narrative genre*: the sense of quest and struggle in Paul (which in turn puts the story in touch with the tragic genre) stands in contrast to the comic optimism of the imperial narratives.[97]

Why, it might be asked at once, is this inference of the narrative category underlying this passage (and hence Paul's understanding of the relation between human and nonhuman redemption) of any significance? Without wishing to anticipate too much our later discussions, we see three interlocking reasons.

First, we note Jewett's forcefully made point that this may be read as a "counter-narrative"—it seeks to establish a story of the situation of the creation (including humans) that is at odds with another powerful and influential narrative wholly or partly located in a different genre, and/or with different main characters.

Second, if it be conceded that the texts from Romans 8 and Colossians 1 that form the focus of this section of the book are the principal Pauline loci at which we learn about God's concern for the whole creation, then the narrative genre in which they are couched may be taken to have some normative character. We shall be seeking in chapters 7 and 8 to outline a Pauline ecotheology and a Pauline ethic of environmental care, and beyond that to indicate the contours of an ecotheological ethic that learns from the New Testament (and also from contemporary science). The character of the cosmological narrative underlying that ethic will therefore be much influenced by the narrative genre of key New Testament texts.

Third, and to return to the particular text, Romans 8:19-23, which is the focus of this chapter, there is the important question as to whether this frustratingly brief passage carries in itself any implicit ethical imperative. As we indicate below (see §6.3) there are reasons to be more cautious and careful than much ecotheological appeal to this favorite text has been. But we also conclude that there are indeed significant ethical implications readily inferred from a contemporary reading of this passage, and that these become most clear when its narrative genre is taken into account (see §6.4) and when it is related to the wider contours of Pauline theology and ethics (see chaps. 7–8).

We take up the themes of liberation and glory, and their relation to the motif of reconciliation, in chapter 7. We turn now to a detailed analysis of the other Pauline text frequently cited in ecotheological discussion: Colossians 1:15-20.

Chapter 5

THE RECONCILIATION OF ALL THINGS (COLOSSIANS 1:15-20)

5.1 INTRODUCTION

In turning to the letter to the Colossians we turn to a text in the Pauline corpus whose authorship is disputed. Among the Pauline letters, Colossians is probably the one where the arguments for and against Paul as author are most finely balanced. While a significant number of contemporary scholars regard Colossians as pseudonymous—on the grounds of its developed christological, cosmological, and eschatological views, and its somewhat distinctive style and ethical teaching[1]—an equally significant number argue for its authenticity.[2] After all, there is considerable variation of style and theological emphasis among the undisputed Pauline letters. Of all the disputed letters, Colossians seems to stand closest to the undisputed Paulines in its content and style. James Dunn, for example, regards Colossians "as a bridge between the undisputed Paulines and those members of the Pauline corpus that are generally considered post-Pauline."[3] Dunn considers it most likely that Paul himself did not write the letter, but that Paul may have outlined his main concerns to a secretary (perhaps Timothy), who then produced the letter. In this sense, Dunn suggests, "we have to call the letter 'Pauline' in the full sense of the word, and the distinction between 'Pauline' and 'post-Pauline' as applied to Colossians becomes relatively unimportant."[4]

We have already made clear our decision to focus on relevant texts in the Pauline corpus as a whole, rather than only on those that can safely be regarded as authentic. And in terms of the kind of analysis and interpretation we attempt here, the authorship question is of comparatively little importance. The letter to the Colossians has its canonical status and theological influence whether or not Paul himself was its author. And whether Paul wrote it or not, we need carefully to consider how far its distinctive material implies a particular story of creation, which may or may not be similar to that of Romans 8.

Our particular interest is in Colossians 1:15-20, the most discussed part of the letter,[5] long identified as a distinct section known as the "Colossian hymn," and often thought to incorporate earlier credal or hymnic material focused on Christology.[6] Various structural analyses have been offered, as well as reconstructions of possible earlier forms of the "hymn," later edited and incorporated into the letter. Despite the competing reconstructions, commentators broadly agree on dividing the hymn into two strophes (1:15-17, 18-20)—with or without a middle transitional stanza—and on identifying a move in the focus of the hymn from creation (vv. 15-17) to redemption (vv. 18-20). Suggestions as to earlier forms of the hymn have also led to reflections on the possible distinctions between the thought-world of the hymn itself and the epistle author's own worldview and motivations in amending this putative earlier version. Indeed, earlier theories focused on the concept of a gnostic heavenly redeemer, suggesting that the central form of Colossians 1:15-20 was not only a preexisting but actually a pre-Christian hymn, based on a gnostic-type myth.[7] Although widely rejected now due to lack of evidence, this suggestion did highlight the potential significance of seeking the possible earlier form of the hymn and religio-historical parallels to it. Nonetheless, some commentators see no need to postulate any prior editorial stages or earlier author(s), regarding the hymn as most plausibly produced in its current form by the author of the letter.[8]

Together with Romans 8:19-23, Colossians 1:15-20 is probably the most frequently cited passage amongst ecotheologians seeking support for creation care from within the Pauline corpus. It is the apparently cosmic canvas of the hymn's declaration of the role and work of Christ that has caused it to loom large within Christian writings on attitudes toward the nonhuman elements of the environment. Indeed, as Alexander Wedderburn notes with regard to the topic of creation care, "Colossians has, perhaps of all the New Testament writings, the strongest claim to be heard on this theme."[9] The key contribution this text appears to offer is an affirmation that, in Steven Bouma-Prediger's words, "Christ's work is as wide as creation itself."[10] The cosmic scope of the hymn is expressed in a number of ways as we shall see below.

5.2 THE EMERGENCE OF AN ECOLOGICAL READING OF COLOSSIANS 1:15-20

In the history of interpretation of the Colossian hymn, the all-encompassing scope of the creation in which Christ is involved, as depicted in the first stanza, has never been in any doubt. However, nonhuman physical elements of creation do not generally feature in the debate around this passage. With regard to the second stanza, focused on redemption, there has been speculation on the nature of the agents referred to when considering what is entailed in "reconciliation" in verse 20 (used by some to imply universalism) and the possible inclusion of spiritual entities within its scope. Origen notes that it specifically includes supernatural entities (*Princ.* 4.4.3).[11] Elsewhere (*Hom. Luc.* 10.3), he seems to interpret "things heavenly" to mean the faithful dead in Christ—Abraham, Isaac, and Jacob—and makes no mention of any agent other than humanity. Chrysostom indicates that, although the passage only describes Christ as head of the church, he understands the passage to indicate that Christ is head of the universe in its fullness (*Hom. Col.* 3). However, the implications of this for nonhuman physical creation are not explored. When dealing with the reconciliation of "all things," Chrysostom explains that, since heaven is already at peace with God, "things in the heavens" refers to reconciliation between humankind and the angels in heaven, who had up till that point been enemies of each other (*Hom. Col.* 3). Aquinas (*ST* 3.22.1), and then Calvin (*Inst.* 3.4.27), speak of the reconciliation of all things solely in terms of believers, with no mention of other agents or creatures.[12]

The lack of explicit reflection on the possible connections between this passage and "nature" continues through into twentieth- and twenty-first-century scholarship; unlike ecotheologians (see below), very few commentators or biblical scholars of the past century have drawn any link between the hymn and its application to nonhuman life.[13] All seem to agree that τὰ πάντα (vv. 16, 17, 20) means exactly what it says—that is, *all* (created) things—particularly when taken in conjunction with πάσας κτίσεως (v. 15), ἐν τοῖς οὐρανοῖς καὶ ἐπὶ τῆς γῆς (v. 16; cf. v. 20),[14] πρὸ πάντων (v. 17), and ἐν πᾶσιν (v. 18). Yet most commentators do not specifically mention nonhuman creation in their discussion of the passage. "Nature" is not explicitly excluded but neither is it discussed. Moreover, many (apparently prompted in some cases by a desire to guard against possible universalist interpretations of the latter stanza) go further, limiting the scope of the hymn by pointing out its context; the apparently cosmic scope of reconciliation is seen as qualified by the reference to the church (v. 18) and the following verses (vv. 21-23), which address the believing recipients of the letter.[15] According to many commentators, while the original form of the hymn might well have implied a cosmic reference, the focus of the author of Colossians is anthropological and ecclesial.[16]

Others also pick up the personalistic overtones of ἀποκαταλλάσσω in verse 20 and consequently, while admitting the possibility that τὰ πάντα may include nonhuman referents, see the author's main focus as being on *persons*, that is rational beings, whether human or spiritual in nature. Roy Yates, seeing in verses 21-23 "a kind of commentary on the hymn which interprets and applies the cosmic work of Christ to the readers,"[17] poses the following question: "since reconciliation properly relates only to persons, how can it be applied to the universe?" Similarly, and some years earlier, C. F. D. Moule commented that it is hard to envisage how all of animate and inanimate creation may be reconciled. He points out that "St Paul readily resolved τὰ πάντα into personal beings" and that such an interpretation is supported by the hymn itself (1:16) and by later references in the letter to disarming rulers (2:15) and worship of angels (2:18).[18] Based on what he sees as the anthropocentric focus of Paul's uses of reconciliation language in 2 Corinthians 5:18-20 (see §7.4 below), Howard Marshall argues for a similar perspective in Colossians 1: "[t]here is no question of the reconciliation of inanimate nature, but rather Paul's thought is of the rulers and powers in verse 16."[19] Lars Hartman reminds us that the author would have understood himself as part of a "cosmos that was alive, filled and swayed by all sorts of living powers" and that "the planets were living creatures, belonging to the same world as man"; he does not mention the rest of creation.[20] Ian Smith illustrates how interpretations of the hymn's focus are tied into the understanding of the error or "heresy" which the author was seeking to address.[21] His identification of the error as a form of Jewish mysticism, which saw asceticism (Col 2:16-23) and submission to personalized elemental spirits (Col 2:8) as a means to acquire a superior level of spirituality, results in his finding that the Christology of the hymn "particularly applied to cosmic powers."[22] Perceptively, Wedderburn admits the possible inclusion of physical creation but points out that "it is not 'all things' that are a problem for the letter; animals, plants, etc., are not an issue, but rather heavenly powers and people who fear them and venerate them."[23] Indeed, given the types of possible "heresies" in the Colossian church, it is likely that, for both author and recipients, the import of Christ's position of supremacy over any earthly and heavenly authorities would have been one of the most significant and relevant features of the hymn.[24]

Other commentaries and monographs, especially in more recent years, do take seriously the cosmic scope of both creation and redemption in our passage and its relation to "nature," though they vary in the degree to which they explore its implications.[25] In 1982, in his essay "Christ and All Things," Markus Barth argued that attempts to downplay references, here and elsewhere, to the universal effects of the work of Christ in redemption, and thereby to promote a more anthropocentric soteriology, are not substantiated by study of the New Testament; moreover, interpreting such material against the backdrop of the Old Testament themes of creation, kingship, wisdom, and eschatology may clarify the theme of Christ's omnipotence over all things. Noting warnings against the "ruthless exploitation of nature," M. Barth claims that "the blunt exclusion of everything natural from Christological research and proclamation is neither true to the substance of the New Testament nor does it meet any needs of modern man."[26] More recently, Dunn comments poetically on the scope of the hymn's vision:

> The vision is vast. The claim is mind-blowing. It says much for the faith of these first Christians that they should see in Christ's death and resurrection quite literally the key to resolving the disharmonies of nature and the inhumanities of humankind . . . In some ways still more striking is the implied vision of the church as the focus and means toward this cosmic reconciliation—the community in which reconciliation has already taken place (or begun to take place) and whose responsibility is to live out . . . as well as to proclaim its secret.[27]

Yet Dunn does not explicitly make mention of any ecological significance to this vision, nor offer any comment on what "the disharmonies of nature" might have been perceived to be. Some commentators go somewhat further. Lewis Donelson notes "that the basic orientation in this hymn coheres with the modern Christian environmental movement."[28] Markus Barth and Helmut Blanke stress the universality of the hymn's referent and go on to observe that "[i]t is a basis for thoughtful reflection in the face of threats, exploitation, and destruction of creation by man, who seems to recognise no superior being besides himself."[29] N. T. Wright, noting that "all creation is to be transformed in the cosmic results of the resurrection," draws the conclusion that, if the lordship of Christ embraces every aspect of life, then Christians should promote "the ecological order of creation."[30] Similarly, John Barclay suggests that "the scope of its claim that Christ is 'all in all' serves as a powerful incentive for Christian engagement with the world, not least in a concern for 'the integrity of creation.'"[31] Andrew Lincoln concurs, claiming that "being concerned for animal welfare, and struggling to prevent the collapse of the ecosystem through the pollution of air, soil, and water have everything to do with this passage's celebration of cosmic reconciliation."[32] Most recently, Douglas Moo sees it as a mistake to limit the passage's application to humanity: "[t]he 'peace' that God seeks is a peace that not only applies to humans in their relationship to God but also to humans in their relationship with one another (hence the mandate for social justice) and to humans in their relationship with the natural world (hence the mandate for a biblically oriented environmentalism)."[33]

In summary, even since the emergence of ecotheological concern, it seems that many commentators still understand the letter's author as focusing primarily on humanity, with the possible inclusion of person-alistic spiritual entities—a topic related to the so-called false teaching at Colossae. Some, however, relate this passage to human relationship with, and responsibility toward, the nonhuman creation. Within this latter group, broadly speaking, the strength of the connection made between the Colossian hymn and the need for ecologically sensitive behavior seems to have increased with the passage of time, concomitant with the increasing severity of the environmental crisis and its progres-sively larger public profile.

The differing approaches to the focus of our passage would also appear to be determined, at least in part, by the relative weight ascribed to the cosmic scope of the hymn itself and the letter writer's relating of this material to the believers in Colossae. The hymn is generally acknowledged as encompassing all things, at a cosmic level, while the author focuses most of the attention of the letter on the lives of the believers, and the possible influences of a false teaching (the "Colossian heresy") on their ethical behavior. Colossians 1:15-20 is immediately followed by a reminder to the hearers that *they* have been reconciled (vv. 21-22). This authorial focus is seen by some commentators as qualifying the implications that might be drawn from the hymn alone.[34] Given the cosmic scope of the hymn and the anthropocentric applications (and references to spiritual beings) elsewhere in the letter, it has seemed to some that the Colossian hymn in itself offers more pretext for ecotheo-logical appropriation than a wider consideration of its context in the letter might allow.[35]

As may be expected, use of this passage by ecotheologians develops its implications well beyond the necessarily brief comments found in exegetical commentary. Ecotheological interpretation generally picks up on one or more features of the hymn that imply a cosmic scope to the work of Christ in both creation and redemption. First, there is the repeated use of τὰ πάντα ("all things"); second, the idea that the goal or purpose of all things is found in Christ (εἰς αὐτόν, vv. 16, 20); and third, the reference to an apparently all-encompassing reconciliation (v. 20).

Ecotheological reflection on this text can be seen as early as 1961, in Joseph Sittler's famous address to the World Council of Churches. Although his keynote speech, "Called to Unity," was primarily focused on a call to ecumenical cooperation, Sittler was the first to suggest an ecological significance to the cosmic Christology presented in Colossians: "the sweep of God's restorative action in Christ is no smaller than the six-times repeated *ta panta* . . . and all things are permeable to his cosmic redemption because all things subsist in him."[36] Sittler insisted that "[a] doctrine of redemption is meaningful only when it swings within the larger orbit of a doctrine of creation" and described care of the Earth as a "christological obedience." Seeing the magnitude of the threat to nature, Sittler argued that it was time to explore the untapped potential in this cosmic Christology, a potential that could lead from doctrine to ethical engagement: "The way forward is from Christology expanded to its cosmic dimensions, made passionate by the pathos of this threatened Earth, and made ethical by the love and the wrath of God."[37] Indeed, already in the 1950s, with remarkable prescience, Sittler was articulating the need for a "theology for earth," a theology that would rekindle a positive view of the Earth as bound up in God's redemptive work.[38]

Subsequently, others have drawn more developed ecologically relevant conclusions from this passage. Sean McDonagh sees in Colossians 1:15-18 an indication that Jesus' ministry "was not confined to teaching, healing and reconciling humans and all creation with God," but more than this: "he is the centre of all creation."[39] Thus, "[a]ll creation is united in Christ and therefore everything has a future in God, through Christ."[40] In a study on the environment and Christian ethics, citing Colossians 1:19-20, Michael Northcott notes that "[t]he orientation of creation towards its eschatological transformation is brought nearer and anticipated in the events of reconciliation and restoration which are begun in the death and resurrection of Christ. Christ's triumph over death has import for the whole cosmos."[41] Brennan Hill sees implications here for Christian discipleship:

> The applications of this Pauline theology [in Col 1:15-20] are obvious. God is the source of all things . . . God has plans for the fulfillment of creation, and Jesus Christ plays a central role in bringing this plan to fruition. Disciples of Christ, then, are called to discern God's plan for creation and resist those who would bring destruction to the earth. It is clear that irresponsible destruction of the environment is a moral offense against God's plan and stands as an impediment to Christ's work of bringing all to fulfillment.[42]

For David Russell, the cosmic perspective of Colossians 1 gives clear grounds for opposing readings that see redemption as primarily, if not exclusively, concerned with humanity: "to state that creation was made for Christ and is fulfilled only in its relationship to him is to reject above all the primary anthropocentric interpretation of texts regarding redemption."[43] Vicky Balabanski suggests that the essentially Stoic ideas on which the author draws imply a "permeation cosmology" which can help us to move "beyond anthropocentrism," since the passage includes τὰ πάντα, "the whole biosphere," in the scope of God's reconciliation.[44] Thus, for Christians, "the peace-making through Jesus' blood on the cross is a dynamic process . . . It enables us to move towards a bio-centric cosmology, learning and relearning respect for the impulse towards life in all creation."[45] Perhaps Steven Bouma-Prediger "earths" the idea most clearly. Quoting Dunn's comment (cited above), Bouma-Prediger finds in Colossians 1:15-20 an important depiction of the universal scope of God's reconciling work in Christ.[46] He later comments: "Christ's work is as wide as creation itself. It is nothing short of the restoration and consummation of all creation . . . if Jesus did not die for white-tailed deer, redheaded woodpeckers, blue whales, and green Belizean rain forests, then he did not die for you and me . . . Thus, our work is to be patterned after Christ's reconciling reign as cosmic Lord."[47]

By contrast with the rather limited ecotheological reflections of the commentators, then, ecotheologians have found great significance in this text. Before we turn to our own constructive exegetical engagement with Colossians 1:15-20, undertaken, as with Romans 8, by means of an examination of the narrative structure of the passage, we turn first to a brief consideration of the likely background(s) of the hymn, particularly insofar as these proposed backgrounds and influences are relevant to, or incorporated into, ecotheological readings.

5.3 THE BACKGROUND OF THE COLOSSIAN HYMN AND THE WORLDVIEW OF THE EPISTLE

Appeals to this passage in ecotheological writing center on the scope of τὰ πάντα, used in relation to both creation and reconciliation. Robin McL. Wilson notes that τὰ πάντα in this form, article plus neuter plural, "was in New Testament times the regular expression for the created universe."[48] However, given the differing understandings of the letter's focus, as expressed in the commentaries and studies discussed above, situating the author's terminology in its wider socio-historical context may help to indicate what scope was intended, and how far readers of the letter were likely to hear the hymn as referring to the whole cosmos.

Parallels in Greco-Roman philosophy

A cosmic understanding of the scope of Colossians 1:15-20 has been supported by reference to the wider world of Hellenistic philosophy. The "pronouncedly Greek point of view" of the letter[49] and the claim that some of its theology of Christ's role in creation "seems only fully understandable in the context of contemporary Middle Platonist thought"[50] has led to comparisons' being made with contemporary writings that have terminology in common with the Colossian hymn.

One such common feature is the use of the metaphor of the body (1:18) which was used in contemporary discourse in both political and religious contexts (if in fact such a distinction has any meaning in the first century); parallels were frequently drawn in Greco-Roman literature between the body of the individual, the family, organizations, the state, and the cosmos.[51] However, it is the widespread imagery of the cosmos as a larger version of the microcosm of the human body which mostly concerns us here. Contemporary thinkers sometimes spoke of the cosmos as the body of a living being, as an εἰκών of the deity (cf.

1:15),[52] with the deity as manifest throughout it,[53] or acting as its head.[54] It is not insignificant that this imagery was appropriated to depict the role of the Roman emperor, and its appearance in the hymn may, therefore, have provided something of a parallel and a contrast with imperial propaganda.[55]

The metaphor of the body is employed to speak of the church as the body of Christ in the undisputed Pauline letters (Rom 12:5; 1 Cor 6:15, 10:17, 12:12-27), as well as in Colossians and Ephesians, whose authorship is debated and where the metaphor's use is distinctively developed (Col 1:18, 24; 2:19; 3:15; Eph 1:22-23; 2:16; 4:4, 12-16; 5:23, 30). In Ephesians there is reference to the body growing and coming to maturity (Eph 4:12-16) but, more significantly, both there (Eph 5:23) and here in Colossians (1:18), Christ is described as the *head* of the church, his body.[56] Considerations of balance and parallelism between strophes have led many to accept that "the church" was an addition to an earlier hymn which spoke of the *cosmos* as his body.[57] But even in the hymn as it now appears the focus on the head and the repeated use of τὰ πάντα might well have evoked the commonly used imagery of the universe comprising the body of the deity more strongly than other Pauline instances of "body" language.[58]

Other concepts and vocabulary suggest connections between the Colossian hymn and the prevalent philosophical notion of the cosmos as an integrated organism. One is the imagery of the cosmos being "held together" (συνέστηκεν, v. 17), in the case of Stoic thought by the agency of πνεῦμα.[59] Another is the employment of a set of prepositions related to Christ which are similar to those found together in Stoic literature, namely ἐν, διά, and εἰς (Col 1:16; cf. vv. 19-20). The most commonly cited example in Stoic thought is found in Marcus Aurelius' *Meditations* (4.23) on nature: ἐκ σοῦ πάντα, ἐν σοὶ πάντα, εἰς σὲ πάντα.[60] Again, it is significant to note that this philosophical terminology is expressed by an emperor, giving a political valence to this notion of the cosmos as an integrated body. The prepositions which occur in this "so-called Stoic omnipotence formula"[61] are also found in the undisputed Pauline letters (notably Rom 11:36 and 1 Cor 8:6), and are commonly seen as reflecting the different forms of causation in Greek philosophy.[62]

Finally, the concepts of cosmic reconciliation and peacemaking (v. 20) may be seen as paralleled by the philosophical idea of the universe being in tension, and the holding together of contrary principles within a harmonious whole, as described, for example, by Dio Chrysostom.[63] Given the contiguous nature of created elements in Greek thought, with the presence of πνεῦμα, albeit in different forms, in everything from inanimate objects through to humanity,[64] such a philosophical background to the Colossian hymn would lend support to an interpretation that saw here a vision of an integrated destiny for all things, including nature, rather than a primarily anthropocentric concern—a vision set in parallel, and perhaps conscious contrast, to an imperial vision of the integration of all things under the headship of the emperor.[65]

Parallels in the Old Testament and Hellenistic Judaism

While there are clearly some striking parallels with Greco-Roman philosophy in this passage, the influence may not have come directly but rather, as is often pointed out, via the Hellenistic influences on Jewish thought. Certainly, some see the hymn as showing evidence of both Jewish and Greco-Roman influences[66] while others find a much stronger influence of Hellenistic Judaism than of specifically Greek philosophy. Bruce, for example, claims that "while it is easy to see affinities between Paul's language here and Stoic terminology, Paul's thought is derived not from Stoicism but from Genesis and the OT wisdom literature, where Wisdom is personified as the Creator's assessor and 'master workman.'"[67] Vincent Pizzuto, noting that the prepositions found in Colossians 1:16 are not identical to the Stoic formula in Marcus Aurelius (there is no ἐξ αὐτοῦ of Christ), concludes that they probably came to our text "through the monotheistic filter of Second Temple Judaism" and that their use was influenced by Paul's letters.[68]

Further examples to support such claims are drawn from Jewish Wisdom literature and specifically the parallels between our passage and the ways in which Jewish writers speak of both Wisdom and Logos.[69] Wisdom, sometimes spoken of as the image of God (Wis 7:26; cf. Col 1:15), is involved in creation (Prov 3:19, 8:27-30; Wis 8:4-6; 9:2, 9), and pervades all things (Sir 1:9; Wis 7:22-24), holding them together (Wis

1:6-7; cf. Col 1:17, using συνέχω)[70] and bringing order (Wis 8:1). The Logos is also spoken of as holding all things together (Sir 43:26).[71]

Further support for locating the thought of the Colossian hymn in a Hellenistic Jewish context is drawn from similarities found within the writings of Paul's Hellenistic Jewish contemporary, Philo.[72] Philo sees Wisdom as the beginning, and the image of God (*Leg.* 1.43; *Ebr.* 31) and the Logos as God's firstborn (*Conf.* 146; *Agr.* 51). It is also notable that he speaks of the cosmos as being composed of separate elements which are held together by God (*Her.* 23, using συνέχω),[73] or the divine Word (*Her* 23; *Fug.* 112; *Mos.* 2.133; *QE* 2.118; cf. also *Plant.* 8–10). The language of divine peacemaking in Colossians 1:20 also finds echoes in Philo; he speaks of God as the peacemaker (εἰρηνοποιός)[74] and peacekeeper (εἰρηνοφύλαξ; *Spec.* 2.31 [§192]) and he describes God's Word as an intermediary between God the peacekeeper and humanity (*Her.* 205–6). Consequently, although λόγος and σοφία do not appear in the text of Colossians as synonyms for Christ (but see 3:16) and although the terminology employed is often different, the similarity between concepts used to speak of Christ in Colossians and of these two attributes of the divine in Hellenistic Jewish writings has led some to the conclusion that this hymn is entirely a reflection and development of contemporary Jewish Wisdom speculation (though it is recognized of course that this tradition was in turn influenced by Greek philosophy).[75]

Other features of the hymn have been suggested as having backgrounds in Jewish festival and sacrificial traditions.[76] However, neither of these suggestions has met with much support.[77] In the LXX, sacrifice is not described using ἀλλάσσω or its cognates; instead we find ἐξιλάσκομαι (e.g., Lev 4:20 LXX) which does not appear in the New Testament. Cilliers Breytenbach has shown that the language of reconciliation is used more often in political than religious settings.[78] More generally, Breytenbach argues strongly that reconciliation language (καταλλάσσειν κτλ.) does not stand in a close relationship to atonement language (ίλακέσθαι κτλ.).

Some of the core motifs of the Colossian hymn, then, may be found expressed in similar ways in Jewish writings, which has led some writers to conclude that there is no need to look elsewhere for its sources and worldview.[79] However, these ideas and concepts are mostly found in the writings of *Hellenistic* Judaism. Moreover, one area in which there do not seem to be any parallels between Jewish wisdom literature and the worldview of the Colossian hymn is in the consideration of *telos*, which we will go on to examine in more detail below.[80] Overall, however, Gordley's claim that the hymn engages Greco-Roman philosophical ideas with concepts drawn from Judaism seems to provide a plausible summary of the background to, and worldview(s) of, the hymn.[81]

Distinctive features of the hymn

Despite a range of close and significant parallels in both Jewish and Greco-Roman literature, there are aspects of the hymn that reflect its distinctively early Christian, and specifically Pauline, character. Whether they are later additions to an earlier form of the hymn, or simply part of the writer's composition, the phrases "the church" (v. 18b) and "by the blood of his cross" (v. 20b), clearly mark this passage as relating to the narrative of the Christ-event, with the crucifixion and resurrection (alluded to in v. 18) marking a turning point in the story (see below).

Another marked peculiarity of this passage is its use of the unusual word ἀποκαταλλάσσω to express the idea of reconciliation; this word appears in Greek only in Colossians 1:20 and 22, and in Ephesians 2:16. There is no evidence of its use elsewhere in Greek literature or in the LXX, suggesting that it may have been coined by the author of Colossians (assuming the majority view that Colossians predates Ephesians).[82] In the undisputed letters, when Paul speaks of reconciliation he uses the verb καταλλάσσω without the prefix (Rom 5:10, 11:15; 1 Cor 7:11; 2 Cor 5:18).[83] Adding the prefix may serve to intensify the meaning.[84] In this instance, both Bruce and Porter suggest that the use of the prefix ἀπο- intensifies the sense of "reconciliation," possibly with reference to the enormity of the claim being made, that the entire universe was to be reconciled to the Creator through the work of Christ on the cross.[85]

Conclusions

As is often the case in New Testament studies, competing proposals are made concerning the most pertinent influences upon the content of Colossians in general and the Colossian hymn in particular. Whichever "background" is deemed of primary influence, or if, as seems more likely, the mixture of influences suggests the author's location in a cultural world from which we cannot neatly separate distinct streams of influence, there are good reasons to conclude that the hymn, and τὰ πάντα in particular, does refer, and would have been heard to refer, to the whole cosmos—to "nature," or the "creation"—and thus includes this physical (and spiritual) universe within the scope of God's creative and reconciling work. Moreover, the hymn makes clear that Christ is central to this work, both in creation and redemption. The image of the cosmos as a body—here, the body of Christ—is no doubt considerably muted by the author's ecclesially focused use of the body metaphor. But the existence of all things in, through, and for Christ—"holding together in him" (v. 17)—implies that everything is encompassed by Christ, incorporated in him, and, therefore, caught up in the reconciliation accomplished by his death.

5.4 A NARRATIVE APPROACH TO COLOSSIANS 1:15-20

In considering how to engage this passage fruitfully in ecotheological reflection, one immediate issue requiring a decision is whether to treat the hymn in isolation from its literary context, perhaps in a reconstructed earlier form, or as it currently stands, embedded in the letter to the Colossians. While there are potentially interesting insights to be gained from the former approaches—not least in terms of stronger indications of the idea of the cosmos as the body of Christ—it seems to us that any appropriation in the context of Christian theological engagement must interpret the hymn in its literary and canonical, as well as historical, context. Whatever the hymn's background, if we wish to engage in a theological and ethical appropriation of the text in ongoing reformulation of the Christian tradition (see chap. 2 above), then it is the current passage, in the context of the letter, with which we have to deal, rather than a reconstructed earlier, original hymn, even if the latter might better meet our requirements for an ecologically friendly reading. As we turn, then, to an analysis of the text in narrative terms, we shall continue to focus on the hymn itself, but will interpret it within the context of Colossians (though noting where the hymn's focus might be different from that of its surrounding material).

Unlike Romans 8, the Colossian hymn gives few explicit indications of a narrative content or implicit substructure. Indeed, Schweizer maintains that "there is no narrative at all."[86] However, despite the lack of explicit narrative indicators, it is possible—and, we believe, fruitful—to explore the narrative implicit in the content of the passage. Stephen Fowl sees in the Colossian hymn a text that encapsulates the story of Christ, with the rest of the letter seeking to draw the recipients into the Christ story.[87] Similarly, Donelson suggests that the hymn "tells . . . the story of Jesus and the cosmos" with Colossians 1:15-16 forming "a creation story, told through the lens of Jesus."[88] The degree of realized eschatology in the hymn—in part, it seems, a reflection of its character as poetic hymn—makes it particularly difficult to discern where the hymn is referring to past, present, or future (see below). Indeed the temporal distinctions here are even more blurred than in Romans 8. This does not mean, however, that no temporal narrative structure can be discerned, only that the distinctions are far from neat. In some cases, while it is possible to place the underlying narrative events in some kind of order, it is not altogether clear which "events" are completed and which are still in progress.

5.5 THE STORY OF CREATION IN COLOSSIANS 1:15-20

As with Romans 8, we first present a brief outline of the narrative implied by Colossians 1:15-20. Following the outline we proceed to expand and justify the various points we have discerned.

Past (with ongoing present reality)

I. Everything (τὰ πάντα) that was made, in the heavens and on the Earth, visible and invisible—the whole κτίσις—was made in and through Christ, the image of God and "firstborn [πρωτότοκος] of all creation" (1:15-16).

II. Something occurred, subsequently it would seem, which necessitated the process(es) of reconciliation and peacemaking between "all things" (1:20). What caused this problem remains unstated.

III. Christ's death on the cross (v. 20), subsequent both to the original creation and the implied problem, is the means of this reconciliation and peacemaking, and his resurrection marks him as "firstborn [πρωτότοκος] from the dead."

Present (continuing from or consequent upon past events)

IV. Christ has primacy over "all things" (πρὸ πάντων) and everything is held together by, or exists in, him (v. 17).

V. Christ is (ἐστιν) the head of his body, the church (v. 18; cf. 2:9-10).

VI. Through the Christ-event, God reconciled (ἀποκαταλλάξαι) everything to Christ (εἰς αὐτόν), making peace (v. 20). This reconciliation involved the pacification/disarmament of "the rulers and authorities" (2:15).

VII. Believers have been reconciled (1:21-22) and now live with Christ (2:13); they have been transferred from the power of darkness into the kingdom of light (1:13), buried and raised with Christ (2:12; cf. 3:9-10). Elsewhere in the letter it is clear that this renewal and reconciliation also has a future dimension (cf. 1:5, 24, 27-28; 3:4, 10-11).

Future (continuing from or consequent upon past and present events)

VIII. Christ will come (ἵνα γένηται) to have first place (πρωτεύων) in the (implied) renewed creation (v. 18).

IX. All creation finds its goal and purpose, its *telos*, in Christ (εἰς αὐτόν, v. 16; cf. v. 20), implying that there remains a forward-looking aspect to the processes of renewal and reconciliation.

I. The creation of all things (τὰ πάντα)

As with our examination of Romans 8:19-23, the obvious starting point to any underlying narrative is the act of creation. Like other New Testament texts, Colossians echoes, or at least assumes, something akin to the creation account of Genesis 1, but, using language which parallels that used of Wisdom and reflects Greek philosophical terminology concerned with cosmology (see §5.3 above), depicts Christ as the one in and through whom God created "the heavens and the Earth" (Col 1:16). This declaration coheres with the depiction of Christ's role in creation elsewhere in the New Testament (John 1:1-3; 1 Cor 8:6; Heb 1:2) and reflects an integration of Christ into the story of God's creation of the heavens and the Earth (cf. Gen 1:1–2:25).[89] As we have seen, τὰ πάντα refers to everything, indicating the universal and cosmic scope of the hymn's concerns. This view of all things as the work of the one (good) creator, in and through Christ, implies the intrinsic goodness of all created entities, including the nonhuman elements, a repeated emphasis in the first creation narrative in Genesis 1 (vv. 1:10, 12, 18, 21, 25, 31); there is no dualism here, no denigration of the material universe as the product of an evil or lesser deity.

The ἐν αὐτῷ of verse 16 is generally interpreted instrumentally, indicating Christ as God's (personal) *agent* in creation (cf. BDF §219).[90] On this reading, ἐν αὐτῷ ἐκτίσθη is essentially equivalent to δι' αὐτοῦ . . . ἔκτισται at the end of the verse. However, Moo argues for the locative "in," as the likely meaning of ἐν in this verse.[91] We would add that a locative sense is particularly likely if the notion of the universe as Christ's body continues to pervade the hymn: the uses of ἐν in verses 17-19 (esp. τὰ πάντα ἐν αὐτῷ συνέσηκεν), as well as 3:11 ([τὰ] πάντα καὶ ἐν πᾶσιν Χριστός) would support this reading of ἐν in verse 16.

Commentators generally agree that the description of Christ as πρωτότοκος πάσης κτίσεως (v. 15) and πρὸ πάντων (v. 17) relates to Christ's position of supremacy over creation rather than implying that Christ is a creature, the first created being.[92] Certainly, what is being stressed is "Christ's preeminent place in the created order"[93] — a use of πρωτότοκος that also coheres with its meaning in verse 18 — and verse 16 "indicates that Christ is in a quite different category from creation, since all things (*ta panta*) are said to have been created 'in him,' 'through him' and 'for him.' "[94] The repeated use of τὰ πάντα underlines the all-encompassing nature of the claims. Colossians 1:16 also describes Christ as the goal of all that has been created (εἰς αὐτόν) and so this event, although located in the past, is in fact the beginning of a story which implies and assumes a future fulfillment in Christ (see below).

II. The problem

The fact that God (subsequently) acts in Christ to reconcile all things implies a need for reconciliation and "making peace." As in Romans 8, however, where the causes of the bondage to decay and the subjection to futility remain unstated, here too there is no explicit indication as to what necessitates reconciliation of τὰ πάντα, nor what was the nature of the event that led to this becoming necessary. Indeed, compared with Romans 8, Colossians 1 offers even less of a clue as to the causes of the "problem."[95] For those who assume an anthropocentric focus here, the answer is obvious: the fall of humanity into sin.[96] If we assume a wider focus, then we need, as with Romans 8, to consider that the author may have envisaged a broader narrative of disruption, with enmity and corruption in the natural (and spiritual?) as well as the human world, arising from, or concomitant with, the breakdown in relationship between humanity and God.[97] Colin Gunton, for example, sees in Colossians 1:20 an indication of creation as an incomplete "project" which has been thrown off course and then brought back to its destiny by the Christ-event.[98]

Also relevant here is the use of the ἀπο- prefix in ἀποκαταλλάσσω. Porter notes that one of the two possible meanings of this preposition is "back," and that, in conjunction with καταλλάσσω, this could imply a restoration of previously disrupted relationships.[99] Porter himself rejects this interpretation because he judges that there is no other evidence for a reversal or reestablishment of a preexisting state in this passage, and because the "peacemaking" also found in Colossians 1:20 does not necessarily involve *restoration* of peace. Indeed, given (for example) Paul's use of καταλλάσσω to convey the restoration of relationship between husband and wife (1 Cor 7:11), it would seem that the ἀπο- prefix is not necessary to convey the sense of a restoration of relationship to an earlier, "conciled" state of affairs. As we suggested earlier, it would seem more likely to be used in an emphatic sense here, presumably to stress the huge scope of the reconciliation of which it speaks. However, with or without ἀπο, it also seems more likely, pace Porter, that the reconciliation the author has in view does imply some prior state of harmony, later disrupted. Precisely this understanding of reconciliation as implying a return to an earlier state is apparently understood by Tertullian[100] as well as many modern commentators. Marshall, for example, suggests that the verb "stresses more the thought of the restoration of a previously existing relationship."[101]

Given the fact that peacemaking implies a movement from estrangement toward right relationship and that all things are said to be initially created in, through, and for Christ, it seems exegetically plausible to read reconciliation in the sense of restoring things to the way they should be, the righting of a disrupted relationship. This in turn implies that a wrong turn has been taken at some point, although we can be even less sure than with Romans 8:19-23 as to the exact nature of the breakdown in right relationship, particularly insofar as it concerns the nonhuman creation. Furthermore, it is important to stress both that the Colossians' narrative is focused forwards, giving little to no indication as to what the supposed "pre-problem" state might have been, and also that the reconciliation achieved in Christ is much more than a kind of return; instead, as we shall see below, it is an attainment of the goal or telos of all creation.[102] This is a rather crucial and difficult point in relation to a scientifically informed contemporary appropriation of this narrative, as we shall see in the following chapter (see §6.4).

III. Reconciliation through the Christ-event

Whether or not the phrase "through the blood of his cross" (v. 20) was present in any supposed earlier version(s) of the hymn, it is crucial to the passage as the author presents it. God's work[103] of reconciliation and peacemaking was achieved through the crucifixion of Christ, though the author does not indicate any specific "theory" as to how this was achieved by this means (see further VI below).

Just as the opening lines of the hymn depict Christ as the first-born (πρωτότοκος) of all creation (v. 15; see I above), so his resurrection (clearly implied, if not specifically mentioned as such) marks him as firstborn (πρωτότοκος) from the dead (v. 18). As mentioned above, most commentators take πρωτότοκος in verse 15 to indicate Christ's supremacy, not his identity as part of creation. Here too it makes sense to see a stress on Christ's preeminent and unique place in the renewed creation—he is ἀρχή, as well as πρωτότοκος ἐκ τῶν νεκρῶν—but the resurrection also seems to mark Christ as the first to participate in new life, leading where others will follow (cf. Rom 8:29-30). The resurrection demonstrates the fact that a new beginning has been made; Christ is the founder and forerunner of a new humanity.[104] More than this, however, Christ's resurrection inaugurates the renewal of creation. Indeed, Moo suggests that the first strophe of the hymn deals with creation while the second is concerned with "new creation."[105] Colossians' primary focus, and that of the hymn specifically, may be anthropological and ecclesial, but there is a much wider scope in view. The language of "new creation" does not, of course, appear here explicitly (cf. 2 Cor 5:17; Gal 6:15; see §7.5 below), but since the "story" the hymn tells moves from the creation of all things to the subsequent reconciliation of all things in Christ, some such notion of cosmic renewal is clearly appropriate. Nonetheless, we should perhaps be more cautious than Moo (and others) about invoking the language of "new creation" specifically: the story of creation and renewal as the Colossian hymn tells it—with τὰ πάντα created, reconciled, and finding a *telos* in Christ—strongly implies that the same "creation" is in view throughout (just as Romans 8 tells the story of ἡ κτίσις, not one of old creation and new creation). There is no hint here of any "new" creation which might replace the old; this is instead the story of τὰ πάντα through the "events" of creation, problem, and resolution.

IV–V. All things existing in Christ, head of the church

With verses 17-18, often seen as a bridge or hinge between the two parts of the hymn dealing respectively with creation and redemption, we move toward the subject of the implications of the Christ-event.[106]

As with πρωτότοκος in verse 15, so too commentators agree that πρὸ πάντων (v. 17) describes Christ's position of supremacy over creation rather than implying that he is a creature.[107] In the phrase τὰ πάντα ἐν αὐτῷ συνέστηκεν we find perhaps the strongest expression of the idea that the whole universe actually exists in Christ,[108] a cosmology parallel in significant ways to what Balabanksi calls the "permeation cosmology" of the Stoics (see §5.3 above). Indeed, it seems likely that the echoes of both Jewish Wisdom, and of the Stoic concept of πνεῦμα, serve to emphasize the integrity of the whole created order, which, as a whole, finds its being in Christ. If an earlier version of the hymn omitted the words τῆς ἐκκλησίας in verse 18, then here too there may have been a further description of a kind of christological cosmology, with the whole universe as Christ's body. But even with the more ecclesially focused text we have, verse 17 clearly affirms the present existence of all things in Christ.

VI–VII. The reconciliation of all things, and specifically of believers, in Christ

Alongside the declaration that all things were created and exist in Christ, also crucial for ecological interpretation of this passage, as we have seen, is the announcement of reconciliation and the making of peace. In interpreting this element of our story, we face two important issues: one concerns the scope of the reconciliation, the other concerns its temporal location (past, present, or future). As we saw when surveying previous commentary on this passage, a number of interpreters have insisted that reconciliation must have a primarily human (or at least personalistic) focus. Certainly, for the author of Colossians, the main focus is on the reconciliation enacted for members of the church (1:21-22) and the pacification of the hostile powers and authorities, all of whom have been brought under the lordship of Christ (2:10, 15).[109] Yet the scope of τὰ πάντα is undoubtedly cosmic and universal (see I and IV above). Indeed, the gloss on τὰ πάντα in verse 20 seems almost deliberately to counter any exclusively anthropocentric interpretation: the reconciliation of τὰ πάντα, the peacemaking achieved by the blood of the cross, explicitly encompasses τὰ ἐπὶ τῆς γῆς and τὰ ἐν τοῖς οὐρανοῖς (cf. also 1:23). As noted in II above, the author gives no indication as to precisely what is the nature of the problem and enmity that gives rise to the need for reconciliation. Nor does he offer any indication as to what "reconciliation" in the world of nature might mean.[110]

Commentators often remark upon the degree to which the eschatology of Colossians is more realized than it is in Paul, and that expressed by the hymn more realized than in the rest of the epistle. This latter difference may well be explained by the particular character of the hymn; as has been remarked, the language of worship and credal confession is likely to express as sure and present realities what is elsewhere recognized to remain in the realm of only partially realized future hope.[111]

The reconciliation of all things announced in verse 20 has been interpreted by some commentators as being already accomplished.[112] Certainly the letter's recipients are depicted as having already been reconciled (1:21-22) and already raised with Christ (2:12) although their glorification lies in the future when Christ appears (3:4). By contrast, Paul speaks of Christians as having died with Christ yet waiting for a future resurrection (Rom 6:4-5; cf. 1 Cor 15:22), and as groaning and hoping, along with the whole creation, as they anticipate a future liberation (Rom 8:18-25). Nonetheless, the differences between Colossians and the undisputed Paulines can be exaggerated, and the extent to which Colossians' eschatology is realized overplayed.[113] In the undisputed Paulines there are statements that stress the "already" aspect of the process of transformation (e.g., 2 Cor 5:17-18), and in Colossians there are clear indications of the "not yet": the present remains a time of pressing *toward* the goal of toil, hope, and suffering (1:23-29), a time when believers face the challenge of orienting their lives in accordance with God's call, anticipating future glory (3:1-17; cf. 3:24, 4:12). The author writes of the recipients as having been raised with Christ (3:1), but nevertheless goes on to instruct them to put to death whatever is earthly (3:5); they are said already to have clothed themselves with the new but nevertheless are urged to clothe themselves with virtues appropriate to God's people, such as love (3:12, 14). In other words, despite the realized eschatological declarations of the hymn, and similarly realized statements elsewhere in Colossians, it is clear that the author assumes there to be a future dimension to this process, a "not yet" as well as an "already," in a way which is at least broadly coherent with this dynamic elsewhere in the undisputed Pauline letters. Whatever we consider to be implied in the reconciliation of "all things," it is evident that this process has a past, present, and future dimension: reconciliation was achieved through Christ's death on the cross, is (thus) a current experience of believers, but, like the Christians' journey to glory, remains to be brought to full and final fruition.

Indeed, the Christian recipients of the letter, already reconciled to God yet hoping for and awaiting a future glory, have their hope precisely because of the way in which their own "story" has been caught up into the narrative of Christ, a story which begins at the creation of "all things" and will end with Christ's being all in all (3:11). As Fowl puts it, "they are a community founded in the stories of the life, death and resurrection of Christ";[114] but in the Colossian hymn their story is embedded within a larger and longer narrative stretching from the creation of the universe to its consummation in Christ. Their story, in other words, is part of the story of everything (τὰ πάντα); as in Romans 8, though differently expressed, their suffering and hope are located within the wider story of the whole creation.

VIII–IX. The consummation of all things in Christ

We have already commented immediately above on the extent to which the vision of reconciliation in Colossians implies a future as well as present dimension. The somewhat realized eschatology of Colossians, and of the hymn in particular, should not be overstressed; a future orientation and anticipated completion is equally apparent in the letter. There are two specific points in the hymn, despite its generally realized form of expression, that would seem to point to such a future orientation.

One such point is in verse 18: Christ is ἀρχή, and firstborn from the dead, ἵνα γένηται ἐν πᾶσιν αὐτὸς πρωτεύων. As Moo points out, although most commentators assume that Christ's preeminence is "an established fact," the periphrastic construction in verse 18 may convey "God's intention of ultimately bringing all creation under his rule in Christ . . . Christ rules the church with the purpose [ἵνα γένηται] of bringing all things ultimately within the scope of that rule."[115] Moo's comment perhaps downplays too much the extent to which Colossians presents Christ as already ruler of all powers and authorities (2:10, 15), but it does helpfully indicate that there is at least, even in the hymn, an "already/ not-yet" tension, not simply an "already." Indeed, the ἵνα γένηται may suggest that, despite the lofty declarations of what is apparently already achieved in Christ, appropriate for the language of worship and hym- nody, the writer is aware that the processes of reconciliation and peace- making are underway, but far from complete.

A similar sense of future fulfillment is indicated in the use of εἰς in verse 16, where all things are described as εἰς αὐτὸν ἔκτισται. The same preposition is used to indicate Christ as the focus for universal reconciliation—assuming that the referent is Christ and not God (v. 20).[116] A comparable expression is found in 1 Corinthians 8:6, but there, while τὰ πάντα are said to come from God the Father (ἐξ οὗ), through Jesus Christ (δι᾽ οὗ), the teleology includes only "us" (ἡμεῖς), and makes God the Father the goal (εἰς αὐτόν), Christ the means (δι᾽ αὐτοῦ). The hymn's formulation thus goes further than the undisputed Paulines (cf. also Eph 1:10).[117] In Colossians the direction or purpose concerns "all things" and relates to Christ; there is also a clear parallel between the activities of creation and redemption. If the reconciliation of "all things" is proleptically announced at the close of the hymn, then the reconcilia- tion of the letter's recipients in verse 21 could be viewed as the firstfruits of that eschatological event; the church is "the sign and seal of the new creation taking shape on earth."[118] As we have already noted (see III above), while there is good reason to see the Colossian hymn as talking about the renewal of creation, some caution is in order before importing the language of new creation into the hymn's interpretation. Perhaps better is a comment like that of Christian Stettler, which more appropri- ately stresses that this is, throughout, the story of the whole creation, τὰ πάντα, which finds its ultimate fulfillment in Christ: "the bringing into being of the whole creation for the Messiah (v. 16) first comes to fulfill- ment in the reconciliation of all things to Jesus (v. 20)."[119]

5.6. SUMMARY AND NARRATIVE ANALYSIS

What then can we conclude about the shape of the story of creation in Colossians, and specifically in the Colossian hymn? A brief summary might run as follows.

Everything made was created in and through Christ, God's co-agent in the work of creation and, in some sense, the "location" of creation, which exists "in" him. Some form of enmity seems to have disrupted the relationships within this created order, such that reconciliation and peacemaking became necessary. This was achieved in the Christ-event: the death of Christ brought about the needed reconciliation, and the resurrection marks the inauguration of the renewal of creation. This accomplishment is depicted and understood as, in a sense, already achieved; but it is also clear that the process is ongoing and awaits future completion, both for believers and (implicitly) for the wider creation. The present remains a time of toil, suffering, and hope. Christ is the one for whom all things were made, and in whom they find their *telos*.

In terms of the analysis of narrative and plot, the central character in Colossians 1:15-20 is τὰ πάντα: four times the phrase is used (plus the phrases πρὸ πάντων and ἐν πᾶσιν in vv. 17-18). Beginning with the making of τὰ πάντα (v. 16) and ending with the reconciliation of τὰ πάντα (v. 20) this is *the story of everything*. As the epistolary context of the hymn shows, the immediate focus of the author is on the implications of this story of everything for the members of the churches at Colossae: *they* have been rescued from the powers of darkness (1:13) and reconciled from a state of enmity by incorporation into Christ (1:21-22); and it is they who are urged to press on in their journey, to embody the peace of Christ in their everyday lives and interactions (3:1-17). But if this is the story of everything, and also specifically the story of the Christians of Colossae, it is, more fundamentally, the story of Christ: it is in and for Christ that all things exist, and in the body of his flesh that believers are reconciled (1:22). The achievement of the Colossian hymn is to tell the story of everything as the story of Christ; or, put differently, to incorporate (literally) everything into Christ (cf. 3:11).[120] Yet as in Romans 8, the central *actor* in the story encapsulated in the hymn is scarcely visible, at least in terms of explicit references. God is mentioned explicitly only once, in the description of Christ as the εἰκὼν τοῦ θεοῦ (v. 15), and implicitly as the one whose fullness dwells in Christ (v. 19; cf. 2:9). Yet God is assumed as the Creator, who makes all things in and through Christ, and the one who acts to reconcile all things in Christ. Nonetheless, it remains striking that the language of Colossians is much less explicitly theocentric than is Paul's elsewhere, notably in 2 Corinthians 5:19 (θεὸς ἦν ἐν Χριστῷ . . .), and 1 Corinthians 8:6 and 15:28 (see chap. 7 below). Here in Colossians, God's being is so fully identified with Christ's that the explicit identification of God as character and actor is decidedly muted.

Indeed, the plot of the story—scarcely visible in the acclamatory, realized language of the hymn—is most evident in the prepositions which describe the relationship of all things to Christ: ἐν, δία, εἰς. These prepositions, especially δία and εἰς, convey, albeit in highly compressed form, a sense of narrative direction and purpose. It was in and through Christ that all things came to be. Yet from the very beginning their purpose and goal was also Christ; the outcome of the process of reconciliation and making peace is that [τὰ] πάντα καὶ ἐν πᾶσιν Χριστός (3:11).

We saw above that behind the thought-world of the hymn may lie Stoic cosmologies based on a cyclical narrative of the cosmos "evolving" to a point at which a conflagration returns it to a primordial state.[121] In terms of Frye's analysis of narrative genres this Stoic position is from a human point of view an ironic, or at best a tragic, narrative, since there is no consummation, neither unity with the divine, nor success in a quest despite the efforts of evil. There is at best a purification which stems from the acceptance of what is inevitable.[122] Balabanski notes that

> [t]he religious affirmation that salvation was to be found in the one in whom and through whom all things exist must have been appealing to those who accepted the cosmological framework of Stoicism, but found the ethical idealism of Stoicism too hard to attain or who could not perceive any salvation in the Stoic teaching that willing acceptance of the external situation constitutes freedom.[123]

This is a telling passage, particularly in the light of her conviction that "Stoicism was very likely the most widely accepted worldview in the Western world," appealing "to all classes, attracting slaves and labourers as well as kings and emperors."[124] She shows plausibly that "the Stoic cosmological framework lent itself to Christological reflection."[125] But she perhaps understates the extent to which the eventual text of the letter subverts the narrative genre of Stoic cosmology and so, at the same time, counters the imperial version of that narrative.

Whether the prevailing cosmology in the circles to which the Colossian letter was addressed was predominantly Stoic, or that of a Hellenistic Judaism influenced by Stoic and Middle Platonic motifs, and whether the telling final phrase "having made peace by the blood of his cross" (1:20) is authentic to the original hymn or not, the rhetoric of the final version of the hymn is undoubtedly that of transformation. It makes a very strong claim on those who "could not perceive any salvation in the Stoic teaching." Whatever might have been thought to have been the state of humans before the redemptive work of Christ, whether it be subjection to disordered powers or more directly to the blocking effects of sin, that state has been transformed. Reconciliation has been achieved; peace has been made. Even more markedly than in the undisputed letters of Paul, a union with Christ has been effected which is the resurrection state, life hidden with Christ in God (3:3; see also 1:13, 2:9-13, esp. v. 12). This reconciled, resurrected state is claimed as achieved, yet also clearly remains a future hope, just as does the ultimate reconciliation of all things to (εἰς) Christ. And the wider literary context of the hymn makes clear that the members of the ἐκκλησία, the community in which this reconciliation is prefigured, continue a hopeful struggle toward this goal (1:5-11, 23-29; 3:1-10).

At first sight this cosmology would be assigned to the genre of a "comic" union with the divine, in which believers are invited to claim through baptism a life hidden with Christ in God, a life in the fullness of God (rightly identified by Petr Pokorný with the indwelling of the Holy Spirit).[126] Peace has been made, in this narrative, but not the *pax Augusta*. As Sylvia Keesmaat makes clear, the peace made by Christ is very different from the peacemaking of the Empire; it is effected not through using crucifixion as a weapon of oppression but through suffering it as a means of atonement.[127] So as we saw in our analysis of the Romans text in §4.5, we may once again be looking at a counter-narrative, not merely to the prevailing cosmology of Stoicism, but also in rejection of the imperial hegemony.

As these concluding reflections will already have indicated, there are both similarities and differences between Colossians 1:15-20 and Romans 8:19-23. In the next chapter we shall compare their two "stories of creation" in more detail, and explore further the issue of their narrative category. We shall then be in a position to consider, critically, what these two texts together might contribute to the shaping of the kind of hermeneutical lens with which we might begin to construct an ecological Pauline theology.

Chapter 6

THE CONSTRUCTION OF A PAULINE HERMENEUTICAL LENS

6.1 INTRODUCTION

Having examined in some detail the two Pauline texts most frequently cited in ecotheological discussion, our next step is to compare these two passages and their narratives of creation. This task will occupy the first section of this chapter. A second task, however, is also crucial, and one we attempt in the second section. This is to reflect, critically, on the ways in which these texts might or might not straightforwardly imply an ecofriendly theology, or mandate any particular approach to environmental ethics. Despite the frequent appeal to these texts, which is often such as to imply that their content, rightly understood, is sufficient to indicate the importance of Christian action to protect and preserve the Earth, we consider that their contribution is more ambivalent and complex than often acknowledged. This does not mean that they cannot contribute positively to an ecotheological ethics, but does mean that that contribution needs critical and constructive engagement, of the kind we outlined in methodological terms in chapter 2.

In the third main section of the chapter, therefore, we move toward such a constructive engagement with these texts and the narratives of creation they reflect, considering what their ecotheological and ecoethi-cal significance might be. Writing from within a context informed by both ecological concerns and the insights of evolutionary science, we explore how they might contribute to a Pauline hermeneutical lens that can help to shape an ecological reading of Pauline theology and ethics.

6.2 TWO NARRATIVES OF CREATION: ROMANS 8:19-23 AND COLOSSIANS 1:15-20

In comparing the stories of creation found in Romans 8:19-23 and Colossians 1:15-20 in order to allow those narratives to inform a wider ecological reading of Pauline theology, we must steer a course between two extremes. One, often reflected in the instincts of biblical scholars, is always to stress the differences between various texts, wary of any (theologically driven) harmonization. The other, often characteristic of theological or apologetic engagement with the Bible, is to system-atize the material without sufficient caution, prematurely or uncritically drawing a single doctrine or message from diverse texts.

At a broad level, the narratives reflected in, or assumed by, our two texts tell a similar story with a similar shape: a story of creation, prob-lem, and resolution. This basic shape also coheres with what is presented elsewhere in Paul as the essential shape of the story of Christ: a story of descent and ascent, in which Christ enters the realm of the corrupted age, suffers its consequences, rises victorious, and is enthroned as Lord (2 Cor 8:9; Phil 2:5-11). Writing on Philippians 2:5-11, for example, Stephen Fowl comments that "what we have here is a down/up pattern with the change in direction occurring in the transition between vv. 8 and 9."[1] The story of Christ and the story of creation cohere not merely coincidentally, but because they mutually inform each other (cf. Rom 5:12-21). And the Colossian hymn combines them especially clearly, with the move from creation through some form of problematic state to reconciliation explicitly located within the story of Christ, whose death on the cross was the crucial turning point and means to achieve recon-ciliation and establish peace.[2]

Moving to a greater level of specificity, it is interesting to compare how Romans 8 and Colossians 1 differently tell, or do not tell, aspects of this basic narrative of creation. This is most clearly set out in tabular form:

Basic narrative	Rom 8:19-23	Col 1:15-20
Creation	(Not explicitly mentioned: implicit in κτίσις.)	Explicitly described as done (by God) in and through Christ.
Problem	Explicitly described as bondage to decay—God's subjection of the creation to futility being both an aspect of the problem and in some way also a precursor to the resolution.	(Not explicitly described: implicit in the need for reconciliation and making peace.)
Resolution	Explicitly described as hope of liberation to share in freedom and glory.	Explicitly described as reconciliation and peacemaking.

Each passage omits explicit description of one stage in the narrative: in Romans 8 it is the original act of creation that is only implicitly referred to; in Colossians 1 whatever is problematic in the created order remains only implicit. But, as we have shown in the preceding chapters, these aspects of the story of creation are clearly enough implied.

There are, of course, significant differences in the language used to describe the story of creation. With its greater focus on the present state of groaning and suffering—a focus which relates the story of creation to the specific circumstances of the Christians in Rome—Romans 8 labels the consequences of creation's problematic state and depicts a hope for liberation and glory. With its focus on the pacification of the powers and authorities and the ending of enmity, Colossians speaks instead of reconciliation and peacemaking.

Also strikingly distinctive is the christological focus of the Colossian hymn: the story of creation, as we have seen, is here subsumed into the story of Christ, in, through, and for whom all things came to be, and by whose cross and resurrection reconciliation was achieved and new life begun. This is a difference not only between Colossians 1 and Romans 8, but more generally between the more theocentric undisputed Paulines and the highly christologically focused Colossians and Ephesians, most sharply epitomized in the contrast between 1 Corinthians 15:28 and Colossians 3:11 (see further §7.4).[3]

One significant similarity, though expressed in different ways, is found in the anthropocentric focus of both passages. In Romans 8, the children of God stand at the heart of the story; it is their revealing that creation awaits, and their freedom and glory creation longs to share. In Colossians 1, despite an importantly cosmic scope of concern, the specific focus, when the hymn is set in its epistolary context, falls on the impact of Christ's reconciling deed for "us," the Christians to whom the author writes (cf. 1:13-14, 21-22), those who now comprise the church, the body of which Christ is the head (1:18, 22). This, of course, is a crucial issue for many ecological interpreters, and one that requires critical and careful reflection (on which see §6.3). To anticipate our argument below, our conclusion is that we should not reject anthro-pocentrism — as in the approach adopted by the Earth Bible Project (see chap. 1 above). Rather, an ecological theology informed by bibli-cal texts, and specifically by the Pauline material, will need to retain anthropocentrism, but to qualify and understand it in a particular way. This approach, we argue, offers more fruitful potential for reshaping the Christian theological tradition — and for generating ecotheological ethics — than an outright rejection of all forms of anthropocentrism. Such a rejection represents too great (and problematic) a break with that tradition.

Colossians and Romans, then, present broadly compatible stories of the cosmos, reflecting a shared narrative of creation, problem, and resolution. Moreover, in both cases it is possible to represent the bibli-cal text as taking a stand for a cosmology in tension with a dominant narrative in the Greco-Roman milieu (see §§4.5, 5.6). Paul in Romans 8 seems to appeal to a story of struggle, a romantic quest-story into which the believers are caught up, co-groaning with the creation, in rejection of the comic narrative of fruitfulness of creation under Caesar (chap. 4). The Colossian hymn seems to assert a largely comic narrative[4] of reconciliation of the cosmos with God in Christ, in rejection of the illusory *eirenopoiesis* of the imperial cult (chap. 5). Beyond that, the hymn may be seen as reframing a Stoic cosmology of ironic acceptance of the cosmic powers—and their inevitable cycle of growth and destruction—into a narrative of transformation.

The two narratives from Romans and Colossians do differ in a number of respects. Importantly, they employ different images of creation's renewal or restoration: freedom and glory on the one hand, reconciliation and peace on the other. It is not necessarily the case that these images are incompatible with one another; indeed, they plausibly form part of a range of images with which the process of renewal can be depicted. But they are different images, and raise different possibilities and different questions for shaping an ecological ethics. Indeed, before we begin to develop our more constructive ecotheological engagement with these texts, we wish to highlight some of the reasons why the move from text to ecological theology and ethics is less straightforward than often assumed.

6.3 REASONS FOR CAUTION
Theo/Christocentrism, Anthropocentrism, and Eschatology

Although our narrative analysis of both Romans 8:19-23 and Colossians 1:15-20 has, in many ways, supported their relevance to the concerns of ecotheology, we also consider it important, not least in view of many too quick or easy moves from these texts to Christian environmentalism, to consider some of the critical difficulties in making such connections. Careful analysis of both texts shows that their contribution to ecotheology and environmental ethics is far less straightforward than many appeals to them would suggest. There are a number of specific aspects to notice in this regard.

First, in both cases, the focus is fundamentally theocentric (Romans 8) or christocentric (Colossians 1). It is God, Paul implies in Romans 8:20, who has subjected the creation to futility. This is a motif elided by many ecological writers in their anxiety to profit from the notion of creation groaning in travail, but its presence here makes it harder to evoke the narrative as simply or unproblematically "ecofriendly." Moreover, the liberation which is anticipated is dependent on the action of God. There is no *explicit* statement in Romans 8—considered by itself—that humans are expected to play any substantive role in "liberating" κτίσις. The chapter, taken overall, primarily encourages them to endure their suffering, a groaning in which the whole of creation shares, because of the certainty of God's final deliverance. Thus, any ethical mandate "to work toward the goal of creation's final transformation," or even "to be involved in working toward those ends that God will finally secure through his own sovereign intervention"[5] needs to emerge from an imaginative and creative engagement with the text, and with the wider resources of Pauline (and, more broadly, Christian) theology.

In Colossians 1:15-20 it is God (implicitly) who has acted in Christ, not only in creation but also in reconciling all things, something the hymn depicts as already accomplished. As we noted in the previous chapter, Eduard Schweizer sees the depiction of total reconciliation as the hymnic language of worship which cannot be pressed for doctrine.[6] Hence Schweizer insists that "a *doctrine* of the redemption of the universe cannot be based on Colossians."[7] Moreover, the primary focus for the author's notion of reconciliation is the "powers and authorities," spiritual as well as earthly, angelic as well as human, as 1:16 makes clear (cf. also 2:15). Such a focus should serve to remind us that the author's cosmology and priorities are very different from those of most modern Westerners, and certainly by no means straightforwardly identifiable with ecological concern for the (material) planet Earth. We have seen in the previous chapter how, despite the realized eschatological language of the hymn, the letter as a whole makes clear that there is also a future dimension to the process of reconciliation, and an associated set of ethical responsibilities. Nonetheless, despite the depiction of a reconciliation in Christ that is truly universal and cosmic in its scope, there are no ecologically related ethical implications explicitly drawn from this in the text. As in Romans 8, this work of cosmic reconciliation is the work of God in Christ, not primarily of humans, and the ethical instructions that do feature in Colossians concern the relationships of Christians with one another (3:8-17) or in the household context (3:18–4:1). It would of course be anachronistic to expect the author of an ancient letter to see ecoethical implications in a passage such as the Colossian hymn. But this only serves to underscore the point that we cannot find ecotheology and ethics directly or explicitly, even in these "favorite" biblical texts.

A second key issue is the anthropocentrism of these texts. In Romans 8:19-21, the redemption of the children of God stands at the center of the story, as the focus for creation's hopes, and the anthropocentrism is more evident still when the passage is set within the wider context of Romans 8 as a whole. Writing of our other key "mantra-text," Marianne Thompson observes, "While Colossians does also speak of the reconciliation of 'all things,' the renewal of human beings in the image of God stands at the heart and center of God's new work of creation. There is an inescapable anthropocentrism in God's creative and redemptive purposes, as the Incarnation itself bears witness."[8]

For some ecotheological writers this is a regrettable tendency which has to be removed from any adequate contemporary ecological theology. The writers in the Earth Bible Team, for example, reading through the lens of "ecojustice principles" which include the "intrinsic worth" and "interconnectedness" of all things and the "mutual custodianship" of Earth and its responsible inhabitants, tend to react with suspicion to any anthropocentrism in the biblical texts. Indeed the principles themselves imply a clear opposition to any such anthropocentrism, whether in the texts or their interpreters. Such a human-centered focus is to be resisted by those seeking a renewed ecological engagement with Scripture by "reading from the perspective of Earth."[9] Does this mean that these texts, in the end, have to be treated with critical suspicion and rejected as positive sources for ecological theology?

It is worth at this point drawing on a distinction proposed by Lukas Vischer between anthropomonism and anthropocentrism. The former, Vischer suggests, is the view that it is only human beings who are of concern in the redeeming purposes of God; human interests are exclusively important such that "humans . . . can dispose of all things . . . for their own purposes." The latter, by contrast, accepts that human beings are of central importance in the divine economy of salvation and are "called to fulfil a special and specific role in [the] world," but does not thereby imply that there is no value or eschatological purpose for the rest of creation.[10]

Another significant distinction has recently been drawn by David Clough.[11] Clough accepts that texts like Romans 8:19-23 imply a kind of instrumental anthropocentrism—that is, that human beings are in some way central to the process by which God is bringing about the liberation of the whole creation. But Clough denies that the biblical texts imply or require any kind of "teleological anthropocentrism," that is, the view that humans have some ultimate value or central place in the (redeemed) creation, or that all things were created so as to give rise to humanity as the source of ultimate creaturely value. We share with Clough a resistance to this kind of teleological anthropocentrism, and to any form of anthropomonist theology or ethics. However, we hold that a chastened and humble instrumental anthropocentrism, which strongly resists anthropomonism, can appropriately remain key to an ecological theology, not only because, as Richard Bauckham points out, human beings evidently do, de facto, have "unique power to affect most of the rest of creation on this planet,"[12] but also because it is human beings whom we address and to whom we look for responsible action in relation to creation's future.

Romans 8 may indeed provide interesting resources for such an ecological anthropocentrism, since it depicts creation, humanity, and the Spirit as conjoined in a chorus of hopeful groaning, and links creation's hope with that of humanity, and specifically that of the "children of God."[13] The Christian believers are significant here, not because they represent the few who alone will be redeemed—an anthropomonist and exclusivist doctrine of salvation—but because they are the ones in whom the promise of renewal and transformation is already coming to fruition: just as they have the firstfruits of the Spirit, so, in a sense, they are the firstfruits of a redeemed creation, the "deposit" that guarantees the remainder (cf. 2 Cor 1:22, 5:5).

Likewise, Colossians' focus on the church can be read in a similar way, with the Christian community representing "the sign and seal of the new creation taking shape on earth,"[14] and with "the redemption of the cosmos" being "prefigured" in the church.[15] At the same time, any ecological anthropocentrism needs to be carefully and cautiously stated, avoiding overstatement about humanity's power.[16]

A third problem concerns the texts' eschatological focus, whether in the forward-looking form of Romans 8 or the more realized form of Colossians 1:15-20. In the case of Romans 8:19-23, the implied narrative is profoundly eschatological, and depicts the final liberation of creation—like the redemption of human bodies—as something which lies beyond the present era in which suffering and mortality are inescapable. In the case of Colossians, the eschatology is presented in a more realized mode, but still anticipates a future glory (1:27). The author urges believers to "seek the things that are above" (3:1), and assures them, "When Christ your life appears, then you too will appear with him in glory" (3:4, NAB). A good deal of effort has gone into attempts to show that biblical eschatology does not envisage the (imminent) *destruction* or annihilation of the Earth, but rather its *transformation*;[17] but even if this is convincing—which seems unlikely, at least for some texts[18]—the gain is much less than is generally recognized. Even a transformed creation, no longer subject to physical suffering and death, is so radically different from the creation we inhabit that it is not immediately clear how classic ecofriendly campaigns (such as recycling) might "help" to reach that end, particularly when the achievement of the renewal of creation is so decisively presented as the action of God in Christ, not of the Christian believers.[19] Indeed, as we have already noted above, another key difficulty in moving from these texts to Christian environmentalism is that they do not draw any particular environmental-ethical implications or explicit injunctions from their depictions of creation groaning for liberation, or receiving full reconciliation in Christ.

All this, combined with the fact that Paul's narratives are, of course, infused with ancient cosmological and mythological presuppositions that are radically different from those of contemporary science, should greatly heighten our caution in appealing to Romans 8 or Colossians

1 as a sufficient or self-evident basis for Christian environmentalism. Indeed, we agree with Neil Messer when he writes in connection with Romans 8 that "considerable reticence is in order as to the nature of this futility and the manner of this liberation."[20] There is—despite the many brief appeals to these texts in ecotheological writing—no easy means to "read-off" any *particular* contemporary ethical responsibilities or policies from Romans 8:19-23, Colossians 1:15-20, or indeed any other biblical text. The problems and issues we have sketched above should together indicate that drawing on these texts to develop an ecotheology or to outline an ethical response to our environmental challenges will require an imaginative, theologically and scientifically informed engagement, one that goes well beyond what Paul and his contemporaries might have envisaged. We now proceed to attempt such an engagement.

6.4 A PAULINE HERMENEUTICAL LENS

As we noted in chapter 2, drawing on the work of Conradie, traditions of biblical interpretation operate with certain lenses at their heart: justification by faith, liberation, stewardship, and so on. These lenses, which Conradie terms "doctrinal keys,"[21] derive from both the biblical text and the contemporary context of the reader, and are constructed in the meeting of these two horizons. Once constructed, such lenses offer further potential for fruitful reading of biblical texts and for generating theology and ethics. In what follows we use the term "hermeneutical lens" (see our analysis in §2.4), recognizing both that the lens is constructed on the basis of an interpretive process involving the juxtaposition of our contemporary contextual understandings with our core biblical texts, and also that we use the lens first to reread those same texts in a hermeneutical spiral (see below), and then to reread the wider Pauline corpus. The emphasis is therefore on hermeneutics rather than doctrine.

There are good reasons why Romans 8:19-23 and Colossians 1:15-20 have been favorite texts for ecotheologians, in particular their explicit references to the nonhuman creation and its redemption. Put in terms of the approach summarized above, we might say that they offer the potential to generate a particular kind of hermeneutical lens that, given the priorities of our contemporary context, deserves to be made central to a new reading of Paul. At the same time, we have shown that the contribution of these texts to ecotheology and ethics is less straightforward and obvious than is often assumed; hence the need for a critical and constructive engagement. It is precisely this kind of nuanced and critical approach that an explicit discussion of hermeneutical lenses makes possible.

We are well aware that other passages could be chosen as focal material, and in chapter 7 we look briefly at some ecotheologies that might result from such choices. We would simply reiterate here that to select the largest corpus of doctrinal and ethical material in the New Testament, and then to focus on the two passages that are agreed by most commentators to have explicit reference to the nonhuman creation, is at least a plausible choice of shaping construct for a Christian interpreter (cf. Introduction above). What we are adding to Conradie's scheme is the possibility that close reading and narrative analysis of the key biblical texts themselves may provide vital shaping of the lens through which the wider Pauline corpus will be read. Conradie suggests that in a particular exercise of interpretation, such as an ecological interpretation, a doctrinal construct (such as stewardship) may shape the reading of a biblical narrative. In our approach, much of the shape of the lens (though not its whole character or its choice as lens) is derived from engagement with the biblical text itself (acknowledging that no such engagement comes without its own presuppositions) rather than from outside. This approach stands in contrast to the "ecojustice principles" advocated by the Earth Bible Project, which eschew any explicit connection between the biblical tradition and the content of the principles, deriving the latter instead from dialogue with the contemporary fields of ecology, and so forth (see §§1.3, 2.3).

As we noted in §2.4, there is an inevitable degree of circularity in the hermeneutical process, since hermeneutical lenses are both products of the tradition and the means for its critical rereading and reconfiguration. Some form of circularity is also inherent in relating parts to whole, and so on. Similarly, a reading is always from the outset shaped by a contemporary context, whether or not that is acknowledged, yet at the same time we read the texts in order to generate new insights and proposals: a reading is neither "neutral" and disinterested nor simply predetermined by the presuppositions of the interpreter. There is, as many have pointed out, an ongoing spiral of interpretation, in which an "interested," contextually shaped perspective generates a reading of a text that is more than simply a confirmation of positions already held, but instead contributes constructively to the interpreter's theology and ethics, and thus shapes further rereadings.[22] Our hermeneutical lens, based initially on our engagement with these two key texts, will, then, be developed and presented in three phases. First we offer some general reflections on the focus of our key texts, deploying the methods of contemporary biblical exegesis, including narrative criticism, and an awareness of the context of the letters of which the texts are a part, to suggest contributions they can make to an ecotheological lens. Second, we bring the texts into conversation with contemporary scientific perspectives, which form part of our contemporary context and (as we shall show) necessarily shape our hermeneutical lens, placing limits upon what can be thought theologically about the created world, its past, present, and future. We then proceed to employ this scientifically informed perspective in dialogue with our key texts to see how such a developing lens — constructed, of course, provisionally and heuristically with a constant eye on its theological and ethical fruitfulness — might start to shape the contours of an ecotheological ethic.

Key ecotheological contributions from Romans 8 and Colossians 1

One focus that both Romans 8 and Colossians 1 offer, in their different ways, is a clear declaration that *the scope of God's saving action in Christ is nothing less than the whole of creation*. While other Pauline texts affirm God's creation (through Christ) of all things (notably 1 Cor 8:6), no others are so clear or developed in *including all creation equally within the forward-looking process of redemption*. The cosmos, from this perspective, is not merely the stage on which the drama of human redemption takes place but is itself fully bound up in the story of renewal and liberation, at the center of which stand the small communities of Christians who, in the Pauline vision, embody and anticipate this hope.

As such, Romans 8 and Colossians 1 offer resources for refocusing the reading of the Pauline tradition, away from the long-established preoccupation with human salvation and relationship with God. As Brendan Byrne comments,

> Since Augustine in the fifth century . . . the issue of justification by faith has dominated the interpretation of Paul in the Western theological tradition. This ensured that interpreters of Paul were engaged in a virtually exclusive preoccupation with relations between human beings and God. What Paul thought or wrote about human relationship to the nonhuman created world scarcely entered the picture.[23]

However, as we have already noted, and will explore in more detail below, this anthropocentric focus is not only a characteristic of Paul's interpreters but also of Paul himself. We cannot pretend that Paul's main focus is anything other than humanity, and specifically the communities of believers whose corporate life Paul seeks to shape and sustain. The Pauline letters have only rather little to say, in explicit terms at least, about "human relationship [and, we might add, God's relationship] to the nonhuman created world." But this is where our own priorities and preoccupations come into play. Just as previous readings of Paul (and the Bible more generally) have been decisively shaped by the contexts of, say, medieval monasticism, Nazi Germany, apartheid South Africa, impoverished Latin America, and so on, so our own reading demands to be shaped by the pressing issue of the state of the Earth and the impact of human activity upon it.

Placing our two chosen texts at the center of our reading of the Pauline tradition also carries certain consequences for our construal of Pauline theology. One implication is a shift of focus onto what has been called the "universal" strand in Paul's views on salvation. Sven Hillert has persuasively drawn attention to two such strands in Pauline thought, which he labels "universal" and "limited" salvation.[24] Some Pauline texts depict salvation as having a universal scope (e.g., Rom 5:18), while others stress the contrast between the saved minority and those who are lost (e.g., 1 Cor 1:18). Hillert resists any harmonization of these two strands, and insists that both remain important and valuable in theological reflection.[25] An ecologically orientated engagement with Paul, and one that stresses the contribution of texts like Romans 8 and Colossians 1 will, unavoidably, emphasize the universal scope of God's saving work. It is, in the language of Romans 8, the whole creation (πᾶσα ἡ κτίσις) that yearns to share in the liberation and glory of the children of God (vv. 21-22), or, in the language of Colossians 1, all things (τὰ πάντα) that are caught up and reconciled in Christ (v. 20). Elsewhere too Paul's letters stress the universality of Christian hope (Rom 5:18, 11:32-36; 1 Cor 15:22) and envisage the ultimate incorporation of all things into God/Christ (1 Cor 15:28; Col 3:11).

Some commentators resist any universalist interpretation of Paul, keen to stress (often for theological reasons) the equally significant emphasis on the salvation (only) of the elect.[26] This applies even to some who stress the positive ecological implications of Paul's theology. For example, Moo accepts that Colossians 1:20 envisages a cosmic scope to reconciliation in Christ, and sees the passage as providing a "mandate for a biblically oriented environmentalism," but rejects a universalist implication, distinguishing between unbelieving humanity and the wider creation: "Colossians 1:20 teaches, then, not 'cosmic salvation' or even 'cosmic redemption,' but 'cosmic restoration' or 'renewal.'"[27] One might question, however, whether such distinctions can be drawn. Can there be a *cosmic* renewal, in the terms set out in Colossians 1:20, in which all things are not included, and if they are included, how can they not be "saved"? And can a Christian mandate for environmental action possibly be grounded on a vision of the renewal of all things in Christ, if, in fact, God's salvation will only include some? Perhaps the suspicions of some evangelicals that ecotheology implies that dangerously liberal notion of universal salvation are essentially correct![28] If God's renewal of creation is to include all things—pelicans and sparrows[29] as well as dodos and woolly mammoths, not to mention plants, rocks, and rivers—then it is hard to see how this all-encompassing scope can fail to include all humanity, subject presumably to God's respecting of the ultimate free choice of humans to reject the divine reconciliation. At the very least, we might say that Pauline theology strongly urges us, and presents as a basis for action, to *hope* for the salvation of all creation.

Our engagement with the key texts, then, leads to an insistence that the scope of God's salvific work is the whole of creation; in narrative terms, they tell a story not just of human degradation and redemption but of the whole creation's being trapped in futility and subsequently redeemed. In depicting the creation in this way, these texts imply both its value and goodness and its ultimate purpose or *telos*. There is implicit in them a sense of creation's intrinsic worth, its inherent value and goodness; it is not merely the (disposable) stage on which the drama of human salvation takes place. There is also a strong sense of creation's "purpose," its own eschatology, since its destiny is its participation in the glory and liberation of the children of God (Romans 8), or being caught up in the reconciliation of all things in Christ (Colossians 1). These values are (as we have deliberately expressed them) similar to some of the ecojustice principles adopted by the Earth Bible Team (see §1.3) and are important foundations for an ecological theology which, in the face of a heavily anthropocentric tradition, seeks to develop and deepen a focus on the story of God's loving and saving relationship with the whole of creation.

In conjunction with this focus on the whole of creation being caught up in God's work, another feature also arises from consideration of both our key texts, namely the involvement and responsibilities of the redeemed people of God. As we have already noted above (see chaps. 4–5), neither of our passages contains explicit ethical instruction relevant to ecological issues—unsurprising, given the focus and preoccupations of these texts in their original contexts. Nonetheless, the references to the "children of God" (Rom 8:19) and to "the church" as the body of Christ (Col 1:18, 22) identify believers as key characters in the drama within which creation, all things, will be freed from bondage and reconciled.

In other words, and to summarize concisely, our hermeneutical lens is one that sets the focus on the whole of creation as central character in a narrative of beginning, problem, and glorious resolution in and through Christ, a narrative into which the Christian believers are caught up and in which they have a central place. We infer from our textual studies a characteristic shape to this narrative of salvation—one with comic elements (in Frye's terms), yet also strongly influenced, certainly in the case of the passage in Romans, by romantic motifs of unfinished quest.[30] We also noted the way the texts appeared to reject other types of narrative shape—the invocation of a spurious golden age (Romans 8), or of an inexorable ironic cycle (Colossians 1). The narrative shape underlying these texts confirms our sense that a Pauline ecotheology will have as underlying cosmological narrative a view that is forward-looking, reliant on the great work of God but also accepting an intrinsic element of human struggle, rejecting not only illusory solutions but also views that imply that there is no solution, no *telos* or transformed future for creation.

Dialogue with science: contemporary interpretive insights

As we indicated in chapter 2, a hermeneutical lens may (and arguably must) also be constructed in dialogue with concerns from disciplines beyond those of theology and biblical studies. Our larger context, that of global ecological crises in the form of climate change, pollution, and loss of habitat for wildlife, amongst others, is necessarily shaped by findings from the natural and Earth sciences. Without their input we would not be posing the questions which this study sets out to answer. When it comes to constructing our hermeneutical lens, the most important scientific disciplines are those of evolutionary and ecological science. In order to appropriate terms such as "creation groaning" within a contemporary hermeneutic we need the best and most durable insights of the sciences into how creatures do indeed flourish and suffer. As Willis Jenkins puts it simply but tellingly, in order for our behavior "to conform to God's passion for earth and its flourishing, then we must know just how the earth flourishes."[31] Ecology brings us to understand the range of conditions that enables the greatest number and diversity of creatures to flourish—particularly vital at a time when human activity threatens so much of this flourishing. Evolutionary reconstructions of the history of the biosphere indicate to us how that diversity came to be possible (and also what conditions tend to destroy it).[32]

One conclusion that emerges from those sciences, of particular importance to the present study, is that there are good reasons for rejecting what John Polkinghorne has called "the ancient Christian understanding that a perfect creation has been marred by a Fall, either that of Adam or a prior angelic rebellion."[33] These reasons may be briefly summarized as follows:

(1) A fall of creation caused by human sin cannot do justice to the vast eras of evolutionary time before anything like a human moral agent existed, and in which there is good evidence that creaturely suffering and extinction were intrinsic to the natural order. There is no scientific evidence that a time ever existed when life on Earth was characterized by peaceful relations between creatures, when, for instance, there was no animal predation or death.

(2) A fall of creation caused by primordial angelic rebellion,[34] or some other mysterious cause,[35] suffers from two major problems, one theological and the other scientific. Theologically, it places another power of comparable force to God at work in the processes of creation, a power capable of frustrating the purposes of the creator at every turn. Put simply, a narrative of creation that depends on such a frustrating power as the source of all violence and suffering in the creation implies that God desired to create straw-eating lions (cf. Isa 11:7), and this power was able to prevent God from doing so. This is at variance with all that the tradition has wanted to confess in terms of God's sovereignty and creation ex nihilo. Scientifically, a primordial fall is problematic because it ignores the point that it is the very processes that involve creaturely suffering that engender creaturely sophistication, and intricacy and diversity of function. As Southgate has pointed out at length, building in particular on the work of Holmes Rolston, creation understood evolutionarily is inherently ambiguous. It can be, must be, understood as both "very good" and "groaning in travail"; the very suffering of which it is filled is productive of the extraordinary values it manifests.[36]

The scientific evidence for predation, disease, and by implication suffering, throughout many million years of the evolutionary narrative, and the consequent rejection of the concept of an original perfect creation marred by a "fall," have led Southgate and a number of other writers reflecting on Romans 8:19-23 in the light of the evolutionary narrative[37] to note that there is an extraordinary consonance between Paul's language of the creation subjected to futility (as a divine passive) and evolutionary descriptions of creaturely life. These reflections inform and shape the way we read our key texts and construct a sense of their meaning for us.

At once we must note where this interdisciplinary engagement is taking us. In bringing insights from our own scientifically informed post-Darwinian context to bear upon our interpretation of these texts, we inevitably go beyond a historical concern with what Paul might have meant when he wrote of creation's futility and groaning. Paul could not have known anything of the narrative of Darwinian evolution, and we do not for a moment suppose that some implicit awareness lay behind his language. But equally, we cannot now read such language, or seek to frame ecotheological ethics on the basis of it, without an awareness of what the sciences now tell us about creaturely flourishing. If the sciences and the biblical texts are to be in conversation as a basis for theological and ethical reflection, then we must take the controversial step of allowing dynamics from outside the thought-world of the author to have a significant impact on our reading lens.[38] (It may be argued that biblical interpreters have always done this, their reading being shaped, sometimes unconsciously, sometimes polemically, by the cosmological narratives, scientific and philosophical speculations of their time.)

Pursuing this approach, then, we would want to explore the possibility of reading the "futility" to which God subjected creation as the futility of the evolutionary process. In such a process "there is . . . a time for every matter under heaven: a time to be born, and a time to die" (to quote from the famous opening of Ecclesiastes 3, the likely source in the LXX of ματαιότης in Rom 8:20; see §4.4 III). There is, as we have indicated, great value generated within this "futile" cycle of birth and death.[39] But the process of evolution is profoundly ambiguous, abounding in suffering and tragedy, but also beauty and ingenuity of strategy. Occasionally a species does transcend its own nature and give rise to fresh possibilities, which in turn fall into their rhythm of birth and death. Southgate's theological formulation of this is that once the process of what he terms "selving" and "self-transcendence"[40] had attained a certain level of complexity, God was able—through the incarnation of the divine Son within a human creature—to inaugurate the process of redemption. Out of the "futility" of the evolutionary process, and the extinction of over 98 percent of the species that have ever lived, came, precariously and eventually, "hope." The rhythm of nature's birthing and dying, with all the creaturely suffering that we have seen necessarily attends it, awaited the ultimate self-transcendence of the humanity of the Christ, whose dying and rising again inaugurated a new era of possibilities. In this era human beings can find their liberty, and in doing so be transformed from one degree of glory to another (2 Cor 3:18), and the creation itself will find liberation.[41]

With reference to our present study, this scientifically informed reflection suggests that the incarnation, itself made possible by the arising within the "futile" evolutionary process of a creature capable of self-sacrificial love, in turn made possible a new way of human existence (cf. 2 Cor 5:16, ἀπὸ τοῦ νῦν . . .). It also leads us to consider how evolved humanity is able to gain understanding of ecosystems, and modify them, to a degree impossible for other creatures. This potential of the human species, together with the calling in the Pauline corpus for believers to act in specific ways according to their new existence, may have implications for how we understand the revelation of the children of God (and the functioning of the church as body of Christ) in our key texts. We will consider this further in chapter 8.

We remain cautiously agnostic as to the best reading of Paul's phrase "bondage to decay" within a scientifically informed reappropriation of the text. Reference to decay is tempting to analyze in thermodynamic terms,[42] but we sense that that takes us too far from Paul's seeming emphasis on the "bondage" as the "problem" in which creation has become embroiled. However, it is worth noting, as we discussed in chapter 4, that Romans 8:19-23 does not refer directly to a specific "fall-incident" as recorded in Genesis 3. The reference may have been, in Paul's understanding, a broader one to humans' property of sinfulness, and the corruption of "all flesh," as catalogued in different ways through the primordial history in Genesis 3–11. In evolutionary terms, as Southgate has shown, "all flesh" finds its identity through "selving,"[43] and hence self-assertion in competition with the interests of other entities. Living entities are therefore indeed in a sort of "bondage" to that process—though a necessary and unsurprising one. The δουλεία τῆς φθορᾶς, read thus, becomes then a part of the problem of creaturely behavior,[44] rather than the outcome of a specific and all-corrupting act of rebellion.

There is therefore a consonance, both at the key terms "subjection to futility . . . in hope" and "bondage to decay," between a "fall-free" reading of our Romans text and contemporary scientific understandings of evolution.[45] This consonance, we hope to show below, can be generative for our approach to understanding human beings' calling in respect of the nonhuman creation.

The Colossian hymn, as we noted at the beginning of this chapter, gives no account of the "problem" besetting creation, only that it required (costly) reconciliation, a view fully compatible with the scheme we are elaborating here. Reading the hymn from a scientifically informed perspective makes it impossible to appropriate the term "reconciliation" as implying a return to a previously ideal state characterized by peaceful relationships between humanity and other creatures, or even within the nonhuman community itself. However, even if the notion of reconciliation in Colossians likely has some sense of restoration in view, a mending of distorted and broken relationships (see §5.5 II above), it is focused forward, as it were, on the reconciliation that God has achieved in Christ and will work to bring to full completion. Colossians' eschatology is, as we have noted, more realized than is that of Romans, but the letter as a whole makes clear that the realized perspective of the hymn is set within a still-future focus, a narrative trajectory not unlike the future-focused one of Romans 8.

What, it may be asked, are the consequences of such scientifically informed contributions to our lens? They are best expressed in narrative terms. As there was no fall from a golden age of creaturely harmony, so we shall not attempt to develop a reading of Pauline theology or ethics based on a restoration of such an age.[46] Yet our key texts force us to speak of a transformation of the present, inaugurated by the redemptive action of God in Christ and giving rise to a genuinely novel state, expressible in terms of the reconciliation of all things, and in terms of a freedom that is also to do with glory. Furthermore, our reading suggests a special role for humanity within this narrative, in its having potential, as a redeemed creature, to act in wise and healing ways impossible for other species. We develop these themes in chapter 7, and the ethics to which they might lead below and in chapter 8. It is enough for now to note that our ecotheological ethics, constructed on the basis of this scientifically informed lens, will be genuinely forward-looking and eschatological—it will look for the new, a transformed matrix of relationship between God and creatures, not back toward some primordial wisdom we supposedly possessed in the past, nor merely to some sort of maintenance of the existing order.

Starting to shape the contours of an ecotheological ethic

This brings us up against the question already raised in §6.3, as to what the ethical implications might be of this reading of our key texts. Do the texts that sit at the center of our hermeneutical lens, Romans 8:19-23 and Colossians 1:15-20, carry in themselves any ethical imperative, either to refrain from harmful behavior, or to cooperate with God in the transformation of the cosmos? As we have already indicated, there are reasons to be cautious in claiming that ethical imperatives can straightforwardly be found in the texts alone. But we would also argue that there are indeed significant ethical implications readily inferred from both Romans and Colossians *if we read them through a lens constructed on the basis of exegesis of both texts, in conjunction with reflection on contemporary science.* A consideration of the narrative genre of the story underlying the text, and further theological reflection on the implications of a "fall-free" reading, helps to identify and develop these implications.

To refine the question in respect of Romans 8: Does the passage suggest that humans and the nonhuman creation are simply caught up in the great transformative work of God in Christ and through the Spirit, in a way that implies nothing for human care of the nonhuman creation? A purely comic understanding of the story of salvation might well imply this. What was not recognized is suddenly plain; troubled relationships are resolved in glorious union. However, we began to identify in chapter 4 a story that also has the character of a quest. Those in Christ are involved in a *process* (involving co-groaning with the creation, and somehow comparable to the process of childbirth), and the liberation of the nonhuman creation in some way depends—so the passage implies—on that process, one in which the children of God discover their own freedom, a freedom that has the character of glory. In that process, in the story of quest through struggle to glorious freedom, lies the basis for an ecoethical appropriation of Romans 8.

The "children of God" have a "freedom," a freedom that is glory,[47] which the creation longs for (8:19) and expects to share (8:21).[48] As we noted in chapter 4, these children of God are therefore crucial and central characters in the story, for their moment of glorious revelation is the essential precursor to any liberation of the creation (8:19). As with Pauline eschatology generally—with its "already/not yet" character—so too with the freedom of the children of God: this is a freedom that they already possess and yet struggle and groan toward in an ongoing story that bears the character of hope.

If we press the question: Why should creation wait on tenterhooks for the revelation of the children of God, why does its liberation await the freedom of their glory?—we might answer in a traditional fall-based reading merely that creation needs to be released from the corrupting effect of human rebellion. Since that release is a divine initiative—Christ becoming sin for the believers, that they might become the righteousness of God (2 Cor 5:21)—any ethical implication for the redeemed human might be taken to be merely negative: "sin no more." However, on the sort of "fall-free" reading to which our reflection on evolution leads us, the freedom of the glory of the children of God becomes the realization of the potential in human beings, liberated by their participation in Christ. It was to make possible the liberation of that potential that creation was subjected to futility in hope. The final liberation of creation might then be taken to await human discovery of the significance of that potential, the effect of the freedom that comes from being not merely creaturely selves but self-transcended selves,[49] after the example of Christ and in fellowship with him. Our narrative reading has suggested that this is best understood as a process, whereby Christians in following their hero-figure in a quest for their full identity "become what they are." It would be very curious if that process, that adventure of responding to the Spirit and thereby deepening the experience of glory,[50] despite all the obstacles and "labor pains" that were experienced in Pauline communities, had no ethical aspect—if the "putting on" (to borrow an image from Colossians) of a freedom that was necessary for the liberation of the rest of creation carried no implications for working out a pattern of behavior consonant with a transformed relationship with that creation. And here the Colossian vision of reconciliation, achieved in Christ but still to be worked out, might also inform our sense of what that pattern of behavior might need to look like (see below).

That is *not* to overstate the power of human care of creation. We do not, Romans 8 tells us, even know how to pray, let alone heal the cosmos. But that there are ecoethical implications of this passage, even when read with all due caution, is in our view an important element of its contemporary hermeneutical appropriation. As we indicated above, these have sometimes been too blithely drawn in passing by ecotheologians, but we would argue, after close reading of the text, that they may have been too little considered by commentators. As we noted above, Robert Jewett may be guilty of some anachronism in attributing so much ecological concern to Paul. However, reading Paul explicitly and consciously with our hermeneutical lens, we conclude that Jewett is right to suppose that there is a key connection to be inferred between the liberated life of the children of God and the liberation of the nonhuman creation. Jewett laments that

> [a]lthough the future tense of the verb Paul selects, ἐλευθερωθήσεται ("it will be freed") clearly correlates with the "revelation of the sons of God" in v. 19, the inference is rarely drawn concerning the means by which God intends to restore the natural world. Schlier is exceptional in referring to "the responsibility that Christians have not only for themselves but also for the realm of pure creatureliness."[51]

Jewett goes on, however, to regret that Schlier "restricts this responsibility to the arena of a proper existential attitude toward nature, refraining from any discussion of ethical responsibility."[52] Jewett writes elsewhere that "the altered lifestyle and revised ethics [of the children of God] begin to restore the ecological system that had been thrown out of balance by wrongdoing and sin."[53] He concludes that "[o]vercoming ecological disorder is depicted here as a divine gift enacted as a result of God's restoration of humanity to its position of rightful dominion, reflecting God's intended glory."[54] Or as Sigve Tonstad puts it, quoting Jewett, "Nature will accept as children of God those who 'demonstrate' they are God's children by 'exercising the kind of dominion that heals rather than destroys.'"[55]

This motif is also taken up by N. T. Wright, who is clear that the eschatological state of believers will involve "new responsibilities within the new creation."[56] Interestingly, Wright does not think that creation will share the glory (of believers), but rather that "[c]reation will enjoy the freedom which comes when God's children are glorified—in other words, the liberation which will result from the sovereign rule . . . of all those who are given new, resurrection life by the Spirit."[57] We have already indicated our sense that both Romans 8 and Colossians 1 do indeed imply a more resolute focus on the high calling of humanity—a form of "anthropocentrism"—than is fashionable in ecotheology, but we would draw back somewhat from Wright's reading. Moreover, our rather different understanding of "glory" (on which see chap. 7) leads us to question his insistence that even in the consummated state of "freedom" the nonhuman creation will not know that glory. Reading the passage in the light of our hermeneutical lens of "all things" being reconciled to God, we suggest that the Romans passage conveys the key insight that only as humans are released from their sinfulness—by that deeper experience of God's glory made possible by the work of Christ and in the power of the Spirit—will the rest of creation also be freed for its final incorporation into the life of the God who will be "all in all" (1 Cor 15:28).

What then of Colossians 1:15-20 and the implications of the narrative genre of this text? In §4.5 we proposed that in the Romans text the transformation is still incomplete—the children of God are still on a quest, on the result of which the relief of the groaning of the rest of creation will depend. Does this, then, represent a very different eschatology, and hence a different category of narrative, from that to be found in Colossians (or yet in other areas of the authentic Paulines, on which see chap. 7 below)?

In the more realized eschatology of the Colossian hymn the "futile" cycle of creation (to borrow a concept from the scientifically influenced reading of Romans 8 that we proposed above) is broken forever by the costly sacrifice of the incarnate Christ. Is there, then, in the eschatology of Colossians a role for the human believer, such as might be related to the eschatological responsibility we inferred from Romans 8? We have already noted how, despite the realized language of the hymn in particular, the letter to the Colossians is equally clear that Christian life in the present remains one of forward-looking hope, struggle, and ethical demand. It is particularly interesting to reflect on the enigmatic statement in 1:24, with its audacious reference to Paul's "completing what is lacking in the afflictions of Christ" (ἀνταναπληρῶ τὰ ὑστερήματα τῶν θλίψεων τοῦ Χριστοῦ), a reference which, for obvious reasons, has caused commentators considerable theological difficulty.[58] Although the reconciliation seemed completed through the cross (1:20), the author still goes on to find a significance for the human struggle and suffering that follows from following, and being found in, Christ.[59] Again it is our conviction that such a text as Colossians 1:24 can be read eco-theologically, in register with 1:20 (and, as we shall see in chap. 7, the reading we propose of 2 Cor 5:17). If the struggles of the apostle have significance for the church in completing the work of Christ, and we recognize from 1:20 the cosmic scope of that work, it seems reasonable to extrapolate to the conclusion that the struggles of the believer, like those of Christ, may have liberative force for the creation as a whole.

This understanding is strengthened if we take the Colossian letter as a whole, and consider the incorporation of believers into the ongoing narrative of God's redemption of the whole cosmos. Taking into consideration the ongoing co-groaning of believers with creation and with the Spirit, and the liberative potential of the "revealing" of the children of God in Romans 8, such a reading of the ὑστερήματα has a profound logic to it.[60] Christ's sacrifice inaugurates the new epoch; it overcomes the spiritual resistances that stand in the way of humans' cooperating with God in the consummation of creation; it is in that sense an already realized reconciliation. But the subsequent struggles of the community in Christ, though made possible only by Christ's liberating sacrifice, are themselves effectual and necessary.

We therefore see Colossians 1:24, read with 1:20, as providing a hint of the importance of the human struggle in respect of the healing of the biosphere. Balabanski too takes up the notion of a process (rather than a straightforward comic resolution of the "problem" of creation). In advancing an argument that the hymn sees Christian reflection building on a Stoic cosmology of divine panimmanence, she wants to stress that "the peacemaking through Jesus' blood on the cross is a dynamic process. It is not a single event. It enables us to move towards a bio-centric cosmology, learning and re-learning respect for the impulse towards life in all creation."[61]

We noted above (§6.2) that our key passages differ in the images they use to depict the destiny of the cosmos: Romans 8:19-23 talking of freedom and glory, the Colossian hymn employing language of peacemaking and reconciliation. It is in this relational language in Colossians, used by some to dismiss its relevance to nonhuman creation (see §5.2), in which we find another indication that the Colossian hymn offers, albeit implicitly, some resources for ecotheological ethics. The making of peace, or reconciliation, is language which speaks of a change in relationship and in attitude and, we will argue, in behavior toward the other. If God has reconciled all things in Christ, then the task of those "in Christ" is to express and enact reconciliation in their relationships and deeds. While Colossians sees this in terms of interhuman (and primarily interecclesial) relationships, a constructive engagement with the text might well develop this further, not least given the clear indications that the processes of reconciliation encompass "all things."

There remains, of course, the difficult question as to what the "reconciliation" in view might be construed to mean, in a scientifically and ecologically informed context. As we saw in chapter 5, the author's focus is on the pacification of the powers and authorities, a motif comparable with depictions of the empire's achievements, as Maier has shown.[62] Once again, despite the many ecotheological appeals to this text and its notion of reconciliation, it is less than obvious what "reconciliation" might be taken to imply as an ecotheological and ethical vision. It is all very well to say, as does Sibley Towner, commenting on the vision in Isaiah 11, that "[i]f peace is the hallmark of the new age (Isa. 11:1-9), then our work in this time of tribulation is to abolish war and to effect reconciliation between people, as well as between people, wolves, and snakes."[63] But it is less obvious what a call to effect reconciliation between wolves and snakes could possibly imply in terms of ethical mandate and practical action during "this time of tribulation."

One possible implication of the vision of God's reconciling, peace-making act is that humans should align themselves with this vision by ceasing to kill and eat animals, an ethical stance we shall explore in chapter 8. But wolves (*pace* the saint of Assisi) are not going to respond to a therapeutic program intended to teach them peaceable, non-violent coexistence with lambs, any more than lions are capable of nourishing themselves on straw (cf. Isa 11:6-9). In any case, evolutionary science has taught us not only that there never was a pre-predatory paradise but also that the forms of living creatures reflect their patterns of life, including hunting prey or fleeing from predators. As Holmes Rolston has so helpfully put it, "The cougar's fang has carved the limbs of the fleet-footed deer, and vice versa."[64]

Another possibility, drawing on ecological concepts, is to envisage at least the this-worldly dimension of cosmic reconciliation as a process in which each is given their proper place, where living space is allowed for all. On this view, reconciliation would not imply that lions switch to an herbivorous diet, nor even that humans become vegetarians, but that all the diverse species of the planet find room for their flourishing. This interpretation of reconciliation would find significant points of anchor in the Colossians' account, which focuses on the bringing of all things under the lordship of Christ, and on the proper ordering of relationships that this renewed life implies. While it is certainly open to serious ethical questioning, the moral vision of the household code (3:18–4:1), for example, suggests that the life of the reconciled community is expressed not in equality of authority, and certainly not in sameness, but rather in relationships ordered according to one's position and conducted with love, justice, and equity (cf. 3:19, 4:1). We may well find the picture of human relationships within the household objectionable, for all sorts of reasons, but the broader sense of what reconciliation might imply could have ecotheological relevance.

Such a construal of reconciliation immediately raises the question of human responsibility, of the ethical mandate implicit in the Colossian vision. Humanity might, then, conceive of a vision of reconciliation in terms of working to sustain (and, *a fortiori*, not to destroy) ecosystems in which there is "place" for all the diversity of creatures, and none suffers such competition as to drive it to extinction. In light of the huge changes wrought upon the terrestrial environment by human technologies and ingenuity, there is, it seems, the possibility for future change and for humanity to play a significant role in reacting to the current "groaning." (These are ideas to which we return in chap. 8.)

So, just as Romans 8 contains no *explicit* ecoethical instruction, but, when read from a scientifically and ecologically informed perspective, conveys a strong if implicit imperative in its depiction of the children of God as those characterized by a glorious freedom that the nonhuman creation somehow awaits, the Colossian hymn too, read in the same way, and in its epistolary context, implies an ethical imperative in its vision of the reconciliation of all things. There is no *stated* demand for Christians to work for reconciliation in the natural world, whatever that might mean, nor even for reconciliation among humans. But the vision of reconciliation majestically depicted in the hymn is clearly a goal, the *telos* of all created things, which requires a patterning of relationships and action to embody it. This is a high human calling to which the readers of the letter are repeatedly summoned (1:9-12, 23; 3:1–4:2). We return to this theme of reconciliation, and its relevance to our understanding of other Pauline passages, in chapter 7.

These short but crucial texts in the Pauline corpus that discuss the fate of the nonhuman creation can, then, be read within a narrative shaped in part by the "comic" motifs of the reconciliation of difficulties and mystical union with the divine, but also by the "romantic" struggle of the believing community toward a transformed state, a process that will have implications for the wider creation. This narrative shape can be seen as a counter to competing narratives of the Hellenistic world, both the false comedy of the *pax Augusta* and the inexorable ironic rhythms of the Stoic cosmos. This narrative shape of struggle and transformative quest also has connections with Paul Fiddes' formulation of a "line of tension" in the Christian narrative—humans are continually exploring what it means to have freedom and yet finitude.[65]

In respect of Romans 8:19-23, we conclude, with Jewett and the support of diverse other thinkers, that in the passage from Romans 8, the as-yet-not-fully-realized working-out of the believers' salvation, the quest for their own transformation and freedom, does imply some kind of active commitment to the healing of relationships with the nonhuman world, to the freeing of the nonhuman creation from whatever types of "bondage" currently hold it, a task led by the Spirit in that Spirit's liberating of humanity. That is not to say that this passage leads to any easy prescriptions in environmental ethics. But, in a reading consciously and explicitly focused on ecological concerns, and informed by contemporary science, an ethical imperative can be seen in the identification of the children of God as crucial to the process of creation's liberation, and as somehow bound up with their experience of freedom and glory.

Our ecoethical inferences from Colossians also contribute to a lens by which to read the Pauline corpus in terms of a salvific *process*. In this process the human struggle to live—in relationship to the nonhuman creation—within the reality of Christ is a significant component, and therefore a significant stimulus for ecological ethics. What reflection on the Colossian hymn contributes in particular to our hermeneutical lens is the theme of reconciliation, which will be a major focus as we start to read more widely in the Pauline writings in the next chapter.

6.5 CONCLUSION

This chapter has served both a constructive and a critical purpose. Comparing the narratives of Romans 8:19-23 and Colossians 1:15-20, set out in detail in the previous two chapters, we found a broadly compatible shape, though with significant differences, not least in terms of the imagery used to depict the ongoing and future renewal of creation. We have also stressed a critical point: that despite frequent appeals to these favorite texts, they cannot in any simplistic way supply a Christian endorsement of the imperatives of environmentalism. These texts do have an important contribution to make, but any theological or ethical appropriation requires much work beyond the elucidation of the meaning of the text in its original context.

These two texts, and the stories of creation's past, present, and future they imply, provide an important focus for an ecological engagement with Paul, a hermeneutical lens to refocus our reading of the Pauline tradition. In this focus creation as a whole comes center stage, fully incorporated in the redeeming, reconciling, and liberating purposes of God in Christ. Influenced by what we perceive to be the thrust of the key texts, and by our scientifically informed and ecologically concerned context, the focus comes to be on an anticipated future transformation of creation, rather than on the restoration of a past paradise. And in this transformation the children of God, the church, come to be seen as significant characters: implicit within both key texts is a call to the involvement of believers in the ongoing narrative of God's work in healing, liberating, and reconciling the cosmos. We anticipate therefore that there will be significant ethical implications to be teased out from the depiction of the importance to the nonhuman creation of the freedom and glory of the children of God, and of the reconciliation achieved in the church and the cosmos (toward which there remains a hopeful struggle). Nonetheless, these implications will require careful elaboration in the light of the wider Pauline corpus.

Our next step, then, is to attempt a broader engagement with the Pauline letters, focused through the kind of hermeneutical lens we have derived from our reading of the stories of creation in Romans 8:19-23 and Colossians 1:15-20. If we place center stage the conviction that the whole creation is bound up in the story of Christ, currently groaning and suffering, but already anticipating its liberation and full reconciliation, and if we focus on the nature of the future transformation and the role of redeemed humanity in this process, how then might we reread other Pauline texts and reappropriate the central themes of Paul's theology and ethics? In the next section of the book, we turn to the task of addressing this question.

PART III

Pauline Ecotheology and Ecoethics

Chapter 7

AN ECOLOGICAL READING
OF PAULINE THEOLOGY

7.1 INTRODUCTION

In the previous section of this book we focused on the two Pauline texts most frequently cited in ecotheological discussion, Romans 8:19-23 and Colossians 1:15-20. These are the obvious places to begin an ecotheological engagement with the Pauline corpus, even if, as we have attempted to indicate, the texts do not quite so easily or obviously yield ecoethical guidance as is often assumed. Nonetheless, as we have also shown at some length, these two passages do provide important foundations for a Pauline ecotheology and ethics, with their drawing of the whole creation into a vision of God's liberating and reconciling work, at the center of which stands redeemed humanity, with its calling to live in a way that reflects the freedom and peace that God in Christ has made possible.

In the last chapter we developed our hermeneutical lens, drawing together elements of the Pauline narrative of creation, as it is variously presented in Romans 8:19-23 and Colossians 1:15-20, indicating how that narrative might be construed when brought into dialogue with contemporary science, and outlining how that scientifically informed reading conveys both theological and ethical implications, particularly with regard to human responsibility. We argued that both Romans 8 and Colossians 1, read in this way, could be seen to convey ecologically relevant ethical implications for believers, caught up as they are in the process by which God is redeeming the whole cosmos.

The task of the current section, divided into two chapters, is to use the preceding analysis, and specifically the kind of reading lens we have developed, as a basis for a much broader ecological reading of the Pauline material. In part, this reflects a conviction that ecotheological engagement with the Bible must go beyond favorite and obvious texts, and must begin to generate new readings of the biblical tradition (in parts, and also as a whole).[1] It also reflects our chosen methodology, derived from the work of Conradie, which sees hermeneutical lenses as a fruitful way to make sense of the process of biblical interpretation. Placing ecological concerns and key creation-focused texts at the center of our inquiry can and should lead to a rereading of the wider Pauline corpus, shaped around these foci. As we proceed with such a reading, the two main aspects of our method will continue to determine our approach.

First, we are clear that what we attempt is a constructive, ecologically informed reading, not one that pretends to be determining what Paul "really" says, as if such an aim could be detached from the ways in which our contemporary context shapes our questions, priorities, and perceptions. As we sought to show in chapter 2, approaches that claim to be presenting (or, more precisely, recovering) what the Bible says mask the active agency and interpretative contribution of the reader. This point is further reinforced by an examination of the various attempts to discern the heart of Pauline theology (see below). Our approach, by contrast, is clear and explicit about the way in which particular concerns and questions arising from our specific contemporary context shape the appropriation of the Bible. Second, we continue to focus on the narrative shape of Pauline theology, seeing here a particularly fruitful way to allow this biblical material to inform and shape a contemporary ecotheology and ethics.

In this chapter we begin with some general observations about Pauline theology and the search for "keys" with which to understand it. This long-established and ongoing scholarly quest is of interest not only for historical reasons but also because the various proposals both reflect and imply different contextually related priorities and concerns. The various proposals for the key to Pauline theology, and our own preferred focus, thus reflect particular interpretative priorities; our own reading is, of course, shaped by the interest in ecological questions. With our focus already set both on the narrative structure of Pauline theology and on the inclusion of the whole creation in God's reconciling and liberating purposes, we outline a new reading of Pauline theology that moves from creation through reconciliation to new creation and eschatology. The vital theme that our "lens" drew from the Colossian hymn was that of reconciliation. We inferred that this is best understood as a process involving the whole of creation, inaugurated and effected by God in Christ, but also involving, as we came to see, the struggles of the believing community in whom Christ is the hope of glory. In this chapter we explore the potential of that theme of reconciliation to stand at the center of our ecological construal of Pauline theology. We consider, for example, whether the key reconciliation text in 2 Corinthians 5 can plausibly be read with the same cosmic scope as we attribute to our key texts, and what such a reading might mean for the phrase "new creation," καινὴ κτίσις. We shall show that, as with the texts in Romans and Colossians, it is possible to read the redemptive work of God in Christ as a *process* into which believer and wider creation are caught up.

From there we go on to reflect on how we might connect reconciliation with the motifs of freedom and glory in the Romans passage. That in turn will open up themes with major implications for ethics, especially the theme of "other-regard." We connect this with the theme of glorification we find in Romans 8, and the kenosis that might make that process possible. In other words, our reading lens leads to a reconfiguration of Pauline theology in which we discern a story of reconciliation and redemption that encompasses the whole creation, a story whose shape carries both theological and ethical implications.

Finally, we give an overview of the shape of our Pauline ecotheology, assessing its potential contribution to a contemporary ecotheology by comparing and contrasting it with a range of the implicit narratives (and their biblical sources) that are represented in recent ecotheological writing.

7.2 THE QUEST FOR THE KEY TO PAUL'S THEOLOGY

There is a long history of attempts to interpret Paul in ways that seek to capture and express what lies at the heart of his gospel, the essence of his thought.[2] Indeed, this history may well go back to the writing of Ephesians, in many ways a magisterial summary of central themes in Pauline theology.[3] Such interpretations represent attempts "to restate Paul's theology as a coherent, self-consistent, and self-sustaining whole."[4] This inevitably involves constructing an entity we choose to refer to as "Paul's theology," systematizing and actively rendering coherent an incomplete set of letters written over a period of years to address a variety of different situations and circumstances, of which our knowledge is limited to historical and sociological reconstructions based on very limited external evidence.[5] Indeed, one of the things the various scholarly proposals reveal is the extent to which the process of interpretation is similar to that which Conradie outlines: rather than simply observing, neutrally, as it were, all the various pieces of Pauline theology and then discerning what is most prominent, attempts to articulate what lies at the center of Pauline theology are, whether acknowledged or not, attempts to *construct* coherence and meaning, in ways shaped not only by the texts but also by the reader's contemporary context and priorities.

For these reasons, some have been suspicious of the very attempt to do "Pauline theology," arguing in some cases that Paul is simply too inconsistent for such systematizing efforts to convince,[6] and in others for an approach that focuses on the theology of each individual letter, certainly before any attempt is made at synthesis.[7] An influential attempt to straddle the difficult gap between occasional correspondence and systematic thought is that of J. Christiaan Beker, who argues that Paul's theology has coherence within contingency.[8] In other words, there are coherent convictions at the heart of Paul's thought, but these are brought to bear in varied and contingent ways in different situational letters.

Our own approach, building on the methodological stance outlined earlier, attempts, like Beker's, to mediate between coherence and contingency. Clearly, the Pauline letters—the undisputed letters and the disputed letters too—form a diverse set of correspondence. The language, topics, and theological emphases vary widely.[9] It behooves the interpreter to take account of these differences and attempt to do justice to the epistolary context of particular passages. At the same time, there is a reasonably consistent set of theological convictions running through this corpus of letters. Moreover—and here we reiterate the stance we articulated in chapter 2—we fully recognize that in articulating a theological "center" to Pauline theology we are engaged in a constructive exercise, one in which we *make* something coherent, rather than pretend simply to discover something already there. Any attempt to do Pauline theology will involve prioritising certain texts, marginalizing others, and reading texts in a particular way, shaped by the (perceived or unacknowledged) priorities and commitments of the reader.

A long tradition, stemming from Augustine and then Luther, sees the heart of Paul's gospel as being justification by faith. Stephen Westerholm charts the emergence of the so-called "Lutheran" Paul,[10] following on from the early teaching of Augustine, through Luther's major exposition of "Paul's gospel of man's free justification by faith in Christ Jesus."[11] This Lutheran reading clearly involves a focus on certain key texts, which are taken to be central in expressing the heart of Paul's gospel. As Westerholm notes with reference to Galatians 2:16: "No text was more central to Luther's understanding of Paul."[12] Luther describes justification by faith as both "the chief doctrine" and "the true meaning" of Christianity.[13]

Criticisms of this perspective were famously expressed by Wilhelm Wrede and Albert Schweitzer. Wrede saw justification by faith as a "polemical doctrine," intended primarily to defend the place of the Gentiles within the people of God, while Schweitzer described it as a "subsidiary crater," not the real center.[14] One of the reasons why these and other scholars argue that justification by faith is not the central key to Paul's whole theology is that such language is virtually absent from some of Paul's letters, notably 1 Thessalonians.[15] Wrede proposed a broader understanding of the redemption at the heart of Paul's theology:[16] its scope was the human race being delivered from spiritual powers and forces, law, and not just personal sin, and its focus was not so much on individuals but the whole human race.[17] Schweitzer argued that the key to Paul's theology was the mystical notion of union with Christ:

"This being-in-Christ is the prime enigma of the Pauline teaching: once grasped it gives the clue to the whole . . . The doctrine of righteousness by faith is therefore a subsidiary crater, which has formed within the rim of the main crater—the mystical doctrine of redemption through the being-in-Christ."[18] Equally significant for our purposes is the observation that the preoccupation with "justification by faith" as the heart of Pauline theology necessarily reflects an anthropocentric focus.[19] While this was fully understandable in a context unaware of the global dimensions and environmental consequences of human activity, it generates a theology inadequate to the concerns and challenges of an ecological age.

Schweitzer's conviction that the idea of participation in Christ lay at the heart of Paul's theology has been especially influential. More recent scholarship continues to argue for some form of a participationist understanding of Paul. In his massively influential *Paul and Palestinian Judaism,* E. P. Sanders, along with exposing what he sees as the Christian caricatures of Judaism—as a religion of "legalistic works righteousness"— evident in much traditional "Lutheran" scholarship, argues that "the participatory categories" are without doubt "where the heart of Paul's theology lies."[20] Paul accepts and repeats early Christian tradition about the atoning death of Christ, but his own emphasis and contribution is to focus on the idea of participation in Christ:

> The prime significance which the death of Christ has for Paul is not that it provides atonement for past transgressions (although he holds the common Christian view that it does so), but that, by *sharing* in Christ's death, one dies to the *power* of sin or to the old aeon, with the result that one *belongs to God* . . . The transfer takes place by *participation* in Christ's death.[21]

More recently still, Douglas Campbell has argued for a participatory understanding of Paul's gospel in the context of a forceful and theologically driven assault on the "justification by faith" model.[22] Campbell identifies three main options in seeking a center to Paul's theology (along with another alternative, the insistence that Paul's theology lacks coherence, an option Campbell labels anti-theological, or AT).[23] These three options are justification by faith (JF), represented by Luther and Lutheran interpreters, such as Bultmann; salvation history (SH), variously represented in the work of W. D. Davies, Oscar Cullmann, N. T. Wright; and finally, Campbell's favored model, pneumatologically participatory martyrological eschatology (PPME), which he sees anticipated to some extent in the work of Schweitzer, Wrede, Adolf Deissmann, and more recently Sanders.

Campbell's work is particularly significant in making the theological agenda explicit and of fundamental importance. While he aims to show that JF—his main target of attack—is exegetically unsatisfactory, and that the PPME model can offer a cogent exegesis of the Pauline texts, it is equally clear that the argument is not driven solely, or even mainly, by historical-exegetical concerns. Rather, Campbell sees the JF model as disastrously flawed *theologically* and as carrying a host of regrettable theological and ethical implications which the PPME model avoids.[24] Indeed, despite such concerns and commitments being frequently concealed beneath scholarly exegesis, it is not difficult to see that construals of Paul's theology are, and have always been, shaped by theological concerns arising from the interpreter's context.[25] In our own context, quite apart from other reasons to favor the participatory reading of Paul's theology, a participatory focus offers more promise to develop an ecological Pauline theology than a focus on justification by faith, as we shall see below.

Other focal themes have sometimes been identified, notably reconciliation, which we shall also discuss and develop below. Indeed, we shall build upon some earlier proposals in arguing that reconciliation—specifically cosmic reconciliation—can and should be placed at the heart of an ecological Pauline theology. Yet we shall also weave into this construal a participatory and eschatological reading of Paul, a reading that will have a clear and intimate connection with ethics, a topic we take up in more detail in the following chapter. Also influential, as we have already indicated in chapter 3, is the recent development of a narrative approach to Pauline theology (see §3.2). As will be clear from our treatment in chapters 4–6, this focus on narrative structure underlies our reading of Pauline texts.

Some interpreters have stressed that there is no single theme at the heart of Paul's theology but rather a cluster of themes or symbols which should not be subsumed under a single key. Beker, for example, stresses the *theocentricity* of Pauline thought: its focus is "God's eternal purpose and plan in the movement of salvation-history from Christ to God's apocalyptic triumph."[26] But Beker sees the "coherent center" of Paul's thought as "a symbolic structure" with a range of symbols such as "righteousness, justification, reconciliation, freedom, adoption, being in Christ, being with Christ, glory, and so on."[27] These are applied in ways contingent to each situation addressed. Similarly, Dunn warns us that "[t]o play off justification by faith and participation in Christ, or the gift of the Spirit, against each other, or to attempt to subsume one within the other, is to fail to recognize the richness of each and the limitation of each."[28] There is indeed a danger with selecting a single theme as the "center" of Pauline theology that we thus impose a particular interpretative grid, or lens, which neglects a range of other material. As Jouette Bassler puts it, opposing such attempts to systematize Paul's theology, "the path of Pauline interpretation is littered with the textual debris of this drive toward theological consistency."[29]

Another way to consider this issue is to recall the criteria Ian Barbour sets out to measure the success of theories in both science and theology: agreement with data, coherence, and scope (see §2.4). An engagement with Paul, even if theologically driven and consciously constructive, will gain plausibility and persuasive appeal the more it takes account of the full range of Pauline material. As we have tried to show, attempts to make sense of the Pauline letters, and to appropriate their content for contemporary theology and ethics, inevitably involve some prioritizing and arrangement of the material in which certain texts or themes are placed at the center, owing to the concerns which drive our particular reading. We have already placed two texts at the beginning and center of our ecological reading of Paul, for good reasons already recognized, implicitly or explicitly, by those who have appealed to these texts in ecotheological writing. However, as we proceed to a broader engagement with Pauline theology, from a perspective (inevitably) shaped by placing these texts at the center, Barbour's criteria become particularly relevant. Our reading will therefore seek not simply to propose a single key—cosmic reconciliation—as the heart of an ecologically reinterpreted Pauline theology but rather to gather a range of images and motifs around the focus suggested by our lens. In other words, we seek not to isolate one Pauline motif or theme that might be fruitful for an ecological theology and ethics but rather to see how the range of Pauline material might be given coherent shape when focused and reread in the light of ecological concerns.

Yet the last of Barbour's criteria is equally important, that of fertility. In other words, given the demands and priorities of our present context, will our interpretation of Paul be theologically and ethically fruitful and suggestive, will it generate relevant and significant insights and actions? For obvious reasons, earlier attempts to crystallize Paul's governing theme, the center of his thought, have mostly focused on humanity and the question of humanity's relationship with God (cf. §6.4 above). The nonhuman creation has seldom been explicitly drawn into the picture. The priorities of the present time, however, impel us to reassess this focus and ask how the resources of Pauline theology might be differently construed and appropriated.

In the previous section of this book we concentrated on the two Pauline texts most obviously relevant to ecotheological concerns. We developed an analysis of their narrative of creation and articulated a lens which brings into focus key ecotheological and ecoethical themes: the resolution of the problem in creation, the inclusion of all things in God's saving purposes, and the associated responsibility of humanity, standing at the center of this story of reconciliation and freedom. Our task now, reading with the lens we developed at the end of the previous section, is to sketch the contours of an ecological reading of Pauline theology. This in turn will deepen and enrich the hermeneutical lens, which serves to shape the way in which we see what the Pauline letters contain and also to shape our sense of the connections between those texts and our own context. Given the focus on the story of creation in our reading of Romans 8 and Colossians 1, we here engage Pauline theology in a way determined by this basic narrative shape, beginning with creation and moving through reconciliation and new creation toward the eschaton.

7.3 GOD'S CREATION AND ITS GOODNESS

The Pauline letters do not focus significantly on what we might call the doctrine of creation. Indeed, this is one of the main reasons why Romans 8 and Colossians 1 have been so important for ecological engagement with Paul. But there are other texts that also indicate Paul's conviction that God (through Christ) is the creator of all things, and on this basis imply some sense of the goodness of the whole creation. This is the first element of the story of creation, as we outlined it in the previous chapter; our hermeneutical lens, shaped through our reading of Romans 8 and Colossians 1, thus facilitates our wider engagement with the Pauline literature.

The most important of these creation texts is 1 Corinthians 8:6, a credal confession of what N. T. Wright calls christological monotheism, in which Christ is woven into the framework of a declaration derived from the Jewish *Shema* (Deut 6:4).[30]

> ἀλλ' ἡμῖν εἷς θεὸς ὁ πατὴρ ἐξ οὗ τὰ πάντα καὶ ἡμεῖς εἰς αὐτόν, καὶ εἷς κύριος Ἰησοῦς Χριστὸς δι' οὗ τὰ πάντα καὶ ἡμεῖς δι' αὐτοῦ.

> yet for us there is one God, the Father, from whom are all things and for whom we exist, and one Lord, Jesus Christ, through whom are all things and through whom we exist. (NRSV)

Like Colossians 1, and using some of the same phrasing (notably τὰ πάντα, and the prepositions διά and εἰς), this text stresses that all things came from God through Christ.[31] The focus here is less heavily christological than in Colossians, with the explicit mention of God as the one from whom all things came, and Christ as the one through whom they were made (cf. Col 1:16). Unlike Colossians, however, the forward-looking focus, the teleology, is resolutely anthropocentric: ἡμεῖς εἰς αὐτόν . . . ἡμεῖς δι' αὐτοῦ. Just as Colossians 1 shows how these ideas and phrases can be taken up into a more cosmologically focused vision, so 1 Timothy 2:5 provides an example of how the credal language can equally be developed in a more anthropocentric direction, depending, at least in part, on the point the author wants to make and the context they are addressing.[32] Other Pauline texts more briefly allude to the conviction that God is creator of all things (Rom 4:17: "the God . . . who calls into being the things that do not exist").

A significant implication of identifying the whole world as that which God has made is that all things thus have an intrinsic goodness. Paul does not explicitly cite or echo the repeated declaration of the creation account in Genesis 1 that all created things are "good." But his conviction that God is creator of all things does seem to convey something like this implication. Toward the end of the extended section of ethical instruction related to the issue of εἰδωλόθυτα (1 Cor 8:1–11:1), at the opening of which stands the credal confession we have just examined, Paul quotes Psalm 24:1: "The Earth and its fullness are the Lord's" (NRSV).[33] What is significant is that Paul uses this Scripture as a basis for his striking insistence that the Corinthian Christians should consider themselves free to eat *everything* sold in the marketplace.[34] While Paul is uncompromising in his insistence that the Corinthians should avoid participation in Gentile idolatry and sacrifice (10:14-22), he equally insists that food in itself is not a source of contamination or evil—because it is part of the (good) world that God has made. Drawing on similar ideas in Romans 14–15, Paul explicitly states that "nothing is unclean (κοινόν) in itself" (Rom 14:14), that "all things are clean (πάντα μὲν καθαρά)" (14:20). To be sure, Paul gives relational reasons in both 1 Corinthians 8–10 and Romans 14–15 why certain foods might need to be avoided—out of concern for one's ἀδελφοί in Christ—but there is, he stresses, no intrinsic or inherent source of moral corruption in the material things of the world God has made.[35] And it is significant that this is expressed even in a letter (1 Corinthians) where the "world" is generally depicted in somewhat negative terms, owing—so Edward Adams has argued—to Paul's sense that he needs more strongly to reinforce a sense of distinction between the church and its wider society.[36]

This conviction is also expressed in an explicitly antiascetic context in 1 Timothy 4:4, perhaps with a direct intertextual relationship to 1 Corinthians 10:25-30, or at least a shared Jewish influence in terms of offering thanks when partaking of food.[37] Indeed, 1 Timothy 4:4 declares the goodness of creation more explicitly than does 1 Corinthians 10:25-26 (again with an emphatic πᾶν at the opening of the phrase): πᾶν κτίσμα θεοῦ καλόν. . . . Indeed, the Pastoral Epistles have long been seen as more "world-affirming" than the undisputed Pauline letters, and criticized as such for their promotion of a more "bourgeois" pattern of Christian ethics.[38] The Pastorals' accommodation to the world and affirmation of it can be seen as deeply dangerous when our focus falls on, say, the unjust social structures and oppressive institutions of society, which the church should challenge rather than accept. But when times call for a reconsideration of our attitudes to the material world—are we humans interconnected parts of the whole creation, or special "spiritual" charac-ters, of whom the elect may hope to be rescued from a doomed and evil Earth?—then perhaps the world-affirming stance of these texts may have a positive contribution to make. In the context of an ecologically focused concern, the world-affirming character of the Pastorals may constitute an important emphasis, especially in contrast to an asceti-cism which regards the Christian's calling as withdrawal from the evil material world.[39] This provides one illustration of how the value and the danger of texts changes with changing times and issues, and how differ-ent lenses shape and configure our reading.

Overall, then, we can see in the Pauline letters a confirmation of the opening part of the story of creation, as we discerned it above: all things have been made by God, through Christ, and, as such, have an intrinsic goodness and worth.

7.4 COSMIC RECONCILIATION

Most of the attention in the Pauline letters, however, falls not on God's work of creation but rather on what God has done in Christ to resolve the problem within the created order—the second stage in the narrative structure we outlined in chapter 6. Understandably, therefore, most of the scholarly debate concerning the heart of Pauline theology, as we saw briefly above, has focused on the best way to grasp the kind of trans-formation, the mode of salvation, which is here in view. The two most influential alternatives are to see this transformation as effected either through a process of justification by faith, or by participation in Christ.

In the context of the present investigation it is worth noting that, on the justification by faith model, the focus almost inevitably rests more or less exclusively on human beings in relation to God, their guilty status, and on the crucial significance of the faith they are invited to have. The perceived theological dangers of this emphasis on human faith—how does this not become a "work," or (more subtly) a contractual basis for the receipt of God's salvation? —have long been recognized and debated, and still form a crucial basis for theological opposition to the justification by faith model.[40] Indeed, to mention briefly another area of heated debate in contemporary Pauline studies, one of the theological attractions of the understanding of πίστις Χριστοῦ as subjective genitive ("the faith[fulness] of Christ") is that it shifts the focus away from human response to divine initiative: human beings are set right with God not by works of law, nor even by their own faith, but rather through the faithfulness of Jesus Christ.[41]

On a more participation-focused model, the emphasis falls on the incorporation of human beings in(to) Christ; it is their identification with him, their being "in him," that most fully encapsulates the nature of their transformation and effects their transition from death to new life. Insofar as the Pauline letters depict the incorporation not only of human beings but of all things (τὰ πάντα) in(to) Christ, this model is clearly more easily open to an ecological reading.[42] Indeed, we argue that a participatory focus is both exegetically cogent and fruitful for ecotheological and ethical interpretation of the Pauline material. As we have seen, Colossians offers a particularly explicit and striking example of the vision of incorporation into Christ, not only in the hymn of 1:15-20, but also in what Wayne Meeks has called the baptismal reunification formula of 3:11, [τὰ] πάντα καὶ ἐν πᾶσιν Χριστός.[43] The context of this panenchristic vision is focused on overcoming the divisions among the human community, just as it is in the earlier occurrences of a similar formula in Galatians 3:28 and 1 Corinthians 12:13.[44] But the use of τὰ πάντα allows, and perhaps directly implies, a wider vision of the ultimate incorporation of all things into Christ. This is certainly how the author to the Ephesians depicts in concise and summary form the *telos* of the divine plan of salvation (Eph 1:10).

Indeed, just such a vision of cosmic redemption is found in 1 Corinthians 15:28. In his lengthy and famous response to the

Corinthians who doubt the promise of resurrection, Paul sets out his reasons for affirming this hope, beginning from the resurrection of Christ (vv. 12-19) and finding in this (as the "firstfruits," v. 20) the basis for belief in a wider resurrection to come. Notable here is one of the more clearly participatory (and universal) salvific statements in Paul: "for as in Adam all (πάντες) die, so in Christ all shall be made alive (πάντες ζωοποιηθήσονται, v. 22; cf. Rom 5:12-21). Paul sets out an order of events that will happen before the end (v. 23) and then depicts this "end" (τὸ τέλος) as the time when Christ hands the βασιλεία over to God, God having first brought all things (τὰ πάντα—a frequent motif in vv. 27-28) into subjection under Christ. The only exception to this process is God himself, the subjector (ὁ ὑπόταξας, v. 27; cf. Rom 8:20), to whom, then, the Son will be subjected (ὑποταγήσεται): ἵνα ᾖ ὁ θεὸς [τὰ] πάντα ἐν πᾶσιν (v. 28).[45]

This is a striking statement in many ways. It is, of course, virtually identical to the phrase in Colossians 3:11. While the focus in Colossians is heavily christocentric, here it is firmly theocentric, implying a subordinationist Christology that fits uneasily with later Trinitarian doctrine.[46] But for our purposes this important difference and the related doctrinal questions need not delay us. Whether the Pauline vision is panenchristic or pantheistic, it is a vision of the incorporation of all things, without exception, into the divine life. This is what constitutes the *telos* of τὰ πάντα. Supporting the idea that cosmic redemption is in view in Paul's theology, E. P. Sanders sagely comments:

> 1 Cor 15:27f. seems to support the view of the ultimate redemption of the creation, and there are no statements to the contrary. Once Colossians is excluded from consideration, the cosmos is seen to play a smaller role in Paul's thought than it appears to in the descriptions of scholars who take Colossians to be authentic, but one must allow that here Colossians is building on a genuine Pauline view: the cosmos will be redeemed. Paul's general focus, however, is on the world of men.[47]

What Sanders helpfully and appropriately highlights here is that, on the one hand, Colossians is an especially important text where the whole cosmos comes explicitly into view but that, on the other hand, and crucially, this vision of cosmic redemption nonetheless represents a "genuine Pauline view." Sanders' closing comment, that Paul's "general focus . . . is on the world of men [sic]," is also undoubtedly true. We have already had cause to comment on the anthropocentrism of Paul and its implications for an ecotheological engagement with his letters (§6.3 above), but will need to return to this topic again below.

Also central to the Colossian hymn, of course, is the description of the achievements of God in Christ as reconciliation. In the context of the Colossian hymn, this seems clearly to be a process that encompasses not only human beings but the whole cosmos also. It is important to ask, then, whether the theme of cosmic reconciliation can be seen elsewhere in Paul's letters, and even perhaps as a central key for an ecological reading of his theology.

Among the various attempts to convey the heart of Pauline theology, Ralph Martin has offered a book-length study in which it is *"the theme of reconciliation* that is offered as expressing the centre of Paul's thought and ministry."[48] This theme clearly invites careful consideration from an ecological perspective.

Reconciliation language is a distinctively Pauline theme in the New Testament. Both noun (καταλλαγή) and verb (καταλλάσσω) appear only in the Pauline letters in the New Testament, and are heavily concentrated in 2 Corinthians 5:18-20.[49] Colossians and Ephesians use the related (and still rarer) prefixed form of the verb (ἀποκαταλλάσσω).[50] But reconciliation language is clearly not as prominent in the Pauline letters as the language of justification/being made righteous (especially passive uses of δικαιόω)—though this too is heavily concentrated in certain texts, notably Romans 2–8 (esp. Romans 3) and Galatians 2–3, and most prominent in the declaration encapsulated in Galatians 2:16 (cf. Rom 3:28). An argument that reconciliation can stand at the heart of Pauline theology cannot rest on frequency of use. But discerning the heart of Pauline theology has never been a matter of counting words.

As we have indicated in our methodological discussions (esp. chap. 2), any attempt to place a certain theme or motif at the center of our interpretation of Paul entails some prioritization and privileging of that selected motif and the texts in which it is apparent. Moreover, that prioritization will most likely reflect the perceived (or unperceived) priorities and convictions of the interpreter, priorities that derive, at least in part, from the interpreter's contemporary context. Hence we have, in light of the ecological concerns that motivate our study, placed two key texts at the center of our inquiry and engaged these texts in constructing our hermeneutical lens. This is not to say that proposals as to the heart of Pauline theology can sit light to exegesis; as attempts at *reading* they require precisely a careful attempt to give a plausible and coherent interpretation of the content of the texts. But it is to say, following the approach we have developed based on the work of Conradie, that the kind of lens that shapes a reading of Paul emerges both from the texts and from the content of the interpreter, and is *made* in the encounter between the two. In terms of Barbour's criteria, any claim concerning the heart of Pauline theology has to succeed in terms of accounting for as wide as possible a range of the data, in a cogent and coherent way, and—crucially—in a way that is theologically and ethically fruitful.

That said, we should immediately acknowledge, as we noted above, the inherent difficulties in placing *one* central theme at the heart of a reading of Pauline theology. Any attentive reading of the letters will reveal that there is a diversity of images and motifs, with certain themes prominent in some letters and virtually absent from others. If we do place a notion of reconciliation at the center of our reading of Pauline theology, we should do so in a way that is attentive to the other themes and motifs which cluster around the center and which represent varied expressions of Paul's soteriological convictions.

The most important reconciliation text in the undisputed Pauline letters is 2 Corinthians 5:18-20.[51] Having declared that there is "new creation" in Christ, a point to which we shall return, Paul announces:

Τὰ δὲ πάντα ἐκ τοῦ θεοῦ τοῦ καταλλάξαντος ἡμᾶς ἑαυτῷ διὰ Χριστοῦ καὶ δόντος ἡμῖν τὴν διακονίαν τῆς καταλλαγῆς, ὡς ὅτι θεὸς ἦν ἐν Χριστῷ κόσμον καταλλάσσων ἑαυτῷ, μὴ λογιζόμενος αὐτοῖς τὰ παραπτώματα αὐτῶν καὶ θέμενος ἐν ἡμῖν τὸν λόγον τῆς καταλλαγῆς. Ὑπὲρ Χριστοῦ οὖν πρεσβεύομεν ὡς τοῦ θεοῦ παρακαλοῦντος δι' ἡμῶν· δεόμεθα ὑπὲρ Χριστοῦ, καταλλάγητε τῷ θεῷ.

All this is from God, who reconciled us to himself through Christ, and has given us the ministry of reconciliation; that is, in Christ God was reconciling the world to himself, not counting their trespasses against them, and entrusting the message of reconciliation to us. So we are ambassadors for Christ, since God is making his appeal through us; we entreat you on behalf of Christ, be reconciled to God. (NRSV)

Paul's opening phrase, τὰ δὲ πάντα ἐκ τοῦ θεοῦ (v. 18), recalls again the creation theology we explored above and, depending on our reading of "new creation" (see below), opens up the possibility of a cosmic scope to Paul's vision here. Indeed, this is also suggested in verse 19, where Paul declares that it was indeed the whole *cosmos* that God was in Christ reconciling to himself.[52] However, given the focus on "us" (ὑμᾶς) in verse 18, to which verse 19 forms an amplifying parallel,[53] and the glossing of the declaration of cosmic reconciliation with the phrase "not counting their trespasses against them," it is hard to deny that Paul's *primary* focus is anthropological—that the primary referent of κόσμος is, in Reimund Bieringer's words, *die Menschenwelt*, the world of human beings.[54] Yet this does not rule out, we would argue, taking the scope of God's reconciling act, as depicted here, to include all things, to encompass the whole cosmos.

It is evident that reconciliation—in the broader sense of the overcoming of divisions and the creation of unity—is, for Paul, one of the key achievements of what God has done in Christ.[55] The ways in which Paul conceives and expresses this vision of unity or oneness reflect the particular contexts and arguments in which he is engaged. A prominent focus in Galatians and Romans, picked up as a *Leitmotif* by the author of Ephesians, is the unity and equality of Jew and Gentile. In 1 Corinthians it is the factional divisions in the church that evoke Paul's appeal that they be united (1:10).[56] For rather obvious reasons—he was not faced with the need to respond to a global ecological crisis caused by humanity's exploitation of the planet—Paul did not reflect on this unity as a potentially *cosmic* achievement, though the author of Colossians hints at this idea. As we have already noted (§6.3), there are wide differences in the cosmological presuppositions between the ancient world and our modern one, such that even in the truly cosmic vision of Colossians, it is spiritual powers and authorities that are mostly in view rather than the whole living biosphere relevant to our ecological concerns. Here in 2 Corinthians, Paul's vision of reconciliation is focused on the relationships of humans with God and with one another; but, as with the Colossian hymn, this does not preclude its constructive development beyond this, given new and pressing issues to address. Indeed we would argue that, broadly construed as the drawing together of all things into Christ (and/or God), cosmic reconciliation can stand at the focal center of our reading of Pauline theology and at the center of our rendering of Paul's story of creation, reinforcing the basic structure outlined in the previous chapter.

7.5 NEW CREATION

Also crucial to consider are Paul's rare but significant references to "new creation" (καινὴ κτίσις). Insofar as this phrase encapsulates a sense of the goal toward which the story of reconciliation and renewal in Christ is heading, it is potentially of considerable relevance to an ecological engagement with Paul. In 2 Corinthians 5 it occurs in a famously elliptical phrase: εἴ τις ἐν Χριστῷ, καινὴ κτίσις, "if anyone in Christ, new creation." The translator clearly needs to supply verbs, and the choices made often give the individual person the identity of "new creation": "if anyone is in Christ, he is a new creation" (ESV, NIV).[57] But the ellipsis leaves room for a range of possible interpretations, discussed at length in the history of interpretation.[58] The only other occurrence (in Paul) is similarly terse: οὔτε γὰρ περιτομή τί ἐστιν οὔτε ἀκροβυστία ἀλλὰ καινὴ κτίσις, "for neither circumcision nor uncircumcision is anything, but new creation" (Gal 6:15).

These two instances of "new creation" are the only occurrences in the entire Bible, though the phrase is generally seen—like the occurrences in intertestamental Jewish literature (e.g., Jub 4.26; 1 En. 72.1)— as originating as a motif in the eschatological hopes of the prophets, especially Deutero-Isaiah (see esp. Isa 43:18-19). This motif is developed in Trito-Isaiah into a depiction of the eschatological renewal of creation and specifically the idea of a "new heaven and new earth" (e.g., Isa 65:17-25, 66:22).[59]

A key question for our purposes is whether the specific phrase "new creation" should be taken to refer primarily to the transformation of the whole cosmos or to the conversion and renewal of individual human beings. Both views have been argued in recent scholarship. Ulrich Mell, for example, argues against reading 2 Corinthians 5:17 (and Gal 6:15) as anthropological "conversion" texts—as in the rendering *ein neues Geschöpf*, "a new creature"—and for understanding them as referring to a cosmic eschatological transformation which the Christ-event has wrought.[60] In regard to Galatians 6:16, he writes, "The cross as an event of divine restoration is a world-transforming, cosmic event in that, in the 'middle' of history it separates a past world before Christ from a new world since Christ . . . It is not the human being who is called 'new creation' but, from a soteriological perspective, the world!"[61] Similarly in 2 Corinthians 5:17, "As the initiator of a new order of life (and a new order of creation), Christ represents a cosmic saving event, in which the human being is in principle bound up."[62] Thus, in Paul, "new creation" is not equivalent to "new person" but is rather a *cosmic* category, referring to the new world that the Christ-event has inaugurated.[63] It is worth noting that Mell does not see this as a point of ecological relevance—the motif is seen as a "leading concept of Paul's theological anthropology"—but one that construes Paul's point as focused not on the ontological transformation of the individual convert but on God's world-transforming action in Christ, which the believer "verifies" in her own experience.[64]

By contrast, Moyer Hubbard's 2002 monograph argues for a thoroughly anthropological reading of the two texts in Paul, proposing that in each case, the focus of Paul's thought is on the Spirit-wrought transformation of the individual believer, her transition from death to life. Particularly prominent in Hubbard's argument is the attempt to set the two Pauline texts in their context in Paul's letters and thought. Thus, after examining the death-to-life imagery in Romans 6 and 7, and Paul's focus on the Spirit as the bringer of new life, Hubbard concludes an exegesis of 2 Corinthians 5:17 with the proposal that "[t]he primary purpose of Paul's stark καινὴ κτίσις statement in 2 Corinthians 5.17 is to portray conversion as a complete and irrevocable break with one's former way of life."[65] Or more forcefully still: "in 2 Corinthians 5.17 καινὴ κτίσις is an anthropological motif relating to the new situation of the individual 'in Christ.'"[66] A similar conclusion goes for Galatians 6:15, such that, for both texts, "Paul's new creation expresses a reality *intra nos* not a reality *extra nos*, and functions as an alternative formulation of his central Spirit affirmation — *the Spirit creates life*."[67]

A thorough comparison and critique of these works would require another lengthy work, and a few comments pertinent to the present task must suffice. In brief, it seems to us that while Hubbard makes a significant case for seeing Paul's focus as primarily anthropological, there is much about Mell's cosmic interpretation that proves more compelling.[68] Indeed, the recent arguments of Tony Jackson have strongly supported the view that Paul's "new creation" texts express an "eschatologically infused soteriology which involves the individual, the community and the cosmos and which is inaugurated in the death and resurrection of Christ."[69]

Despite the force of Hubbard's case that Paul's primary concern in this text and elsewhere is anthropological, focused specifically on the experience of human beings like Paul himself, who have found themselves taken from death to life, there is a danger of misconstruing Paul if this focus is taken to imply that the transformation in view is that of the individual and that Paul's thought is in this sense anthropocentric. For a start, one must emphasize, as the "apocalyptic" readers of Paul since Käsemann have done, that the focus of Paul's thought is on the epoch-making action of God in Christ; it is more properly seen as theocentric or christocentric than anthropocentric. As Mell rightly points out, what Paul sees as the achievement of the Christ-event is the inauguration of a new world, an eschatological *Umbruch*;[70] the ἀπὸ τοῦ νῦν of 2 Corinthians 5:16 is not conversion terminology but eschatological terminology.[71] This transformation is, as Bultmann emphasized long ago, evident only from the perspective of faith, both for individuals and for the world; it is no more "empirically" visible in Paul's still dying body than it is in the world.[72]

Moreover, while Paul's primary focus is undoubtedly on humanity, the background to the term "new creation" in the prophetic and apocalyptic depictions of the renewal of the whole creation strongly suggests that a notion of the Christ-event as having inaugurated a truly *cosmic* transformation may well be in view. Mell has shown this to be exegetically plausible in the two places where Paul uses this motif. There are indeed hints in these verses in 2 Corinthians 5 that we should (or reasonably may) take καινὴ κτίσις in a cosmic rather than individual sense. It is notable that Paul does not say, in glossing what this new creation implies, that the old person has passed away, to be replaced by a new person. He does not speak here of the "outer person" (ὁ ἔχω ἄνθρωπος) and the "inner person" (2 Cor 4:16), nor of the "new person" (ὁ καινὸς ἄνθρωπος; cf. Eph 4:24). Nor does he speak of the making of one new human, transcending the former division of humanity into Jew and Gentile (Eph 2:15) — a depiction from the author of Ephesians, who, unlike the author of Colossians, focuses not on the cosmic scope of the reconciliation God has achieved in Christ but on the human level, on the reconciliation between Jew and Gentile.[73] Instead, Paul speaks of τὰ ἀρχαῖα passing away, replaced by καινὰ (or, according to a widely attested textual variant, καινὰ τὰ πάντα, a reading that certainly suggests that a cosmic and universal renewal was understood here).[74] And this is immediately followed, as we noted above, by the assertion τὰ δὲ πάντα ἐκ τοῦ θεοῦ, a phrase that recalls similar formulations elsewhere in Paul, where the work of God in creation is in view (1 Cor 8:6, 11:12), as well as the more christological formulations of Colossians 1:15-20. The Christ-event, in Paul's view, not only makes possible the transformation of individual believers but also, and more fundamentally, marks the decisive eschatological interruption which announces the end of the old age and the beginning of the new (cf. 1 Cor 10:11: τὰ τέλη τῶν αἰώνων).

In both "new creation" texts, then, Paul's thought may plausibly be construed as focused less on the individual's new identity — a focus that may owe more to Western individualism than to Paul, as Krister Stendahl long ago argued[75] — and more on the sense that what God has achieved (or is in the process of bringing about) in Christ is a cosmic "new creation": anyone who is in Christ belongs to, participates in, this new creation, in which the former distinctions (between Jew and Gentile, etc.) no longer count for anything.[76] The work of God in Christ is a renewal of the cosmos, an inauguration of the promised eschatological new creation, not merely the transformation of individual believers.[77] In this sense, at least, Paul's theology here is arguably less anthropocentric than that of his interpreters, with *their* focus on what Barrett calls "the work of God *in nobis*, that is, the new creation that takes effect in and for a man who by faith comes to be in Christ."[78]

7.6 PARTICIPATION IN CHRIST

At the center of the Pauline story of creation, then, stands the transforming act of God that provides the solution to the problem afflicting both humanity and the wider nonhuman creation. This transforming act can best be summarized as one of reconciliation. Reading from the perspective of our ecologically focused hermeneutical lens, with Colossians 1 (and Romans 8) at the center of our vision of the wider Pauline material, this can plausibly be seen as a vision of cosmic reconciliation that includes and incorporates all things.

As we mentioned above, however, any attempt to identify a heart to Pauline theology that focuses on one theme alone is likely to fail Barbour's test of "scope": it will simply leave aside too much of the relevant material. It is more promising to see how coherently a range of motifs and themes can be configured around this proposed central notion.

Already evident in our treatment of 2 Corinthians 5:14-21 is the importance of participatory categories in Paul—here we echo the proposals of Schweitzer, Sanders, Hooker, Campbell, and others (see §7.2). Long ago, Adolf Deissmann identified the prominence and importance of the participatory language so frequently and distinctively used by Paul, the description of believers as "in Christ," "in him," "in the Lord," and so on.[79] Indeed, a Christian can effectively be described in Pauline terms as an "in-Christ," an ἄνθρωπος ἐν Χριστῷ (2 Cor 12:2).[80] This incorporative language is central not only to Paul's descriptions of the believers' participation in Christ but also to the Pauline vision of the cosmos, as we have seen in Colossians (focused on Christ) and 1 Corinthians 15:28 (focused on God). Moreover, another prominent theme in the Pauline letters, as we noted above, is the vision of God's accomplishment in Christ as that of making many into one, overcoming distinctions and divisions. The ritual of baptism enacts and represents this process of incorporation into a unity (Gal 3:26-28; 1 Cor 12:12-13), while the Lord's Supper confirms and demonstrates it (1 Cor 10:16-17).[81]

In terms of how Paul envisages this process taking place there are two key sets of terminology: that of being righteoused/justified and that of being reconciled. As we have seen, the two images are set in close parallel in both Romans 5:9-11 and 2 Corinthians 5:14-21. The language of righteousness and justification relates more exclusively to human beings — there is no instance where a cosmic "justification" is in view—and it has specifically to do with sin and judgment, escaping from wrath (cf. Rom 5:8-9). Reconciliation, on the other hand, is extended in a cosmic direction, encompassing all things, most crucially, of course, in Colossians 1:20; and it has to do with enmity and hostility as the causes of alienation (cf. Rom 5:10), such that it is a process that brings about peace.

In a recent work, Willard Swartley has drawn particular attention to this theme of peace, arguing that this should be the central key: "Paul, more than any other writer in the NT canon, makes peace, peacemaking, and peacebuilding central to his theological reflection and moral admonition."[82] Interacting with Martin's work on reconciliation, Swartley argues that the stress should fall on "peace" rather than "reconciliation," given, for example, Paul's characterization of God as "the God of peace," a characterization taken to indicate what is most crucial about God's being and action.[83] However, the distinction to be drawn is that reconciliation is the *process* by which God *establishes peace* in a cosmos previously ruptured by hostility and alienation. (Peacemaking [εἰρηνοποιέω], after all, is found as such only once in the Pauline corpus, at Colossians 1:20.[84]) Swartley more or less concedes this point when he writes,

> the notion of making peace between humans and God and between formerly alienated humans is so central to the core of Pauline doctrinal and ethical thought that it is impossible to develop a faithful construal of Pauline thought without peacemaking and/or reconciliation at the core.[85]

Swartley also places the focus here on humans and their relationship to God, without, surprisingly, any reflection on the ecological implications and relevance of this vision of universal peace. This is understandable to a point, and correct insofar as this is where the weight of Paul's concern lies.[86] Yet, as we have seen not only in Romans 8:19-23 and Colossians 1:15-20 but also in 1 Corinthians 15:28 and 2 Corinthians 5:14-21 (and cf. Eph 1:10), Paul's focus is both broader and more theocentric (or christocentric) than anthropocentric. As scholars such as Beker and Sanders have stressed, Paul's message "is not about man and does not describe him" but is rather about "what God had done in Christ," an act which is *of cosmic significance and affects 'all things.'*"[87] This makes Paul's theology amenable to an ecological rereading. Paul's predominant concern is with the conversion of human beings and with the communities of believers whose corporate life he seeks to shape; but his theology is centered on *the act of God in Christ which affects the whole cosmos and has inaugurated the renewal of that cosmos—what Paul describes as new creation.* This renewal entails the overcoming of hostility and enmity, the establishment of peace, the incorporation of all things as one in Christ/God, and depends, fundamentally, on the reconciling act of God in Christ. This cosmic focus on universal reconciliation opens up possibilities for an ecologically relevant reading of Paul's theology; but it does not of itself directly or straightforwardly convey obvious ecoethical implications (see further chap. 8 below).

What does, however, make a profound and central contribution to Pauline ethics—and to their ecological implications, as we shall see in the following chapter—is the notion of the believer's participation in Christ. While this notion of participation is, as we have seen, one that encompasses τὰ πάντα and is thus the *telos* of the whole creation, it has a particular focus and ethical resonance for Christian believers, whose participation in Christ consists of a sharing in the pattern of his paradigmatic story of self-giving for others. For at the heart of the story of creation, from its origins through problem to resolution (see chap. 6), is the story of Christ, who enters the world to redeem it, and is raised to glory as the firstborn of the new creation.

Paul summarizes this story most famously and tellingly in the Philippian hymn (Phil 2:5-11).[88] Like Colossians 1, this richly christological text, with its crucial and influential doctrinal declarations, has been subject to enormous discussion, "an uncontainable deluge of scholarly debate, quite possibly more so than any other New Testament text."[89] Despite earlier attempts to deny that the passage had an ethical focus, it is now widely accepted that, whether shown by the incarnation or by his subjection to crucifixion, Christ's humility and self-lowering are presented as an ethical example of putting the good of others before one's own rights, interests, possessions, or comfort (e.g., Phil 2:4, 21).[90] The paradigm, here in Philippians 2 and elsewhere, is of one who chose not to act in a way to which he was entitled but instead chose self-denial for the benefit of others (Rom 15:1-3; 1 Cor 10:32–11:1; Phil 2:5-8). And participating "in Christ" means sharing his story, conforming to the shape of that story as it moves through costly self-giving for others to eschatological glory. This costly self-giving, which we shall place as one key theme at the center of our engagement with Pauline ethics in the following chapter, may, picking up the language of the Philippian hymn (ἐκένωσεν, v. 7), be described as a form of kenosis, specifically, we shall argue in chapter 8, an ethical kenosis.[91] And, as the Philippian hymn clearly shows in the case of Christ, the eschatological consummation of this process of participation in Christ is participation in glory (cf. 2 Cor 4:17).

7.7 THE ESCHATON
Freedom, Glory, Consummation

As we have already seen in chapter 1, biblical eschatology raises difficult questions for any ecological engagement with the Bible. Does the promise of God's future and final transformation effectively (or at least potentially) devalue the present material world and negate any human responsibility to care for it (cf. also §6.3)? This difficulty might lead some to argue that environmental ethics should be derived from other, non-eschatological biblical resources, such as the command to love one's neighbor or a sense of "natural" law. However, Paul's theology (and, consequently, also his ethics, on which see chap. 8 below) is so profoundly and thoroughly eschatological that this cannot be an option for an ecological engagement with the Pauline letters. As Victor Furnish writes with regard to Paul, "eschatology is not just one motif

among numerous others, but helps to provide the fundamental perspective within which everything else is viewed."[92] Indeed, Christian
theology and ethics—built as they are around the central conviction
that God has acted in Christ to save the world—must be fundamentally eschatological in their orientation. As Helmut Thielicke writes,
"Theological ethics is eschatological or it is nothing."[93] Moreover, given
the texts we have placed at the center of our hermeneutical lens and the
shape of the narrative we have discerned at their heart, our ecotheological engagement with Paul could hardly be other than profoundly and
thoroughly eschatological.

Pauline eschatology clearly has an inaugurated character; as many
have long noted, it can be encapsulated in the catch phrase "already
but not yet."[94] While some texts—including Colossians 1:15-20 and
2 Corinthians 5:17—convey a more realized perspective, others (such
as Rom 8:19-23) focus more heavily on the "not yet," on the suffering
and struggle that define present existence, oriented as it is toward the
promised future. As we have already seen in relation to Romans 8 in
particular, the implied Pauline narrative is one in which such suffering and struggle characterize the experience of the children of God, as
they pursue their hopeful calling. But the eschatological transformation,
which is already begun, shapes and defines the character of that calling,
and the identity and practice of those who respond to it.

Indeed, the inaugurated character of Pauline eschatology (and of
other New Testament eschatologies) offers a theological basis for an
engaged environmental ethics that does not succumb to the potential
problems mentioned above (cf. §6.3; also §§1.2, 1.4, 2.1). The final consummation is not something simply to be awaited as a matter of entirely
future experience, nor is it something that implies only God's action—
though God remains the central and determinative actor in the drama.
Rather, the character of the end already shapes the character and experience of the Christian community now—in which reconciliation, unity,
freedom, and peace are (meant to be) found. And the conduct of the
renewed, reconciled, people of God is meant to display their identity
as members of God's new creation, dead to sin and living in Christ,
which implies imperatives to act in ways congruent with that future

hope, pursuing the vision of the unity and incorporation of all things in Christ/God. To say this is not to imply that humans presume the ability, or even the vocation, to usher in the final end; this remains the victory and work of God. But they do have a responsibility to act in ways that reflect their participation in that story of redemption, and reflect the point in the story where they are located—that is, at some point before its consummation but empowered by a vision of its goal.[95]

In Romans 8, of course, the future hope of creation is described as a "liberation" from bondage to decay, a sharing in the freedom which (already, if only partially) characterizes the children of God. Freedom is, indeed, one of the characteristics of new life in Christ that Paul mentions in a number of places, so much so that Allen Verhey can see freedom as *the* fundamental value in Pauline ethics.[96] This may somewhat exaggerate its prominence and importance, but it nonetheless has a central significance, especially for an ecological reading in which Romans 8:19-23 occupies a central place. What is striking is that freedom seems to be a quality that Paul can depict Christians as already having (Gal 2:4, 5:1, 13)—albeit a freedom that is profoundly qualified by the imperatives of love and concern for others (cf. 1 Cor 10:23; cf. 6:12), so much so that Paul depicts himself as voluntarily enslaved, for the sake of winning others (1 Cor 9:19). Yet the freedom of *creation* seems, at least so far as Romans 8 depicts it, to be a future hope, albeit one closely related to the freedom of the children of God (Rom 8:21). The same may go for glory, another term that Paul not infrequently uses to describe the character of Christians' transformed lives as well as their future hope (2 Cor 3:17-18). (We discuss the theme of glory more fully below.) Paul is clear that freedom and glory remain, at present, thoroughly enmeshed in a context of suffering and struggle, in bodies that remain weak and dying (2 Cor 4:7-11, 6:4-10), but it seems a cogent exegesis of the Pauline letters to see the freedom and glory of the children of God as a matter of present experience as well as future hope; while the freedom and glory of the whole creation are still anticipated, and bound up with the coming into vision of the children of God.

What this implies is that, in part at least, the ethical responsibility of the children of God—a topic we turn to in more depth in the following chapter—consists in their living in a way consistent with their renewed identity, expressive of freedom and glory, as well as of the fundamental goals of reconciliation and peace. And the final end of the Pauline story of God's redemption of the cosmos is attained in the incorporation of all things into Christ/God, an ultimate panentheistic unity.

Toward a creative ecotheological appropriation of the Pauline corpus

As we noted in the previous section of this book, when comparing the stories of Romans 8 and Colossians 1, the images with which these two texts depict the eschatological vision are different: freedom and glory, liberation from futility on the one hand, reconciliation and peace on the other. Where there is some extremely generative theological work to be done—going beyond the close reading of individual texts, but potentially very important for ecological ethics and spirituality—is in linking these motifs.

The scope of the present study provides little opportunity to chart this course in detail, and we have been cautious, in all this work, about over-ambitious systematization that parts company with the detail of the texts. But we give here an indication of the direction in which we consider further explorations could be made. What the Christ-event makes possible is an eschatological state of freedom and reconciliation. Freedom in Paul is closely associated with the work of the Spirit (2 Cor 3:17; Gal 5:1-27). Manifesting the fruit of the Spirit is both a sign of being reconciled to God, other humans, and creation, and in itself a process that makes for greater depths of relationship, indeed of communion, with others and with the Lord. The condition of freedom, then, is conferred by the Spirit on the believer who is reconciled by the work of Christ, and it is a condition that makes possible a life manifesting the fruits of that Spirit. Can we then say more about the process of living in that freedom? It seems to us that the process can be envisaged in two ways, which we discuss separately but which must be understood together; the one development does not take place without the other, and we shall identify the key concept that connects them.

The first way in which reconciliation might be extended and deepened is through the redeemed believer's freedom extending and enriching their love of other creatures. This is the motif of "other-regard" which Horrell has shown to be at the center of Paul's approach to theological ethics[97] and which, in the following chapter, we shall develop in an ecological direction, specifically in terms of an ethical kenosis. A crucial step, we shall argue, is to extend this other-regarding love and concern beyond the ecclesial and even human community to encompass all creatures.

The other way, which is not so much complementary to the first as another way of expressing the same process, is the deepening of the believer's participation in the life of God. In the previous chapter we noted, and endorsed, Jewett's conviction that δόξα in Romans 8:21 needs to be read not against its background in Classical Greek but with the full force of the Hebrew כבוד: the glory of the liberated children of God is the glory—the weight, the honor, the profound and ultimate importance—of participating in the life of the resurrection, in all that is possible to be experienced of the life of Godself.[98] Hans Urs von Balthasar writes of "the freedom of the glory of the children of God" (Rom 8:21) as "a freedom in which the children of God will be at home wholly in themselves and wholly in God, a glory which will be wholly theirs and wholly God's."[99] The children, in their present life, have the firstfruits (ἀπαρχή) of that life with God in their experience of the Spirit (Rom 8:23). In 2 Corinthians 3, Paul talks of the believer's progression "from one degree of glory to another," a process associated with the contemplation of the glory of God in the face of Jesus Christ.[100] To look away from the self, "from our embarrassed self-concealment,"[101] and contemplate the reality, the radiance, of Christ's life is both to be transformed and to be incorporated into that life. Von Balthasar again: "there is no seeing without being caught up."[102] It is not hard to make a connection between this progressive process of glorification of the (freed and reconciled) believer, as a part of καινὴ κτίσις, and the "freedom of the glory of the children of God" in Romans 8:21, and hence to infer that the sharing of this liberation by the rest of the creation depends on that process of progressive glorification of believers, on that contemplation of Christ.

Why there should be, in Paul's vision, this dependence of the rest of the creation on human glorification is difficult to say. Negatively, one could say that healing of the profound sinfulness of humans—which clearly continued to be a struggle for Paul's communities and remains so to the present—is required for them to show the depth of other-regard that will truly transform the fabric of relationship within the created order. Any consideration of the ecological performance of the human species over the last 10,000 years suggests the reality of that view. More positively, one could express the need for humans to discover their true vocation in the image of God, responding with self-giving love to the divine initiative of self-giving.[103] It is perhaps in the particular way in which humans are called to participate in the story of Christ that we are to find the reason why, in Pauline terms at least, they have such a significant role. Just as Christ's self-emptying, dying, and rising are at the center of the redemption and reconciliation of the universe, so, next in line, as it were, are the children of God whose contemplation and imitation of Christ's costly, self-giving love is a crucial part of both the process of the reconciliation of the cosmos (cf. 2 Cor 5:18-20; Col 1:20) and the believers' path to glory.

We have sketched here two ways in which the Spirit might draw the believer deeper into the reconciled state, in ways that also participate in God's initiative of reconciliation. The first was the extension and deepening of other-regard, a thoroughly Pauline expression of freedom (1 Cor 9:19; Gal 5:13), the second was the progressive glorification of the believer in deepening communion with God. We have stressed that these two processes cannot be separated in the economy of salvation. It falls now to ask if there is a further Pauline theme that unifies them.

Our answer here is that the theme is kenosis. It is the emptying of the self, after the example of Christ in Philippians 2:7, that permits the other to be regarded fully for and in itself, to be contemplated as what God has made it and in what God intends for it.[104] But the resources for the emptying of the self come from the freely entered into contemplation of Christ. Paul expresses this in different ways in different places: transformation by the renewal of the mind (Rom 12:2); having the mind that was in Christ (Phil 2:5); glorification through the contemplation of the face of Christ (2 Cor 3:18). All of these can find their unity in the scheme we are developing here, in which that contemplation in freedom is the deepening glory of the children of God. That deepening glory stems out of so profoundly contemplating Christ's self-giving as to become part of God's self-giving to the world,[105] and hence to purify utterly the regard for the other creature.

This is high-flown sentiment, and in danger therefore of becoming abstracted, inadequately earthed in our task of formulating ecological theology. To earth it we draw on an exercise often done with students at Exeter in Southgate's modules exploring possible models of the relationships between God, humanity, and the world. A spectrum can be discerned within ecotheological views of the calling of the human being, from at one end a humble biocentrism, a search to be in Aldo Leopold's terms a plain citizen of the biosphere, through various manifestations of the stewardship approach, to at the other extreme a "created cocreator" position which asserts that humans are to take an active role in improving, healing, indeed redeeming the biosphere.[106] The students are asked to indicate their view of the human vocation by taking a position on a line corresponding to a place on this spectrum, and then justifying that position. The most acute thinkers among them often remark that it is necessary to start from the biocentric end of the spectrum in order most truly to take up a role as cocreators. That perfectly illustrates the centrality of ethical kenosis and its importance in this eschatological ecotheology that we are generating. These students are articulating a key dynamic in the Christian story. They identify (unconsciously, in most cases) the possibility that humans might follow the "trajectory of the Redeemer" as charted by the Philippian hymn. Believers' participation in Christ means that his story becomes their own too. Incarnation involves engaging with the grain of created reality in a way that exposes the Logos of God to every type of struggle to which human narratives give testament.[107] Kenosis is the necessary prelude to full participation in glory. Costly self-lowering in imitation of Christ is the route to communities of equality, harmony, and shared creativity.[108] Full exposure to the ironies and limitations of human life allows the Redeemer to become the hero of the quest, and through his resurrection to draw all the elements of creation into unity with himself. And the believer can follow—can be involved in the cotravailing of creation, can suffer meaningfully, in a process of struggle and rebirth, as part of Christ's process of reconciliation of the world to God. From a Pauline perspective, humans cannot set out about the exercise of their freedom except from the mind that was in Christ Jesus. But the right expression of that mind, as it moves from one degree of glory to another, issues in a vocation that the κτίσις longs to see, and which is in itself transforming. Theologically, we might summarize it by saying that we have to start from kenosis in order to be part of "enosis"[109] and "theosis," God's fullness interpenetrating created persons and ultimately filling the whole experience of the created world.[110] What this means in practice for ethics will occupy us in the next chapter.

7.8 PAULINE AND OTHER POSSIBLE ECOTHEOLOGICAL NARRATIVES

Before we leave our theological work and embark on more specifically ethical reflection, it will be helpful to compare the shape of our developing Pauline ecotheology with that of other contemporary ecotheologies. Our approach is informed by analysis of the implicit cosmological narrative underlying various schemes, and how that narrative might be understood in terms of narrative genre.

First, we offer a concise summary of what we propose as an ecologically oriented construal of Pauline theology, a construal rooted first in our close reading of Romans 8 and Colossians 1 and subsequently, with those texts at the center of our reading lens, extended into the broader resources of the Pauline corpus. The basic shape of the Pauline story, we have shown, moves from creation through problem to resolution. Paul gives only relatively little attention to describing the opening events in the story, the act of creation itself, though he says enough to indicate that this is the work of God through Christ, and that this implies an intrinsic goodness in all created things. He depicts the problem clearly enough too, particularly in describing Adam's sin, and human rebellion in general, as the reason for the universal sentence of death. Yet the Pauline letters give little explicit indication as to what is perceived to be the cause and character of the wider problem in creation, except in the depiction of it as in bondage to decay, subject to futility, and in need of reconciliation. These depictions, as we noted, are much more concerned to look forward, in hope, to focus on the accomplishment of God in Christ which will ultimately lead to the incorporation of all things into God/Christ. Paul's story of creation, then, is a profoundly eschatological story, focused on the inaugurated future, the new creation which the Christ-event has already, if not fully, brought into being. It is also a story of continuing struggle and suffering, both for believers and for the rest of creation, as they live in the end times, at the ends of the ages, already transformed but yet subject to suffering and decay, groaning in anticipation of the liberation still fully to come. More than this, it is a story in which the children of God, redeemed humanity, play a crucial and central role, as they participate in the story of Christ. Their transformation in Christ, their new life, enabled and empowered by the Spirit, carries with it profound theological and ethical implications; they have a responsibility to live in a way that reflects and coheres with their status as freed, renewed, reconciled people. In Frye's terms, this is a romantic story with a strong comic element, one in which a parlous state is transformed, through struggle and in solidarity with the power of goodness, into one of hope and eventual unity with the divine.

Contemporary ecotheologies, often without reflecting explicitly on their implied narrative character, offer a range of kinds of story. We detect two narrative motifs common to a variety of ecotheological proposals. The first is a longing for a vanished Golden Age, and a proposal that all might be well if there were a return to that society, that way of humans' being in nature. As Frye shows, this is a characteristic of many comic formulations.[111] The Age is rediscovered when a range of difficulties, at first perhaps impressive, is overcome, and unity and harmony restored.

We find this trope in a diversity of ecotheologies. An example is Lynn White's famous and notorious paper in *Science*, to which we have already given consideration in chapter 1. It is often forgotten, when White's article is cited, that White did not just condemn the anthropocentrism he saw as so dominant, and expressed in the conviction that "God planned all [creation] for man's benefit and rule."[112] He proposed an alternative, a counter-narrative, of what humans could and should be. He invoked the possibility of a new Franciscanism, after the example of the saint who, he claimed, "tried to substitute the idea of the equality of all creatures, including man, for the idea of man's limitless rule of creation."[113] White, then, idealizes the community around Francis, and on the basis of that vision advocates what might be termed a strategy of receptiveness: we need to recover our sense of the enchantment and inspiritedness of the world, of "a unique sort of pan-psychism of all things animate and inanimate," and of our participation in its glorification of the transcendent God.[114] The implicit narrative structure underlying this proposal is indeed based on the overcoming of an apparent contradiction,[115] namely that the first biblical account of creation by an all-benevolent creator appears to license selfish domination by humans. Once humanity reattunes itself to the natural world, recognizing "the spiritual autonomy of all parts of nature," after the example of Francis, all may yet be well.[116]

Another type of Golden Age story is what Rosemary Radford Ruether (not uncritically) has recounted as the fall story of ecofeminists, namely that harmonious matrifocal societies were swept away by male violence and domination, and that what is required is a return to that type of society, and to its attunement to the rhythms of the Earth.[117] There is a strong element in such schemes of countering the anthropocentrism of the tradition, and of the need for repentance of past abuses and oppressions. (Here, perhaps, the comic genre of a narrative of attaining union with the Earth, with God understood as the divine matrix underlying the powers/energies of the Earth[118] has a romantic element of struggle and quest about it; the "powers" of patriarchy and ecological abuse are identified but not yet broken.[119])

A third type of ecotheology that harkens back to a Golden Age is one underlying many evangelical formulations that lead to an ethic of stewardship. As Jenkins helpfully shows, stewardship is a very diverse ecoethical strategy that supports and is supported by a wide range of theology and spirituality.[120] However, common to almost all such schemes would be a longing for the pre-lapsarian state of humans in which they exercised proper dominion, a dominion that enabled the nonhuman world to be itself. In Beisner's work, for example, redeemed humanity is meant to transform "wilderness" into "garden," reversing the effects of the fall and the related curse upon the Earth (see §1.4). Such formulations are often quite strongly "Pauline" as the term is often used.[121]

However, it will be clear from the analysis presented in chapter 6 and augmented above that we do not consider any such narrative of nostalgia as doing justice to the Pauline material. Paul's theological vision is resolutely forward looking and eschatological through and through. Furthermore, some of these schemes, insofar as they assume the idea of a pre-fall humanity whose proper dominion can somehow be restored, must be rejected on scientific and paleoanthropological (as well as theological) grounds.

Indeed, paradoxically there may be in some thinking about stewardship an implicit narrative that is not so much comic as ironic. In a view of stewardship as "preservation" there is a hope of preserving the future no worse than the present.[122] There is an implication here (which most of the relevant ecotheologians would probably hotly deny) that indeed things tend to get worse, and stewardship is important to protect God's Earth because we do not expect its miraculous deliverance or transformation, at any rate anytime soon.

This brings us to consideration of the other major narrative trope we discern in contemporary ecotheologies, which is that of irony. If the best that can be hoped for is the proper operation of the cycles of nature, without interference from humans—since we understand them inadequately, and when we meddle with them, we do so badly—then the underlying narrative is one of inexorabilities, in which our part as characters is to be stoically accepting. It is perfectly possible to construct a thoroughly "biblical" ecotheology of this type by using, for example—as controlling text in the construction of the hermeneutical lens—sections of the book of Ecclesiastes. Ecclesiastes begins with the concept of "vanity," which in the LXX is rendered by the same word, ματαιότης, that Paul uses in Romans 8:20. It goes on to assert that to everything there is a season, everything passes, yet God's purposes remain unknowable, and before long the theme of vanity returns (Ecclesiastes 3). Such an ecotheology would imply an ethic of acceptance of the rhythms of nature, and of the futility of all human aspiration. It is also perfectly possible, indeed more than tempting, to construct an ecotheology in purely ironic mode, based on the secular conclusion that the world "just is the way it is." Such views have recently been proposed by Jim Cheney[123] and Wesley Wildman.[124]

Our other example of ironic ecotheology is the invocation of a very different text from the New Testament examples with which we have been working: Job 38–41. We treat this invocation at more length as it has had relatively little critical attention as yet.[125] Like Job in the story, anthropocentric presumptions about our ability to influence nature positively are subjected—by ecotheologians working with this passage—to ironic ridicule.[126] The reader is reminded of the vast scale of creation, which in the end is God's sphere of influence, not a human fiefdom. These approaches may be termed strategies of renunciation, in terms of our attempts to control the rest of creation. There is also a strong appeal to mystery, as to our understanding of the suffering with which the biosphere is filled.[127]

A very explicit example is Bill McKibben's *The Comforting Whirlwind: God, Job and the Scale of Creation* (1994). McKibben points to the "deeply sarcastic" answer God gives Job in an effort to undercut anthropocentric presumptions.[128] For McKibben the divine speech shows us "the rich, tough, gristly fabric of life";[129] it gives excerpts from "a rich, complicated novel without any conclusion."[130] Tellingly and chillingly, it depicts "a world without people"[131]—a thought-experiment recently repeated in a very different way by Alan Weisman.[132] McKibben is explicitly using the Job passage to provide a counter-narrative to those who would embrace a stewardship model of the human calling.[133] And the thrust of his book is very much toward renunciation, renunciation of our "decreating" ways, as after Hiroshima and Nagasaki we were able to renounce the use of the atom bomb. Such renunciation would re-equip us to be "the animal that appreciates"[134] the wonder and mystery of creation (in all its undoubted ambiguity and irony).[135]

Job is specifically invoked by Clare Palmer as a counter to the concept of humans as stewards. She writes, "Here, God is 'watering a land where no man lives, a desert with no-one in it.' God is directly involved with the land and has no gardener. Humanity is irrelevant . . . The animals . . . are not made to be human companions, nor even made with humans in mind."[136] William P. Brown too sees the narrative of Job as setting the human calling within strict bounds: "No longer is conquering and controlling nature part of the equation for discerning human dignity."[137]

In this appeal to Job 38–41 we see a kind of counter-narrative being set up. In opposition to a prevalent discourse, preoccupied with the centrality of humans, comes an appeal to a particular biblical passage which can be read as having a distinctive narrative shape, and that shape, it is argued, should take the hearts, minds, and actions of the readers in a very different direction from the one to which the tradition has often pointed. We noted this phenomenon of a counter-narrative both in respect of Paul's rejection of the Augustan Golden Age (see chap. 4), and in the writer to the Colossians' rejection of a pure-Stoic cosmology (see chap. 5).

Lisa Sideris, in an article praising the work of Holmes Rolston, also invokes the Book of Job in her rejection of the notion that humans can profitably tamper with the evolutionary process, productive as it is of value innately bound up with disvalue.[138] Interestingly, Rolston's own language does not remain within the ironic mode; he writes of nature as a passion play, a *via dolorosa*, a slaughter of the innocents—the language of tragedy is continually invoked.[139]

Denis Edwards is another scholar who, like Rolston, has been much concerned with suffering in evolution, and for whom the book of Job is therefore an important clue to the limits of our understanding of the Godhead and God's ways with creation. But Edwards does not remain in Job; he also invokes the cross as our guarantee that God is to be trusted, and in more recent work Edwards has stressed his conviction that in some form or other the victims of evolution are held in a continuing way in the love and life of God.[140] The narrative does not remain in the ironic mode we would be left with if the book of Job ended at chapter 41, nor do we have to settle for the banal, almost self-satiric ending that was given to Job in the canonical text. For Edwards, God's love in

Christ leads to a deeper, more profound union from which no character need be lost. Irony is subverted by eschatological commedia.

This brief survey shows something of the range of implicit narratives that sustain contemporary ecotheologies, and the various biblical texts from which they derive, or find support. We do not want to suggest that only one ecotheological narrative can be "biblical" and also theologically and ethically fruitful. However, we do want to propose that there are good reasons why a narrative of the kind we have inferred from our examination of key Pauline texts should underpin a scripturally informed Christian ecotheology. With its focus on the Christ-event as the crucial moment in the story of God's transformation and redemption of the whole cosmos, its forward-looking and hope-filled vision,[141] its sense of vocation and responsibility for humanity, this narrative is appropriately and thoroughly eschatological, and related profoundly and centrally to the heart of Christian doctrine. We therefore propose that it offers an appropriate basis on which to construct a Christian ecological ethic.

7.9 CONCLUSION

It is entirely appropriate and unsurprising that the Bible underdetermines the narrative shape of the theologies that can be distilled from it. The great story of God's relation to creation that the biblical writers convey contains a plurality of narrative modes, and we have seen that appeal to different controlling texts will license different types of model. A hermeneutical lens constructed on the basis of Job 38–41 will tend to lead to a different emphasis from that suggested by Romans 8:19-23 or Colossians 1:15-20. It will therefore necessarily be the case that the Bible underdetermines approaches to what we now call our "environment" and understand in "ecological" terms (two concepts that would have been largely alien to ancient writers). We can see even in patristic exegesis a great range of hermeneutical strategies, indeed a conviction that a range of types of reading is necessary to do justice to the richness of the text.[142] Yet there are, as we noted in our introduction, good reasons for giving close attention to Paul in any Christian theological engagement with the Bible, given his profound influence on Christian theology, particularly in the Protestant tradition, and the central place he gives to the Christ-event in inaugurating the renewal of all creation. The Pauline letters, we hope to have shown, offer rich resources for an ecologically orientated construal of Christian theology. Despite the preoccupation with humanity in the dominant interpretive traditions, Pauline theology is focused on the world-transforming act of God in Christ, an act with cosmic dimensions and implications. Just as humans are transferred from old to new creation by their incorporation into Christ, dying with him and beginning a new life, empowered by the Spirit, so too the whole creation is in process of being reconciled and incorporated into Christ, and so into the life of the One who will in the end be all in all. Through our narrative analysis, we have shown something of the shape and character of the Pauline story of creation, shown how profoundly eschatologically orientated that story is, and indicated how the depiction of humanity's role within that eschatological story can lead to fruitful ecoethical implications. What remains for the final chapter is to explore how discussions of Pauline ethics might further inform that picture of humanity's ecoethical responsibilities, and to discuss in dialogue with contemporary scientific and ethical understandings how those responsibilities might be worked out in practice.

Chapter 8

PAULINE ETHICS THROUGH AN ECOTHEOLOGICAL LENS

8.1 INTRODUCTION

In the previous chapter, and indeed at various points in our study of Romans 8:19-23 and Colossians 1:15-20, we have seen how Pauline theology and ethics are intrinsically and inextricably interconnected. The redemption and renewal that God has already but not yet achieved in Christ not only describe the status of the new convert but also convey implications for the convert's behavior and responsibilities. The task of this final chapter is to focus on these ethical dimensions of our reading of Paul, and to explore how these connect with issues and dilemmas in contemporary environmental ethics. While we have stressed throughout that the move from exegesis to application is not simple or straightforward, we nonetheless want to show that there are ways in which the Pauline vision can shape and inform our response to current ethical challenges.

In this chapter, then, we offer first a brief overview of attempts to encapsulate the center of Pauline ethics. We state our own proposal that the moral norms of the Pauline ethic are best captured by a focus on christologically grounded other-regard and corporate solidarity. This leads us to a consideration of the potential for developing Paul's notion of other-regarding moral responsibility beyond the limits of the human community. We then apply our thinking through focused consideration of three questions: what shape ethical kenosis might take, in what way ethics can be eschatological, and what place a sense of corporate solidarity can have, ecologically applied. In each case we give examples of the application of our proposals, proposals that express the human calling to embody and enact the reconciliation and liberation that God wills for the whole cosmos.

8.2 CONSTRUING PAULINE ETHICS
Other-regard and Corporate Solidarity

Somewhat surprisingly, there have been far fewer studies devoted to Paul's ethics than to his theology.[1] In part this is because, as Hans Hübner points out, ethics is not an independent theme in the study of Paul, but is bound up with many other much-discussed topics, such as law, righteousness, and so on.[2] There has nonetheless been a wide variety of different approaches to the subject, sometimes complementary and sometimes competing. For example, some have stressed the Jewish character of Pauline ethics, the influence of the Jewish Scriptures on their content and shape, and their character as a form of halakhah for Gentiles.[3] Others, by contrast, have stressed the parallels with Greco-Roman moral philosophy, specifically with Cynic-Stoic patterns of discourse and exhortation.[4] Without denying the complexity of the issues and the nuances of the existing research, we hold that both spheres of influence are important in any attempt to grasp and understand the shape of Pauline exhortation.[5]

Another suggested influence on the shape and content of Pauline ethics is the teaching of Jesus. This is a proposal classically made by Alfred Resch and W. D. Davies, and more recently articulated by David Wenham, for whom there is "massive overlap" between the teaching of Jesus and Paul, with many echoes of Jesus' teaching in Paul's letters.[6] Yet the number of explicit references to Jesus' teaching is extremely small (1 Cor 7:10-11, 9:14, 11:23-25; less securely, Rom 14:14; 1 Thess

4:15-17), and it is difficult to establish the case that a decisive shape is given to Paul's ethics by this *teaching* as such.[7]

What does seem well established, and already indicated in our preceding chapters, is the strong and intimate connection between theology and ethics in Paul, a connection often expressed in terms of the connection between indicative and imperative.[8] Paul's declarations as to the indicative of salvation—you are (already) part of God's new creation, dead to sin and alive in Christ—are also expressed in imperative exhortations—so count yourselves dead to sin, and set your minds on the things of the Spirit (Rom 6:11-13, 8:5-13, etc.). In short: "be what you are."

This classic formulation of the connection between theology and ethics in the Pauline letters has certainly been challenged and reformulated,[9] but what seems secure is the intimate connection between the two, however this is grasped and expressed. In the terms we have already discussed above, the indicative of God's reconciling act in Christ, stressed, for example, in 2 Corinthians 5:18-19 and Colossians 1:20-22, also carries an imperative, to announce and embody a message of peace, unity and reconciliation (2 Cor 5:20; Col 1:23, 3:1-15). This also indicates how eschatology and ethics are intimately bound up in Paul: the moral imperatives are expressions of the character of the new creation, which is and is not already here.[10] The shape of Christian ethics is given, for Paul, by the character of God's salvific and eschatological act in Christ, an event that has decisively inaugurated the new age. One of the significant contributions of the narrative approach we have developed through this book is to indicate how Christian ethics finds its definition from the particular point in the story where we are located: in the period of struggle at the overlap of the ages, straining toward the hope of the consummation of God's project of redemption, acting in ways already defined by the character of that new creation, yet without pretending that human action will of itself usher in that eschaton, the onset of which finally depends on God.

Paul's profoundly theological ethics are, then, thoroughly eschatological, but they are also thoroughly *christological*. Again, this is a theme that has emerged in previous studies. Rather than find the basis for Paul's ethics in the *teaching* of Jesus, it is more compelling to find it in Paul's Christology: Wolfgang Schrage notes that "christology is for Paul the fundamental ethical principle," while Richard Hays states that "the fundamental norm of Pauline ethics is the christomorphic life."[11] Hays specifies this further when he defines the two key norms of Pauline ethics as "the unity of the community and the imitation of Christ."[12] In a recent study of Pauline ethics, Horrell has developed this exploration of the christological basis by proposing that "*[t]he 'metanorms' of Paul's ethics are most concisely described as corporate solidarity and other-regard*" and that "[i]n both cases, these moral imperatives are grounded in Paul's theology, and especially his Christology."[13] Corporate solidarity is grounded in the notion of the community as the body of Christ (1 Cor 12:12-26; Rom 12:4-5), entered by baptism (1 Cor 12:13; Gal 3:26-28) and celebrated in the Lord's Supper (1 Cor 10:16-17), and underpins Paul's appeals for unity and reconciliation.[14] "Other-regard" is rooted in the example of Christ, whose self-giving for others is set forth by Paul as the paradigm for Christian action (Rom 15:2-3; 1 Cor 11:1; Phil 2:4-11).[15] But what this earlier study does not do is look beyond the human community, to consider how these moral norms of Pauline ethics might be related to the ecological challenges that face us.

In chapter 6 we derived a hermeneutical lens that among other things placed the theme of cosmic reconciliation at the heart of our reading of Pauline theology. The validity of this was tested in our explorations in chapter 7. We also argued that this motif not only contained a declaration about God's action (an "indicative") but also had ethical implications (an "imperative"). This allowed us to conclude that Christians are called to act in ways that promote peace and reconciliation, and foster and deepen right relationships, but what exactly this should mean in relation to environmental concerns is less clear. For a start, in thinking about the themes of peace and reconciliation some historical and contextual differences are obvious. Paul's social context, broadly speaking, is that of an agrarian society—living on sometimes marginal land and coping with the challenges of such a lifestyle, including vulnerability to changes in weather, crop infestation, and predation of livestock and threat to humans—overlaid by the urban infrastructure of the Greco-Roman world, and by the demands of the imperium for grain to feed both its cities and its armies. Such a context focuses minds, more sharply than does a modern Western lifestyle, on the competition for limited food supplies between humanity and other life forms.

As Miroslav Volf notes, even full intra-*human* reconciliation is a "messianic problem," which awaits its completion in the hands of God. Nevertheless, as Volf goes on to suggest, we can in the meantime "struggle for *a non-final reconciliation based on a vision of reconciliation that cannot be undone.*"[16] However, envisioning reconciliation among creatures in the present creation, where some provide necessary food for others, is even more difficult.[17] What should such reconciliation consist of, and in what ways might humans seek to foster it? We indicated in §6.4 one possible way to understand this in terms of making space for creaturely flourishing, and we go on in §8.4 to consider some more specific possible out-workings of this vision, such as efforts to reduce or eliminate the killing of animals by humans, and to prevent the extinction of species.

In terms of an ethical pattern for relations with others, it is the christological paradigm of self-giving for the sake of others that forms a central moral norm in Pauline ethics. This is for Paul focused on the relationships ἐν ἐκκλησίᾳ, and the merit or otherwise of one's actions is to be determined by the degree to which they promote κοινωνία and do good to the community of faith.[18] As Horrell has shown, in Paul this other-regard can even act as a "meta-norm" by which other commands of God may be relativized or adapted in the light of specific circumstances.[19] Such a meta-norm may then render otherwise legitimate courses of action unacceptable. Care for other believers extends as far as putting the welfare of the ἀδελφοί above the preferences or desires of self, however legitimate those desires might be. Such a demand overrides even fully justified "rights" (1 Cor 8:9–9:23; Rom 14:1–15:7). For instance, Christians are free to eat all foods, since "nothing is unclean in itself" (Rom 14:14), but this freedom may need to be set aside out of concern for another sister or brother who finds such eating unacceptable (14:15-21).

With our reading of the Pauline letters refocused through a lens that places at the center God's reconciling concern for all creation, and all creation's participation in God's saving and glorifying purposes, we find reason to broaden the community of others to which this instruction relates; this is obviously in accord with the greater appreciation science brings us of the mutual interdependence within ecosystems of which humanity is a part. In this context Paul's instruction concerning the restriction of one's own rights for the sake of others, love for neighbors, and the inextricable interconnectedness of the body finds new resonance and relevance—for example, in cases where our human "rights" impinge on the continued flourishing of other species.

As we noted above (§7.6), one of the most influential texts encapsulating this christological pattern of self-giving for the sake of others is Philippians 2:5-11.[20] Paul relates this christological paradigm to specific cases. For instance, when he earths the ethical praxis of regard for others in the issue of money, he appeals to the example of Christ, who being rich became poor for the sake of others (2 Cor 8:9). Paul expects believers in Corinth to support other churches in need, at least partly because at present the intended givers have more than enough; he implies that the Corinthians will not be "hard pressed" following their giving but that their "plenty" will supply the need of those receiving the gift, resulting in "equality" (2 Cor 8:13-15; see also Rom 12:13, 15:26; 1 Cor 16:1-2). In other words, in the interest of benefitting others, they are not giving up their needs but only their surplus. The Pauline writings condemn greed, πλεονεξία, as a vice of the Gentile world (Rom 1:29; Eph 4:19), which the writer to the Colossians identifies with idolatry (Col 3:5); Paul vehemently denies such a motivation in his own behavior (1 Thess 2:5; cf. 2 Cor 7:2).[21]

Such instruction, related by Paul to contexts of inter-human and inter-ecclesial relationships, may be reread and refocused when we place at the center of our interpretation a lens that involves all creation in processes of reconciliation and redemption in Christ. The community of "others" to whom costly regard is owed may be broadened not only beyond the ecclesial community but beyond the human community too. We now proceed to explore this proposal further.

8.3 BEYOND THE HUMAN COMMUNITY
Other-regard and Ethical Kenosis

As we have acknowledged throughout our discussion of Pauline texts, there is little doubt that Paul has the human (and specifically, ecclesial) community primarily in view. Paul is concerned with how those in Christ should treat other people; there is no explicit discussion of human interaction with other elements of the creation. Indeed, when he does cite a text concerned with what we might call animal welfare, he insists that it functions only as a directive about human rights and responsibilities (1 Cor 9:9: "Is God concerned for oxen?"). Furthermore, when we examine the way in which Paul builds the bases for his churches' ethical behavior, we find that his approach is relational and arises from the identity of believers as siblings in the family of God (e.g., Rom 8:12-17; Phil 2:14-15). Paul's other-regarding ethic is focused on human relationships, and specifically relationships ἐν ἐκκλησίᾳ; believers are to behave thus because they are fellow members of the body of Christ (e.g., 1 Cor 1:10; Rom 14:10-21). It is clear that there is therefore no obvious or easy way to read-off any Pauline contribution to debate on how humans relate to the nonhuman environment.

Paul's ethical exhortations may nonetheless give us some hints in the direction of an extension of their realm of concern beyond the ecclesial and human community. To begin with, despite their generally ecclesial focus, Paul's ethical exhortations are also concerned with behavior toward those outside the community; there is a call to do good and show love for "all" and for enemies, not just the ἀδελφοί (Rom 12:14-17; Gal 6:10; Phil 4:5; 1 Thess 3:12, 5:15). There is also an apparent assumption (as in Rom 12:17), that there will be at least some overlap between what insiders and outsiders consider to be "good."[22] Such an ethic of universal human concern, also expressed in the command Paul cites to love one's neighbor as oneself (Rom 13:9; Gal 5:14; cf. Lev 19:18), offers the potential to undergird some forms of ecological reflection, since the injunction to love or do good to all (human) neighbors can promote action to mitigate the effects of environmental degradation or change where this influences human health or welfare, for example, in flooding exacerbated by global warming.[23] But this remains a theological ethic that is essentially anthropocentric.

A first step beyond this exclusively anthropocentric concern may be taken when we place at the center of our inquiry those texts in Paul that we have already identified as crucial for ecotheological interpretation: Romans 8:19-23 and Colossians 1:15-20 (see chaps. 4-6). As we have shown in detail above, these texts strongly suggest a reading of Paul's story of redemption such that it clearly encompasses the whole creation. And while these texts are the most developed and important on this theme, other Pauline texts can coherently be read around this central focus on the inclusion of all creation in God's redeeming and reconciling purposes (see chap. 7).

It remains an imaginative step to broaden the scope of the other-regard to which Paul calls believers not only beyond the church community but also beyond the human community. But in the present context of an ecological crisis precipitated by the activities of a human population of over six billion, possessed of hugely powerful technologies for the altering of environments, a context hugely different from anything within the realm of Paul and his contemporaries' understanding, this step seems important. It is a step that moves beyond the substance, but, we would argue, not fundamentally against the grain, of Paul's thought. If Christ's death encompasses "all things" in its reconciling, peacemaking action, then the "living for others" which follows as the ethical consequence of this act may certainly be argued, logically if not in Paul's own expressions of the notion, to include all things, τὰ πάντα, within its scope.

It is perhaps worth noting, too, that this extension of other-regard beyond the human community is in a sense no greater an interpretive move than the move to extend the language of kinship beyond the Christian community: for Paul it is clear that ἀδελφοί are those in Christ, members of the churches, yet contemporary Christians have often adapted this language to speak of all humans as "brothers and sisters." We may not want or need to take the radical step of extending kinship language to the nonhuman creation,[24] but extending the community of moral concern to "all things" is, we would argue, a crucial move for any engagement of Pauline ethics with contemporary environmental concerns.

So rather than seeing nonhuman creation as merely the stage on which the drama of human redemption takes place, or as a store of resources at humanity's disposal, we propose that other life-forms be included within the community of others for whom costly other-regard should be shown. We saw in the previous chapter how kenosis after the example of Christ could act as a unifying theological concept underpinning the motifs of reconciliation and participation in glory. Christ's self-emptying also serves as an ethical paradigm, providing motivation and legitimation for humans to place the survival needs, or "goods," of other species at a higher priority than humanity's own nonessential resource requirements. The Pauline model would suggest a certain "equality" of provision and concern: in Paul's use of the christological paradigm in 2 Corinthians, it is the relatively strong and powerful who are challenged so to act; this is not an ethic that legitimates the meek submission of the weak, but one that calls for costly self-giving on the part of the *relatively* strong. However, there is also the example of the Macedonians' giving "beyond their means," from their "deep poverty," out of their desire to serve the saints in need (2 Cor 8:1-5). This suggests that a Christian approach might see some sacrifice or curtailment of legitimate human aspirations as justified in meeting the needs of other species. Christ's kenotic self-giving is the model for Christian action in relation to all "others." Yet it is equally clear that this Pauline model provides no clear or obvious answers to concrete ethical dilemmas.[25] Nonetheless, we propose that a paradigm of ethical kenosis might well stand at the heart of an ecological ethics that stands in faithful continuity with the Pauline tradition.[26]

In situating kenosis at the heart of our ethical framework we must at once be aware of the critique of the term from a feminist perspective. Sarah Coakley has offered a judicious analysis of this critique and a response to it.[27] As Coakley points out, although we may deploy the hermeneutics of suspicion in relation to the language of self-sacrifice, "it does not follow that *all* attempts to rethink the value of moral *kenosis*, or of 'sacrificial' love, founder on the shoals of gender essentialism."[28] Indeed, while the Pauline model of ethics certainly requires critical appraisal, it avoids some of the obvious dangers of a self-humbling ordinance, since it does not urge the socially weak or vulnerable to suffer silently in imitation of Christ. Rather it appeals in particular to the socially *strong* to follow the example of Christ's self-lowering, seeing a reversal of status and hierarchy as one characteristic of the body of Christ.[29]

The first element in ethical kenosis, after the example of Christ, may be termed kenosis of aspiration. Like Christ, the believer is called not to make of status a "snatching-matter,"[30] not to aspire to high status, but rather to "look to the interests of others" (Phil 2:4). The essence of a kenosis of aspiration is of resisting the temptation to grasp at something, or (depending on our understanding of the much debated ἁρπαγμός) to cling tightly onto a role or position, rather than willingly following obediently in God's purposes for the good of others, even when costly suffering is the result.[31] The consequence of such grasping or clinging is at once to fail to respect fully the status of the other creature, and to fail to follow Christ.

With kenosis of aspiration, however, must go a kenosis of appetite. It is possible to think of sin as "a compulsion towards attitudes and actions not always of [humans'] own willing or approving," a power which prevents humankind from recognizing its own nature.[32] This may be a compulsion to desire status over against God, the compulsion on which the Genesis 3 account focuses. But it may be a compulsion to gain power over others or to use sex for sex's sake or to satisfy a craving for an excess of intake of alcohol, drugs, food, or sensation of whatever kind. All these draw us into idolatry; they make of a substance or experience a kind of substitute god.[33] All drain away the freedom that comes from worshipful dependence on God. Such appetite consumes more of the world's fullness[34] than is our share. The application of this principle of kenosis of appetite is widespread; it applies to deforestation to expand farmland for excess export crops, but also to the high-food-mile demands of the West that fuel so many unsustainable practices, to the taking of spurious long-haul flights as well as the frittering away of carbon-intensive energy in so many human dwellings.

A particular aspect of the kenosis of appetite, which links it to the kenosis of aspiration, is the kenosis of acquisitiveness. Just as we as humans must be willing to order our ambitions and our experiences in accord with the freedom of the redeemed order, so we must order our acquisition of the material trappings of life, which again are often acquired at the expense of the well-being of other creatures. The Pauline material does not, of course, uniquely or unambiguously generate specific indications as to what it might mean to live more lightly on the Earth, to lessen the impact of our ecological footprint. But it does, crucially, provide a model for placing such patterns of practice at the heart of Christian ethics, as a central part of what following (or, better, imitating) Christ implies.[35]

These types of ethical kenosis make possible a deepened other-regard, which furthers and intensifies the great reconciliation that Jesus' own kenotic life initiated. This other-regard may be expressed as the desire, on the part of anyone who truly loves, that the other, the beloved, should flourish in his/her/its otherness. Love between humans, in different modes depending on whether it be the love of parents for children, lovers for each other, friends for each other, or the hard, willed love for stranger or enemy, is in each case non-coercive longing for the other to flourish. So also love between humans and the nonhuman creation depends on a real desire to know the other and respect the other for itself, and a recognition too of the other as creature belonging to and in relation with God.

Such a love has to be a tough, discerning love, not mere sentiment but a real outworking of desire purified by kenosis. It is a love that recognizes that other creatures may have to be fenced away from human habitation, or controlled by pharmaceuticals or pesticides, for the human good, but still celebrates the wonder of their existence, and desires coexistence, indeed that the other might know fullness of flourishing as itself, and opportunity for self-transcendence. Humans are to be part, so we inferred from our creative appropriation of the Pauline corpus, of God's transforming the world, making it more than it currently is. Humans can have a part in God's starting to heal that world's ambiguity and travail.

In order to apply this thinking on kenotic other-regard to real cases we focus on two further questions. First: can ethics meaningfully be eschatological? Second: can the motif of corporate solidarity, identified above but so evidently anthropocentric—and arguably exclusive—in its original context, find ecoethical expression?

8.4 ETHICS AS ESCHATOLOGICAL

We have seen that reflection on the shape of key Pauline texts that address directly the theme of creation's redemption suggests a process of continued struggle. Moreover, particularly in Romans 8:19-21, though also implied in texts such as Colossians 1:24, there is a sense that the human vocation is a vital part of that struggle. Human freedom is in the familiar phrase "now but not yet," and on the fulfillment of that freedom—at least on our reading of Romans 8:19, 21—the transformation of creation depends. This view then gives rise to proposals for ecotheological ethics which take this eschatological vocation of the human seriously.

Eschatological ethics does not have to imply extremes of behavior, nor a hostile negation of the world as it is. It can be prudential, indeed pragmatic, as Paul's sexual ethics in 1 Corinthians 7 suggest (7:2-6, 12-16, 27).[36] Even Paul's famous ὡς μή, repeated five times in a series of clauses calling for some kind of "detachment" from the world—comparable to similar phraseology in Stoic-Cynic writings[37]—can be read not as implying a lack of care *for* the world but rather as precisely an indication of the Christian's freedom, a freedom not to be determined by the desires and appetites of the world. As Bultmann classically puts it, "Given freedom from death, *freedom from the world and its powers* are also given. The man of faith is freed from the care of one who relies upon himself, has the world (supposedly) at his disposal, and yet is its victim."[38] Or as Gordon Fee comments, "one lives in the world just as the rest—marrying, sorrowing, rejoicing, buying, making use of it—but none of these determines one's life. The Christian is marked by eternity; therefore he or she is not under the dominating power of those things that dictate the existence of others."[39] It is not hard to see how this kind of asceticism, often criticized as implying a rejection of the material world, could add an eschatological undergirding to the kinds of ethical kenosis we have sketched above:[40] Paul challenges his readers to live as those who are free from the acquisitive desires and appetites of the world in its present form, shaped as they are by the new creation that is already taking shape yet is still to come.

We encounter in the literature two main alternatives to such an approach to eschatology. The first is to reject eschatological formulations, as they have emerged, "severed from historical hope," in Christianity from Paul onwards—to regard them as part of the array of dualisms that has corrupted the ecological potential of Christian thought through the ages.[41] Ecotheological ethics would therefore be done from the doctrine of creation alone.

The other alternative to the type of appropriation of eschatology we propose here seems to us to be the existentialization or demythologization of this motif, an approach typically associated with the work of Bultmann.[42] On one variant of this the New Testament's reach into human relationships with the nonhuman creation is simply ignored. Indeed as we have seen there have been commentators both on Romans 8 and on Colossians 1 whose approach has been narrowly human centered (see §§4.2, 5.2). Even were such exegesis warranted on the basis of the grain of the texts, it would omit crucial resources for creation care, resources that, as we have shown, begin to emerge from a more holistic reading.

However, we detect an alternative, much more sophisticated form of existentialization in the detemporalized eschatology of Kathryn Tanner. She claims that in the face of the scientific predictions as to the future of the universe it is best to reframe the doctrine of the eschaton in a way analogous to the doctrine of creation. Just as science tells us the universe may have had no beginning, yet the doctrine of creation may be taken to affirm the ontological dependence of all created space-time from moment to moment on God, so science tells us the universe may have no meaningful end, but only a drift away into futility, but eschatology can be about hope and purpose in the present. An eschatological orientation for Tanner is an orientation toward the condition the New Testament calls eternal life, a present orientation to the kingdom of God, rather than a future hope.[43] Tanner's work is carefully and elegantly constructed, and seems realistic about the problems of a scientifically informed eschatology.[44] However, we question whether her narrative does full justice to the narrative shape that we have inferred from our key Pauline texts. Her approach seems more like a contemporary reappropriation of the demythologized approach propounded by Bultmann, admixed with a certain "Stoicism" about the state of the world. The implication of what she writes is that the great cosmic cycles will eventually resolve the fate of the universe; meanwhile, the Christian, in whom eternal life is already immanent, is to endure the state of things and keep her orientation toward that immanence.

Our approach here is more in keeping with the "proleptic ethics" of Ted Peters, which he defines as "taking creative and transformative action in the present stimulated by our vision of the future."[45] It is an effort to cooperate with the ways of God by which the eschaton will be brought in, without making the overblown claim that human action could itself usher in the consummation of the new creation. The struggle and suffering that that effort involves is not merely seen as a condition of the age, but part of the process of divine transformation of the world. We take with all seriousness Volf's caution that too confident an eschatological ethic could be oppressive, even totalitarian.[46] But we consider that in respect of the nonhuman creation an eschatological approach can hope to side with the purposes of God, in extending other-regard, in recognizing the need to extend our ideas of community beyond the human, and to give voice to the voiceless (see below), but also in working—to the best of our extremely limited ability—to help creation transcend the "futility" to which God subjected it in hope, hope for the glorious liberty of humans and, ultimately, of the whole creation.

Andrew Linzey has also framed an eschatological ecoethic, much influenced by Romans 8. In turning now to practical outworkings of our ethical scheme, we begin by considering his proposal that vegetarianism be adopted as an eschatological sign.

Vegetarianism as an anticipation of the peaceable kingdom

In the context of a broader argument for a theology that takes the status and rights of animals seriously, a kind of liberation theology for animals, Linzey presents a case for "vegetarianism as a biblical ideal."[47] Linzey finds in Romans 8:19-21 a decisive text indicating how humans are "to exercise a priestly ministry of redemption . . . the releasing of creation from futility, from suffering and pain and worthlessness."[48] Like other vegetarians before and since, Linzey appeals to the depictions of both the original creation in Genesis 1:29-30 and the peaceable future kingdom in Isaiah 11:6-9 as indications that "God's will is for peace," for an end to killing, including the killing of animals. He points out that in the biblical account such killing was allowed only as a concessionary permission in the context of human sinfulness (Gen 9:3-5).[49] Thus, "[t]o opt for a vegetarian life-style is to take one practical step towards living in peace with the rest of creation. One step towards reducing the rate of institutionalized killing in the world today."[50] After seeking to address the potential problem that "Jesus was no vegan and probably no vegetarian," Linzey concludes his argument with an appeal to vegetarianism as a means of "approximating the peaceable kingdom."[51] This is an eschatological ethic in the sense that it regards a commitment to vegetarianism as a step in tune with the vision of a future peace in the messianic age: "Forward, we may say, not backward to Genesis."[52]

There are aspects of this ethical argument that are compelling. Just as many have taken the prophetic vision of people hammering swords into ploughshares (Mic 4:3) as a motivation and mandate for ending war, a call to peacemaking, so it makes sense to see the vision of a future peace encompassing humans and animals as an ethical challenge, a call to live "already" what is clearly "not yet." Yet we also find reasons to question the argument for eschatological vegetarianism as an ethical enactment of the Pauline (and more broadly biblical) vision.[53]

First, there are problems with making any appeal to the original state of creation, particularly when this is associated with a view of the violence of predation as a sign of nature's "fallenness."[54] Not only is it impossible to square the notion of a pre-predatory paradise with the scientific evidence, but it is precisely through the processes inherent in nature as we know it that the goods of creation have been brought about. As Southgate puts it,

> [t]he competition and struggle for resources intrinsic to the evolution-
> ary process, and which give rise in nature to strategies of predation,

suffering and extinction, are the *very processes* that refine the character-istics of species and propel them towards greater sophistication . . . So far from the universe being fallen from a perfection initially given it by God, through the rebellion of created beings, it seems plausible that the sort of universe we have, in which complexity emerges in a process governed by thermodynamic necessity and Darwinian natural selection, is the only sort of universe that could give rise to the range, beauty, complexity and diversity of creatures the Earth has produced. On this view, this *is* the sort of universe God originally intended.[55]

This is not to say, as Southgate makes clear, that the universe is all that it is intended to become; God's eschatological intention is to liberate the creation from the futility and decay that have (necessar-ily) characterized its existence. Indeed, our eschatological narrative, derived from close engagement with Pauline texts, precisely indicates a "romantic" story of eventual victory and release, won through struggle and suffering. Within such a narrative, eschatological arguments for vegetarianism might retain their cogency as a conscious if partial antici-pation of the peaceable future of a creation redeemed.

Second, however, we must acknowledge that predation, and the multitudinous networks of predator-prey relationships, quite apart from being intrinsic to all that has emerged as the goodness of creation, are unalterably part of the functioning of the world as we know it. We may envisage an ultimate eschaton, in which God renews creation in such a way that predation and violence are no more, but it is neither realistic nor desirable for humans to seek to alter or redeem predator-prey rela-tionships here and now. Effecting reconciliation between animals, as well as between humans and animals, cannot mean seeking to change the food chains of ecosystems.

The Christian vegetarian will immediately reply, with some justifi-cation, that while it may not be possible, this side of the eschaton, for lions to nourish themselves on straw, it is certainly possible for humans, at least for those who have the necessary resources and opportunity, to nourish themselves adequately on a vegetarian diet. There are indeed many cogent (non-eschatological) ethical reasons to greatly reduce our consumption of meat—a point that deserves to be stressed.[56] But we remain to be convinced that a commitment to vegetarianism is the best ethical response to the eschatological vision. This is in particular because an argument can be made that keeping (and killing and eating) animals as a part of a system of agriculture, in certain forms, can reflect a positive and valuable pattern of human-animal relationships, and one that makes ecological sense in terms of sustainability. Describing the patterns of hill farming characteristic of Dartmoor, an area of moorland in southwest England, Southgate makes the case that the human-animal relationships that have profoundly shaped the landscape and ethos of the area can be seen as relationships characterized by care and friendship, even when those relationships involve the killing of animals.[57] The very particular kind of relationship between humans and domestic pets should not be seen, *pace* Stephen Webb, as the paradigmatic model for human-animal relationships.[58] Thus it may be argued that

> the breeding, rearing, and management of animals in the context of healthy methods of farming (including genuinely humane killing) can be considered a form of care and friendship between species that is an authentic part of the human vocation . . . certain sorts of community would be lost in a move to strict vegetarianism, which might therefore be seen as a move away from, rather than toward, the Isaianic vision.[59]

This argument can be further strengthened from an ecological and scientific point of view. As Michael Pollan so well shows, animals play a crucial role, particularly in a model of small-scale, sustainable farming, in the recycling of nutrients through manure, reducing the need for chemical fertilizers and oil-based products and transportation.[60] Yet as Pollan also powerfully argues, a humane pattern of animal husbandry would be very different from the industrial operations prevalent today. Just as Karl Barth suggested that Romans 8:18-19 should be written "in letters of fire . . . across every hunting lodge, abbatoir and vivisection chamber," such that the killing of animals could only take place "as a deeply reverential act of repentance, gratitude and praise on the part of the forgiven sinner,"[61] so Pollan argues for a "glass abbatoir," literally or figuratively, so that we have to contemplate what we do there:

The industrialization—and brutalization—of animals in America is a relatively new, evitable and local phenomenon: No other country raises and slaughters its food animals quite as intensively or as brutally as we do. No other people in history has lived at quite so great a remove from the animals they eat. Were the walls of our meat industry to become transparent, literally or even figuratively, we would not long continue to raise, kill and eat animals the way we do. Tail docking and sow crates and beak clipping would disappear overnight, and the days of slaughtering four hundred head of cattle an hour would promptly come to an end—for who could stand the sight? Yes, meat would get more expensive. We'd probably eat a lot less of it, too, but maybe when we did eat animals we'd eat them with the consciousness, ceremony, and respect they deserve.[62]

In short, it is not necessarily the case that a commitment to vegetarianism best expresses the ethical implications of the eschatological vision we have derived from our study of Pauline texts. These texts have generated an eschatological narrative structure in which humans have a responsibility to express their new identity as freed, reconciled creatures in working for reconciliation, peace, and liberation throughout all creation. But this vision, particularly when brought into dialogue with scientific and ecological insights, might, we would argue, be better enacted in a commitment to generous and reverential patterns of human-animal relationships, to small-scale, sustainable, and locally focused agriculture rather than to vegetarianism.

Reducing extinction as an eschatological task

Having investigated one possible proposal in eschatological ethics we now turn to consider another. We showed in chapter 6 that the "futility" of creation (Rom 8:20) may be read, in the light of evolutionary science, as being the pattern of suffering and extinction out of which values of beauty, complexity, adaptiveness, and ultimately consciousness emerge in the biosphere.[63] This pattern has resulted in millions of extinctions, including over 98 percent of all the species that have ever lived.

Southgate has proposed that we can not only take seriously Moltmann's understanding of Christ as evolution's redeemer,[64] but also the possibility of human partnership in this process. Southgate does not suppose that humans could end or transform the process of predation—only God could do that. But he makes the bold proposal that *a sign of our liberty, as children of God starting to be part of the liberation of the whole creation, would be that human beings, through a blend of prudential wisdom and scientific ingenuity, cut the rate of natural extinction.*

Extinction is an intrinsic part of the way that wild nature "works." But the extinction of a species means the loss of a whole way of being alive on the planet, a whole aspect of the goodness of creation, a whole way of praising God. Part of fulfilled human calling might be, by dint of our knowledge and ingenuity, to have a share in eliminating that phenomenon from the biosphere. That would mean humans' acquiring a great deal more wisdom as well as a great deal more knowledge than we currently possess. So one great human priority at present must be to gather (noninvasively) as much knowledge and wisdom as we can about the nonhuman world, and to reduce the very high rate of *human-induced* extinction to which the biosphere is currently subject.

But our proposal goes beyond that to suggest that humans could also make appreciable progress toward ending the process of biological extinction, and thereby take a very significant step toward the healing of creation.

The ending of some not-wholly-anthropogenic extinctions is widely accepted as entirely desirable and ethically warranted. The giant panda is an animal which has captured human imagination. It is not—for whatever series of reasons—one of evolution's "successes"; it has a low reproduction rate and its population is easily threatened by any diminution in the quality of its environment. Even were its bamboo forests not under threat from human activity, the panda might struggle to survive. But strenuous attempts are nevertheless made to preserve it both in the wild and in captivity.

Rolston is clear that anthropogenic extinctions differ from natural as profoundly as murder from death by natural causes: "Though harmful to a species, extinction in nature is no evil in the system; it is rather the key to tomorrow."[65] The crux of our disagreement with him is that Rolston is still looking to the natural unfolding of the creation, whereas we regard this as the eschatological phase of history, in which humans should be looking to their own liberation and to the relief of creation's groaning.

Our Pauline ecotheological narrative, developed in the preceding chapters, sees the present as a time of continued struggle and suffering, yet also as the "endtime," in which the decisive defeat of the evil age and the inauguration of the new creation has been accomplished in the death and resurrection of Christ. This calls for an utterly new perspective on the world, what Martyn has called "a new way of knowing."[66] From the perspective of "new creation," the processes of evolution—in which new possibilities are explored via natural selection, with concomitant levels of extinction—may be regarded as part of the old age, with its futility and death (and extinctions). Now is the time for the renewal of creation, a time in which new possibilities of reconciliation and self-transcendence among already existing species will be explored. The Colossian hymn stresses that this transformation is first and foremost the work of God in Christ. However, our reading of both Colossians and Romans, and of Pauline theology and ethics more generally, implies that God's reconciling, liberating work, anticipated and visible especially in the church, also entails ethical responsibility on the part of humans. Human beings have a key role in working out in their practices and relationships what it means to live as renewed creatures in a creation straining toward its ultimate renewal. In terms drawn from Romans 8, the final, glorious phase of the labor pains of creation await our coming to live in freedom. And a sign of that freedom would be that humans seek to prevent any species presently companioned by the Spirit from disappearing from the network of possibilities within creation.

This call to work toward the ending of the extinction of species might also be seen as part of a scientifically informed notion of reconciliation. As we stressed in §6.4, and in our discussions above assessing the case for eschatological vegetarianism, we cannot cogently conceive of a this-worldly imperative to end predation and inter-species competition. What we might well do is to seek to ensure, insofar as our wisdom allows us to do, that ecosystems around the world are sustained and sustainable—a vision of reconciliation as enabling ordered, nonoppressive relationships in which there is "space," in all senses of the word, for the diverse community of others to flourish. This would include a concern not only for iconic species such as giant pandas and polar bears (on which see below) but also for all the myriad life-forms on which such species, as well as we ourselves, are dependent.

This might mean keeping some species in artificial environments, if competition would ordinarily mean their extinction. It might entail major (humane) culls of populous competing species. The cooperation of the human communities that live in the vicinity of endangered ecosystems would be essential. The cultural understandings and sense of place of such communities would need to be treated with the utmost respect, and they would need to be compensated for changes in their lifestyle. So once again we are thrown back on the need for kenotic restraint and costly self-giving on the part of the affluent. Ideally the flourishing of indigenous populations should be alongside that of the nonhuman biota, but there may be places and situations (as with the preservation of the tiger) where it is essential to have uninhabited areas in which endangered species can thrive.

We restate our conviction that where the Pauline writings locate us is in the already-but-not-yet of the eschaton. This, then, is the age in which God's hope for the creation is vindicated and enacted, reconciliation achieved, the age of the healing of creation's travail, beginning from the coming into liberty of the renewed and reconciled children of God. Biological extinction, while it has been a necessary part of the process that has made possible all the beauty, diversity, and richness of this creation, as well as creaturely freedom, is a profound disvalue. As Thomas Berry puts it,

> [e]xtinction is a difficult concept to grasp. It is an eternal concept. It's not at all like the killing of individual life forms that can be renewed through normal processes of reproduction. Nor is it simply diminishing numbers. Nor is it damage that can somehow be remedied or for which some substitute can be found. Nor is it something that only affects our own generation. Nor is it something that could be remedied by some supernatural power. It is, rather, an absolute and final act for which there is no remedy on earth as in heaven.[67]

Berry is writing of anthropogenic (human-induced) extinction, but his observations apply equally to all extinctions. Our argument therefore advocates as an eschatological sign the reduction even of non-anthropogenic extinction. As Jenkins points out, the full diversity of other species matters not only for themselves, but also indeed for our own experience of life with God.[68]

8.5 CORPORATE SOLIDARITY

As we noted above, the other great meta-norm of Pauline ethics, aside from other-regard, is that of corporate solidarity, expressed in such classic passages as 1 Corinthians 12:12-26 and Romans 12:4-5. Paul sees the Christian community as one body, in Christ (Rom 12:4-5), even as the body of Christ (1 Cor 12:27). Baptism and Eucharist enact and display this membership of one corporate community (Gal 3:26-29; 1 Cor 10:16-17). But as this is an ἐκκλησία of human beings, and a small minority community at that, how can this meta-norm offer any contribution to an eschatological ethic with an ecological reach?

We note the following points: first, our recognition, as indicated in chapter 6, that our hermeneutic necessarily implies a universal ambit to salvation. On this view, every creature, human and other, is on the way to salvation; every creature has a part, actual or proleptic, in the community of Christ's redemptive purpose. The Colossian hymn in particular suggested a model of the whole community of creation as incorporated and reconciled in Christ, though we found this panenchristic or panentheistic vision expressed also elsewhere in the Pauline corpus (see §7.4). Moreover, a characteristic of the community in Christ, as revealed in particular in 1 Corinthians 12, is that of fellowship and interdependence in the Spirit. In the Pauline writings κοινωνία is that fellowship in community that enables the giving and receiving of gifts of all kinds.

Indeed, Paul's depiction of the body, with its diverse, interrelated, mutually dependent parts, contains a number of features worth noting. Using the concept of the body to depict human society or even the whole cosmos was nothing unusual (cf. §5.3). But what is striking about Paul's presentation is his insistence that God has given greatest honor and importance to the apparently weakest, least honorable members.

There is here a strong rhetoric of reversal, an insistence that God's ordering of the body is such as to turn upside down the normal expectations of importance and priority (cf. vv. 22-24).[69] And what this reversal makes possible is a certain equality of care and concern, such that every member's joy or grief calls for an empathetic response from all other members of the community. While it is clear that Paul is here talking about the relationships within the Corinthian ἐκκλησία, our ecologically oriented hermeneutical lens has already made clear our proposal to broaden the notion of the body and of community to encompass "all things," a proposal to which the Colossian hymn in particular makes a crucial contribution.

This understanding enables us to open up the concept of community in ways that are the very reverse of exclusive, or strongly hierarchical. When the focus is on the interdependence that community makes possible, we can also see the link with our core theme of reconciliation. Interdependence may helpfully be seen as "gift-exchange," a terminology developed in particular by Anne Primavesi.[70] If community grows and flourishes by the deepening interdependence of its members, then it does so also by progressively more complete reconciliation of what prevents mutual understanding and exchange.[71] As we as humans depend more and more on the other's energies and gifts, we are progressively freed from the idol of autonomy, and have to live more and more authentically from the matrix of our relationships. Again we see the pattern we articulated in the last chapter: kenosis, renunciation of self-asserted self-importance, makes possible both more genuine freedom and more profound reconciliation.

In Pauline thought the interdependence of humans in community is underpinned by the work of the Holy Spirit (1 Cor 12: 4-26; cf. also 2 Cor 13:13). The making of community, then, is the process of συνοίκησις of which Sigurd Bergmann writes;[72] it requires that we find ways to make the Spirit of God at home. The most characteristic of such actions is the one that, in celebration and epiclesis, constitutes the human community in Christ, meeting together for the Lord's Supper. But again, our view of this is not an exclusive one, but seeks an inclusive, indeed a cosmic, understanding of Eucharist.[73] The fruit of such a process of συνοίκησις is the love, joy, and peace mentioned in Galatians 5:22. Such fruits come to their fullness, then, in community, a community in the Holy Spirit that, we argue, from the perspective of our constructive and ecologically informed rereading of Paul, can and should be taken to extend beyond human beings alone.

The language of community has been perhaps too blithely evoked by ecotheological writers, often attracted to the simplicity and cogency of Aldo Leopold's "land ethic."[74] The term is not without its problems, and is helpfully discussed by Celia Deane-Drummond.[75] Scientifically, Leopold's formulation of a stable and beautiful biotic community is problematic, given the modern recognition that "biotic communities" are not static entities; they unfold dynamically around complex "attractors" in phase space. Ethically, too strong an emphasis on interspecies community can run into the same type of difficulties as an emphasis on rights for nonhuman subjects.[76] Human community is full of quasi-contractual mutual obligations—rights interwoven with responsibilities. Where a whole range of subjects are accorded rights without being able to sustain any responsibilities, many understandings of community begin to fail.

However, a deep truth remains in this language of community, in the sense that humans are undoubtedly and inalienably dependent not only on each other but also on a whole range of other organisms. It has become increasingly evident that these networks of interdependence include not just our intestinal flora, the crops we might grow, and the animals we might keep, but relationships at great distances. To breathe we depend on photosynthesis for our oxygen, to eat protein we are dependent ultimately on the fixation of atmospheric nitrogen by legumes, but far less obviously, for example, we are dependent also on the recycling of atmospheric sulphur by marine algae.[77] There are many other examples. In turn, it is increasingly the case that systems of nonhuman creatures only flourish where humans have taken positive decisions to encourage, or at least to permit, such flourishing. Even great marine ecosystems such as coral reefs will only continue to flourish if humans positively address the current rises in ocean temperature. Much use of the language of community has been oriented toward conferring moral status on nonhuman entities. But a more helpful emphasis is on recognizing our dependence on other creatures, and how it binds us together with them, as receivers of their gifts, and, one hopes, as generous givers of our gifts to them.[78]

As we have already noted, there is evidence that Paul's particular concern, within the community in Christ, was for the poor, a concern which he records sharing with the leaders of the church in Judaea (Gal 2:10).[79] Indeed it is very striking how much effort he seems to have exerted on the collection for the poor of Jerusalem (Rom 15:26; 2 Cor 8-9), seeking generous giving by appealing to the example of Christ.[80] Concern for the poor seems to have been a common factor between the diverse and sometimes competing factions of the emerging church.[81] In turn it reflects a strong motif of divine care for the poor, which is found in various traditions within the Hebrew Bible.[82]

However, the poor are not simply to be defined as those who are currently materially poor.[83] One significant dimension determining the underlying condition of the poor is that their future flourishing is threatened, and they lack the power, the voice to assert themselves and to remedy their situation. Hence the association of the poor in the New Testament with those who hunger, thirst, and mourn (Matt 5:3-4; par. Luke 6:20-21); with the blind, the lame, lepers, and the dead (Matt 11:4-5); the maimed, the lame, the blind (Luke 14:13, 21), and the "wretched, pitiable, poor, blind and naked" (Rev 3:17).[84] All share this underlying condition of being unable to flourish, or restore their state to one of flourishing, and many biblical texts assert God's closeness to them and concern for their restoration.

Here is a further dimension to the expanded sense of corporate concern that emerges from our consideration of Pauline thought. Within this enhanced sense of community engendered by our interdependence with others and our common path to salvation, particular ethical concern attends the vulnerable, the voiceless, the weak. We have suggested elsewhere that this is a promising contribution that Christian ethics can make to the new problems posed by climate change.[85] The future generations of humans in communities living in low-lying areas, and in areas especially vulnerable to hurricanes and typhoons, already have their flourishing threatened by the thoughtless (and indeed in a sense oppressive)[86] actions of the presently rich. An argument could well be made that those future generations are the most profoundly voiceless persons affected by the present crisis, and that their flourishing is profoundly at risk—to the extent indeed that some traditional island communities are literally losing the ground on which they are based.[87]

In the light of the powerful passage on extinction quoted from Thomas Berry above, the same argument may be pushed yet further. It is not only future human generations, but future generations of non-human species whose flourishing is under profound threat, and whose voice is barely heard when humans are considering their medium-term interest. These too—it might be held—are the new "poor," the beleaguered, those whose future is proscribed by the actions of the powerful, those, therefore, so the biblical tradition seems to imply, particularly of concern to God.[88]

As a practical outworking of this thinking, consider as a thought-experiment an effort to establish polar bears—a magnificent, iconic species native only to the sea ice of the Arctic, and therefore potentially doomed by global warming—in Antarctica. Could they survive such a journey? Will there be, on the melting fringes of late twenty-first century Antarctica, sufficiently stable habitats of ice on water, with sufficiently stable sources of food, to enable them to establish themselves? These are huge imponderables. But we suggest that the ethical reflection of this chapter moves us in the direction of very active consideration of such measures. It insists on an extended other-regard, involving the sacrificial use of resources by those with resources to give. It refuses to exclude from community even creatures with vastly different ecologies from our own—even, indeed, the one creature known routinely to hunt humans. And the Pauline model of costly concern for the weak, and for a model of the body-as-community in which the apparently weakest, most insignificant members are given greatest importance and honor, would imply that such concern be demonstrated for creatures of all sizes and shapes, even those with much less appeal than the impressive polar bear. These meta-ethical principles do not necessarily tell us which costly choices to make, and that indeed is a characteristic of such principles.

Both the general extension of ethical concern to all creatures, and the stress we have noted on the priority of the voiceless and those whose flourishing is most threatened, add power and poignancy to these ecological dilemmas. And the inclusion of potential future generations of creatures resists the discounting of the future on which other systems of valuing are based.[89] Polar bears have become dependent on our activities to a new extent, and may need to rely on our ingenuity and giftedness in unprecedented ways. But the enormous effort and care required of such a project as polar bear relocation, its costliness and precariousness, would have another value. It would not only serve the needs of that species. Whereas Barlow and Martin describe the proposed introduction of the Florida torreya into more northern latitudes as "easy, legal and cheap,"[90] clearly many assisted migrations would be neither easy nor cheap. Such thought-experiments, even before they actually came to implementation, would act as a rhetorical device to make yet more plain to those who influence the course of the most carbon-intensive economies in the world just how vital a change of overall policy has become. There is a whole complex of measures—economic, fiscal, technological, sociopolitical—which needs to be put in place to mitigate the impact of climate change, and most of these measures will be easier, cheaper, and more dependable as means of preventing mass extinction than great projects in assisted migration.[91] To have to think through the latter emphasizes the vital importance of the former.

Innumerable unsolved problems face the formulation of environmental ethics. One of these of which we are especially aware is that an ethics of other-regard and corporate solidarity faces continual tensions about the relative demands of individual "others" and community health in general and the relative worth of human and nonhuman flourishing. In arguing for an "other-regard," which humans work out in terms of an ethical kenosis, a self-giving for the sake of other species, we do not mean to imply that the good of another species, or of individuals within another species, should rank more highly, or even equally, with the good of humans. The issue of the relative moral status of human and other species is of course a complex and controversial one, which we do not intend to debate here. But what we do mean to argue is, first, that nonhuman creatures should, in our rereading of Pauline ethics, be counted as "others" worthy of moral concern—such that ecoethical actions are not only based on the (highly important!) welfare needs of other humans. And second, that these "others" are worthy precisely of a costly, generous, and self-limiting regard from humans, in particular from those humans with the highest levels of comfort and consumption, whose ecological impact on the Earth is greatest—such that the flourishing of creation is not only measured in terms of its ability to support human flourishing.

When the ambit of ethical concern and of involvement in community is extended, the problem merges with a classic problem in environmental ethics as to the respective goods of individual and system.[92] Our own scheme, by taking the eschatological character of our ethics seriously and thereby introducing a duty to seek to bring to an end biological extinction, raises the contentious issue of how to allow other species to flourish when the human population is still expanding. It also elevates the interests of rare species over common, in ways that others will no doubt want to contest. But these are questions that it is important to consider, given the current global context.

8.6 CONCLUSIONS

So we reach the end of our attempt to set out a hermeneutically explicit and ethically engaged reading of Paul in relation to the ecological issues that press upon us. As we bring the argument to a close, it is appropriate to draw together some overall conclusions, as well as specific findings from this final chapter.

First, it is important to reiterate that what we have attempted is an explicitly constructive, creative, and hermeneutically informed reading of Paul, a reading shaped by the particular context we inhabit and informed by the contemporary science so crucial to understanding issues of ecology. We consider that what we propose is an important stance insofar as it articulates an approach somewhere between the readings of "recovery" that imply that the Bible presents a "green" message, once we realize what is there, and critical readings of resistance, such as those found in the Earth Bible series, which set out their "canon" in the form of modern ethical principles independent of the Bible (see chaps. 1–2).

We do not pretend to be presenting what Paul "really said" or thought; nor do we pretend that Paul—or any other biblical tradition— could alone supply clear and substantial ethical guidance on matters related to our complex contemporary environmental challenges. But we do intend to allow the Bible—and Paul in particular—a generative and constructive role in the formulation of ecotheology and ethics, such that these can plausibly be presented as Christian contributions, persuasive reappropriations of the tradition. In this work an engagement with science is crucial, and, as will be clear from the present chapter, the move from broad theological and ethical principles to specific and concrete proposals is difficult and inevitably open to much uncertainty and debate. Indeed, our final proposals have consciously been tentative and brief, since our main concern throughout this book has been to establish a method of reading Paul ecologically—establishing what the broad shape of his theology and ethics might look like when read from this perspective—rather than to arrive at specific prescriptions.

This method has placed at its center both the notion of a hermeneutical lens, derived from the work of Conradie (see chap. 2), and an attempt to discern the narrative shape underlying the key Pauline texts (see chap. 3). Despite their differences, which should not too quickly be dissolved, we found in Romans 8 and Colossians 1 a coherent narrative of creation, which moved through the stages of beginning and problem to resolution. What these texts clearly indicate is that Paul's story of God's saving purposes encompasses the whole creation, not just (elect) humans. More specifically, using these crucial texts to establish our hermeneutical lens, we found in them a broadly "romantic" type of story, in Frye's terms, in which the final state of creation's glorious reconciliation and freedom is attained only after struggle and suffering. Moreover, the depiction of the characters in the story clearly implied a crucial role for human beings, specifically the members of the Christian communities, whose new life in Christ entails ethical responsibilities and imperatives: those in Christ are called to live in a way coherent with their new identity, expressing their freedom, enacting peace and reconciliation, and imitating Christ's self-giving for others (see chaps. 4–6).

Romans 8 and Colossians 1 use different images and motifs in describing the future hope of all creation: in Romans 8 the picture is of liberation and glory after futility and bondage, while in Colossians 1 the dominant image is that of reconciliation. The images from Romans 8, we have suggested, lend themselves especially well to an appropriation informed by evolutionary science. The idea of reconciliation, on the other hand, needs careful thought before it can be related to ecological issues, though we have argued that it is a crucial theme in terms of the ecological reading of the Pauline tradition.

The wider landscape of Pauline theology also offers much fruitful material for an ecological engagement. The broad narrative of creation-problem-resolution can be seen in various texts outside the eco-favorites of Romans 8 and Colossians 1, and specifically the idea that all things were created by God through Christ and will in the end find their *telos* in God/Christ, in whom all things will finally be incorporated. Amidst the various proposals for discerning the "heart" of Pauline theology, an eschatological and participatory reading of Paul seems to make good exegetical sense and to offer the most fruitful potential for ecological engagement. Moreover, the motif of cosmic reconciliation can arguably stand at the center of Pauline theology, again with a sense both of exegetical integrity and of ecotheological fruitfulness. This kind of Pauline narrative ecotheology will inevitably be thoroughly eschatological, infused with a sense that we stand at a particular and crucial point in the story, where God's decisive action to liberate the cosmos has already taken place in the Christ-event, but where the fulfillment of that goal is yet to be achieved, such that the present remains a time of straining forward, caught in the tension between the now and the not yet. This hope-filled eschatological narrative contrasts with some other (implicit) narratives in contemporary ecotheology but, we would argue, has a strong claim to be seen as expressing the fundamental narrative shape of a Christian ecotheology, at least insofar as such a narrative seeks to be informed by the New Testament in general and Paul in particular (see chap. 7).

The central idea of participation in Christ also has ethical dimensions, since it points to the believer's responsibility to live in Christ, which means conforming to the pattern of Christ's self-giving for others. This pattern of other-regard, specifically construed as ethical kenosis, we have argued, stands at the center of Pauline ethics. And once we have taken the crucial step of broadening the community of "others" to include the whole creation—a step that makes sense, given the Pauline vision of the value and incorporation of all things into Christ—that Christ-like other-regard is owed to all species and forms of life, not just to fellow Christians, or fellow humans. Moreover, the other key meta-norm in Pauline ethics, the idea of the community's solidarity as one body in Christ, can also be construed in an ecological direction, implying relations of care and mutuality throughout the created order.

These key arguments imply a certain anthropocentrism in our Pauline ecotheology and ethics, in ways that some will doubtless find problematic. Yet if our theological and ethical reflections remain informed by Paul, and the Pauline tradition, it can hardly be otherwise. The Pauline letters in general, and the specific texts on which we have focused, place the communities of human believers in Christ at the center of the story, seeing in them an anticipation and embodiment of the renewal of all things that God is in the process of bringing to fulfillment. Yet the form of anthropocentrism this implies is, we have argued, not one in which humans lay claim to a sense of superiority or ultimate importance. Rather, the anthropocentrism is one that places ethical responsibility upon those in Christ, a responsibility to live out their freedom in Christ in costly self-giving and regard for others, in working for peace and reconciliation through the whole creation, in limiting their own appetites and acquisitiveness out of generous love for those who are relatively weak and poor. It is in this sense that humans stand at the center of God's reconciling and liberating work.

We have argued that this ecological construal of Pauline theology and ethics offers much of value and gives a general shape to both ecotheology and ecoethics. The narrative shape of Pauline theology and the ethical norms that follow from participation in Christ show the fruitfulness of such an engagement with Paul. We have also explored some more concrete outworkings of this broad ethical framework, in assessing the case for Christian vegetarianism—a case we did not entirely affirm—and in arguing for human action to protect species from extinction. It is important to reiterate, however, that the move from the broad ethical shape derived from the Pauline material to the specifics of policies and actions is a complex and uncertain one in which we need all the resources of science and contemporary ethics to guide and inform our reflections. It is of fundamental importance to have established the broad shape of a Pauline ecological ethics, and we hope this is one of the significant contributions of our work, but we recognize that the move from this to decisions on specific measures and commitments remains tentative. Whatever is made of our particular reflections on such matters—and we look forward to further fruitful dialogue and debate—we hope to have shown how Paul can help to inform and to shape the theological and ethical framework within which Christians can develop their contributions to such questions.

NOTES

Introduction

1   For recent presentation of the evidence, see the latest publications available from the Intergovernmental Panel on Climate Change (IPCC) at http://www.ipcc.ch/index.htm (accessed August 4, 2009). For an accessible introduction, see Mark Maslin, *Global Warming: A Very Short Introduction* (Oxford: Oxford University Press, 2004).

2   For a critical overview of a wide range of biblical texts, see David G. Horrell, *The Bible and the Environment: Towards a Critical Ecological Biblical Theology*, Biblical Challenges in the Contemporary World (Oakville, Conn.: Equinox, 2010).

3   Pioneering in this regard is the work of the Earth Bible project under the leadership of Norman Habel. For details and publications, see chapter 1 below.

4   The claim that Paul was the "real founder of Christianity" was made from a critical perspective by Friedrich Nietzsche. The idea that Paul may be credited with being the "second founder of Christianity" is a description accepted with approval by Martin Hengel and Anna Maria Schwemer, *Paul between Damascus and Antioch: The Unknown Years* (London: SCM Press, 1997), 309.

5   Cf. Fernando F. Segovia and Mary Ann Tolbert, *Reading from This Place*, 2 vols. (Minneapolis: Fortress, 1995).

Chapter 1

1   Lynn White Jr., "The Historical Roots of our Ecologic Crisis," *Science* 155 (1967): 1203–7.

2   "... der meistzitierte Autor im Rahmen der ökotheologischen Diskussion" (our translation); Heike Baranzke and Hedwig Lamberty-Zielinski, "Lynn White und das Dominium Terrae (Gen 1,28b). Ein Beitrag zu Einer Doppelten Wirkungsgeschichte," *BN* 76 (1995): 56. Baranzke and Lamberty-Zielinski note the flood of studies that have followed White's article (32), and examine the impact of his work on studies of Gen 1:28 and the theme of human dominion over the earth. Similarly, Gene Tucker comments that White's article led to a veritable "cottage industry" of responses from biblical scholars: Gene M. Tucker, "Rain on a Land Where No One Lives: The Hebrew Bible on the Environment," *JBL* 116 (1997): 3–4. For further references and discussion, see, e.g., Udo Krolzik, *Umweltkrise, Folge des Christentums?* (Stuttgart: Kreuz, 1979); Lawrence Osborn, *Guardians of Creation: Nature in Theology and the Christian Life* (Leicester: Apollos, 1993); Colin A. Russell, *The Earth, Humanity, and God* (London: UCL, 1994), 89; Wilfried Lochbühler, *Christliche Umweltethik: Schöpfungstheologische Grundlagen, Philosophisch-ethische Ansätze, Ökologische Marktwirtschaft*, Forum Interdisziplinäre Ethik 13 (Frankfurt am Main: Peter Lang, 1996), 76–77; Peter Harrison, "Subduing the Earth: Genesis 1, Early Modern Science, and the Exploitation of Nature," *JR* 79 (1999): 86–109; Alister E. McGrath, "The Stewardship of the Creation: An Evangelical Affirmation," in *The Care of Creation*, ed. R. J. Berry (Leicester: InterVarsity, 2000), 86–89; Richard J. Bauckham, *God and the Crisis of Freedom: Biblical and Contemporary Perspectives* (Louisville, Ky.: Westminster John Knox, 2002), 129–33. For a recent discussion of the extent to which White has been allowed to shape the debate, see Willis Jenkins, *Ecologies of Grace: Environmental Ethics and Christian Theology* (New York: Oxford University Press, 2008), 10–15. A comparable critique of the negative ecological implications of Christianity's doctrine of humanity's place in creation was mounted by Carl Amery, *Das Ende der Vorsehung: Die Gnadenlosen Folgen des Christentums* (Hamburg: Rowohlt, 1972), though Amery, like White, does not engage in detail with biblical texts or biblical scholarship.

3   White, "Historical Roots," 1205. It should be noted here that White implies that this anthropocentrism is a negative and destructive facet of Christianity. For a recent mention of anthropocentrism as a more ambiguous factor in ecological writing, see Marguerite Shuster, "The Redemption of the Created Order: Sermons on Romans 8:18-25," in *The Redemption*, ed. Stephen T. David, Daniel Kendall, and Gerald O'Collins (New York: Oxford University Press, 2004), 321–42. For further discussion of this important issue, see §6.4.

4   White, "Historical Roots," 1205.

5   White, "Historical Roots," 1206.

6   White, "Historical Roots," 1207. See §7.7 for further discussion of White's proposal for a new Franciscanism.

7   White, "Historical Roots," 1205, 1206. This need for a rethinking of belief found an important parallel outside Christian thought in Arne Naess' call for a "deep, long-range ecology movement" ("The Shallow and the Deep, Long-Range Ecology Movement. A Summary," *Inquiry* 16 [1972]: 95–100). See also Ian Barbour's exchanges with White in the early 1970s, discussed in Christopher Southgate, "Environmental Ethics and the Science-Religion Debate: A British Perspective on Barbour," in *Fifty Years in Science and Religion: Ian G. Barbour and His Legacy*, ed. Robert J. Russell (Aldershot: Ashgate, 2004), 241.

8   Nonetheless, some of those responding to White's challenge write as if he had specifically engaged in biblical exegesis; e.g., Baranzke and Lamberty-Zielinski, "Lynn White," 32–33, who speak of White's "Bibelinterpretation" and his accusation against "die biblischen Schöpfungstexte, darunter vor allem Gen 1,26-28."

9   White, "Historical Roots," 1205.

10   Cf. Tucker, "Rain," 3–4.

11   David W. Orr, "Armageddon versus Extinction," *Conserv Biol* 19 (2005): 290–92; Keith D. Dyer, "When Is the End Not the End? The Fate of Earth in Biblical Eschatology (Mark 13)," in *The Earth Bible*, vol. 5, *The Earth Story in the New Testament*, ed. Norman C. Habel and Vicky Balabanski, (Cleveland, Ohio: Pilgrim, 2002), 44–56.

12   See Dyer, "When Is the End Not the End?" 45–49. Cf. also Lochbühler, *Christliche Umweltethik*, 76–77.

13   Dyer, "When Is the End Not the End?" 48–49. See also the discussion in Edward Adams, "Retrieving the Earth from the Conflagration: 2 Peter 3.5-13 and the Environment," in *Ecological Hermeneutics: Biblical, Historical, and Theological Perspectives*, ed. David G. Horrell, Cherryl Hunt, Christopher Southgate, and Francesca Stavrakopoulou (New York: T&T Clark, 2010), 108–20.

14   Ernst M. Conradie, "Towards an Ecological Biblical Hermeneutics: A Review Essay on the Earth Bible Project," *Scriptura* 85 (2004): 126.

15   Conradie, "Towards," 126.

16   Francis Watson, "Strategies of Recovery and Resistance: Hermeneutical Reflections on Genesis 1–3 and Its Pauline Reception," *JSNT* 45 (1992): 82.

17   Watson, "Strategies," 80.

18   Conradie, "Towards," 124; H. Paul Santmire, *Nature Reborn. The Ecological and Cosmic Promise of Christian Theology* (Minneapolis: Fortress, 2000), 7. Cf. The Earth Bible Team, "Guiding Ecojustice Principles," in *The Earth*

Bible, vol. 1, *Readings from the Perspective of Earth*, ed. Norman C. Habel (Cleveland, Ohio: Pilgrim, 2000), 39; Elisabeth Schüssler Fiorenza, *In Memory of Her* (London: SCM Press, 1983), 18.

19   Fiorenza, *In Memory*, 140–51.

20   Fiorenza, *In Memory*, 168–73; Elisabeth Schüssler Fiorenza, "Missionaries, Apostles, Co-workers: Romans 16 and the Reconstruction of Women's Early Christian History," *Word and World* 6 (1986): 420–33.

21   On these examples, see further Fiorenza, *In Memory*, 45–48; Fiorenza, "Missionaries"; Morna D. Hooker, "Authority on Her Head: An Examination of I Cor. XI.10," *NTS* 10 (1964): 110–16, later published in eadem, *From Adam to Christ: Essays on Paul* (Cambridge: Cambridge University Press, 1990). For a brief overview, see David G. Horrell, *An Introduction to the Study of Paul*, 2nd ed. (New York: T&T Clark, 2006), 114–20.

22   Cf. Watson, "Strategies," 83. The drawing together of both "suspicion and retrieval" as a necessity in hermeneutics is particularly associated with the work of Paul Ricoeur, on which see Anthony C. Thiselton, *New Horizons in Hermeneutics: The Theory and Practice of Transforming Biblical Reading* (Grand Rapids: Zondervan, 1992), 344–78.

23   Cf., e.g., Mary Hayter, *The New Eve in Christ* (Grand Rapids: Eerdmans, 1987); Ben Witherington III, *Women in the Earliest Churches*, SNTSMS 59 (Cambridge: Cambridge University Press, 1988); Ben Witherington III, *Women and the Genesis of Christianity* (Cambridge: Cambridge University Press, 1990).

24   *The Green Bible* (London: HarperCollins, 2008), I–15 (from the preface).

25   Norbert Lohfink, *Theology of the Pentateuch: Themes of the Priestly Narrative and Deuteronomy*, trans. Linda M. Maloney (Edinburgh: T&T Clark, 1994), 8.

26   Lohfink, *Theology*, 12–13.

27   Lohfink, *Theology*, 17.

28   Bauckham, *God*, 141.

29   Bauckham, *God*, 141–42. For similar and earlier arguments, see Krolzik, *Umweltkrise*; Harrison, "Subduing."

30   Bauckham, *God*, 159.

31   Bauckham, *God*, 160.

32   Bauckham, *God*, 167.

33   Bauckham, *God*, 158; emphasis added.

34   Bauckham, *God*, 176–77; further Richard Bauckham, "Joining Creation's Praise of God," *Ecotheology* 7 (2002): 45–59.

35   See, e.g., William Dyrness, "Stewardship of the Earth in the Old Testament," in *Tending the Garden*, ed. Wesley Granberg-Michaelson (Grand Rapids: Eerdmans, 1987), 50–65; McGrath, "Stewardship"; Douglas John Hall, *The Steward: A Biblical Symbol Come of Age* (1982; rev. ed., Grand Rapids: Eerdmans, 1990). Stewardship tends to be a prominent theme in Christian

environmental declarations and initiatives; see, e.g., "An Evangelical Declaration on the Care of Creation," in Berry, *Care*, 17–22; Interfaith Council for Environmental Stewardship, "The Cornwall Declaration on Environmental Stewardship" (2000), http://www.cornwallalliance .org/docs/the-cornwall-declaration-on-environmental-stewardship.pdf (accessed July 31, 2009); The John Ray Initiative, http://www.jri.org.uk (accessed August 26, 2009); *The Green Bible* (e.g., I-26–28; 1226). See also "Common Declaration on Environmental Ethics: Common Declaration of John Paul II and the Ecumenical Patriarch His Holiness Bartholomew I," http://www.vatican.va/holy_father/john_paul_ii/speeches/2002/june/ documents/hf_jp-ii_spe_20020610_venice-declaration_en.html (accessed August 4, 2009); The International Theological Commission, "Communion and Stewardship: Human Persons Created in the Image of God," http:// www.vatican.va/roman_curia/congregations/cfaith/cti_documents/rc _con_cfaith_doc_20040723_communion-stewardship_en.html (accessed August 4, 2009).

36 See below §2.1 with nn. 9–11; also further discussion in §7.8.

37 Osborn, *Guardians*, 86.

38 See, e.g., James Jones, *Jesus and the Earth* (London: SPCK, 2003).

39 Tim Cooper, *Green Christianity. Caring for the Whole Creation* (London: Spire, 1990), 218; James A. Nash, *Loving Nature: Ecological Integrity and Christian Responsibility* (Nashville: Abingdon, 1991), 143; Michael S. Northcott, *The Environment and Christian Ethics*, New Studies in Christian Ethics (Cambridge: Cambridge University Press, 1996), 224–25; Edward P. Echlin, *The Cosmic Circle: Jesus and Ecology* (Blackrock, Colo.: Columba, 2004), 94–96.

40 See Matt 6:26-29; Mark 4:1-20, 26-32; John 15:1-8; as treated, e.g., in Sean McDonagh, *The Greening of the Church* (Maryknoll, N.Y.: Orbis, 1990), 159; Cooper, *Green Christianity*, 172; See also Ian Bradley, *God Is Green: Christianity and the Environment* (London: Darton, Longman, & Todd, 1990), 78; Richard Bauckham, "Reading the Synoptic Gospels Ecologically," in Horrell, Hunt, Southgate, and Stavrakopoulou, *Ecological Hermeneutics*, 70–82.

41 Adrian M. Leske, "Matthew 6.25-34: Human Anxiety and the Natural World," in Habel and Balabanski, *The Earth Story in the New Testament*, 21.

42 Leske, "Matthew 6.25-34," 24.

43 Leske, "Matthew 6.25-34," 26–27.

44 McDonagh, *Greening*, 158.

45 McDonagh, *Greening*, 158–59. Cf. more recently Sean McDonagh, *Passion for the Earth* (London: Geoffrey Chapman, 1994), 140: "It would be a distortion to pretend that care for creation is a central theme of the Gospel of Jesus. Nevertheless a Christian theology of creation can learn much from the attitude of respect which Jesus displayed toward the natural world.

He enjoyed an intimacy with nature which is evident from his parables — the sower and the seed (Matt 13:3-9, 18-23), the vine and the branches (John 15:1-17; Mark 12:1-12). He illustrated his stories by referring to the lilies of the field (Luke 12:27), the birds of the air (Matt 6:26), and foxes and their lairs (Luke 9:58)." For another example, see Echlin, *The Cosmic Circle*, 95: "Jesus preached God's kingdom using metaphors and parables drawn from food growing. . . . The Jesus of the gospels was sensitive to the changing seasons, weather, seeds, soil, growth, harvest, and the treasure of local rural wisdom about working with a local biosystem."

46 McDonagh, *Greening*, 162–64 and, e.g., Nash, *Loving Nature*, 125; Northcott, *Environment*, 202–5.

47 Ernest Lucas, "The New Testament Teaching on the Environment," *Transformation* 16, no. 3 (1999): 97.

48 Steven Bouma-Prediger, *For the Beauty of the Earth: A Christian Vision for Creation Care* (Grand Rapids: Baker Academic, 2001), 77.

49 Thomas Finger, *Evangelicals, Eschatology, and the Environment*, The Scholars Circle 2 (Wynnewood, Pa.: Evangelical Environmental Network, 1998); Douglas J. Moo, "Nature in the New Creation: New Testament Eschatology and the Environment," *JETS* 49 (2006): 449–88; David M. Russell, *The "New Heavens and New Earth." Hope for the Creation in Jewish Apocalyptic and the New Testament*, Studies in Biblical Apocalyptic Literature 1 (Philadelphia: Visionary, 1996).

50 Watson, "Strategies," 81.

51 See, e.g., Fiorenza, "Missionaries," 422–23; Elisabeth Schüssler Fiorenza, "The Will to Choose or to Reject: Continuing Our Critical Work," in *Feminist Interpretation of the Bible*, ed. Letty M. Russell (Philadelphia: Westminster, 1985), 130–31.

52 Santmire, *Nature Reborn*, 6.

53 Mary Daly, *Beyond God the Father: Toward a Philosophy of Women's Liberation* (London: Women's Press, 1986); Daphne Hampson, *After Christianity* (London: SCM Press, 1996).

54 Phyllis Trible, *Texts of Terror: Literary-Feminist Readings of Biblical Narratives* (Philadelphia: Fortress, 1984). See also Diana Lipton, "Remembering Amalek: A Positive Biblical Model for Dealing with Negative Scriptural Types," in *Reading Texts, Seeking Wisdom*, ed. David F. Ford and Graham Stanton (London: SCM Press, 2003), 139–53. However, Trible's work well illustrates the point that feminist readings can and do operate in both modes of recovery and resistance; for a feminist reading of recovery dealing with the creation of Adam and Eve, see "A Love Story Gone Awry" in Phyllis Trible, *God and the Rhetoric of Sexuality* (London: SCM Press, 1978), 72–143.

55 Kathleen E. Corley, "1 Peter," in *Searching the Scriptures*, vol. 2, *A Feminist Commentary*, ed. Elisabeth Schüssler Fiorenza (London: SCM Press, 1995), 354–57.

56 T. Lemaire, cited in Roger Burggraeve, "Responsibility for a 'New Heaven and a New Earth,'" *Concilium* 4 (1991): 116.

57 In Norman C. Habel, ed., *The Earth Bible*, vol. 1, *Readings from the Perspective of Earth* (Cleveland, Ohio: Pilgrim, 2000), 24. For a fuller explanation of these principles see also The Earth Bible Team, "Guiding."

58 The Earth Bible Team, "Ecojustice Hermeneutics: Reflections and Challenges," in Habel and Balabanski, *The Earth Story in the New Testament*, 2. For discussion of these principles, see The Earth Bible Team, "Conversations with Gene Tucker and Other Writers," in *The Earth Bible*, vol. 2, *The Earth Story in Genesis*, ed. Norman C. Habel and Shirley Wurst (Cleveland, Ohio: Pilgrim, 2000), 21–33.

59 Dyer, "When Is the End Not the End?" 48–49.

60 Gene McAfee, "Chosen People in a Chosen Land: Theology and Ecology in the Story of Israel's Origins," in Habel and Wurst, *The Earth Story in Genesis*, 158.

61 Howard N. Wallace, "Rest for the Earth? Another Look at Genesis 2.1-3," in Habel and Wurst, *The Earth Story in Genesis*, 56.

62 Keith Carley, "Psalm 8: An Apology for Domination," in Habel, *Readings*, 121.

63 Carley, "Psalm 8," 122.

64 Norman Habel, "Introducing the Earth Bible," in Habel, *Readings*, 30.

65 Norman C. Habel, "An Ecojustice Challenge: Is Earth Valued in John 1?" in Habel and Balabanski, *The Earth Story in the New Testament*, 76–82.

66 Habel, "An Ecojustice Challenge," 82.

67 Elizabeth Wainwright, "Which Intertext? A Response to 'An Ecojustice Challenge: Is Earth Valued in John 1?'" in Habel and Balabanski, *The Earth Story in the New Testament*, 83.

68 Norman C. Habel, "Geophany: The Earth Story in Genesis 1," in Habel and Wurst, *The Earth Story in Genesis*, 46–47. Cf., similarly, Norman C. Habel, "Introducing Ecological Hermeneutics," in *Exploring Ecological Hermeneutics*, ed. Norman C. Habel and Peter Trudinger, Society of Biblical Literature Symposium 46 (Atlanta: SBL, 2008), 6–8.

69 The Earth Bible Team, "Guiding," 38.

70 Habel, "Introducing the Earth Bible," 33, explicitly draws on Fiorenza's feminist hermeneutic of suspicion *and* retrieval in articulating a hermeneutic for the Earth Bible project; see also Habel, "Introducing Ecological Hermeneutics." Similarly, Conradie, "Towards," 127, maintains that "[a]n ecological hermeneutics . . . has to operate not only with a hermeneutic of trust but also one of suspicion."

71 Wayne Grudem, *Systematic Theology: An Introduction to Biblical Doctrine* (Leicester: InterVarsity, 1994), 459–66.

72 John Paul II, "Apostolic Letter *Mulieris Dignitatem*," Libreria Editrice Vaticana (1988), http://www.vatican.va/holy_father/john_paul_ii/letters/documents/hf_jp-ii_let_29061995_women_en.html (accessed January 8, 2007). This diversity of roles is further expounded in John Paul II, "Letter to Women," *Libreria Editrice Vaticana* (1995), http://www.vatican.va/holy_father/john_paul_ii/letters/documents/hf_jp-ii_let_29061995_women_en.html (accessed January 8, 2007), with reference to the Gospel accounts of Christ only choosing men as disciples.

73 Manfred Hauke, *Women in the Priesthood? A Systematic Analysis in the Light of the Order of Creation and Redemption*, trans. David Kipp (San Francisco: Ignatius, 1988), 332–33 (Eucharist); 202–3, 347–56 (subordination).

74 Loren Wilkinson, "New Age, New Consciousness, and the New Creation," in Granberg-Michaelson, *Tending the Garden*, 25. For instance, Cumbey outlines similarities she sees between Christian environmental thinking and New Age philosophy, particularly appeals to the immanence of God in creation (Constance E. Cumbey, *The Hidden Dangers of the Rainbow: The New Age Movement and Our Coming Age of Barbarism* [Shreveport: Huntington House, 1983], 162–69). See also Constance E. Cumbey, *A Planned Deception: The Staging of a New Age "Messiah"* (East Detroit, Mich.: Pointe Publishers, 1985), 43, where she points out that the "environmental saving measures" put forward by New Agers "almost universally promote animism and pantheism"; and 110–23, where she is suspicious of anyone advocating international controls of anything (e.g., food distribution, economics, environment) or anyone wanting to "transform" the world. Interestingly, she identifies these policies as a "political agenda" (111). See also Dave Hunt, *Peace, Prosperity, and the Coming Holocaust: The New Age Movement in Prophecy* (Eugene, Ore.: Harvest House, 1983). Cf. the comments of Osborn, *Guardians*, 27–28.

75 Wilkinson, "New Age," 24.

76 Orr, "Armageddon." For a number of responses to Orr, see *Conserv Biol* 19.6 (2005).

77 A significant publication in this regard is E. Calvin Beisner, *Where Garden Meets Wilderness: Evangelical Entry into the Environmental Debate* (Grand Rapids: Eerdmans, 1997), on which see below. For a survey of the diverse Evangelical reactions to the environmental debate in the USA, see Harry O. Maier, "Green Millennialism: American Evangelicals, Environmentalism, and the Book of Revelation," in Horrell, Hunt, Southgate, and Stavrakopoulou, *Ecological Hermeneutics*, 246–65.

78 Todd Strandberg, "Bible Prophecy and Environmentalism," http://www.raptureready.com/rr-environmental.html (accessed December 18, 2007);

Spencer Strickland, "Beware of Global Warming! (2 Peter 3:6-7)," http://
jeremiahdanielmccarver.wordpress.com/2008/08/07/beware-of-global
-warming-2-peter-36-7/ (accessed April 2, 2009).

79   Cf. Osborn, *Guardians*, 27, who comments, citing Cumbey as the key example in the literature, "Some fundamentalists expect the imminent demise
of the earth on biblical grounds and, for them, the environmental crisis is
merely additional evidence that God's Kingdom is not of this earth. They
argue that since this world will pass away our treatment of it is ultimately
a matter of indifference. To such people, Christians who are concerned
about the environment have sold out to the New Age movement." Cf. also
61–62.

80   Hal Lindsey, *The Late Great Planet Earth* (London: Lakeland, 1971) and
the series of books starting with Tim LaHaye and Jerry B. Jenkins, *Left
Behind* (Wheaton, Ill.: Tyndale House, 1995). These books have been
enormously successful: Lindsey's book has sold over 40 million copies
(Michael S. Northcott, *An Angel Directs the Storm: Apocalyptic Religion and
American Empire* [New York: I. B. Tauris, 2004], 66) and by January
2002 the *Left Behind* series had sold 32 million copies (Crawford Gribben,
"Rapture Fictions and the Changing Evangelical Condition," *Lit Theol* 18
[2004]: 78).

81   See Gribben, "Rapture Fictions," 77–79; Maier, "Green Millennialism."

82   Paul Boyer, *When Time Shall Be No More: Prophecy Belief in Modern American
Culture* (Cambridge, Mass.: Belknap, 1992), 331–37; cf. Osborn, *Guardians*,
61–63. The attitude engendered by premillennialism, of "indifference, if
not actual hostility toward all remedial agencies designed to improve the
present order of existence," was noted with regard to social reform early
in the last century (Shirley Jackson Case, *The Millennial Hope: A Phase
of War-time Thinking* [Chicago: University of Chicago Press, 1918], 240).
Anti-environmental attitudes amongst contemporary Christians have
been attributed to fundamentalism by Douglas Lee Eckberg and T. Jean
Blocker, "Christianity, Environmentalism, and the Theoretical Problem of
Fundamentalism," *JSSR* 35 (1996): 343–55.

83   E.g., James McKeever, cited in Boyer, *When Time*, 333–34.

84   Boyer, *When Time*, 337.

85   Tony Campolo, *How to Rescue the Earth without Worshipping Nature: A
Christian's Call to Save Creation* (Milton Keynes: Word, 1992), esp. 94–96.
See also R. S. Beal Jr., "Can A Premillennialist Consistently Entertain
a Concern for the Environment? A Rejoinder to Al Truesdale," *PSCF*
46 (1994): 172–77, and the portrayal of premillennial thought as hav-
ing a positive attitude toward tackling current problems in Robert G.
Clouse, ed., *The Meaning of the Millennium: Four Views* (Downers Grove, Ill.:
InterVarsity, 1979), esp. 68–69.

86   Beisner, *Where Garden*, 65–66, 164, 170.
87   Beisner, *Where Garden*, 110.
88   Beisner, *Where Garden*, 48–49, 53, 117–23. It is perhaps worth noting that different attitudes to wilderness might be a significant indicator of different stances toward the environment.
89   Beisner, *Where Garden*, 25.
90   Beisner, *Where Garden*, 107; cf. 125, etc. For further treatments of this important part of Romans 8 see chaps. 4, 6, and 7.
91   Maier, "Green Millennialism."
92   E.g., Lindsey states that a cardinal rule of biblical interpretation is to seek the literal meaning of the text (Lindsey, *Late Great*, 50), but he then proceeds to read the plague of Zechariah 14:12 as describing the results of a thermonuclear blast (Lindsey, *Late Great*, 175).
93   Northcott, *An Angel*.
94   See Lindsey, *Late Great*, 69, 72–80, although Arab involvement in alliance with Russia is seen as being due to an extension of Communism through Africa.
95   Boyer, *When Time*, 326–31.
96   Conversely, it is possible that political commitments may in turn influence theological approaches: separating out various factors is difficult.
97   Boyer, *When Time*, 141. For similar reports of Watt's testimony see Mark Tracy, "The Ronald Reagan Years—The Real Reagan Record: Environment" (2003), http://www.geocities.com/thereaganyears/environment .htm (accessed January 2007); for his own account, see Greg Lakes, "Headwaters News: James Watt," Center for the Rocky Mountain West at the University of Montana (2003), http://www.headwatersnews.org/ p.watt.html (accessed February 20, 2007). He was also reported as having said, "My responsibility is to follow the Scriptures which call upon us to occupy the land until Jesus returns" (*The Washington Post*, May 24, 1981).
98   See John Hinderaker, "Bill Moyers Smears a Better Man than Himself" (2005), http://powerlineblog.com/archives/2005/02/009377.php (accessed July 31, 2009).
99   Andrew Sibley, *Restoring the Ethics of Creation: Challenging the Ethical Implications of Evolution* (Camberley: Anno Mundi Books, 2005), e.g., 146–47.
100 It is relevant to note here that The Earth Bible Team's ecojustice principle of "interconnectedness"—"Earth is a community of interconnected living things that are mutually dependent on each other for life and survival" (see The Earth Bible Team, "Guiding," 44–46)—represents a contrary insistence that humanity is fully "part of nature," against any notion of human uniqueness and intrinsic superiority (cf. The Earth Bible Team, "Guiding," 45). It should also be noted that a creationist position is not necessarily opposed to environmental care, see, e.g., Ralph E. Ancil, "Environmental

Problems: A Creationist Perspective Our Biblical Heritage [sic]," *Creation Social Science and Humanities Quarterly Journal* (1983), http://www.creationism .org/csshs/v06n4p05.htm (accessed May 14, 2006); Ralph E. Ancil, "Man and His Environment: The Creationist Perspective," *Creation Social Science and Humanities Quarterly Journal* (1989), http://www.creationism .org/csshs/v12n4p19.htm (accessed August 5, 2009).

Chapter 2

1   Albert Schweitzer, *The Quest of the Historical Jesus*, ed. John Bowden (1913; repr., London: SCM Press, 2000), 6. The full quotation runs as follows: "[E]ach successive epoch of theology found its own thoughts in Jesus; that was, indeed, the only way in which it could make him live. But it was not only each epoch that found its reflection in Jesus; each individual created Jesus in accordance with his own character. There is no historical task which so reveals a man's true self as the writing of a Life of Jesus." A precise image which illustrates the point is used by George Tyrrell, criticizing the portrait of Christ presented in the work of Adolf von Harnack: "The Christ that Harnack sees, looking back through nineteen centuries of Catholic darkness, is only the reflection of a Liberal Protestant face, seen at the bottom of a deep well" (*Christianity at the Crossroads* [London: Longmans, Green, 1910], 44).

2   Clearly the word "plausible" could be unpacked and discussed at some length. Essentially what we mean to include here is any reading that does not so obviously do violence to the text as to render that reading thereby hardly conceivable as an interpretation.

3   James Barr, "Man and Nature — The Ecological Controversy and the Old Testament," *BJRL* 55 (1972): 30. Cf. also Lohfink, *Theology*, 1–17; Bernhard W. Anderson, "Creation and Ecology," in idem, *Creation in the Old Testament* (Philadelphia: Fortress, 1984), 152–71.

4   Bauckham, *God*, 158.

5   Harrison, "Subduing," 88–90.

6   See esp. N. T. Wright, *The New Testament and the People of God* (London: SPCK, 1992), 282–85, 332–33; idem, *Jesus and the Victory of God* (London: SPCK, 1996), 360–65; idem, *New Heavens, New Earth: The Biblical Picture of Christian Hope* (Cambridge: Grove, 1999).

7   Edward Adams, *The Stars Will Fall from Heaven: Cosmic Catastrophe in the New Testament and Its World*, LNTS 347 (London: T&T Clark, 2007).

8   This problem is exemplified in *The Green Bible*, published in 2008: the aim of this "green-letter edition" is to highlight texts which show that the Bible's message calls humans to care for creation. For a critique, see David G. Horrell, "*The Green Bible*: A Timely Idea Deeply Flawed," *ExpTim* 121 (2010): 180–85.

9   Wesley Granberg-Michaelson, "Introduction: Identification or Mastery?"
     in Granberg-Michaelson, *Tending the Garden*, 4. There is here a series
     of references to what "the Bible" teaches: "the Bible sees the nature of
     humanity's dominion as service for the sake of all creation" (3); "The Bible
     fights against the kind of dualism that modern Christians want to read
     into its pages" (3–4); "the Bible's picture of the intended relationship of
     God, humanity, and the created world . . ." (4), etc. See also Dyrness,
     "Stewardship," 53–54; Loren Wilkinson et al., *Earthkeeping: Christian
     Stewardship of Natural Resources* (Grand Rapids: Eerdmans, 1980), 203–38;
     and now, also, *The Green Bible*.
10   John Reumann, *Stewardship and the Economy of God* (Grand Rapids:
     Eerdmans, 1992), 7, 16, 18, respectively.
11   For further critique of the ethical value of the notion of stewardship see
     especially Clare Palmer, "Stewardship: A Case Study in Environmental
     Ethics," in *The Earth Beneath: A Critical Guide to Green Theology*, Ian Ball et
     al. (London: SPCK, 1992), 67–86, e.g., "The political message encoded
     in stewardship is one of power and oppression; of server and the served"
     (76). Assumptions underlying the concept include "a strong sense of
     humanity's separation from the rest of the natural world . . . that the natu-
     ral world is a human resource, that humans are really in control of nature,
     that nature is dependent on humanity for its management" (77–78). It
     is, in short, Palmer argues, an anthropocentric and patronizing ethic (cf.
     81–84). Similar questions are posed by Bauckham, *God*, 172, who sug-
     gests that "the image of stewardship is still too freighted with the bag-
     gage of the modern project of technological domination of nature. Can
     we entirely free it of the implication that nature is always better off when
     managed by us, that nature needs our benevolent intrusions, that it is our
     job to turn the whole world into a well-tended garden inhabited by well-
     cared-for pets?" See also Richard Bauckham, *Beyond Stewardship: The Bible
     and the Community of Creation*, 2006 Sarum Lectures (London: Darton,
     Longman, & Todd, forthcoming); Christopher Southgate, "Stewardship
     and its Competitors: A Spectrum of Relationships between Humans and
     the Non-Human Creation," in *Environmental Stewardship: Critical Perspectives,
     Past and Present*, ed. R. J. Berry (New York: T&T Clark, 2006), 185–95,
     and our further discussion in §7.8.
12   This is, in a sense, the issue which drives the argument of John Milbank,
     Theology and Social Theory: Beyond Secular Reason (Oxford: Blackwell, 1990),
     and the "radical orthodoxy" that Milbank's work has generated, though
     the approach is utterly different from that taken by fundamentalism.
13   Francis Watson, "Hermeneutics and the Doctrine of Scripture: Why They
     Need Each Other," paper presented at the Australian Theological Forum
     in Canberra, 2008 (publication forthcoming), 18–19 in manuscript.

14 People with no connection with the Christian tradition might, of course, be interested in probing and assessing the Bible's ecofriendliness out of a concern either to expose and critique Christianity's contribution to the ecological crisis (following White), or to persuade Christians to adopt certain stances; but both of these reasons are derivative from the fact that there is a body of people for whom the biblical texts are important in shaping contemporary moral insight and action. We have not here attempted to engage with Jewish readings of relevant Hebrew Bible texts, nor with their significance for contemporary Jewish life and ethics; the approaches to the Bible we have surveyed in this essay are essentially those of (or reacting to) the Christian tradition, and we wish to avoid any impression that Jewish readings could simply be assimilated to Christian ones.

15 Santmire, *Nature Reborn*, 6–9.

16 Santmire, *Nature Reborn*, 7–8

17 Nash, *Loving Nature*, 94. Included in this category could be those writers who find the use of an overarching biblical theme, rather than specific texts, a more fruitful way to find an environmental ethic in the Bible. Nash himself favors the extension of the call to neighborly-love to include our "biotic neighbors [*sic*]" (143) and Celia Deane-Drummond focuses on the Hebrew Scriptures' concept of wisdom (*Creation Through Wisdom* [Edinburgh: T&T Clark, 2000]), while Michael Northcott, in his *Environment*, advocates the application of natural law ethics which reflect both "Hebraic" and Christian ideas of creation, relationality, and the restoration of the natural order. A more radical approach is espoused by Matthew Fox (see, e.g., *Original Blessing* [Santa Fe: Bear, 1983]) with his rejection of what he terms a "fall/redemption spirituality" in favor of a "creation-centered" one. In fact, Santmire classes him as a reconstructionist rather than a revisionist, although Fox might see himself more as working within the authentic tradition (cf. *Original Blessing*, 11).

18 Cf. Karl Barth's famous statement about the task of dogmatics, which "does not ask what the apostles and prophets said but what we must say on the basis of the apostles and prophets" (*Church Dogmatics I.1: The Doctrine of the Word of God*, trans. G. W. Bromiley, 2nd ed. [Edinburgh: T&T Clark, 1975], 16).

19 Cf. Dale B. Martin, *Sex and the Single Savior* (Louisville, Ky.: Westminster John Knox, 2006), 1–16.

20 Ernst M. Conradie, "The Road towards an Ecological Biblical and Theological Hermeneutics," *Scriptura* 93 (2006): 305–14, esp. 305–8. See also Ernst M. Conradie, "Interpreting the Bible amidst Ecological Degradation," *Theology* 112 (2009): 199–207; idem, "What on Earth is an Ecological Hermeneutics? Some Broad Parameters," in Horrell, Hunt, Southgate, and Stavrakopoulou, *Ecological Hermeneutics*, 295–313.

21   Conradie, "The Road," 306 (emphasis in original).

22   Cf. John Thompson's definition of ideology, as "the ways in which mean-
     ing (or signification) serves to sustain relations of domination" (John B.
     Thompson, *Studies in the Theory of Ideology* [Cambridge: Polity, 1984], 4,
     130–31, 134, 141, 146).

23   Conradie, "The Road," 308.

24   We note in this context the very helpful study of Frances Young, *The Art of
     Performance: Towards a Theology of Holy Scripture* (London: Darton, Longman,
     & Todd, 1990).

25   Conradie, "Interpreting"; Conradie, "Ecological Hermeneutics."

26   Conradie, "Interpreting," 200.

27   Conradie, "The Road," 311–12.

28   Conradie, "The Road," 311.

29   Conradie, "The Road," 312. More recently, Conradie has slightly refor-
     mulated this point to indicate that some forms of what may be perceived
     as "doctrinal" influence are inevitable in interpretation. See Conradie,
     "Ecological Hermeneutics."

30   F. Gerald Downing, "Review of Habel, Norman C. and Balabanski, Vicky
     (eds.), *The Earth Story in the New Testament*. The Earth Bible 5. London:
     Sheffield Academic Press, 2002," *BibInt* 12 (2004): 311–13.

31   Augustine, *On Christian Doctrine* 1.35.40: "anyone who thinks that he has
     understood the divine scriptures or any part of them, but cannot by his
     understanding build up this double love of God and neighbour, has not
     yet succeeded in understanding them." Citation is from R. P. H. Green,
     ed. and trans., *Saint Augustine: On Christian Teaching*, Oxford World's
     Classics (Oxford: Oxford University Press, 1997). (We are grateful to
     Dale Martin for alerting us to this text [see his *Sex*, 11–12, 49–50, 168].)
     Cf. also 1.40.44: "So when someone has learnt that the aim of the com-
     mandment is 'love from a pure heart, and good conscience and genuine
     faith' [1 Tim. 1:5], he will be ready to relate every interpretation of the
     holy scriptures to these three things and may approach the task of han-
     dling these books with confidence." The move of placing love of God and
     of neighbor as the heart of the Law has earlier precedents, of course, both
     Jewish and Christian.

32   On Luther's approach to interpreting Scripture, see Roy A. Harrisville
     and Walter Sundberg, *The Bible in Modern Culture: Theology and Historical-
     Critical Method from Spinoza to Käsemann* (Grand Rapids: Eerdmans, 1995),
     15–16; Francis Watson, *Text, Church, and World: Biblical Interpretation in
     Theological Perspective* (Edinburgh: T&T Clark, 1994), 231–36.

33   But see further Christopher Southgate, ed., *God, Humanity, and the Cosmos:
     A Companion to the Science-Religion Debate*, rev. ed. (New York: T&T Clark,
     2005), esp. 213–41.

34 Ian Barbour, *Religion and Science: Historical and Contemporary Issues* (London: SCM Press, 1997), 106–36.

35 Barbour, *Religion and Science*, 109.

36 For a scrupulously careful account of creationism viewed over against evolutionary science and theistic evolution see Ted Peters and Martinez J. Hewlett, *Evolution from Creation to New Creation* (Nashville: Abingdon, 2003).

37 Barbour, *Religion and Science*, 113.

38 Barbour, *Religion and Science*, 113.

39 See Robert J. Russell, *Cosmology: From Alpha to Omega* (Minneapolis: Fortress, 2008), for an examination of the ways in which Christian conviction about eschatology must depart from the current findings of modern science.

40 Stanley Hauerwas and David Burrell, "From System to Story: An Alternative Pattern for Rationality in Ethics," in *Why Narrative?* ed. Stanley Hauerwas and L. Gregory Jones (Grand Rapids: Eerdmans, 1989), 185.

41 We would also want to note, without anticipating too much the material of chap. 3, that the concern for the tragic expressed in the last of Hauerwas and Burrell's criteria presupposes a particular shape to the Christian narrative. No doubt this shape is appropriate to their concern with medical ethics, but for our purposes it will be important to consider the range of shapes in which the narrative of faith can be unfolded, and also the characteristic shapes of the narratives lying within key Pauline texts on the nonhuman creation.

42 For a broader sketch of a critical ecological biblical theology, see David G. Horrell, *The Bible and the Environment: Towards a Critical Ecological Biblical Theology*, Biblical Challenges in the Contemporary World (Oakville, Conn.: Equinox, 2010).

Chapter 3

1 See Rudolf Bultmann, "New Testament and Mythology: The Problem of Demythologizing the New Testament Proclamation [1941]," in *New Testament and Mythology and Other Basic Writings*, ed. Schubert M. Ogden (London: SCM Press, 1985), 1–43; and the discussion in Richard B. Hays, *The Faith of Jesus Christ: The Narrative Substructure of Galatians 3:1–4:11* (1983; rev. ed., Grand Rapids: Eerdmans, 1997), 51–55.

2 George W. Stroup, *The Promise of Narrative Theology* (1981; repr., London: SCM Press, 1984).

3 Alasdair MacIntyre, *After Virtue: A Study in Moral Theory* (London: Duckworth, 1981).

4 See Stanley Hauerwas, *A Community of Character: Toward a Constructive Christian Social Ethic* (Notre Dame, Ind.: University of Notre Dame Press,

1981), esp. 9–35, where Hauerwas uses the novel *Watership Down* to illustrate the importance of narrative in forming and sustaining community. On Hauerwas' approach, see David G. Horrell, *Solidarity and Difference: A Contemporary Reading of Paul's Ethics* (New York: T&T Clark, 2005), 63–70.

5   For a clear introduction to this postmodern context and the place of story within it, see Gerard Loughlin, *Telling God's Story: Bible, Church, and Narrative Theology* (Cambridge: Cambridge University Press, 1996), 3–26.

6   Milbank, *Theology*, 330.

7   Hauerwas, *Community*, 84.

8   In this section, and elsewhere in this chapter, we draw on parts of David G. Horrell, "Paul's Narratives or Narrative Substructure? The Significance of 'Paul's Story,'" in Longenecker, *Narrative Dynamics in Paul*, 157–71.

9   Greimas proposed that narratives could be understood by subordinating events to character (Michael J. Toolan, *Narrative: A Critical Linguistic Introduction*, 2nd ed. [New York: Routledge, 2001], 82).

10   Hays, *Faith of Jesus Christ*.

11   Wright, *New Testament*; Ben Witherington III, *Paul's Narrative Thought World: The Tapestry of Tragedy and Triumph* (Louisville, Ky.: Westminster John Knox, 1994); James D. G. Dunn, *The Theology of Paul the Apostle* (Edinburgh: T&T Clark, 1998); also Michael J. Gorman, *Cruciformity: Paul's Narrative Spirituality of the Cross* (Grand Rapids: Eerdmans, 2001); idem, *Inhabiting the Cruciform God: Kenosis, Justification, and Theosis in Paul's Narrative Soteriology* (Grand Rapids: Eerdmans, 2009). For an overview of this type of development, see Bruce W. Longenecker, "Narrative Interest in the Study of Paul," in Longenecker, *Narrative Dynamics in Paul*, 3–16; Bruce W. Longenecker, "The Narrative Approach to Paul: An Early Retrospective," *CurBS* 1 (2002): 88–111; Horrell, "Paul's Narratives," esp. 168–71.

12   Douglas A. Campbell, *The Quest for Paul's Gospel: A Suggested Strategy*, JSNTSup 274 (New York: T&T Clark, 2005), 70.

13   Campbell, *Quest*, 71. But see our further analysis in §3.3 below, which shows that a problem-solution structure is only one type of narrative "plot."

14   See Hays, *Faith of Jesus Christ*, 51–63, for an overview. E.g., J. Louis Martyn voices his opposition to the notion of a linear *Heilsgeschichte* in Galatians ("Events in Galatia: Modified Covenantal Nomism versus God's Invasion of the Cosmos in the Singular Gospel: A Response to J. D. G. Dunn and B. R. Gaventa," in *Pauline Theology*, vol. 1, *Thessalonians, Philippians, Galatians, Philemon*, ed. Jouette M. Bassler [Minneapolis: Fortress, 1991], 160–79), whereas N. T. Wright, Robin Scroggs, Richard B. Hays, and David J. Lull, in different ways, argue for a "salvation-historical" approach to Paul. In the same volume, Scroggs makes explicit links between "salvation history" and the "now-popular 'story theology'" and advances the bold claim

that "[t]o rethink Paul's theology within the structure of salvation history does the least violence, I believe, to his own conscious thought processes" (Robin Scroggs, "Salvation History: The Theological Structure of Paul's Thought [1 Thessalonians, Philippians, and Galatians]," in Bassler, *Pauline Theology,* 1:215–16).

15 Ernst Käsemann, "Justification and Salvation History in the Epistle to the Romans," in Käsemann, *Perspectives on Paul,* NTL (London: SCM Press, 1971), 64. For an argument that "salvation history" can be disassociated from a notion of evolutionary development, see David J. Lull, "Salvation History: Theology in 1 Thessalonians, Philemon, Philippians, and Galatians: A Response to N. T. Wright, R. B. Hays, and R. Scroggs," in Bassler, *Pauline Theology,* 1:251.

16 In addition to the essays in Bassler, *Pauline Theology,* vol. 1, see Bruce W. Longenecker, ed., *Narrative Dynamics in Paul: A Critical Assessment* (Louisville, Ky.: Westminster John Knox, 2002), and the response by Richard B. Hays, "Is Paul's Gospel Narratable?" *JSNT* 27 (2004): 217–39.

17 J. Louis Martyn, *Galatians,* AB 33A (New York: Doubleday, 1997), 347–48. Cf. also idem, "Events in Galatia," 172–73, for Martyn's opposition to "a *heilsgeschichtlich* reading of Paul": Galatians lacks the sense of "pre-Christ linearity necessary to a meaningful use of that term [*Heilsgeschichte*]. In Galatians, Abraham is a distinctly punctiliar figure rather than a linear one . . . Thus neither history nor story is a word well linked with Paul's portrait of Abraham in Galatians." Cf. also John M. G. Barclay, "Paul's Story," in Longenecker, *Narrative Dynamics in Paul,* 133–56.

18 Martyn, *Galatians,* 389; cf. also 283. Contrast Hays, who writes in criticism of Bultmann: "Bultmann also stressed the event-character of God's action in Christ, but he tended to treat the event as punctiliar. My reading of Paul emphasizes that the salvation event has temporal extension and shape; the event of the cross has meaning not as an isolated event but as an event within a story" (*Faith of Jesus Christ,* 267n1).

19 Campbell, *Quest,* 93.

20 Toolan, *Narrative,* 4–6. And as Seymour Chatman has pointed out, "The principle of causality is so strong in literature that the reader expects it and will in fact infer it even if it is not stated" (quoted in Mark Allen Powell, *What Is Narrative Criticism? A New Approach to the Bible* [London: SPCK, 1993], 40). The temporal trajectory of a cosmology will imply a sequence of causation, a "plot." For a helpful introductory treatment of objections to narrative criticism see Powell, *Narrative Criticism,* 91–98.

21 Northrop Frye, *Anatomy of Criticism* (1957; repr., Princeton: Princeton University Press, 2000); James F. Hopewell, *Congregation: Stories and Structures* (Philadelphia: Fortress, 1987).

22 Christopher Booker, *Why We Tell Stories* (New York: Continuum, 2004).

23   Frye, *Anatomy*, 162.
24   Hopewell, *Congregation*, 58.
25   Hopewell, *Congregation*, 59.
26   Hopewell, *Congregation*, 76.
27   Hopewell, *Congregation*, 76.
28   Frye, *Anatomy*, 191.
29   Hopewell, *Congregation*, 60.
30   Hopewell, *Congregation*, 60.
31   Frye, *Anatomy*, 208.
32   Hopewell, *Congregation*, 61.
33   Hopewell, *Congregation*, 62.
34   Frye, *Anatomy*, 238.
35   Frye, *Anatomy*, 42.
36   As Hopewell puts it, "Their worlds [of these polar opposites — comedy and tragedy, romance and irony] are contradictory: comedy moves from problem to solution, while tragedy moves from solution to problem; romance moves the self to the supernatural, while irony removes the supernatural from the self" (*Congregation*, 61). That is not to say, as Paul Fiddes has shown, that a great, overarching comedy cannot contain tragic *elements*. This is clearly the case with the Christian story of cross and resurrection when told as a whole narrative arc. See Paul S. Fiddes, *Freedom and Limit: A Dialogue between Literature and Christian Doctrine* (Macon, Ga.: Mercer University Press, 1999), 65–82.
37   Hopewell, *Congregation*, 98.
38   Cf. Loughlin, *Telling God's Story.*
39   Here we again echo something of Hauerwas' approach to Christian ethics. See, e.g., Hauerwas, *Community*; Horrell, *Solidarity*, 63–70.

Chapter 4

1   Indeed, a relatively small number of biblical texts are clearly the favorites in ecotheological discussion. See, e.g., the texts cited and discussed in Bouma-Prediger, *Beauty of the Earth*; Hans Halter and Wilfried Lochbühler, eds., *Ökologische Theologie und Ethik*, 2 vols. (Graz: Styria, 1999); Gerhard Liedke, *Im Bauch des Fisches: Ökologische Theologie* (Stuttgart: Kreuz, 1979); Lochbühler, *Christliche Umweltethik*; Bradley, *God Is Green*; Santmire, *Nature Reborn.*
2   John Bolt, "The Relation between Creation and Redemption in Romans 8:18-27," *CTJ* 30 (1995): 34.
3   B. Pyatt et al., "An Imperial Legacy? An Exploration of the Environmental Impact of Ancient Metal Mining and Smelting in Southern Jordan," *J Archaeol Sci* 27 (2000): 771–78.

4   John Seymour and Herbert Girardet, *Far from Paradise: The Story of Human Impact on the Environment* (London: Green Planet, 1990), 45, 53.

5   The term is generally assumed to apply to various combinations of one or more of the following non-overlapping sets: angelic beings, believers, non-believers, nonhuman living creation, the inanimate elements of nonhuman creation.

6   This interpretation of the subject of our passage has remained in Eastern Orthodox teaching and forms part of their contemporary perspective on human responsibility for creation: Michael Prokurat, "Orthodox Perspectives on Creation," *SVTQ* 33 (1989): 331–49.

7   Wilhelm Pauck, ed. and trans., *Luther: Lectures on Romans*, ed. John Baillie, John T. McNeill, and Henry P. Van Dusen, LCC 15 (London: SCM Press, 1961), 237–39.

8   John T. McNeill, ed., *Calvin: Institutes of the Christian Religion*, vol. 1, Books I.i to III.xix, LCC 20, 2 vols. (London: SCM Press, 1960), 717.

9   Sermon 60 in John Wesley, *The Works of the Rev. John Wesley, A. M.*, vol. 6 (London: John Mason, 1829), 245.

10   Alan Scott, *Origen and the Life of the Stars* (1991; repr., Oxford: Oxford University Press, 1994), 127, 147–48.

11   See Bonaventure, "The Tree of Life," in *Bonaventure: The Soul's Journey into God; The Tree of Life; The Life of St. Francis*, trans. Ewert Cousins (London: SPCK, 1978), 131.

12   E.g., Brendan Byrne, *Romans*, SP 6 (Collegeville, Minn.: Liturgical Press, 1996); Charles E. B. Cranfield, *A Critical and Exegetical Commentary on The Epistle to the Romans*, vol. 1, *Romans I–VIII*, ICC, 2 vols. (Edinburgh: T&T Clark, 1975); James D. G. Dunn, *Romans 1–8*, WBC 38A (Dallas, Tex.: Word Books, 1988), 469; Joseph A. Fitzmyer, *Romans: A New Translation with Introduction and Commentary*, AB 33 (New York: Doubleday, 1993), 506; Douglas J. Moo, *The Epistle to the Romans*, NICNT (Grand Rapids: Eerdmans, 1996), 514.

13   E.g., Cranfield, *Romans*, 412; Moo, *Romans*, 514.

14   Karl Barth, *Church Dogmatics IV.2: The Doctrine of Reconciliation*, vol. 2, trans. G. W. Bromiley (Edinburgh: T&T Clark, 1958), 329; Ernst Käsemann, *Commentary on Romans*, trans. G. W. Bromiley (Grand Rapids: Eerdmans, 1980), 232–33.

15   J. Ramsey Michaels, "The Redemption of Our Body: The Riddle of Romans 8:19-22," in *Romans and the People of God*, ed. Sven K. Soderlund and N. T. Wright (Grand Rapids: Eerdmans, 1999), 92–114.

16   C. K. Barrett, *A Commentary on the Epistle to the Romans*, BNTC (1957; rev. ed., London: A&C Black, 1971), 165. This point is made still more forcefully by Anton Vögtle, who concludes that Paul does *not* want to teach about "das Schicksal der Schöpfung in Vergangenheit, Gegenwart

und Zukunft . . . Der Apostel hat wohl überhaupt nur die Situation der noch leidenbedrängten Christen im Auge" ("Röm 8,19-22: Eine Schöpfungstheologische oder anthropologisch-soteriologische Aussage?" in *Mélanges bibliques en hommage au R. P. Béda Rigaux*, ed. Albert Descamps and André de Halleux [Gembloux, Belgium: Duculot, 1970], 365).

17   John G. Gager Jr., "Functional Diversity in Paul's Use of End-Time Language," *JBL* 89 (1970): 329.

18   G. W. H. Lampe, "The New Testament Doctrine of *KTISIS*," *SJT* 17 (1964): 460. More recently, Thomas Schreiner comments that, while the passage talks about creation, it "does not constitute the center stage of Paul's vision" (*Romans*, Baker Academic Commentary on the New Testament [Grand Rapids: Baker Academic, 1998], 437), and Moo claims that "his focus is consistently on anthropology" (*Romans*, 517n50).

19   C. H. Dodd, *The Epistle of Paul to the Romans*, Moffat's New Testament Commentary (London: Houghton, 1932), 134. For a rather different understanding of glory, see Robert Jewett, *Romans*, Hermeneia (Minneapolis: Fortress, 2007), 510–11; N. T. Wright, *The Resurrection of the Son of God* (London: SPCK, 2003), 257–58. Edward Adams, "Paul's Story of God and Creation," in Longenecker, *Narrative Dynamics in Paul*, 19–43, understands this as reflecting "an Adamic soteriology" (29). We take up the theme of "glory" further in chap. 7.

20   See also Bolt, "Relation." With regard to κτίσις in our text, Rudolf Bultmann, *Theology of the New Testament*, vol. 1, trans. Kendrick Grobel (London: SCM Press, 1952), says, "what is meant is evidently the earth and its creatures subordinate to man, not the *cosmic powers* which are enumerated in 8.38f" (230, emphasis in original), but he goes on to insist that "Paul's conception of the creation, as of the Creator, depends upon *what it means for man's existence*; under this point of view the creation is ambivalent" (231, emphasis added).

21   E.g., R. J. Berry, *Ecology & Ethics* (London: InterVarsity, 1972), 28.

22   See, e.g., Ron Elsdon, "Eschatology and Hope," in Berry, *Care*, 161–66; Northcott, *Environment*, 204; Santmire, *Nature Reborn*, 42.

23   Bouma-Prediger, *Beauty of the Earth*, 40. See also N. T. Wright, "Jesus is Coming — Plant a Tree," in *The Green Bible* (London: HarperCollins, 2008), I-72–I-85.

24   See Berry, *Care*, 19.

25   Jürgen Moltmann, *The Way of Jesus Christ: Christology in Messianic Dimensions*, trans. Margaret Kohl (London: SCM Press, 1990), 283. See also McDonagh, *Passion*, 141–42; Cooper, *Green Christianity*, 64–68; Nash, *Loving Nature*, 125.

26   McDonagh, *Greening*, 163. Cf. also the central place given to Romans 8 in Wright, "Jesus is Coming."

27 Sermon 60 in *Works*, 241–52. See also Jeffrey G. Sobosan, *Romancing the Universe: Theology, Science, and Cosmology* (Grand Rapids: Eerdmans, 1999), although he insists that "St Paul apparently never imagines that a butterfly might be raised from the dead" (100).

28 For an ecological treatment of the passage, see Ernst M. Conradie, *An Ecological Christian Anthropology: At Home on Earth?* (Aldershot, Vt.: Ashgate, 2005), 73–77. Conradie discusses issues such as the problem of linking futility with human sin in the light of evolutionary science, and notes that an ecological reading of this passage was "probably not included in Paul's vision" (74).

29 Charles E. B. Cranfield, "Some Observations on Romans 8:19-21," in *Reconciliation and Hope: New Testament Essays on Atonement and Eschatology presented to L. L. Morris on His 60th Birthday*, ed. Robert Banks (Exeter: Paternoster, 1974), 230.

30 John G. Gibbs, *Creation and Redemption: A Study in Pauline Theology*, NovTSup 26 (Leiden: Brill, 1971), 155.

31 Briefer exegetical essays, connecting explicitly with ecological questions, include Wolfgang Schrage, "Bibelarbeit über Röm 8,19-23," in *Versöhnung mit der Natur*, ed. Jürgen Moltmann (Munich: Kaiser, 1986), 150–66.

32 Byrne, *Romans*, 259.

33 Jewett, *Romans*, 513.

34 Jewett, *Romans*, 512.

35 Harry Alan Hahne, *The Corruption and Redemption of Creation: Nature in Romans 8.19-22 and Jewish Apocalyptic Literature*, LNTS 336 (New York: T&T Clark, 2006). See also Horst R. Balz, *Heilsvertrauen und Welterfahrung: Strukturen der paulinischen Eschatologie nach Römer 8,18-39*, BEvT 59 (Munich: Kaiser, 1971); Walther Bindemann, *Die Hoffnung der Schöpfung: Römer 8,18-27 und die Frage einer Theologie der Befreiung von Mensch und Natur* (Neukirchen-Vluyn: Neukirchener Verlag, 1983); Olle Christoffersson, *The Earnest Expectation of the Creature: The Flood-Tradition as Matrix of Romans 8:18-27* (Stockholm: Almqvist & Wiksell, 1990); Hae-Kyung Chang, *Die Knechtschaft und Befreiung der Schöpfung. Eine exegetische Untersuchung zu Römer 8,19-22*, BM 7 (Wuppertal: Brockhaus, 2000).

36 Habel, *Readings*; Habel and Wurst, *The Earth Story in Genesis*; Norman C. Habel and Shirley Wurst, eds., *The Earth Bible*, vol. 3, *The Earth Story in Wisdom Traditions* (Cleveland, Ohio: Pilgrim, 2001); Norman C. Habel, ed., *The Earth Bible*, vol. 4, *The Earth Story in Psalms and Prophets* (Cleveland, Ohio: Pilgrim, 2001); Norman C. Habel and Vicky Balabanski, eds., *The Earth Bible*, vol. 5, *The Earth Story in the New Testament* (Cleveland, Ohio: Pilgrim, 2002).

37 Brendan Byrne, "Creation Groaning: An Earth Bible Reading of Romans 8.18-22," in Habel, *Readings*, 193–203; Marie Turner, "God's Design: The

Death of Creation? An Ecojustice Reading of Romans 8.18-30 in the Light of Wisdom 1–2," in Habel and Wurst, *Wisdom Traditions*, 168–78. More recently, see Sigve Tonstad, "Creation Groaning in Labor Pains," in Habel and Trudinger, *Exploring Ecological Hermeneutics*, 141–49; Brendan Byrne, "An Ecological Reading of Rom 8.19-22: Possibilities and Hesitations," in Horrell, Hunt, Southgate, and Stavrakopoulou, *Ecological Hermeneutics*, 83–93.

38   John T. McNeill, ed., *Calvin: Institutes of the Christian Religion*, vol. 2, *Books III.xx to IV.xx*, LCC 21, 2 vols. (London: SCM Press, 1960), 1006–7.

39   See, e.g., the summary comment on the changed perception of Romans 9–11 in Karl P. Donfried, *The Romans Debate* (rev. ed.; Edinburgh: T&T Clark, 1991), lxx, and the statement in John Ziesler, *Paul's Letter to the Romans* (Philadelphia: Trinity, 1989), 37: "9–11 constitute a climax (even *the* climax) to the total argument."

40   Horst Balz, e.g., though without any connection to ecological issues, sees Romans 8 as the center and high-point of Pauline eschatology (*Heilsvertrauen*, 125, 129); N. T. Wright, more recently, and writing explicitly on the topic of "what God intends to do with the whole cosmos," sees Romans 8:18-28 as "the deliberate and carefully-planned climax to the whole train of thought in Romans 5–8, and indeed Romans 1–8, as a whole" (*New Heavens*, 12). On the other hand, Chang, *Die Knechtschaft*, can open his discussion of Romans 8:19-22 by describing it as a "short excursus" (1; "Der knappe Exkurs über die Schöpfung . . .").

41   E.g., a bald reference to Romans 8:20 has been used to claim that "one of the chief roles of a Christian is to be a co-worker with God in the continuous repair of the created order (which has the tendency to decay into disorganised systems), to bring new things into existence and to establish new patterns of order" (Brian Heap and Flavio Comin, "Consumption and Happiness: Christian Values and an Approach towards Sustainability," in *When Enough Is Enough: A Christian Framework for Environmental Sustainability*, ed. R. J. Berry [Nottingham: Apollos, 2007], 96). On the superficiality of many appeals to this text, cf. also the comment of Byrne, "Creation Groaning," 193.

42   As in Jewett, *Romans*, 512–15. For a more detailed presentation of this perspective on Romans 8, see Robert Jewett, "The Corruption and Redemption of Creation: Reading Rom 8:18-23 within the Imperial Context," in *Paul and the Roman Imperial Order*, ed. Richard A. Horsley (Harrisburg: Trinity Press International, 2004), 25–46.

43   Toolan, *Narrative*, 4–6.

44   Powell, *Narrative Criticism*, 40.

45   E.g., Christoffersson, *Earnest Expectation*, 108; Cranfield, *Romans*, 416; Dunn, *Romans 1–8*, 472; Jewett, *Romans*, 516; although Sanday and

Headlam point out that "the apprehension of it may not have been so common as he [Paul] assumes" (William Sanday and Arthur C. Headlam, *A Critical and Exegetical Commentary on the Epistle to the Romans*, ICC [5th ed.; Edinburgh: T&T Clark, 1905], 209). Tonstad also uses this point in suggesting that Romans 8 should be read in light of its underlying narrative (Tonstad, "Creation," 141).

46   For an earlier, significant attempt to analyse this narrative throughout Romans, see Adams, "God and Creation." Using Greimas' actant model, Adams concludes that there is, within Romans 1–8, "a basic and coherent" account of "God's creative aims from their foundation at the beginning of creation, through their frustration due to Adam's fall and subsequent human fallenness, to their ultimate fulfilment in the eschaton" (33). However, his treatment of Romans 8:19-22 is brief and he does not consider the narrative trajectories involved.

47   It is clear, then, that there can be no neat, linear story in which past, present, and future are easily distinguished, not least given Paul's inaugurated eschatology. Nonetheless, we consider that there is a temporal flow in the implied narrative, such that distinguishing past, present, and future is both legitimate and, we would argue, significant for ecotheological interpretation (see further chap. 7 below).

48   See Watson, "Strategies."

49   Cranfield, *Romans*, 404. It is also notable that both Stoics and Platonists could speak of the whole cosmos as living; see further §5.3 below.

50   Chrysostom makes this link: "What is the meaning of 'the creation was made subject to vanity'? Why that it became corruptible" (*Hom. Rom.* 14). Cf. Dunn, *Romans 1–8*, 470: "ματαιότης can be regarded as nearly equivalent to φθορά . . . so long as the full sweep of *both* words is borne in mind" (emphasis in original). Jewett, *Romans*, 513–15, speaks of vanity and "resultant corruption," while Byrne, *Romans*, 261, sees slavery resulting from subjection.

51   See below for our conviction that the implicit subject of ὑπετάγη must be God.

52   On the parallels between Romans 1:18-23 and 8:19-22, see Nikolaus Walter, "Gottes Zorn und das 'Harren der Kreatur.' Zur Korrespondenz zwischen Römer 1,18-32 und 8,19-22," in *Christus Bezeugen. Festschrift für Wolfgang Trilling zum 65. Geburtstag*, ed. Karl Kertelge, Traugott Holtz, and Claus-Peter März (Leipzig: St. Benno, 1989), 218–26, though Walter argues that κτίσις in Romans 8:19-22 refers to unevangelized, unbelieving humanity (220).

53   Byrne, *Romans*, 260; Dunn, *Romans 1–8*, 470: "the primary allusion is to the Adam narratives."

54   Hahne, *Corruption and Redemption*, 195.

55 See Fitzmyer, Romans, 509. The idea of φθορά having any moral content in
    this context is rejected by others, e.g., Dunn, Romans 1–8, 472, and Hahne,
    Corruption and Redemption, 195. Interestingly, Pseudo-Jonathan's targum
    on Genesis 3:17 comments that the ground was cursed "because it did not
    show forth your guilt" (John Bowker, The Targums and Rabbinic Literature:
    An Introduction to Jewish Interpretations of Scripture [Cambridge: Cambridge
    University Press, 1969], 121).

56 Edward Adams, Constructing the World: A Study in Paul's Cosmological Language
    (Edinburgh: T&T Clark, 2000), 77–80, commenting on the linguistic
    background of κτίσις, notes that its use to denote God's creative activity
    is "a linguistic innovation on the part of the translators of the Greek Old
    Testament" (77). Foerster notes the more usual sense of κτίσις in Greek in
    NT times (founding of cities) and, pointing out the uses of κτίζω to denote
    divine activity in the LXX (4 or 5 in the Pentateuch, none in the historical
    books, 15 in the prophets, 9 in the writings, and 36 in the apocrypha), sug-
    gests that its theological significance only arose after the first works of the
    LXX (the Torah) were translated. It is clear that it emerges most promi-
    nently only in the apocryphal books (Werner Foerster, "κτίζω," TDNT
    3:1025).

57 Adams, Constructing, 178, notes that "Paul, in line with later Jewish reflec-
    tion on that text [Gen 3:17-19] expands the scale of the judgement to
    cosmic dimensions."

58 Christoffersson builds on the idea that the flood story provides the back-
    ground to Paul's use of κτίσις here, and argues that the "sons of God" (v.
    19) is a reference to Gen 6:2, with the development of this story in the
    Enochic traditions lying behind Paul's allusions. However, Paul nowhere
    else makes reference to this tradition or to the story of the Watchers —
    unlike some other New Testament letters (1 Pet 3:19-20; 2 Pet 2:4-5, 3:5-
    6; Jude 6) — and Christoffersson's reading of the υἱοὶ τοῦ θεοῦ in Romans
    8:19 is implausible; see below and Christoffersson, Earnest Expectation.

59 E.g., Cranfield, Romans, 413; Dunn, Romans 1–8, 470. John Murray, The
    Epistle to the Romans, NICNT (Grand Rapids: Eerdmans, 1968) comments
    that "[i]n relation to the earth this is surely Paul's commentary on Gen.
    3.17, 18" (303).

60 See, e.g., Cranfield, Romans, 414; Dodd, Romans, 134; Franz J. Leenhardt,
    The Epistle to the Romans: A Commentary (London: Lutterworth, 1961), 220;
    Moo, Romans, 516. See also Jewett, Romans, 513, who cites a telling parallel
    from a magical spell influenced by Jewish language: ". . . the [holy] and
    honoured name to whom all creation is subjected [ἡ πᾶσα κτίσις [ὑ]πόκειται]."
    The act of subjection has been attributed more directly to Adam; see Byrne,
    Romans, 258; and Byrne, "Creation Groaning." But see Byrne's more recent

essay ("Ecological Reading"), where he somewhat refines his view: "God was the agent of the subjection . . . Adam was its cause."

61 Pauck, *Luther*, 238.

62 McNeill, *Calvin's Institutes 1*, 246.

63 Hahne, *Corruption and Redemption*, 211.

64 *Jub.* 3.24–25 echoes Genesis 3:16-19 (labour and thistles), adding that "on that day the mouths of all the wild animals and the cattle and the birds, and of everything that walks or moves, were shut, so that they could no longer speak (for up till then they had all spoken with one another in a common tongue)" (3.28). Cf. also *1 En.* 80.2-4. *Apoc. Moses* (after Paul) continues this theme, with the fall resulting in animals' disobeying humans (10.1–11.3; 24.4), and leaves' falling from trees (20.4).

65 Hahne, *Corruption and Redemption*, 212–13.

66 *Contra* Christoffersson, *Earnest Expectation.*

67 Cf. Walter, "Gottes Zorn."

68 E.g., Hooker, *From Adam to Christ*, 76–84, who, focusing on Romans 1:23, sees here a clear reference to the story of the fall.

69 As Dale Martin notes, "Paul does not here mention Adam, Eve, the fall, or the universal bondage of humanity to sin . . . the scenario Paul sketches in Romans 1 has to do with the invention of idolatry and its consequences, not the fall of Adam" (*Sex*, 52). Francis Watson, *Paul and the Hermeneutics of Faith* (New York: T&T Clark, 2004), 144, sees this particular verse (Rom 1:23) as an allusion to the account of the golden calf, while Stanley K. Stowers, *A Rereading of Romans: Justice, Jews, and Gentiles* (New Haven, Conn.: Yale University Press, 1994), 86–90, noting the "absence of Adam," prefers to see the decline of a golden age following the hubris shown at the tower of Babel, and the consequent emergence of Abraham's descendants as a nation distinct from others, as the background to the whole of Romans 1.

70 Cranfield, *Romans*, 413–14.

71 Byrne, *Romans*, 260–61. See further under II above.

72 Another suggestion is that it could imply the subjection of creation to the dominion of celestial authorities. Cf. Barrett, *Romans*, 165–66.

73 Otto Bauernfeind, "μάταιος κτλ," *TDNT* 4:523, sees Romans 8:20 as "a valid commentary on Qoh.," and Jewett thinks that this verse would have brought Ecclesiastes 1:2 to mind in the letter's audience (Jewett, *Romans*, 513). Note the critique of this view by Hahne, *Corruption and Redemption*, 190. R. J. Berry, *God's Book of Works. The Nature and Theology of Nature* (New York: T&T Clark, 2003), 231, considers the whole of Qoheleth as a commentary on the Romans passage (albeit anachronistically!).

74 Cf. also N. T. Wright, *Evil and the Justice of God* (Downers Grove, Ill.: InterVarsity, 2006), 116–17. This futility is sometimes attributed directly

to the failure of humankind to play its part in creation; Byrne, *Romans*, 258; Cranfield, *Romans*, 413–14.

75 Leenhardt, *Romans*, 219–25; Moo, *Romans*, 515; Byrne, *Romans*, 258.

76 There is a pre-Pauline link between the judgment and labor pains (1 *En.* 62.4 and 1QH 3.7-18), but a specific link with the Messiah only seems to occur in later writings (Cranfield, *Romans*, 416; E. P. Sanders, *Jesus and Judaism* [London: SCM Press, 1985], 124). Other proposals include Sylvia Keesmaat's argument that the narrative of the exodus provides some of the background story to Paul's thought here (Sylvia C. Keesmaat, *Paul and His Story: (Re)Interpreting the Exodus Tradition*, JSNTSup 181 [Sheffield: Sheffield Academic Press, 1999], 89) and Laurie Braaten's proposal that creation's groaning expresses its mourning over human sin ("All Creation Groans: Romans 8:22 in Light of the Biblical Sources," *HBT* 28 [2006]: 131–59).

77 See Adams, *The Stars*, for a survey of eschatological scenarios.

78 On this theme, see further Katherine M. Hayes, *"The Earth Mourns": Prophetic Metaphor and Oral Aesthetic*, Academica Biblica 8 (Atlanta: SBL, 2002).

79 Luzia Sutter Rehman, "To Turn the Groaning into Labor: Romans 8.22-23," in *A Feminist Companion to Paul*, ed. Amy-Jill Levine and Marianne Bickenstaff (Cleveland, Ohio: Pilgrim, 2004), 80–81, emphasizes the importance of the earth as a place of transformation and notes parallels between ancient views of the earth and the uterus.

80 See nn. 56–57 above.

81 See Rehman, "To Turn the Groaning," 79, who notes this use by Philo (στενεῖν; *Leg.* 3.212) and Josephus (στενάζειν; *J.W.* 5.384).

82 E.g., Barrett, *Romans*, 166–67; Cranfield, *Romans*, 416–17; Dunn, *Romans 1-8*, 472; Byrne, *Romans*, 261; Moo, *Romans*, 518.

83 Cranfield, *Romans*, 417.

84 Cf. Rom 6:4-8, 8:16-17; Gal 2:19.

85 Cranfield, *Romans*, 417, followed by Dunn, notes how "extremely emphatic" is the repeated αὐτοί, "even more so with ἐν ἑαυτοῖς following" (Dunn, *Romans 1-8*, 474).

86 See again Rehman, "To Turn the Groaning," who stresses both the sharing of travail and the shared work of liberation (80–82).

87 Christoffersson, *Earnest Expectation*, 103–4, 120–24.

88 See also υἱοί in speaking of the children of Israel (2 Cor 3:13) and believers, elsewhere in the undisputed Pauline epistles (2 Cor 6:18, citing Hos 2:1 LXX; Gal 3:7, 26; 4:6-7).

89 Byrne, "Creation Groaning," 202, suggests that Paul may avoid mentioning resurrection here precisely because "he wishes to suggest a sense of continuity and transformation rather than destruction and rebirth." Moo, on the other hand, sees "the doctrine of the resurrection of the body"

precisely as demanding "a significant continuity of some kind between this world and the next. In fact, the analogy of the human body, as many interpreters have suggested, may offer the best way to resolve the tension between destruction and transformation with respect to the universe. Here also we find a puzzling combination of continuity and discontinuity" (Moo, "Nature in the New Creation," 469).

90   Cf. Rehman, "To Turn the Groaning," 81.

91   Jewett, *Romans*, 515 with n79.

92   Hahne, *Corruption and Redemption*, 215–16. This raises the much wider issue of whether the NT's "cosmic catastrophe" imagery is symbolic or metaphorical language depicting a radical transformation on the historical plane, as N. T. Wright argues (*New Testament*, 280–86), or whether it envisages a truly cosmic and destructive event, as Edward Adams argues (*The Stars*); cf. §2.1 above with nn. 6–7. Adams also suggests that there are two strands in NT eschatology in this regard, one emphasizing the notion of cosmic destruction and re-creation, the other — notably represented in Romans 8 — focused on the notion of transformation (256–57).

93   Adams, "God and Creation," 38, speaks of "a *creation history* rather than a salvation history" in Romans since the underlying narrative focuses on God's intentions for creation (emphasis in original).

94   Hopewell, *Congregation*, 59–60, 69, 75–79.

95   See Jewett, "Corruption and Redemption"; Jewett, *Romans*, 508–17. See also J. R. Harrison, "Paul, Eschatology, and the Augustan Age of Grace," *TynBul* 50 (1999): 79–91.

96   These are cited in Jewett, "Corruption and Redemption," 27, 30–31, and in Jewett, *Romans*, 509.

97   As a further symbol of this distinction Jewett notes the (complacent?) reclining of the Mother Earth figure in the Augustan Altar of Peace, which he compares with the ἀποκαραδοκία of the κτίσις in Romans (*Romans*, 511).

Chapter 5

1   See, e.g., Eduard Lohse, *Colossians and Philemon*, Hermeneia, trans. William R. Poehlmann and Robert J. Karris (Philadelphia: Fortress, 1971), 180–81; Eduard Schweizer, *The Letter to the Colossians*, trans. Andrew Chester (London: SPCK, 1982 [1976]), 15–19; Roy Yates, *The Epistle to the Colossians*, Epworth Commentaries (London: Epworth, 1993), xi–xii. George H. van Kooten, *Cosmic Christology in Paul and the Pauline School: Colossians and Ephesians in the Context of Graeco-Roman Cosmology with a New Synopsis of the Greek Texts*, WUNT 2.171 (Tübingen: Mohr Siebeck, 2003), gives a detailed discussion of the differences in cosmology between Paul and the writer of Colossians.

2   See, e.g., Peter T. O'Brien, *Colossians, Philemon*, WBC 44 (Dallas: Word Books, 1982), xli–xlix; F. F. Bruce, *The Epistles to the Colossians, to Philemon, and to the Ephesians* (Grand Rapids: Eerdmans, 1984), 28–33; N. T. Wright, *The Epistles of Paul to the Colossians and to Philemon* (Leicester: InterVarsity, 1986); 31–34; Markus Barth and Helmut Blanke, *Colossians: A New Translation with Introduction and Commentary*, AB 34B, trans. Astrid B. Beck (New York: Doubleday, 1994), 114–26; Douglas J. Moo, *The Letters to the Colossians and to Philemon* (Grand Rapids: Eerdmans, 2008), 28–41. For arguments demonstrating continuity with Pauline thought see, e.g., Andrew T. Lincoln, "The Household Code and Wisdom Mode of Colossians," *JSNT* 74 (1999): 93–112, and Todd D. Still, "Eschatology in Colossians: How Realized Is It?" *NTS* 50 (2004): 125–38.

3   James D. G. Dunn, *The Epistles to the Colossians and to Philemon*, NIGTC (Grand Rapids: Eerdmans, 1996), 19.

4   Dunn, *Colossians and Philemon*, 38.

5   "More has been written about these verses than any other passage in the epistle" (Yates, *Colossians*, 14).

6   As Ian K. Smith, *Heavenly Perspective: A Study of the Apostle Paul's Response to a Jewish Mystical Movement at Colossae*, LNTS 326 (New York: T&T Clark, 2006), 147–50, notes, there is now a general consensus that the features of Colossians 1:15-20 justify its description as hymnic material (although see Stephen E. Fowl, *The Story of Christ in the Ethics of Paul: An Analysis of the Function of the Hymnic Material in the Pauline Corpus*, JSNTSup 36 [Sheffield: Sheffield Academic Press, 1990], 31–45, on the suitability of the term for the NT passages to which it is commonly applied). Smith, *Heavenly Perspective*, 150–51 also gives a summary of the huge variations in suggestions put forward for its original form.

7   Ernst Käsemann, "A Primitive Christian Baptismal Liturgy," in *Essays on New Testament Themes*, SBT 41 (London: SCM Press, 1964), 149–68 (original essay was published in 1949). See Robert Jewett, *Paul's Anthropological Terms: A Study of their Use in Conflict Settings* (Leiden: Brill, 1971), 230–37 for a survey of the history of this idea.

8   E.g., O'Brien, *Colossians, Philemon*, 40–42; Wright, *Colossians and Philemon*, 64; Barth and Blanke, *Colossians*, 227–36; Christian Stettler, *Der Kolosserhymnus: Untersuchungen zu Form, traditionsgeschichtlichem Hintergrund und Aussage von Kol 1,15-20*, WUNT 2.131 (Tübingen: Mohr Siebeck, 2000), 345. N. T. Wright, *The Climax of the Covenant* (Edinburgh: T&T Clark, 1991), 100, comments on the debate surrounding the original form of the hymn: "the first task of the exegete—arguably in this case the only possible one—is to deal with the text that we possess."

9   Andrew T. Lincoln and A. J. M. Wedderburn, *The Theology of the Later Pauline Letters* (Cambridge: Cambridge University Press, 1993), 66.

Similarly, Marianne Meye Thompson, *Colossians & Philemon* (Grand Rapids: Eerdmans, 2005), 144, claims that "[i]t would not be overstating the case to argue that Colossians provides more raw material for continuing reflection on creation than any other book of the NT."

10 Bouma-Prediger, *Beauty of the Earth*, 124.

11 Irenaeus (*Haer.* 1.22.1) does not make specific reference to this passage but, with reference to John 1:3, he stresses the all-encompassing scope of πάντα. See also Augustine (*Sermons* 290.2) and a selection of other ancient commentators in Peter Gorday, ed., *Ancient Christian Commentary on Scripture: Colossians, 1–2 Thessalonians, 1–2 Timothy, Titus, Philemon,* ACCSNT 11 (Chicago: Fitzroy Dearborn, 2000), 14–16.

12 See also Aquinas, *ST* 3.35.8 *ad* 1, and Calvin, *Inst.* 2.12.4.

13 E.g., among recent monographs dealing with the letter, see Fowl, *Story*; Matthew E. Gordley, *The Colossian Hymn in Context: An Exegesis in Light of Jewish and Greco-Roman Hymnic and Epistolary Conventions*, WUNT 2.228 (Tübingen: Mohr Siebeck, 2007); Smith, *Heavenly Perspective.*

14 Moo, *Colossians and Philemon*, 121, notes that heaven and earth function as a common biblical merism to indicate the whole universe.

15 Cf. §6.4, with nn. 26–29.

16 See, e.g., Lohse, *Colossians*, 41, 61; Schweizer, *Colossians*, 55–88; Bruce, *Colossians, Philemon, Ephesians*, 74–77; Edward Schillebeeckx, *Christ: The Christian Experience in the Modern World*, trans. John Bowden (1977; repr., London: SCM Press, 1988), 187, 194; van Kooten, *Cosmic Christology*, 127. Lohse, criticizing Sittler (on whom see below), suggests that the theology of the cross "arrests all attempts to utilize the hymn for the purposes of a natural or cosmic theology" (60n211).

17 Yates, *Colossians*, 27.

18 C. F. D. Moule, *The Epistles to the Colossians and to Philemon* (Cambridge: Cambridge University Press, 1962), 71. Interestingly, he goes on to say that "[p]erhaps the best comment on this inclusive hope is Rom. viii, with its promise of redemption for (apparently) Nature as well as Man." Cf. also J. B. Lightfoot, *Saint Paul's Epistles to the Colossians and to Philemon: A Revised Text with Introductions, Notes, and Dissertations* (New York: Macmillan, 1886), 115; G. H. P. Thompson, *The Letters of Paul to the Ephesians, to the Colossians, and to Philemon* (Cambridge: Cambridge University Press, 1967).

19 I. Howard Marshall, "The Meaning of 'Reconciliation,'" in *Unity and Diversity in New Testament Theology: Essays in Honor of George E. Ladd*, ed. Robert A. Guelich (Grand Rapids: Eerdmans, 1978), 127.

20 Lars Hartman, "Universal Reconciliation (Col 1,20)," *SNTU* 10 (1985): 112 and 120.

21 See Smith, *Heavenly Perspective*, 146–47. For surveys of discussion on the "heresy" and possible "errors" see Bruce, *Colossians, Philemon, Ephesians*,

17–26; Dunn, *Colossians and Philemon*, 23–35; John M. G. Barclay, *Colossians and Philemon*, NTG (Sheffield: Sheffield Academic Press, 1997), 39–48; Smith, *Heavenly Perspective*, 19–38. John J. Gunther, *St. Paul's Opponents and Their Background: A Study of Apocalyptic and Jewish Sectarian Teachings*, NovTS 35 (Leiden: Brill, 1973), 3–4, lists over forty different suggestions found in the literature on Colossians. Morna Hooker, however, questions the existence of any such "heresy" at Colossae ("Were There False Teachers in Colossae?" in *Christ and Spirit in the New Testament*, ed. Barnabas Lindars and Stephen S. Smalley [Cambridge: Cambridge University Press, 1973], 315–31).

22   Smith, *Heavenly Perspective*, 172.

23   Lincoln and Wedderburn, *Later Pauline Letters*, 15–16.

24   See Fowl, *Story*, 123–54; Smith, *Heavenly Perspective*, 146–72.

25   Col 1:1–20 is discussed in Gibbs, *Creation*, and the relevance of Colossians' theme to the ecological crisis is noted (155). Gibbs elsewhere links "[t]he holistic view of the world that ecology requires" with "the concept of Christ's lordship over creation and redemption" in both recognized and disputed Pauline writing: John G. Gibbs, "Pauline Cosmic Christology and Ecological Crisis," *JBL* 90 (1971): 472.

26   Markus Barth, "Christ and All Things," in *Paul and Paulinism: Essays in Honour of C. K. Barrett*, ed. M. D. Hooker and S. G. Wilson (London: SPCK, 1982), 160–72, 165.

27   Dunn, *Colossians and Philemon*, 104.

28   Lewis R. Donelson, *Colossians, Ephesians, 1 and 2 Timothy, and Titus*, Wesminster Bible Companion (Louisville, Ky.: Westminster John Knox, 1996), 31.

29   Barth and Blanke, *Colossians*, 197–200; quotation from 246.

30   Wright, *Colossians and Philemon*, 77, 80.

31   Barclay, *Colossians and Philemon*, 95.

32   Andrew T. Lincoln, "The Letter to the Colossians," in *The New Interpreter's Bible, Vol. 11*, ed. Leander E. Keck (Nashville: Abingdon, 2000), 610.

33   Moo, *Colossians and Philemon*, 137.

34   See n. 16 above.

35   Wedderburn notes "the possibility that the hymn, more than the letter itself, may reflect a worldview in tune with current ecological awareness" (Lincoln and Wedderburn, *Later Pauline Letters*, 66). However, Gibbs, *Creation*, 100–101, argues that the hymn is integral to the letter and that its cosmic meaning was not contrary to the epistle's author's intentions.

36   Joseph Sittler, "Called to Unity," in *Evocations of Grace: The Writings of Joseph Sittler on Ecology, Theology, and Ethics*, ed. Steven Bouma-Prediger and Peter Bakken (Grand Rapids: Eerdmans, 2000), 39 (essay was originally published in 1962). The phrase τὰ πάντα appears as such four times,

plus the plural forms πρὸ παντών (v. 17) and ἐν πᾶσιν (v. 18). For other writings on cosmic Christology see, e.g., Allan D. Galloway, *The Cosmic Christ* (London: Nisbet, 1951); Joseph Sittler, *Essays on Nature and Grace* (Philadelphia: Fortress, 1972); Matthew Fox, *The Coming of the Cosmic Christ* (San Francisco: Harper & Row, 1988).

37 Sittler, "Called," 40, 48.

38 Joseph Sittler, "A Theology for Earth," in Bouma-Prediger and Bakken, *Evocations of Grace*, 20–31 (essay was originally published in 1954).

39 McDonagh, *Greening*, 160.

40 McDonagh, *Greening*, 163. Many others make similar comments, e.g., Charles P. Lutz, "Loving All My Creaturely Neighbors," *Trinity Seminary Review* 25 (2004): 98: "ALL things will be reconciled back to God and ALL creatures will be reconciled to one another"; Paulos Mar Gregorios, "New Testament Foundations for Understanding the Creation," in Granberg-Michaelson, *Tending the Garden*, 89; Nash, *Loving Nature*, 125; Santmire, *Nature Reborn*, 42. The Earth Bible series, notably, does not deal directly with this text except in passing, in a discussion of a similar passage in Eph 1: Elmer Flor, "The Cosmic Christ and Ecojustice in the New Cosmos," in Habel and Balabanski, *The Earth Story in the New Testament*, 137–47; but see now Vicky Balabanski, "Critiquing Anthropocentric Cosmology: Retrieving a Stoic 'Permeation Cosmology' in Colossians 1:15-20," in Habel and Trudinger, *Exploring Ecological Hermeneutics*, 151–59, and Vicky Balabanski, "Hellenistic Cosmology and the Letter to the Colossians: Towards an Ecological Hermeneutic," in Horrell, Hunt, Southgate, and Stavrakopoulou, *Ecological Hermeneutics*, 94–107.

41 Northcott, *Environment*, 202. See also Michael S. Northcott, *A Moral Climate: The Ethics of Global Warming* (London: Darton, Longman, & Todd, 2007), 239–40.

42 Brennan R. Hill, *Christian Faith and the Environment: Making Vital Connections* (Maryknoll, N.Y.: Orbis, 1998), 96.

43 Russell, "*New Heavens and New Earth*," 181.

44 Balabanski, "Critiquing," 157, 158

45 Balabanski, "Critiquing," 159; see also Balabanski, "Hellenistic Cosmology."

46 Bouma-Prediger, *Beauty of the Earth*, 108; see 105–10.

47 Bouma-Prediger, *Beauty of the Earth*, 124.

48 R. McL. Wilson, *A Critical and Exegetical Commentary on Colossians and Philemon*, ICC (New York: T&T Clark, 2005), 136. Barth and Blanke, *Colossians*, 199, suggests that the phrase was a means of translating the Hebrew כל, which, in the absence of a specific noun, served to designate the cosmos or universe.

49 Lincoln and Wedderburn, *Later Pauline Letters*, 13; e.g., the reference to "barbarians and Scythians" in Colossians 3:11.

50 Van Kooten, *Cosmic Christology*, 126. Balabanski, "Critiquing," explores the extent of Stoic cosmology within the hymn.

51 See, e.g., Livy, *AUC* 2.32; Epictetus, *Diatr.* 2.10.3–4; Seneca, *Clem.* 1.4.3, 1.5.1. C. K. Barrett, *A Commentary on the First Epistle to the Corinthians*, BNTC (1968; 2nd ed., London: A&C Black, 1971), 287, notes that the metaphor was used in political settings to encourage civic behavior and in Stoic circles to advocate behavior according to the natural order. See esp. Dale B. Martin, *The Corinthian Body* (New Haven, Conn.: Yale University Press, 1995), 15–21, on the ancient world's view of the body as an actual, not just metaphorical, micro-cosmos.

52 *Corp. herm.* 8.2 and 12.15 and Plato's "εἰκὼν τοῦ νοητοῦ θεὸς αἰσθητός" (*Tim.* 92C).

53 See Michael Lapidge, "Stoic Cosmology and Roman Literature, First to Third Centuries A.D.," *ANRW* II.36.3 (1989): 1381–83, for use of this idea by Stoics; Plato, *Tim.* 32B, 32C; Aristotle, *Metaph.* 12. 8; Philo, *Her.* 155.

54 Orphic fragment 168 (Otto Kern, *Orphicorum Fragmenta* [1922; repr., Berlin: Weidmann, 1963]), 201–2.

55 See Harry O. Maier, "A Sly Civility: Colossians and Empire," *JSNT* 27 (2005): 340.

56 On this development in the use of the metaphor see, e.g., Moule, *Colossians and Philemon*, 67; Margaret Y. MacDonald, *The Pauline Churches: A Socio-historical Study of Institutionalization in the Pauline and Deutero-Pauline Writings*, SNTSMS 60 (Cambridge: Cambridge University Press, 1988), 154–55; Margaret Y. MacDonald, *Colossians and Ephesians*, SP 17 (Collegeville, Minn.: Liturgical Press, 2000), 61; Hanna Roose, "Die Hierarchisierung der Leib-Metapher im Kolosser- und Epheserbrief als 'Paulinisierung': Ein Beitrag zur Rezeption Paulinischer Tradition in Pseudo-paulinischen Briefen," *NovT* 47 (2005): 117–41.

57 E.g., Lohse, *Colossians*, 52–56; Ralph P. Martin, *Ephesians, Colossians, and Philemon*, Interpretation (Atlanta: John Knox, 1991), 106; Schweizer, *Colossians*, 58. It was the content of this "recovered" form of the hymn, together with the similarity of the language in Colossians to contemporary philosophical concepts, that led Ernst Käsemann to suggest that the hymn could have been modified from a pre-Christian original ("Baptismal Liturgy," 151–52).

58 Van Kooten, *Cosmic Christology*, 23–30, argues that, while the church is presented as the body of Christ in the Colossian hymn, elsewhere in the letter (2:9, 17, 19) his body is clearly identified with the entire cosmos. See also E. Best, *One Body in Christ: A Study in the Relationship of the Church to Christ in the Epistles of the Apostle Paul* (London: SPCK, 1955), especially 203–7, on

corporate personality. Although his (earlier) study focuses specifically on the use of "body" in the undisputed Paulines, Jewett, *Paul's Anthropological Terms*, 241–45, suggests that the language of believers as the body of Christ may be paralleled in the later-documented Jewish concept of *guf*-Adam, while Moo judges that Paul's concept of Christ as a "corporate person" is "a more immediate influence" than other contemporary metaphors of body (Moo, *Colossians and Philemon*, 127). However, for a dissenting view, see Paul Beasley-Murray, "Colossians 1:15-20: An Early Christian Hymn Celebrating the Lordship of Christ," in *Pauline Studies: Essays Presented to Professor F. F. Bruce on His 70th Birthday*, ed. Donald A. Hagner and Murray J. Harris (Grand Rapids: Eerdmans, 1980), 179–82.

59 This point is made by a number of commentators, including Lightfoot, *Colossians and Philemon*. See also Michael Lapidge, "Stoic Cosmology," in *The Stoics*, ed. John M. Rist (Berkeley: University of California Press, 1978), 170–76, and David E. Hahm, *The Origins of Stoic Cosmology* (Columbus: Ohio State University, 1977), 142–43, for a discussion of Stoic thought. For examples, see A. A. Long and D. N. Sedley, eds., *The Hellenistic Philosophers*, 2 vols. (Cambridge: Cambridge University Press, 1987), §§44F and 67L; Pseudo-Aristotle's *De Mundo* 6.397 and 7.401 and Wilson, *Colossians and Philemon*, 144. Barrett claims that the term may imply "a putting together of sundered fragments": C. K. Barrett, *From First Adam to Last* (London: A&C Black, 1962), 86n4.

60 See, e.g., Lohse, *Colossians*, 49; Dunn, *Colossians and Philemon*, 91. For further examples, see James D. G. Dunn, *Romans 9–16*, WBC 38B (Dallas, Tex.: Word Books, 1988), 701, on Romans 11:36.

61 Barth and Blanke, *Colossians*, 227.

62 Van Kooten, *Cosmic Christology*, 123; Richard Bauckham, "Where is Wisdom to be Found? Colossians 1.15–20 (2)," in Ford and Stanton, *Reading Texts, Seeking Wisdom*, 134.

63 Dio Chrysostom, speaking of concord amongst the elements of the universe (*Or.* 38.10–11; 40.35–37) specifically mentions καταλλαγή (38.11) as a manifestation of the same principle. See also Pseudo-Aristotle's *De Mundo* 6.396 and van Kooten, *Cosmic Christology*, 130–31, noting that the reconciling/harmonizing of "cosmic principles" is paralleled in the action of Osiris and Eros/Aphrodite.

64 Lapidge, "Stoic Cosmology."

65 See Harry O. Maier, "Barbarians, Scythians and Imperial Iconography in the Epistle to the Colossians," in *Picturing the New Testament: Studies in Ancient Visual Images*, ed. Annette Weissenrieder, Friederike Wendt, and Petra von Gemünden, WUNT 2.193 (Tübingen: Mohr Siebeck, 2005), 385–406; Maier, "A Sly Civility."

66 E.g., Gordley, *Colossian Hymn*; Donelson, *Colossians*, 21–28. Cf. also Jack T.

Sanders, *The New Testament Christological Hymns*, SNTSMS 15 (Cambridge: Cambridge University Press, 1971), 75n3. See also Moule, *Colossians and Philemon*, 58; O'Brien, *Colossians, Philemon*, 45–48; Wright, *Climax*, 111–13; Dunn, *Colossians and Philemon*, 89; Barclay, *Colossians and Philemon*, 66–68; Stettler, *Kolosserhymnus*. C. F. Burney, "Christ as the ΑΡΧΗ of Creation," *JTS* 27 (1926): 160–77, reads the Colossian hymn as a exposition of the different meanings of בראשית in Genesis 1.

67   Bruce, *Colossians, Philemon, Ephesians*, 62. He (at 58), and others, find echoes of the Jewish Scriptures at various points in the language of Col 1:15-20; see, e.g., Gibbs, *Creation*, 107–8; O'Brien, *Colossians, Philemon*, 52–53; Lincoln, "Colossians," 599; Smith, *Heavenly Perspective*, 171; Moo, *Colossians and Philemon*, 113–14, 117–19.

68   Vincent A. Pizzuto, *A Cosmic Leap of Faith: An Authorial, Structural, and Theological Investigation of the Cosmic Christology in Col. 1:15-20*, BeT 41 (Leuven: Peeters, 2006), 175–76.

69   See Martin Scott, *Sophia and the Johannine Jesus*, JSNTSup 71 (Sheffield: Sheffield Academic Press, 1992), 89–94, for discussion of the parallels between Wisdom and Logos in Jewish thought around this time.

70   See also a possible translation of Proverbs 8:30 in R. B. Y. Scott, "Wisdom in Creation: The 'āmôn of Proverbs VIII 30," *VT* 10 (1960): 220–22.

71   Smith, *Heavenly Perspective*, 166, notes also a parallel between πρὸ πάντων in Colossians 1:17 and a similar expression used of Wisdom in Sirach 1:4, although this speaks of Wisdom being created.

72   David T. Runia, *Philo in Early Christian Literature: A Survey*, CRINT. Section III: Jewish Traditions in Early Christian Literature 3 (Minneapolis: Fortress, 1993), 84–86, deals with parallels and differences between the cosmology of Philo and that in Colossians. See also Hartman, "Universal," 113–18, and Dunn, *Colossians and Philemon*, 91.

73   Philo uses συνίστημι, but in the context of the human body being held together by God's providence (*Her.* 58).

74   The term is rare in biblical writings, appearing in Matthew 5:9 and in the LXX only (in verbal form) at Proverbs 10:10. Cf. Lohse, *Colossians*, 59n203. See also Werner Foerster, "εἰρηνοποιέω," *TDNT* 2:419–20.

75   A background in Wisdom thought is, however, strongly disputed by others, such as Gordon D. Fee, *Pauline Christology: An Exegetical-Theological Study* (Peabody, Mass.: Hendrickson, 2007), 317–25, who claims that "the 'parallels' are only in the mind of the beholder" (325). This seems an overly strong dismissal of significant similarities.

76   Ernst Lohmeyer, *Die Briefe an die Philipper, an die Kolosser und an Philemon*, KEK 10A (11th ed., Göttingen: Meyers, 1956), 43–46. Stanislas Lyonnet suggested that the idea of peacemaking within nature at Jewish New Year lay behind Colossians 1:20; S. Lyonnet, "L'hymne christologique de

l'épitre aux Colossiens et la fête juive du nouvel an (S. Paul, *Col.*, 1,20 et Philon, *De spec.leg.*, 192)," *RSR* 48 (1960): 93–100.

77　Schweizer, *Colossians*, 74–75 dismisses both Lohmeyer's and Lyonnet's suggested festival contexts, arguing that, while the New Year festival features peacemaking between elements of creation but does not refer to forgiveness, the Day of Atonement concerns forgiveness but not creation. Similarly, Lohse, *Colossians*, 46, claims that reconciliation "does not allude, even remotely, to a connection with Jewish conceptions of sacrifices and of the great day of Atonement." However, Margaret Barker, *The Great High Priest: The Temple Roots of Christian Liturgy* (New York: T&T Clark, 2003), 42–55, sees a link between NT passages speaking of reconciliation and the Temple rituals designed to "restore the bonds which held together the community and the creation" (53).

78　Cilliers Breytenbach, *Versöhnung: eine Studie zur paulinischen Soteriologie*, WMANT 60 (Neukirchen-Vluyn: Neukirchener, 1989), 37–83, esp. 64–65. This is supported by Stanley Porter's extensive study of the use of καταλλάσσω (Καταλλάσσω *in Ancient Greek Literature, with Reference to the Pauline Writings*, EFN 5 [Cordoba: Ediciones El Almendro, 1994], esp. 16), which finds no evidence for its use in religious contexts until its occurrence in 2 Maccabees and the NT.

79　E.g., W. D. Davies, *Paul and Rabbinic Judaism: Some Rabbinic Elements in Pauline Theology* (1948; 2nd ed., London: SPCK, 1955); Smith, *Heavenly Perspective*, 157; Stettler, *Kolosserhymnus*.

80　Schweizer, *Colossians*, 70; Dunn, *Colossians and Philemon*, 92; Lightfoot, *Colossians and Philemon*, 153. On the point that 1:20 indicates a sense of *telos* see, e.g., Stig Hanson, *The Unity of the Church in the New Testament: Colossians and Ephesians* (Uppsala: Almqvist & Wiksells, 1946), 112; Lohse, *Colossians*, 51–52; Barclay, *Colossians and Philemon*, 80; Fee, *Christology*, 302; Fowl, *Story*, 109. Similar formulations are found in the undisputed Paulines but with God (Rom 11:36; 1 Cor 8:6) as object. Bruce, arguing that there is no direct link with Stoic terminology here, notes that the idea of the world being made for the Messiah's sake occurs in rabbinic teaching (Bruce, *Colossians, Philemon, Ephesians*, 64nn119, 121) but Beasley-Murray, "Colossians 1:15–20," 173, disputes this. See *b. Sanh.* 98b.

81　Gordley, *Colossian Hymn.*

82　Friedrich Büchsel, "ἀποκαταλλάσσω," *TDNT* 1:259. On the priority of Colossians, see Lohse, *Colossians*, 4n2.

83　In the LXX, καταλλάσσω is only used to speak of reconciliation in 2 Maccabees (1:5, 7:33, 8:29) and here it is reconciliation of God to people. Its only other LXX use is, curiously, to translate חתת in Jeremiah 48:39 (LXX 31:39). Reconciliation between people (Sir 22:22, 27:21) is expressed by διαλλαγή. Lincoln and Wedderburn, *Later Pauline Letters*, 33n23, note the unusual prepositional use in Colossians.

84   Porter, Καταλλάσσω, 183, notes three potential consequences of the addition of a prepositional prefix to a verb: the prefix may retain its unprefixed meaning, the prefix may confer a new meaning on the verb to which it is attached, or it may intensify the sense of the verb. Cf. G. Abbott-Smith, *A Manual Greek Lexicon of the New Testament* (Edinburgh: T&T Clark, 1936), 51, who suggests that with ἀποκαταλλάσσω, "ἀπο here signifies *completely*," hence "*to reconcile completely*"; Friedrich Wilhelm Blass, A. Debrunner, and Robert W. Funk, *A Greek Grammar of the New Testament and Other Early Christian Literature* (Chicago: The University of Chicago Press, 1961), §318 (5).

85   Bruce, *Colossians, Philemon, Ephesians*, 74n164; Porter, Καταλλάσσω, 184–85. Lightfoot, *Colossians and Philemon*, 157, also notes a possible parallel in Acts 3:21: ἀποκατάστασις.

86   Schweizer, *Colossians*, 85.

87   Fowl, *Story*, esp. 104, 130.

88   Donelson, *Colossians*, 24, 26.

89   Anderson notes that NT teaching on creation presupposes that found within the OT but is viewed christologically (Bernhard W. Anderson, *From Creation to New Creation: Old Testament Perspectives* [Minneapolis: Fortress, 1994], 17–18, 244).

90   E.g., Lohse, *Colossians*, 50–51; Lincoln and Wedderburn, *Later Pauline Letters*, 26; Dunn, *Colossians and Philemon*, 90–91.

91   Moo, *Colossians and Philemon*, 121. Dunn, *Colossians and Philemon*, 91n20, suggests a reference to "the Hellenistic Jewish idea of the Logos as the 'place' in which the world exists."

92   E.g., see O'Brien, *Colossians, Philemon*, 44–48; Bruce, *Colossians, Philemon, Ephesians*, 59–65; Dunn, *Colossians and Philemon*, 89–93; Wilson, *Colossians and Philemon*, 135–36, 143–44; Moo, *Colossians and Philemon*, 119–20.

93   MacDonald, *Colossians*, 59.

94   Barclay, *Colossians and Philemon*, 80.

95   Richard Bauckham notes that the narrative assumes an "intrusion of evil that takes place implicitly between the first and second stanzas of the hymn" but goes on to admit that "Colossians is as reticent about the origins of evil as most of the Bible is" (Bauckham, "Where is Wisdom?" 135). See also Dunn, *Colossians and Philemon*, 84–85, who notes the "tension" between a universe held together "in him" (v. 17) and the later (v. 20) "presupposition of a cosmos disrupted and alienated."

96   As with Romans 8, some assume an unspoken, implicit reference here to the disobedience of Adam, humanity's primeval fall, as the cause of any ensuing cosmic disorder; e.g., Bultmann, *Theology*, 176; Walter T. Wilson,

The Hope Of Glory: Education and Exhortation in the Epistle to the Colossians, NTS 88 (Leiden: Brill, 1997), 188–205; Berry, *God's Book*, 245.

97   Some assume that the author is referring to a feeling common among people at that time, a sense of the *Brüchigkeit der Welt* (Hartman, "Universal," 116; cf. Schillebeeckx, *Christ*, 182, 191; Lohse, *Colossians*, 59; Schweizer, *Colossians*, 217–20; Liedke, *Im Bauch*, 158–61). Others, noting that the hymn encompasses such entities as "powers" and things "in heaven" (1:16, 20), and that similar references occur elsewhere in the letter (1:13; 2:15; cf. 2:18, 20), have spoken in more general terms of creation being under the control of malevolent forces (e.g., Dunn, *Colossians and Philemon*, 97; Barrett, *First Adam*, 86). Contrasting this passage with Romans 8:19-23, Bruce claims that "here it is not simply subjection to futility but positive hostility that is implied on the part of the created universe. The universe has been involved in conflict with its Creator, and needs to be reconciled to him" (*Colossians, Philemon, Ephesians*, 74).

98   Colin Gunton, "Atonement and the Project of Creation: An Interpretation of Colossians 1:15-23," *Dialog* 35 (1996): 35–41.

99   Porter, Καταλλάσσω, 183.

100 *Adv. Mar.* 5.19.5: "For they might have been conciliated (*conciliari*) to a stranger, but reconciled (*reconciliari*) to no god except their own."

101 See Marshall, "Unity and Diversity," 125; also Beasley-Murray, "Colossians 1:15-20," 179). Lohse, *Colossians*, 59n203, says, "cosmic peace has *returned*" (our italics). Similarly, Elmer Flor notes the sense of "re-setting things under one head" which is conveyed by the use of ἀνακεφαλαιώσασθαι in a similar passage in Ephesians 1:10 (Flor, "Cosmic Christ and Ecojustice," 139–41).

102 Cf. Stettler, *Kolosserhymnus*, 345, quoted below (see n. 119).

103 Strictly speaking, "the fullness" is the subject of the verbs here but it is generally accepted to be equivalent to "God in all his fullness." See Schweizer, *Colossians*, 76–79; Bruce, *Colossians, Philemon, Ephesians*, 72–74; Dunn, *Colossians and Philemon*, 99–102.

104 Gibbs, *Creation*, 106.

105 Moo, *Colossians and Philemon*, 126–28.

106 See, e.g., Bruce, *Colossians, Philemon, Ephesians*, 54; Wright, *Colossians and Philemon*, 65; Barth and Blanke, *Colossians*, 193; Dunn, *Colossians and Philemon*, 97; Wilson, *Colossians and Philemon*, 126; Moo, *Colossians and Philemon*, 115–16.

107 See n. 92 above.

108 The use of the perfect tense of συνίστημι may suggest the ongoing nature of this process in Christ; Moo, *Colossians and Philemon*, 125.

109 See, e.g., Fowl, *Story*, 123–54, on the ways in which the superiority of

Christ over the powers is one of the two main themes arising from the hymn and echoed through the letter.

110 Indeed, Bauckham finds it difficult to see why reconciliation of any non-human creation would be needed and what form it might take ("Where is Wisdom?" 136–37).

111 E.g., Schweizer sees the declaration of the accomplishment of total reconciliation as the "hymnic language of worship" (Colossians, 86); cf. also Stettler, Kolosserhymnus, 342.

112 These include O'Brien, Colossians, Philemon, 53; Schweizer, Colossians, 84; MacDonald, Colossians, 64. However, Moo, Colossians and Philemon, 137n219, points out that aorist infinitives (such as used for "reconciliation") and participles (as in "making peace") do not necessarily refer to past events.

113 See Still, "Eschatology in Colossians," for a challenge to an overemphasis on Colossians' distinctive and realized eschatology.

114 Fowl, Story, 130.

115 Moo, Colossians and Philemon, 130.

116 Either reading is possible, since the pronoun may be read as αὐτόν or αὑτόν (= ἑαυτόν) but the christological reading seems to be favored by the parallel in verse 16 as well as by the generally christocentric focus of the hymn. In favor of Christ as referent, see, e.g., Lohse, Colossians, 59n201; Barth and Blanke, Colossians, 214–15; Dunn, Colossians and Philemon, 83n3; 103; Moo, Colossians and Philemon, 133–34. For God, see, e.g., Bruce, Colossians, Philemon, Ephesians, 74; Wright, Colossians and Philemon, 75–76; Wilson, Colossians and Philemon, 154. Nonetheless, as Wilson comments, "it is ultimately God who is at work here . . ." (154).

117 This point is noted by Moule, Colossians and Philemon, 59, and O'Brien, Colossians, Philemon, 40, among others.

118 Barclay, Colossians and Philemon, 87. Cf. also Donelson, Colossians, 27–31, who suggests that verse 20 is an example of "hymnic exaggeration," with the rest of the letter forming "an ethical and ecclesiological commentary" on the cosmic hymn (29). See also Lincoln and Wedderburn, Later Pauline Letters, 29–30.

119 Stettler, Kolosserhymnus, 345, our translation ("das Geschaffensein der ganzen Schöpfung auf den Messias hin [V. 16fin.] kommt erst in der Versöhnung des Alls auf Jesus hin [V. 20a] zur Erfüllung").

120 Colossians therefore represents a particular response to the kind of issue with which Francis Watson grapples in Text, 137–53. Concerned that "[n]arrative theologies sometimes display a tendency towards christomonism in their preoccupation with 'the story of Jesus'" (137), Watson turns to a reading of Genesis 1 in order to set out something of "the universal horizons of the Christian narrative" as "the indispensible hermeneuti-

cal framework within which the story of Jesus must be set" (138). He concludes, "Over against the apolitical parochialism of some postmodern narrative theology, the story of Jesus must instead be interpreted as the midpoint of time, deriving from the universal horizon of the creation of the world and of humankind in the likeness of God, and pointing towards the universal horizon of an eschaton in which the human and non-human creation together reach their appointed goal" (153). For Colossians, the story of Jesus cannot be set *within* the wider horizons of creation and eschaton. Rather, the story of Jesus is universalized and made to encompass everything, temporally and spatially.

121 Although the influence of Stoic thought was very widespread in the Hellenistic world, there is no *direct* reference in Colossians to these cycles, or to ekpurotic conflagration (such as we find in 2 Pet 3:5-7).

122 Simon Blackburn, *The Oxford Dictionary of Philosophy* (New York: Oxford University Press, 1994), 364: "The capstone of Stoic philosophy was an ethic of the consolations of identification with the impartial, inevitable, moral order of the universe. It is an ethic of self-sufficient, benevolent calm, with the virtuous peace of the wise man rendering him indifferent to poverty, pain and death."

123 Balabanski, "Critiquing," 157.

124 Balabanski, "Critiquing," 155.

125 Balabanski, "Critiquing," 158.

126 Petr Pokorný, *Colossians: A Commentary*, trans. Siegfried S. Schatzmann (Peabody, Mass.: Hendrickson, 1991; German original, 1987). For an extended analysis of the worldview of Colossians understood in narrative terms, see Wilson, *Hope*, 188–218.

127 Sylvia C. Keesmaat, "Echoes, Ethics and Empire in Colossians," paper presented at the annual meeting of the SBL, Washington, D.C., November 2006. Cited with permission.

Chapter 6

1 Stephen E. Fowl, "Christology and Ethics in Philippians 2:5-11," in *Where Christology Began: Essays on Philippians 2*, ed. R. P. Martin and B. J. Dodd (Louisville, Ky.: Westminster John Knox, 1998), 142; cf. Wayne A. Meeks, "The Man from Heaven in Paul's Letter to the Philippians," in *The Future of Early Christianity: Essays in Honor of Helmut Koester*, ed. B. A. Pearson (Minneapolis: Fortress, 1991), 329–30; Douglas A. Campbell, "The Story of Jesus in Romans and Galatians," in Longenecker, *Narrative Dynamics in Paul*, 108.

2 It seems to us unconvincing to insist, as Francis Watson does, that the Christ-event is a vertical incursion that interrupts history, and so does *not* form a narrative (Francis Watson, "Is There a Story in These Texts?"

in Longenecker, *Narrative Dynamics in Paul*, 231–39). Cf. also Barclay, "Paul's Story." For more detailed criticism, see Richard Hays' response to Watson in Hays, "Is Paul's Gospel Narratable?" We note, however, Paul Fiddes' cautionary analysis: the richness of the biblical narratives does not reduce easily into a simple pattern, even this classic "U-shaped curve" (see Fiddes, *Freedom and Limit*, 47–64).

3   However, this contrast can be overdrawn; Romans 8:17 identifies the suffering and glorification of the subsequent verses as being "with Christ" while, as we saw in §5.6, God is present, albeit "behind the scenes," in the Colossian hymn.

4   Though the wider context of the letter suggests some romantic elements of struggle in the underlying narrative (see below).

5   Moo, "Nature in the New Creation," 474, 484. See also Jewett, *Romans*, 511–18, and N. T. Wright, "The Letter to the Romans," in *The New Interpreter's Bible*, Vol. 10, ed. Leander E. Keck (Nashville: Abingdon, 2002), 596–97, for commentators on the text confident of its ethical implications. We discuss these issues further in §6.4.

6   Schweizer, *Colossians*, 86–87, 299.

7   Schweizer, *Colossians*, 276 (emphasis in original).

8   Thompson, *Colossians*, 116.

9   E.g., Carley, "Psalm 8"; Earth Bible Team, "Guiding," 44–46; Habel, "Geophany." See also many of the essays in Norman C. Habel and Peter Trudinger, eds., *Exploring Ecological Hermeneutics*, Society of Biblical Literature Symposium 46 (Atlanta: SBL, 2008).

10   Lukas Vischer, "Listening to Creation Groaning: A Survey of Main Themes of Creation Theology," in *Listening to Creation Groaning: Report and Papers from a Consultation on Creation Theology Organised by the European Christian Environmental Network at the John Knox International Reformed Center from March 28 to April 1st 2004*, ed. Lukas Vischer (Geneva: Centre international réformé John Knox, 2004), 21, 22, respectively. The term "anthropomonism" seems to come from Patriarch Bartholomew; see John Chryssavgis, ed., *Cosmic Grace, Humble Prayer: The Ecological Vision of the Green Patriarch Bartholomew I* (Grand Rapids: Eerdmans, 2003), 314.

11   David Clough, *On Animals: Theology* (New York: T&T Clark, forthcoming).

12   Bauckham, *God*, 173.

13   Cf. Byrne, "Creation Groaning," 198–200, who draws a distinction between "negative" and "positive" anthropocentrism.

14   Barclay, *Colossians and Philemon*, 87.

15   Donelson, *Colossians*, 27; cf. above p. 111 with n. 118.

16   As found, e.g., in Stephen Webb's incautious comments, which vastly overstate the extent of human power: "The world is shrinking and humans

are in charge of all of it, for better or worse. We cannot shirk our responsibility for nature. Nature is largely under our control. The only question is how we will exercise that control" (*Good Eating* [Grand Rapids: Brazos, 2001], 24). Floods and tsunamis, droughts and earthquakes, not to mention the broader picture of climate change, illustrate how little *control* we humans have over nature, however significant the impact of our actions.

17 For references see §1.2 with nn. 47–49.

18 See Adams, *The Stars*, for a comprehensive study of NT texts of "cosmic catastrophe," and a strong argument that many if not all of these texts do envisage some form of real cosmic collapse.

19 Here we note Kathryn Tanner's comment: "Where God acts alone to bring in the eschaton . . . Our struggle for the good—painful, effort-filled action that takes time—is therefore devalued relative to God's immediate achievement of the world that is to come; and expectations of the good that is to be achieved by way of our struggles often drop away" ("Eschatology and Ethics," in *The Oxford Companion to Theological Ethics*, ed. Gilbert Meilaender and William Werpehowski [Oxford: Oxford University Press, 2007], 43). See chap. 8 for further engagement with Tanner's views on eschatology.

20 Neil Messer, *Selfish Genes and Christian Ethics: Theological and Ethical Reflections on Evolutionary Biology* (London: SCM Press, 2007), 214.

21 See Conradie, "The Road," and §2.4 above.

22 See Conradie, "Ecological Hermeneutics," for an explanatory diagram.

23 Byrne, "Creation Groaning," 194. See also Bolt, "Relation."

24 See Sven Hillert, *Limited and Universal Salvation: A Text-Oriented and Hermeneutical Study of Two Perspectives in Paul*, ConBNT 31 (Stockholm: Almqvist & Wiksell, 1999), and the earlier comments, which convey this tension *in nuce*, in E. P. Sanders, *Paul* (Oxford: Oxford University Press, 1991), 126–27.

25 Hillert, *Limited*, 237–52. On the universalism of Romans 5:18, see Richard H. Bell, "Rom 5.18–19 and Universal Salvation," *NTS* 48 (2002): 417–32.

26 E.g., O'Brien, *Colossians, Philemon*, 55–57; Schweizer, *Colossians*, 87; Bruce, *Colossians, Philemon, Ephesians*, 75; Wright, *Colossians and Philemon*, 77.

27 Moo, *Colossians and Philemon*, 137 and 136, respectively.

28 Cf. Schweizer, *Colossians*, 260–77 on the influence of Colossians 1:15-20 on the history of discussion of universal redemption (*Allversöhnung*).

29 See Jay B. McDaniel, *Of God and Pelicans: A Theology of Reverence for Life* (Louisville, Ky.: Westminster John Knox, 1989); Denis Edwards, "Every Sparrow that Falls to the Ground: The Cost of Evolution and the Christ-Event," *Ecotheology* 11 (2006): 103–23; Christopher Southgate, *The Groaning of Creation: God, Evolution, and the Problem of Evil* (Louisville, Ky.: Westminster John Knox, 2008), 78–91.

30 For evidence of motifs of struggle and quest in the wider context of the letter to the Colossians see §6.4.

31 Jenkins, *Ecologies of Grace*, 67.

32 To say this is not to suppose that evolutionary descriptions, of themselves, value one state of an ecosystem more than another. That would be wholly misleading, and is perhaps the greatest weakness of the way James Lovelock has drafted his histories of Gaia; see James Lovelock, *The Ages of Gaia: A Biography of Our Living Earth* (Oxford: Oxford University Press, 1989). We have good evidence for a state of the planet known as "snowball Earth," with glaciation even at equatorial latitudes, which preceded the extraordinary phenomenon of the Cambrian explosion (Mark A. S. McMenamin, "Gaia and Glaciation: Lipalian [Vendian] Environmental Crisis," in *Scientists Debate Gaia*, ed. Stephen H. Schneider et al. [Cambridge, Mass.: MIT Press, 2004], 115–27). Evolutionary descriptions must be accompanied by some criteria by which biological states can be valued — whether it be for their current diversity, their potential, their beauty, or whatever may be chosen. Only a valuing scheme which, on some basis or other, accorded more value to a more diverse biosphere, or a biosphere with more potential to give rise to complexity and intricacy of biological function, would be able to state a preference for the one phase of the Earth over the other. The evidence suggests moreover that it is periods of great ecological "impoverishment" such as snowball Earth, or the later phase of the extinction of the dinosaurs, that make possible new phases of rapid evolutionary innovation.

33 John Polkinghorne, "Pelican Heaven," *Times Literary Supplement*, April 3, 2009.

34 The conclusion to which Michael Lloyd finds himself forced in Michael Lloyd, "Are Animals Fallen?" in *Animals on the Agenda*, ed. Andrew Linzey and Dorothy Yamamoto (London: SCM Press, 1998), 147–60.

35 Perhaps most famously in recent theology, Karl Barth's formulation of *das Nichtige* in *Church Dogmatics III.3: The Doctrine of Creation*, trans. G. W. Bromiley and R. J. Ehrlich (2nd ed., Edinburgh: T&T Clark, 1960), adopted in a modified form by Thomas F. Torrance, *Divine and Contingent Order* (Oxford: Oxford University Press, 1981), and recently reappropriated by Neil Messer, "Natural Evil after Darwin," in *Theology after Darwin*, ed. R. J. Berry and Michael Northcott (Carlisle: Paternoster, 2009), 139–54. Celia Deane-Drummond has offered what appears to be a related strategy, writing of "Shadow Sophia" ("Shadow Sophia in Christological Perspective: The Evolution of Sin and the Redemption of Nature," *Theology and Science* 6 [2008]: 13–32).

36 Southgate, *Groaning*; cf. Holmes Rolston, III, "Disvalues in Nature," *Monist* 75 (1992): 250–78; idem, "Naturalizing and Systematizing Evil,"

in *Is Nature Ever Evil?* ed. Willem B. Drees (New York: Routledge, 2003), 67–86.

37   John F. Haught, *God after Darwin: A Theology of Evolution* (Boulder, Colo.: Westview, 2000), 38; Richard W. Kropf, *Evil and Evolution: A Theodicy* (1984; repr., Eugene, Ore.: Wipf & Stock, 2004), 156; Holmes Rolston, III, *Science and Religion: A Critical Survey* (1987; repr., Philadelphia: Templeton Foundation, 2006), 146.

38   Wedderburn argues that it is "open to us to say that there are further depths of meaning in the passage which the writer has not plumbed, but which we may plumb with some confidence that we are not thereby using this text perversely or in a way that runs directly counter to the author's intention in quoting it" (Lincoln and Wedderburn, *Later Pauline Letters*, 42).

39   N. T. Wright also sees the futility of creation in the natural rhythms of the seasons and of birth and death (*Evil*, 117). Richard W. Kropf sees the futility as residing in the operation of chance in the evolutionary process (*Evil and Evolution*, 124). Cf. also Holmes Rolston: "'Groaning in travail' is in the nature of things from time immemorial. Such travail is the Creator's will, productive as it is of glory" ("Naturalizing," 85).

40   Southgate, *Groaning*, 60–73. "Self-transcendence," in these terms, covers any phenomenon in which the narrow self-interest of the creature is transcended. This includes gene exchange in bacteria, symbiosis to give rise to eucaryotes, and cooperation in insect communities, all the way to the sacrificial care of mothers for progeny, the monkeys that call to alert the tribe to predators, the grooming of the hurt chimpanzee after a dispute, and all human cognates, reaching into the possibilities that human love and other-regard can realize. All of these are seen by Southgate as response to the divine invitation of self-giving love; he sees in Jesus both perfect image and perfect response.

41   Southgate, *Groaning*, 94–95.

42   Cf. Robert J. Russell, "Entropy and Evil," *Zygon* 18 (1984): 449–68.

43   Southgate, *Groaning*, 60–73.

44   See also recent writing on (human) original sinfulness in Daryl P. Domning and Monika K. Hellwig, *Original Selfishness: Original Sin in the Light of Evolution* (Aldershot, Vt.: Ashgate, 2006); Gaymon Bennett, Martinez J. Hewlett, Ted Peters, and Robert J. Russell, eds., *The Evolution of Evil* (Göttingen: Vandenhoeck and Ruprecht, 2008).

45   Our appropriation of the scientific narrative has something in common with Sallie McFague's appeal to "the common creation story," in her effort to generate novel and constructive proposals in environmental ethics; however, our own hermeneutical lens seeks not to be *merely* a remythologization with "ethical or pragmatic concern" (*The Body of God: An Ecological Theology* [London: SCM Press, 1993], 81) and it allows the biblical texts

more of a controlling influence than is the case with McFague's own theology. Cf. the critique of McFague's general approach by Daphne Hampson, *Theology and Feminism* (Oxford: Basil Blackwell, 1990), 161.

46 It is very much open to question whether the evidence of the biblical witness itself is to a restoration of an initial harmony. Cf. Oliver O'Donovan, *Resurrection and Moral Order: An Outline for Evangelical Ethics*, 2nd ed. (Grand Rapids: Eerdmans, 1994), 55–56. Hans Urs von Balthasar, *The Glory of the Lord: A Theological Aesthetics, Volume VII: Theology: The New Covenant*, ed. John Riches, trans. Brian McNeil (San Francisco, Calif.: Ignatius, 1989), 297, writes: "The New Testament nowhere speaks of the recovery of a lost glory of the original state, but rather of the eschatological achieving of the righteousness and glory of God in his cosmos." For a reading of Genesis 1–2 as a forward-looking "prophetic" text, see J. W. Rogerson, "The Creation Stories: Their Ecological Potential and Problems," in Horrell, Hunt, Southgate, and Stavrakopoulou, *Ecological Hermeneutics*, 21–31.

47 For this construal, see §4.4 VIII n. 91.

48 As Jewett, *Romans*, 510–11, also points out, δόξα here needs to be read with the force of the Hebrew כבוד. This is a word that connotes weightiness, and hence ultimately substance, importance, depth of reality. See Gerhard Kittel and Gerhard von Rad, "δοκέω κτλ," *TDNT* 2:237–51, for the transformation of δόξα in the NT away from its meaning in classical Greek, under the influence of כבוד. For further discussion of the connotations of כבוד see Carey C. Newman, *Paul's Glory-Christology: Tradition and Rhetoric*, NovTSup 69 (Leiden: Brill, 1992), 17–24; also Walter Brueggemann, *Reverberations of Faith: A Theological Handbook of Old Testament Themes* (Louisville, Ky.: Westminster John Knox, 2002), 87–89; Hans Urs von Balthasar, *The Glory of the Lord: A Theological Aesthetics*, vol. 6, *Theology: The Old Covenant*, ed. John Riches, trans. Brian McNeil and Erasmo Merikakis (Edinburgh: T&T Clark, 1991), 31–37. The glory of the liberated children of God is the glory of participating in the life of the resurrected Christ (Col 3:4; Rom 8:7), in all that is possible to be experienced of the life of Godself. We develop this thought in chap. 7.

49 Southgate, *Groaning*, 65–66, 71–73.

50 Or, as Paul goes on to put it in 12:2, being transformed by the renewal of minds.

51 Jewett, *Romans*, 515. Referring to Heinrich Schlier, *Der Römerbrief*, HThKNT 6 (Freiburg: Herder, 1977), 262–63.

52 Jewett, *Romans*, 515n75.

53 Jewett, "Corruption and Redemption," 35.

54 Jewett, *Romans*, 515.

55 Tonstad, "Creation," 148–49. Cf. also Schillebeeckx, *Christ*, 237: "the creation looks for the redemptive moment when human beings will finally

have mercy on it as good shepherds, caring stewards, so that the cosmos too can take its breath again." Schillebeeckx' mention of "breath" here is very significant in the light of our reflection in this section on the work of the Spirit.

56 Wright, *Resurrection*, 258. Cf. Cranfield, "Some Observations," 227: "[all the components of creation] are prevented from being fully that which they were created to be, so long as man's part is missing."

57 Wright, *Resurrection*, 258. For a radically contrary understanding see Turner, "God's Design."

58 See, e.g., Dunn, *Colossians and Philemon*, 114–17; Wilson, *Colossians and Philemon*, 170–72; Moo, *Colossians and Philemon*, 149–53.

59 There is, then, both *agon* and *pathos* in the believer's following of the hero Christ through the quest (cf. Frye, *Anatomy*, 187).

60 We draw out these thoughts further in chap. 8 when we discuss the extension of corporate solidarity to include the nonhuman creation.

61 Balabanski, "Critiquing," 159.

62 Maier, "A Sly Civility," esp. 340.

63 W. Sibley Towner, "The Future of Nature," *Int* 50 (1996): 33.

64 Rolston, *Science and Religion*, 134.

65 Fiddes, *Freedom and Limit*, 47–64. As we noted above, Fiddes is uneasy with an oversimplified analysis of the biblical narrative in terms of a "U-shaped curve"—paradise, paradise lost, paradise regained—a pattern he finds in Michael Edwards, *Towards a Christian Poetics* (London: Macmillan, 1984). That this is not quite fair to Edwards is shown by this passage: "We are so placed within the process [of salvation], however, that the fulfilling of possibility, the transcending of an initial greatness, is for the future. We experience, at most, only its beginning. Although the world will be renewed, it continues in the meantime to fall around us. The earth will become paradise, but continues cursed. Besides, the property of a dialectic is that its resolution is incomplete, its third term becoming the thesis of a further triad and the origin of a new conflict. Such is the case here. The Resurrection brings not immediate bliss but another series of contradictions, between the forces of rebirth and the death which still asserts itself—between, in the same individual, the 'new man' and the 'old'" (8). See also Luke Ferretter, *Towards a Christian Literary Theory* (Basingstoke: Palgrave Macmillan, 2003), 160–68, for a judicious analysis of Edwards and Fiddes.

There is a link also here to the recent work of Ernst Conradie on redemption seen ecotheologically. Conradie points out that salvation can be seen as a process dominated by the cross and God's forgiveness, hard won but offered as free grace, as a process proleptically completed in the victory of the resurrection, or as a call to follow in the Spirit the example of the incarnate Christ. None of these shapes to the narrative of salvation is adequate by itself. See Ernst Conradie, "The Redemption of the Earth: In Search of Appropriate Soteriological Concepts in an Age of Ecological Destruction," unpublished paper, Yale Divinity School, 2008. Cited with permission.

Chapter 7

1   Cf. the comments of, e.g., Odil Hannes Steck, *Welt und Umwelt* (Stuttgart: Kohlhammer, 1978), 173; Habel, "Introducing the Earth Bible," 33–35; Conradie, "Ecological Hermeneutics."

2   For overviews, see J. Christiaan Beker, *Paul the Apostle: The Triumph of God in Life and Thought* (Edinburgh: T&T Clark, 1980), 13–16; Dunn, *Theology of Paul*, 19–23; Campbell, *Quest*, 29–55; Stanley E. Porter, "Is There a Center to Paul's Theology? An Introduction to the Study of Paul and His Theology," in *Paul and His Theology*, ed. Stanley E. Porter (Leiden: Brill, 2006), 1–19.

3   Cf. J. Christiaan Beker, *Heirs of Paul: Paul's Legacy in the New Testament and in the Church Today* (Edinburgh: T&T Clark, 1992), 68–71.

4   Dunn, *Theology of Paul*, 5.

5   For a summary of these difficulties, and of the various approaches to Pauline theology, see Porter, "Is There a Center?"

6   E.g., Heikki Räisänen, *Paul and the Law*, WUNT 29 (Tübingen: Mohr Siebeck, 1983).

7   See, e.g., the series of volumes produced by the SBL Consultation on Pauline Theology: Bassler, *Pauline Theology*, vol. 1; David M. Hay, ed., *Pauline Theology*, vol. 2, *1 and 2 Corinthians* (Minneapolis: Fortress, 1993); David M. Hay and E. Elizabeth Johnson, eds., *Pauline Theology*, vol. 3, *Romans* (Minneapolis: Fortress, 1995); E. Elizabeth Johnson and David M. Hay, eds., *Pauline Theology*, vol. 4, *Looking Back, Pressing On* (Minneapolis: Fortress, 1997).

8   Beker, *Paul the Apostle.*

9   Among many studies that have drawn attention to some of these contrasts, see John W. Drane, *Paul: Libertine or Legalist? A Study in the Theology of the Major Pauline Epistles* (London: SPCK, 1975); John M. G. Barclay, "Thessalonica and Corinth: Social Contrasts in Pauline Christianity," *JSNT* 47 (1992): 49–74; Adams, *Constructing.*

10   Stephen Westerholm, *Perspectives Old and New on Paul: The "Lutheran" Paul and His Critics* (Grand Rapids: Eerdmans, 2004).

11   From Luther's 1538 commentary on Galatians, translated by Theodore Graebner, http://www.ccel.org/ccel/luther/galatians.iv.html (accessed July 2009).

12   Westerholm, *Perspectives*, 30.

13   Jaroslav Pelikan, ed., *Luther's Works*, vol. 26, *Lectures on Galatians 1535, Chapters 1–4* (1535; repr., St. Louis, Mo.: Concordia, 1963), 118 and 136, respectively.

14   W. Wrede, *Paul*, trans. Edward Lumin (London: Philip Green, 1907); Albert Schweitzer, *The Mysticism of Paul the Apostle* (2nd ed., 1931; repr., London: A&C Black, 1953). For a detailed discussion of their views, and the famous phrases quoted above, see Westerholm, *Perspectives*, 101–16. Both phrases are quoted, e.g., by Philip F. Esler, *Galatians* (New York: Routledge, 1998), 153.

15   See Esler, *Galatians*, 154–59.

16   Wrede, *Paul*, 85–86, 153.

17   See, e.g., Wrede, *Paul*, 115, 132. This focus on Paul's dealing with the human race, or with human groups rather than individuals, and with defending the place of Gentiles within the people of God, was notably taken up in Krister Stendahl's work. Stendahl insisted that "Paul's doctrine of justification by faith has its theological context in his reflection on the relation between Jews and Gentiles, and not within the problem of how *man* is to be saved . . ." (*Paul Among Jews and Gentiles* [Philadelphia: Fortress, 1976], 26).

18   Schweitzer, *Mysticism*, 3, 225.

19   Byrne, "Creation Groaning," 194.

20   E. P. Sanders, *Paul and Palestinian Judaism: A Comparison of Patterns of Religion* (London: SCM Press, 1977), 502.

21   Sanders, *Paul and Palestinian*, 467–68; italics original. Sanders cites passages such as Rom 6:3-11; 7:4; Gal 2:19-20, 5:24; Phil 3:10-11 in support, claiming that, "*It is these passages which reveal the true significance of Christ's death in Paul's thought.*" Morna Hooker proposes the notion of "interchange" as a way to encapsulate the central theological idea, echoing words of Irenaeus: "Christ became what we are in order that we might become what he is" (*From Adam to Christ*, 22). She, like Sanders, finds the notion of participation in Christ "fundamental, not only for his [Paul's] Christology, but for his understanding of salvation, of the nature of the redeemed community, of God's plan for humanity and the world, and of the way of life appropriate for restored humanity" (9; cf. 4, *et passim*).

22   Campbell, *Quest*. The combative language is a deliberate echo of the imagery that pervades Campbell's work. Most recently, Michael Gorman has articulated an important attempt to move beyond the oppositional alternatives of justification or participation (Gorman, *Inhabiting*, esp. 40–104). Gorman argues for an understanding of justification as "a participatory death-and-resurrection experience" (74), though this work appeared too late for us to take it fully into account here.

23   Campbell, *Quest*, 29–55.

24 This argument against JF is now presented in massive detail in Douglas A. Campbell, *The Deliverance of God: An Apocalyptic Rereading of Justification in Paul* (Grand Rapids: Eerdmans, 2009).

25 For an example where the theological motivation is explicit, Käsemann's vigorous rejection of the "salvation-history" approach is driven by his sense of how that theological perspective informed and in some ways legitimated Nazi ideology (see above, p. 51 with n. 15).

26 Beker, *Paul the Apostle*, 365.

27 Beker, *Paul the Apostle*, 16. A broadly similar point was earlier made by Adolf Deissmann, who insists that "all these 'concepts' of justification, reconciliation, forgiveness, redemption, adoption are not distinguishable from one another like the acts of a drama, but are synonymous forms of expression for one single thing . . . We shall not comprehend Paul until we have heard all these various testimonies concerning salvation sounding together in harmony like the notes of a single full chord" (*Paul: A Study in Social and Religious History*, trans. William E. Wilson [London: Hodder & Stoughton, 1926], 176–77).

28 James D. G. Dunn, *The New Perspective on Paul: Collected Essays*, WUNT 185 (Tübingen: Mohr Siebeck, 2005), 88.

29 Jouette M. Bassler, "A Response to Jeffrey Bingham and Susan Graham: Networks and Noah's Sons," in *Early Patristic Readings of Romans*, ed. Kathy L. Gaca and L. L. Welborn, Romans Through History and Culture Series (New York: T&T Clark, 2005), 142.

30 See Wright, *Climax*, 120–36, esp. 125, and the recent monograph by Erik Waaler, *The Shema and the First Commandment in First Corinthians: An Intertextual Approach to Paul's Re-reading of Deuteronomy*, WUNT 2.253 (Tübingen: Mohr Siebeck, 2008).

31 Most scholars agree in seeing a reference to creation here, rather than only a soteriological reference, as argued by Jerome Murphy-O'Connor, "I Cor.,VIII,6: Cosmology or Soteriology?" *RB* 85 (1978): 254–59. James D. G. Dunn, *Christology in the Making* (London: SCM Press, 1980), 179–83, downplays any sense of Christ's preexistence here, but acknowledges an identification of Christ "with the creative power and action of God" (182).

32 On the intertextual relationship between 1 Corinthians 8:6 and 1 Timothy 2:5, see Margaret M. Mitchell, "Corrective Composition, Corrective Exegesis: The Teaching on Prayer in 1 Tim 2,1-15," in *Colloquium Oecumenicum Paulinum*, vol. 18, *1 Timothy Reconsidered*, ed. Karl Paul Donfried (Leuven: Peeters, 2008), 41–62, drawing on the methodology of Annette Merz, *Die fiktive Selbstauslegung des Paulus: Intertextuelle Studien zur Intention und Rezeption der Pastoralbriefe*, NTOA 52 (Göttingen: Vandenhoeck & Ruprecht, 2004).

33   On the details of this complex passage, see David G. Horrell, "Theological Principle or Christological Praxis? Pauline Ethics in 1 Cor 8.1–11.1," *JSNT* 67 (1997): 83–114; Horrell, *Solidarity*, 168–82.

34   Πᾶν stands emphatically at the opening of verse 25.

35   For a detailed consideration of the ethics evident in these two major and related blocks of instruction, see Horrell, *Solidarity*, 166–203.

36   Adams, *Constructing*. Adams sees this as a contrast between 1 Corinthians and Romans, with the latter letter having a generally more positive depiction of the κόσμος.

37   Note the shared concern with whether some foods should be forbidden, the idea of the goodness of God's creation, and the idea that food is partaken with thanksgiving (cf. also Rom 14:6). The established Jewish custom of giving thanks at mealtimes, offering a blessing on the food, is clearly taken over into these early Christian contexts. As C. K. Barrett notes, Psalm 24:1 was used by the rabbis "to justify the use of benedictions over food" (*Essays on Paul* [London: SPCK, 1982], 52).

38   For discussion and critique see Reggie M. Kidd, *Wealth and Beneficence in the Pastoral Epistles: A "Bourgeois" Form of Early Christianity?* SBLDS 122 (Atlanta: Scholars Press, 1990). Cf. also Arland J. Hultgren, "The Pastoral Epistles," in *The Cambridge Companion to St Paul*, ed. James D. G. Dunn (Cambridge: Cambridge University Press, 2003), 141–55.

39   On the affirmation of the "goodness of creation" in 1 Timothy 4:1-5, see Paul Trebilco, "The Goodness and Holiness of the Earth and the Whole Creation (I Timothy 4.1-5)," in Habel, *Readings*, 204–20.

40   Notably in Campbell's work, which firmly opposes a contractual model of the process of salvation. See Campbell, *Quest*; Campbell, *Deliverance*, and §7.2 above.

41   See esp. Hays, *Faith of Jesus Christ*; also, inter alia, Douglas A. Campbell, *The Rhetoric of Righteousness in Romans 3.21-26*, JSNTSup 65 (Sheffield: JSOT Press, 1992), 58–69; Douglas A. Campbell, "Romans 1:17 — A Crux Interpretum for the ΠΙΣΤΙΣ ΧΡΙΣΤΟΥ Debate," *JBL* 113 (1994): 265–86. Those who argue for the objective genitive reading, such as James Dunn and Barry Matlock, make the point that perceived theological attractiveness should not determine grammatical/exegetical decisions. See esp. R. Barry Matlock, "Detheologizing the ΠΙΣΤΙΣ ΧΡΙΣΤΟΥ Debate: Cautionary Remarks from a Lexical Semantic Perspective," *NovT* 42 (2000): 1–23; James D. G. Dunn, "Once More, ΠΙΣΤΙΣ ΧΡΙΣΤΟΥ," in Johnson and Hay, *Pauline Theology* 4:61–81 (now reprinted in the second edition of Hays, *Faith of Jesus Christ*, 249–71); Dunn, *Theology of Paul*, 379–85.

42   Nonetheless, despite what we would see as this potential, most recent readings of Paul, even when taking a participatory perspective, fail to

show any explicit interest in this broadening beyond the realm of human salvation. Cf., e.g., Campbell, *Quest*; Gorman, *Inhabiting*.

43 Wayne A. Meeks, "The Image of the Androgyne: Some Uses of a Symbol in Earliest Christianity," *HR* 13 (1974): 180–81.

44 Cf., e.g., Robin Scroggs, "Paul and the Eschatological Woman," *JAAR* 40 (1972): 291–92; H. Paulsen, "Einheit und Freiheit der Söhne Gottes — Gal 3.26-29," *ZNW* 71 (1980): 78–85; Douglas A. Campbell, "Unravelling Colossians 3.11b," *NTS* 42 (1996): 120–32.

45 The textual evidence for the inclusion (א, D², F, G, Ψ, et al.) or exclusion (A, B, D*, et al.) of the article is rather finely balanced but makes little difference to the meaning of the phrase.

46 Cf. Richard B. Hays, *First Corinthians*, Interpretation (Louisville, Ky.: John Knox, 1997), 266; Beker, *Paul the Apostle*, 356–60.

47 Sanders, *Paul and Palestinian*, 474.

48 Ralph P. Martin, *Reconciliation: A Study of Paul's Theology* (Atlanta: John Knox, 1981), 3 (emphasis in original), here referring also to a proposal to this effect by Peter Stuhlmacher. Cf. the brief overview of Martin's argument in Breytenbach, *Versöhnung*, 28–29, where Breytenbach identifies two essential questions where Martin offers "doch keine neue Perspektive," and on which his own study goes on to focus: from where did Paul derive his notion of reconciliation, and how does it relate to the understanding of the death of Jesus?

49 καταλλαγή (Rom 5:11, 11:15; 2 Cor 5:18-19); καταλλάσσω (Rom 5:10 [*bis*]; 1 Cor 7:11; 2 Cor 5:18, 19, 20).

50 Col 1:20, 22; Eph 2:16. On the sense of ἀποκαταλλάσσω in comparison with the non-prefixed form, see above pp. 105–6.

51 For a more detailed treatment of this text in the context of a discussion of its contribution to an ecological reading of Paul, see David G. Horrell, "Ecojustice in the Bible? Pauline Contributions to an Ecological Theology," in *Bible and Justice: Ancient Texts, Modern Challenges*, ed. Matthew J. M. Coomber (Oakville, Conn.: Equinox, forthcoming).

52 There are various possible construals of the crucial phrase in verse 19a, ὡς ὅτι θεὸς ἦν ἐν Χριστῷ κόσμον καταλλάσσων ἑαυτῷ. Reimund Bieringer, "2 Kor 5,19a und die Versöhnung der Welt," *ETL* 63 (1987): 295–326, explores these thoroughly, arguing that ὡς ὅτι should be taken in the sense "that is" (300–304), and that ἐν Χριστῷ should be taken adverbially: God is the subject, "was reconciling" the predicate, and ἐν Χριστῷ "eine adverbiale Ergänzung des Prädikats" (312; see 304–12).

53 Margaret E. Thrall, *A Critical and Exegetical Commentary on the Second Epistle to the Corinthians I–VII*, ICC (Edinburgh: T&T Clark, 1994), 431: "This verse is a repetition and amplification of what Paul has already said in v. 18."

54 Bieringer, "2 Kor 5," 318. Cf. Adams, *Constructing*, 235. This need not, however, be taken to mean that cosmos is here "given an *exclusively* personal sense" (Thrall, *Second Corinthians*, 435; emphasis added), referring to "the totality of mankind" (Marshall, "Unity and Diversity," 123).

55 Gal 3:26-28; 1 Cor 12:12-27. Cf. Eph 1:10. See further Daniel Boyarin, *A Radical Jew: Paul and the Politics of Identity* (Berkeley: University of California Press, 1994); Horrell, *Solidarity*, 99–132.

56 On 1 Corinthians 1:10 as the fundamental "thesis" around which 1 Corinthians is orientated, see Margaret M. Mitchell, *Paul and the Rhetoric of Reconciliation* (Louisville, Ky.: Westminster John Knox, 1991).

57 Among the commentators, Thrall argues for the personal, anthropological rather than the cosmological interpretation: "Paul is saying that if anyone exists 'in Christ,' that person is a newly-created being . . . the main emphasis must lie on the world of humanity" (*Second Corinthians*, 427–28). Victor Paul Furnish sees Paul's emphasis as on the believer, but locates this within a broader context: "In v. 17 the apostle emphasizes in a more comprehensive way the radical newness of the believer's eschatological existence . . . Those who are *in Christ* . . . have . . . become part of a wholly *new creation* . . . the *new creation* of which Paul conceives has an ontic reality which transcends the new being of individual believers. It is the new age which stands over against the present evil age" (*II Corinthians*, AB 32A [New York: Doubleday, 1984], 332).

58 On which see Ulrich Mell, *Neue Schöpfung: Eine traditionsgeschichtliche und exegetische Studie zu einem soteriologischen Grundsatz paulinischer Theologie*, BZNW56 (Berlin: Walter de Gruyter, 1989), 9–32; more briefly Moyer V. Hubbard, *New Creation in Paul's Letters and Thought*, SNTSMS 119 (Cambridge: Cambridge University Press, 2002), 1–5, who epitomizes the anthropological, cosmological, and ecclesiological alternatives under the phrases "new creature," "new creation," and "new community."

59 For a thorough study of the motif and its development in Jewish literature, see Mell, *Neue Schöpfung*, 47–257. Cf. also the comments of Adams, *Constructing*, 226.

60 Cf. Mell, *Neue Schöpfung*, 352–53.

61 "Das Kreuz als Ereignis göttlicher Reversion ist ein weltbewegendes, kosmisches Geschehen, insofern es in der 'Mitte' der Geschichte eine vergangene Welt vor Christus von einer neuen Welt seit Christus trennt . . . Nicht der Mensch heißt 'neue Schöpfung,' sondern, im soteriologischen Verfassungsdanken, die Welt!" (Mell, *Neue Schöpfung*, 324).

62 "Christus als Initiator einer neuen Lebens(= schöpfungs)ordnung repräsentiert ein kosmisches Heilsgeschehen, in das der Mensch prinzipiell einbezogen ist" (Mell, *Neue Schöpfung*, 371).

63 Mell, *Neue Schöpfung*, 392, cf. 393.

64 Mell, *Neue Schöpfung*, 387, cf. 392. See also 394: "Nicht mit der Bekehrung, sondern schon jenseits der individuellen Verifikation gilt mit dem Datum des Christusereignisses eine neue Soteriologie."

65 Hubbard, *New Creation*, 186.

66 Hubbard, *New Creation*, 183.

67 Hubbard, *New Creation*, 232; cf. again at 236: "new creation in Paul was essentially a reality *intra nos*, not *extra nos*."

68 It is worth noting that Hubbard's critique of Mell, taking its point of departure from a rather dismissive comment by Jerome Murphy-O'Connor, "Pauline Studies," *RB* 98 (1991): 150–51, fails to do justice to the content of Mell's monograph. Hubbard sees Mell's flawed (*traditionsgeschichtliche*) methodology as one that "forces the exegete to concentrate on the secondary sources, leaving much of the primary source material (Paul's letters) untouched. Yet for all Mell's apparent comprehensiveness, it is nonetheless stunning that he focuses solely on the Isaianic oracles in his examination of new creation in the Jewish Scriptures, while also ignoring the anthropological new creation texts of, e.g., *Jubilees* and *1 Enoch*" (Hubbard, *New Creation*, 6). It is only fair to point out, in view of such criticism, that Mell spends nearly 140 pages (compared with 150 or so in Hubbard's book) examining the "Bedeutung und Funktion des Begriffes 'Neue Schöpfung' in der paulininschen Theologie," discusses *1 Enoch* and *Jubilees* (and *Joseph and Aseneth*) at some length (see Mell, *Neue Schöpfung*, 113–78 ["Zur neuschöpfungsvorstellung in der Apokalyptik"] and 226–49 [on *JosAs.*]), and gives exegetical arguments why the Pauline material should not be construed along the lines of an individual conversion-theology as found in Hellenistic Jewish literature like *Joseph and Aseneth* (cf. 305n89, 314–15, 366, 387, 392, 394, etc.).

69 Tony Ryan Jackson, "The Historical and Social Setting of New Creation in Paul's Letters," Ph.D. dissertation, University of Cambridge, 2009, 2–3; cf. 81, 169, *et passim*. As well as showing well how Paul's new creation language implies both anthropological and cosmological dimensions, Jackson's particular and novel contribution is to illuminate this Pauline vision by placing it alongside Roman imperial ideology, with its depiction of a renewal of creation inaugurated by Augustus (see esp. 57–79).

70 Cf. Mell, *Neue Schöpfung*, 365.

71 Mell, *Neue Schöpfung*, 366.

72 Cf. Rudolf Bultmann, "Das Problem der Ethik bei Paulus," *ZNW* 23 (1924): 135–36; English trans. in Rudolf Bultmann, "The Problem of Ethics in Paul," in *Understanding Paul's Ethics: Twentieth-Century Approaches*, ed. Brian S. Rosner (Grand Rapids: Eerdmans, 1995), 211–12. Hubbard seems to distinguish too strongly the "already" transformed experience of the believer from the "not yet" of the creation: he suggests, e.g., in refer-

ence to Romans 8:18-23, that the believer groans because of the already whereas the creation groans because of the not yet (*New Creation*, 224–25). On the contrary, the groaning and suffering of believers seems also to reflect the "not yet."

73   See further van Kooten, *Cosmic Christology*, 156–58, 168–71.

74   Some miniscules (including 33) read τὰ πάντα καινά here, while D² K L P Ψ and a few miniscules read καινά τὰ πάντα. The shorter reading is supported by P⁴⁶ ℵ B C D* F G 048 0243 and some miniscules (including 1739). The longer reading is likely influenced by the opening of v. 18, and the shorter reading is probably to be preferred, though homoeoteleuton could explain why πάντα was accidentally omitted. Cf. Bruce M. Metzger, *A Textual Commentary on the Greek New Testament* (2nd. ed., New York: United Bible Societies, 1994), 511.

75   Krister Stendahl, "The Apostle Paul and the Introspective Conscience of the West," HTR 56 (1963): 199–215; repr. in Stendahl, *Paul among Jews and Gentiles*, 78–96. Stendahl's point was that Paul had been interpreted through the lens of "the introspective conscience of the West," as if he were concerned with the fate of the guilty individual, whereas Paul, possessed of a robust conscience (Phil 3:6), was concerned with the salvation of Gentiles and Jews, and the basis on which God had made this possible.

76   As Ralph Martin sagely comments, "we must be careful not to reduce the phrase to 'new creature' . . . Paul is not describing *in this context* the personal dimension of a new birth; rather he is announcing as a kerygmatic statement *the advent of the new creation 'in Christ*,' the dramatic recovery of the world, formerly alienated and dislocated, by God who has acted eschatologically in Christ, i.e. the world is placed now under his rule" ("Reconciliation and Forgiveness in the Letter to the Colossians," in Banks, *Reconciliation and Hope*, 104). Cf. also Adams, *Constructing*, who suggests that καινὴ κτίσις refers "to the new eschatological world" (227) or "to the new or renewed created order" (235), even if Paul's focus (in both Galatians and 2 Corinthians) is on the believer and the ecclesial community.

77   See esp. Jackson, "The Historical and Social Setting."

78   C. K. Barrett, *A Commentary on the Second Epistle to the Corinthians*, BNTC (London: A&C Black, 1973), 175, quoted in Martin, "Reconciliation and Forgiveness," 104. Again Martin, "Reconciliation and Forgiveness," 104, offers a useful corrective: "The flow of Paul's thought suggests the opposite. It is God's work 'outside of us' (*extra nos*), objectively viewed and independent of human application that Paul has recited . . ." One should note, however, Barrett's comments on verse 16, which indicate a wider perspective: "To know one's environment in a new way, and to be newly related to God through justification, is to live in a new world; a new set of relationships has come into being" (174).

79 Deissmann, *Paul*, 140.

80 Paul never uses the term Χριστιανός, but "in-Christ" is functionally equivalent.

81 See further Horrell, *Solidarity*, 99–132. For a distinctive argument that Paul's main vision is of all humanity incorporated into One, see Boyarin, *Radical Jew*.

82 Willard M. Swartley, *Covenant of Peace: The Missing Peace in New Testament Theology and Ethics* (Grand Rapids: Eerdmans, 2006), 190.

83 See Swartley, *Covenant of Peace*, 190–91 with note 3; Rom 15:33, 16:20; Phil 4:9; 1 Thess 5:23. Swartley argues, e.g., that since God is God of peace we "can expect that this character description of God will be refracted in the whole of Paul's ethics. And so it is . . ." (211).

84 The noun εἰρηνοποιός does not occur at all in the Pauline corpus, and in the NT only in Matthew 5:9. For parallels to this idea, see §5.3 above.

85 Swartley, *Covenant of Peace*, 192.

86 Cf. Sanders, *Paul and Palestinian*, 474, quoted above.

87 Sanders, *Paul and Palestinian*, 446, 444, and 446, respectively (emphasis in original).

88 On Philippians 2.6-11 as a text that encapsulates "Paul's Master Story," see Gorman, *Cruciformity*, 88–92; Gorman, *Inhabiting*, 9–39.

89 Markus N. A. Bockmuehl, *The Epistle to the Philippians*, BNTC (London: A&C Black, 1998), 115.

90 See Horrell, *Solidarity*, 206–14. Paul sometimes mediates this appeal through himself as someone who imitates Christ and may function as an exemplar (e.g., 1 Cor 4:16, 11:1; Phil 3:17).

91 For a comparable stress on kenosis here, see Gorman, *Inhabiting*, esp. 31–36.

92 Victor Paul Furnish, *Theology and Ethics in Paul* (Nashville: Abingdon, 1968), 214.

93 Helmut Thielicke, *Theological Ethics*, vol. 1, *Foundations*, abridged and translated ed., trans. William H. Lazareth (Grand Rapids: Eerdmans, 1966), 47.

94 Dunn, *Theology of Paul*, 466, notes a "consensus of usage."

95 Cf. Miroslav Volf, *Exclusion and Embrace: A Theological Exploration of Identity, Otherness, and Reconciliation* (Nashville: Abingdon, 1996), 110.

96 Allen Verhey, *The Great Reversal: Ethics and the New Testament* (Grand Rapids: Eerdmans, 1984), 107–8.

97 Horrell, *Solidarity*.

98 Frances Young and David F. Ford speak of God's glory as "the dynamic of transformation in Christian life . . . intrinsically social, to be participated in through a community of those who reflect it together" (*Meaning and Truth in 2 Corinthians* [London: SPCK, 1987], 259).

99   Von Balthasar, *Glory of the Lord,* 7:409.
100 See Newman, *Paul's Glory-Christology,* esp. 227–28.
101 Von Balthasar, *Glory of the Lord,* 7:472.
102 Von Balthasar, *Glory of the Lord,* 7:24.
103 For this understanding of the image of God in humans see Christopher Southgate, "Re-reading Genesis, John, and Job: A Christian's Response to Darwinism," paper presented at the fourth meeting of the International Society for Science and Religion, Robinson College, Cambridge, July 5, 2009. To be published in *Zygon: Journal of Religion and Science* (December 2010).
104 Southgate, *Groaning,* 61, 97–98. Cf. Volf, *Exclusion,* 13–31, exploring "The Cross, the Self, and the Other," including "the theme of divine self-donation for sinful humanity and human self-giving for one another" (24).
105 See von Balthasar, *Glory of the Lord,* 7:391–99.
106 Southgate, "Stewardship."
107 So strong and evident are the comic, romantic, and tragic elements in the Gospel accounts that it is worth just drawing attention to the ironic elements: the poor you have always with you (John 12:8), the limitation of Jesus' mission in the story of the Syro-Phoenician woman (Mark 7:26-27), the cry of dereliction, the moment at which Jesus seems as baffled as Job by the mystery of the ways of the Father (Mark 15:33).
108 Cf. Horrell, *Solidarity.*
109 For the concept of *enosis,* "a mysterious but intimate uniting of divine personhood and finite personhood, so that finite lives can become true images of the divine nature and mediators of divine power," see Keith Ward, "Cosmos and Kenosis," in *The Work of Love: Creation as Kenosis,* ed. John Polkinghorne (Grand Rapids: Eerdmans, 2001), 152–66, esp. 164. Ward associates the movement of *enosis* particularly with Galatians 2:20: "It is no longer I who live, but Christ who lives in me."
110 For a recent treatment of Paul that also draws on the language of theosis, a term used in the Eastern Orthodox tradition but largely absent from recent Western theology, see Gorman, *Inhabiting.* For Gorman, "*[k]enosis is theosis.* To be like Christ crucified is to be both most godly and most human. Christification is divinization, and divinization is humanization" (37).
111 Frye, *Anatomy,* 171.
112 White, "Historical Roots," 1205.
113 White, "Historical Roots," 1207.
114 White, "Historical Roots," 1207.
115 Hopewell, *Congregation,* 58.
116 White, "Historical Roots," 1207. However, doubt has been cast on the extent to which Francis, or early Franciscans, can really be annexed as early ecotheologians. See Wes Jackson, *Becoming Native to This Place* (New

York: Counterpoint, 1994), quoted in Jenkins, *Ecologies of Grace*, 266n52, on the "domestication" (rather than the liberation to full flourishing) of the wolf of Gubbio. See also Nesliha Şenocak, "The Franciscan Order and Natural Philosophy in the Thirteenth Century: A Relationship Redefined," *Ecotheology* 7 (2003): 113–25.

117 Rosemary Radford Ruether, *Gaia and God: An Ecofeminist Theology of Earth Healing* (London: SCM Press, 1992), 143–72.

118 Ruether, *Gaia and God*, 253.

119 Willis Jenkins notes the surprisingly strong vein of salvific metaphor in a thinker such as Ruether, who can talk of "redeeming our sister, the earth, from the bondage of destruction" (Jenkins, *Ecologies of Grace*, 102–3, with quotation from 102).

120 Jenkins, *Ecologies of Grace*, 77–92.

121 There are interesting comparisons to be made between Beisner's approach (Beisner, *Where Garden*) and that presented in our analysis. In both analyses, creation is "groaning" and human activity is taken to be capable of at least playing some part in transforming it. The key differences are, first of all, that in our approach there is no appeal to an ideal prelapsarian state, or human role, to which humans might aspire to return, and secondly that we emphasize an ethically kenotic other-regard (see above and chap. 8), whereas Beisner's emphasis is on creation as serving the needs and aspirations of humanity.

122 See Osborn, *Guardians*, 143, on stewardship as preservation; also Southgate, "Stewardship." In Loren Wilkinson et al., *Earthkeeping in the Nineties: Stewardship of Creation* (rev. ed., Grand Rapids: Eerdmans, 1991), the authors talk of the calling of the shepherd to "maintain the flock" (292), and note that the "commons" face despoiling, if they are not already spoiled. Perhaps, therefore, the call to stewardship of the "commons translates to the establishing of governing bodies, capable of restricting the use of the commons" (323).

123 Jim Cheney writes, "Which do we want: a world governed by a God who either treats us like infants or is constrained to act with an inhuman ruthlessness toward our suffering, *or* a world well suited, by and large, to human flourishing, a basically nurturing world that says, in effect, have at it, you are in a world that has brought your species into existence, a world to which the human species has been finely tuned by the forces of evolution? It is a world which will kill you one way or another; it is a world that, given your particular circumstances in life, may leave you one of the wretched of the Earth through no fault of your own: you may not even get a start down the road . . . The earth matrix doesn't care *about* you, but it cares *for* you in the most fundamental way: it is a nourishing matrix for you and your kind—with a little luck on your side that is, and

if your human culture is favourable" ("Naturalizing the Problem of Evil," *Environmental Ethics* 19 [1997]: 312; emphasis in original). This is a fine example of an ironic narrative, outdoing even the writer of Qoheleth in its fidelity to the genre.

124 Wesley J. Wildman, "Incongruous Goodness, Perilous Beauty, Disconcerting Truth: Ultimate Reality and Suffering in Nature," in *Physics and Cosmology: Scientific Perspectives on the Problem of Evil in Nature*, ed. Nancey Murphy et al. (Berkeley: CTNS, 2007), 267–94, has proposed a position that he calls "ground-of-being theism." Wildman's God is the ground of being, whose nature is glimpsable in the beauty but also in the violence of the cosmos. His God is not a determinate entity in all or indeed most respects. Wildman writes, "Cursed to wander in search of secrets, then, let us not waste energy on defending the universe or its divine heart" (267). His type of theism is "an awkward partner for common human moral expectations but deeply attuned to the ways of nature and resonant with the wisdom about suffering that is encoded in many of the world's religious and philosophical traditions" (268). Wildman presses the question, "can this be called a worship-worthy God?" and claims that plausibility is more important than religious appeal. His God is "beautiful from a distance in the way that a rain forest is beautiful" (293). Suffering in nature is "neither evil nor a byproduct of the good. It is part of the wellspring of divine creativity in nature, flowing up and out of the abysmal divine depths like molten rock from the yawning mouth of a volcano" (294).

125 Though see Habel and Wurst, *Wisdom Traditions*, for essays by Habel, Dale Patrick, and Isak Spangenberg dealing with this passage.

126 This is not the only significance of the passage; it might be said that Job's search for the meaning behind his suffering is consummated by an encounter with the divine, an encounter which only such suffering, and such resolute protest, made possible. But viewed in terms of humans' relation to, and role in respect of, the nonhuman creation, Job's inquiry is turned aside in distinctly ironic terms. Any conviction that humans' knowledge and ability offers them a role in improving or healing nature, or sharing in its transformation, is doomed to meaninglessness and futility.

127 So Robert Alter, *The Art of Biblical Poetry* (New York: Basic Books, 1985), 102, commenting on this passage: "The animal realm is a nonmoral realm, but the sharp paradoxes it embodies make us see the inadequacy of any merely human moral calculus . . . In the animal kingdom, the tender care for one's young may well mean their gulping the blood of freshly slain creatures. It is a daily rite of sustaining life that defies all moralizing anthropomorphic interpretation . . . And yet . . . God's providence looks after each of these strange, fierce, inaccessible creatures. There is an underlying continuity between this representation of the animal world and

the picture of inanimate nature in 38.2-38, with its sense of terrific power abiding in the natural world, fructification and destruction as alternative aspects of the same, imponderable forces."

128 Bill McKibben, *The Comforting Whirlwind: God, Job, and the Scale of Creation* (Grand Rapids: Eerdmans, 1994), 35.

129 McKibben, *Comforting Whirlwind*, 55.

130 McKibben, *Comforting Whirlwind*, 57.

131 McKibben, *Comforting Whirlwind*, 36.

132 Alan Weisman, *The World without Us* (London: Virgin Books, 2007). Interestingly, McKibben's is the name endorsing this book on its front cover.

133 McKibben, *Comforting Whirlwind*, 51, describes stewardship as "so lacking in content as to give us very little guidance about how to behave in any given situation."

134 McKibben, *Comforting Whirlwind*, 88.

135 There is a hint here that renunciation can prepare the way for receptiveness, in a way related to the analysis we give above of the centrality of kenosis. Where our scheme differs is as to where, working from our chosen key texts, we find ourselves placed in the story: not in a novel without any conclusion, but in the already-but-not-yet of the Pauline eschaton.

136 Palmer, "Stewardship," 70.

137 William P. Brown, *The Ethos of the Cosmos: The Genesis of Moral Imagination in the Bible* (Grand Rapids: Eerdmans, 1999), 375.

138 Lisa Sideris, "Writing Straight with Crooked Lines: Holmes Rolston's Ecological Theology and Theodicy," in *Nature, Value, Duty: Life on Earth with Holmes Rolston, III*, ed. Christopher J. Preston and Wayne Ouderkirk (Dordrecht: Springer, 2007), 77–101.

139 Note that this is not, as in the Colossian hymn, a narrative in which a past sacrifice leads to a new state of reconciliation. Rather the sacrifice is continual, there is no relief of creation's groaning. Rolston also invokes Romans 8:22: "'Groaning in travail' is in the nature of things from time immemorial. Such travail is the Creator's will, productive as it is of glory" ("Naturalizing," 85). We should not then, in Rolston's view, desire relief from this groaning and cruciform state of creation, because the groaning is productive of glory. Southgate and Robinson describe this emphasis on sacrifice and tragedy in Rolston's work as the "constitutive" element in Rolston's theodicy (Christopher Southgate and Andrew Robinson, "Varieties of Theodicy: An Exploration of Responses to the Problem of Evil based on a Typology of Good-Harm Analyses," in *Physics and Cosmology: Scientific Perspectives on the Problem of Evil in Nature*, ed. Nancey Murphy, Robert J. Russell, and William Stoeger SJ [Berkeley: CTNS, 2007], 69–90). See also Southgate, *Groaning*, 40–54.

140 Denis Edwards, *The God of Evolution: A Trinitarian Theology* (Mahwah, N.J.: Paulist Press, 1999), 36–39; Edwards, "Every Sparrow."

141 It is interesting to reflect on which virtues different narrative genres particularly commend. It seems to us that comic and romantic genres suggest the primacy of hope and faithful resolve, whereas tragedy would commend sacrifice, and irony endurance. All of these are key New Testament virtues, but our comic-romantic narrative implies that hope and faith will be the primary virtues, along with the love that does not grasp at status or insist on its own way (Phil 2:7; 1 Cor 13:5).

142 See Morwenna Ludlow, "Power and Dominion: Patristic Interpretations of Genesis 1," in Horrell, Hunt, Southgate, and Stavrakopoulou, *Ecological Hermeneutics*, 140–53.

Chapter 8

1 For an overview of research, and more detailed consideration of the various proposals briefly indicated here, see Horrell, *Solidarity*, 7–46.

2 Hans Hübner, "Paulusforschung seit 1945. Ein kritischer Literaturbericht," *ANRW* II.25 (1987): 2649–2840, 2802.

3 E.g., Peter J. Tomson, *Paul and the Jewish Law: Halakha in the Letters of the Apostle to the Gentiles* (Minneapolis: Fortress, 1990); Brian S. Rosner, *Paul, Scripture, and Ethics: A Study of 1 Corinthians 5–7* (Leiden: Brill, 1994); Karin Finsterbusch, *Die Thora als Lebensweisung für Heidenchristen*, SUNT 20 (Göttingen: Vandenhoeck & Ruprecht, 1996); Markus N. A. Bockmuehl, *Jewish Law in Gentile Churches* (Edinburgh: T&T Clark, 2000).

4 E.g., Abraham J. Malherbe, *Paul and the Thessalonians: The Philosophic Tradition of Pastoral Care* (Philadelphia: Fortress, 1987); Will Deming, *Paul on Marriage and Celibacy: The Hellenistic Background of 1 Corinthians 7*, SNTSMS 83 (Cambridge: Cambridge University Press, 1995); F. Gerald Downing, *Cynics, Paul, and the Pauline Churches* (New York: Routledge, 1998); Troels Engberg-Pedersen, *Paul and the Stoics* (Edinburgh: T&T Clark, 2000).

5 Cf. §5.3 above, on the background(s) to the Colossian hymn.

6 Alfred Resch, *Der Paulinismus und die Logia Jesu in ihrem gegenseitigen Verhältnis*, TU 12 (Leipzig: Hinrichs, 1904); Davies, *Paul and Rabbinic Judaism*; David Wenham, *Paul: Follower of Jesus or Founder of Christianity?* (Grand Rapids: Eerdmans, 1995), 377.

7 See further Victor Paul Furnish, *Jesus according to Paul* (Cambridge: Cambridge University Press, 1993); Horrell, *Solidarity*, 24–27, with additional references there.

8 See esp. the classic and still important studies of Bultmann, "Ethik bei Paulus"; and Furnish, *Theology and Ethics*.

9 See, e.g., Udo Schnelle, *Apostle Paul: His Life and Theology*, trans. M.

Eugene Boring (2003; English version, Grand Rapids: Baker Academic, 2005), 546–48; Ruben Zimmermann, "Jenseits von Indikativ und Imperativ. Entwurf einer 'impliziten Ethik' des Paulus am Beispiel des 1. Korintherbriefes," *TLZ* 132 (2007): 259–84; David G. Horrell, "Particular Identity and Common Ethics: Reflections on the Foundations and Content of Pauline Ethics in 1 Corinthians 5," in *Jenseits von Indikativ und Imperativ: Kontexte und Normen neutestamentlicher Ethik/Contexts and Norms of New Testament Ethics*, ed. Friedrich Wilhelm Horn and Ruben Zimmermann, WUNT 2.238 (Tübingen: Mohr Siebeck, 2009), 197–212.

10   Cf. J. Paul Sampley, *Walking between the Times: Paul's Moral Reasoning* (Minneapolis: Fortress, 1991).

11   Wolfgang Schrage, *The Ethics of the New Testament*, trans. David E. Green (1982; repr., Edinburgh: T&T Clark, 1988), 181; Richard B. Hays, *The Moral Vision of the New Testament* (Edinburgh: T&T Clark, 1997), 46.

12   Hays, *Moral Vision*, 41. Cf. more recently, Richard A. Burridge, *Imitating Jesus: An Inclusive Approach to New Testament Ethics* (Grand Rapids: Eerdmans, 2007), 83–90.

13   Horrell, *Solidarity*, 274 (emphasis in original).

14   See Horrell, *Solidarity*, 99–132.

15   See Horrell, *Solidarity*, 204–45.

16   Volf, *Exclusion*, 109–10 (emphasis in original). This has echoes of Bonhoeffer's insistence that Christian ethics has to operate in the realm of the "penultimate." See Dietrich Bonhoeffer, *Ethics*, ed. Eberhard Bethge, trans. Neville Horton Smith (London: Collins, 1964), 125–43.

17   Cf. Bauckham, "Where is Wisdom?" 136–38.

18   Furnish, *Theology and Ethics*, 233.

19   See Horrell, *Solidarity*, 214–22, for an example.

20   In the following paragraphs we draw on parts of Cherryl Hunt, "Beyond Anthropocentrism: Towards a Re-reading of Pauline Ethics," *Theology* 112 (2009): 190–98.

21   On this topic, see Brian S. Rosner, *Greed as Idolatry: The Origin and Meaning of a Pauline Metaphor* (Grand Rapids: Eerdmans, 2007).

22   See Horrell, *Solidarity*, 246–72; also Victor Paul Furnish, "Uncommon Love and the Common Good: Christians as Citizens in the Letters of Paul," in *In Search of the Common Good*, ed. Dennis P. McCann and Patrick D. Miller (New York: T&T Clark, 2005), 58–87.

23   See, e.g., Paula Clifford, *"All Creation Groaning": A Theological Approach to Climate Change and Development* (London: Christian Aid, 2007).

24   As does St. Francis, in *The Canticle of the Creatures*, a text, interestingly, selected as the frontpiece in *The Green Bible*.

25   When considering conflicts of interest in human-otherkind interactions, we find apt Stephen Clark's comment that resolution "must be left to concrete occasions and to careful agents, rather than being settled with a flourish of

high principles" (*How to Think about the Earth* [London: Mowbray, 1993]; quoted in Conradie, *Ecological Christian Anthropology*, 126).

26 What follows is drawn closely from the analysis in Southgate, *Groaning*, 101–3; by permission of Westminster John Knox Press. Cf. Andrew Linzey, *Animal Theology* (London: SCM Press, 1994), 45–61, who sees humans as "the servant species" and argues that "human uniqueness can be defined as the capacity for service and self-sacrifice" (45).

27 Sarah Coakley, "Theological Meanings and Gender Connotations," in *The Work of Love: Creation as Kenosis*, ed. John Polkinghorne (Grand Rapids: Eerdmans, 2001), 192–210.

28 Coakley, "Theological Meanings," 208 (emphasis in original).

29 Cf. Horrell, *Solidarity*, 243. In this respect, 1 Peter 2:18–3:6 is a more problematic text, the difficulties of which are sharply exposed by Corley, "1 Peter."

30 Gerard Manley Hopkins' translation of ἁρπαγμός in Philippians 2:6; see Christopher Devlin, ed., *The Sermons and Devotional Writings of Gerard Manley Hopkins* (London: Oxford University Press, 1959), 108.

31 There is much debate over whether ἁρπαγμός should be taken to indicate a grasping for a status which was not previously possessed or a clinging to a status which was already in possession. For a strong argument for the latter see Wright, *Climax*, 56–98. John Reumann, *Philippians: A New Translation with Introduction and Commentary*, AB 33B (New Haven: Yale University Press, 2008), translates ἁρπαγμός as "something of which to take advantage" (333); see his discussion on 345–47.

32 Cf. Dunn, *Theology of Paul*, 112. Also Byrne, "Creation Groaning," on "the sin story."

33 Cf. Rosner, *Greed*, on the connections between (over)indulgence of appetite and idolatry in Paul.

34 We avoid the term "resources" here as that carries the implication that the good things of the world are defined by their availability for use by human beings.

35 Cf. Burridge, *Imitating Jesus*, for whom the central demand of NT ethics is the imitation of Jesus' inclusive, generous, loving practice.

36 Though the thrust of his teaching on marriage indicates an eschatologically driven preference for singleness (7:7-9, 28-34).

37 Cf. Gordon D. Fee, *The First Epistle to the Corinthians*, NICNT (Grand Rapids: Eerdmans, 1987), 340 with nn. 17–18, and further references there.

38 Bultmann, *Theology*, 351 (emphasis in original).

39 Fee, *First Corinthians*, 340–41. Cf. that fine saying of F. F. Bruce's, "A truly emancipated spirit such as Paul's is not in bondage to its own emancipation," quoted in Richard Alan Young, *Is God a Vegetarian? Christianity, Vegetarianism, and Animal Rights* (Chicago: Open Court, 1999), 124.

40   For brief comments on the value of such asceticism, see David G. Horrell, "Biblical Vegetarianism? A Critical and Constructive Assessment," in *Eating and Believing: Interdisciplinary Perspectives on Vegetarianism and Theology*, ed. Rachel Muers and David Grumett (New York: T&T Clark, 2008), 50–51. More broadly, see Leif E. Vaage and Vincent L. Wimbush, eds., *Asceticism and the New Testament* (New York: Routledge, 1999).

41   Such approaches are described, not uncritically, by Rosemary Radford Ruether, *Sexism and God-Talk: Towards a Feminist Theology* (London: SCM Press, 1983), 235–57; quotation from 245.

42   See esp. Bultmann, "New Testament," 1–43.

43   Kathryn Tanner, "Eschatology without a Future?" in *The End of the World and the Ends of God*, ed. John Polkinghorne and Michael Welker (Harrisburg: Trinity, 2000), 222–37; Tanner, "Eschatology and Ethics." For critical discussion of Tanner's work, see also Stephen C. Barton, "New Testament Eschatology and the Ecological Crisis in Theological and Ecclesial Perspective," in Horrell, Hunt, Southgate, and Stavrakopoulou, *Ecological Hermeneutics*, 266–82.

44   "Naturalism is now associated more with fatalism than with confidence in the powers of human achievement: death, transience, and failure seem simply the irremediable stuff of life. Things will ultimately come to a bad end of cosmic proportions if the physicists are right: dissipation or conflagration is our universe's sorry future" (Tanner, "Eschatology and Ethics," 46). Therefore for Tanner "eschatology does not refer to what happens at the end . . . the eschaton—consummation in the good—has to do primarily with a new level of relationship with God" (47–48). It is not clear how her eschatology involves the nonhuman creation in any way.

45   Ted Peters, *Playing God: Genetic Determinism and Human Freedom* (New York: Routledge, 1997), 174. Cf. the quotation from Volf, above n. 16.

46   Volf, *Exclusion*, 109–10.

47   Linzey, *Animal Theology*, 125–37.

48   Linzey, *Animal Theology*, 55.

49   Linzey, *Animal Theology*, 130. For comments on earlier appeals to such texts, see Samantha Jane Calvert, "'Ours Is the Food That Eden Knew': Themes in the Theology and Practice of Modern Christian Vegetarians," in *Eating and Believing: Interdisciplinary Perspectives on Vegetarianism and Theology*, ed. Rachel Muers and David Grumett (New York: T&T Clark, 2008), 124–26. Similar arguments to those of Linzey are also made by Webb, *Good Eating*, 59–81.

50   Linzey, *Animal Theology*, 132.

51   Linzey, *Animal Theology*, 132, 134. For a similar attempt to grapple with the evidence regarding Jesus' diet in the context of an argument for "biblical vegetarianism," see Webb, *Good Eating*, 102–40. For a critique

of these and other appeals to Jesus in this regard, see Horrell, "Biblical Vegetarianism?" 46–49.

52   Linzey, *Animal Theology*, 137.

53   Our points here draw on the more extensive treatments in Southgate, *Groaning*, 116–24; Christopher Southgate, "Protological and Eschatological Vegetarianism," in *Eating and Believing: Interdisciplinary Perspectives on Vegetarianism and Theology*, ed. Rachel Muers and David Grumett (New York: T&T Clark, 2008), 247–65; and Horrell, "Biblical Vegetarianism?"

54   Linzey, *Animal Theology*, 84–85, 98–99.

55   Southgate, "Protological," 249. See further Southgate, *Groaning*, esp. 28–35.

56   Southgate, "Protological," 259–60; Southgate, *Groaning*, 122–24, for brief indications of these.

57   Southgate, *Groaning*, 119–22. Stephen Budiansky, *The Covenant of the Wild: Why Animals Chose Domestication* (London: Phoenix, 1997), points out the symbiotic nature of domestication and the dependence on humans of domesticated species.

58   For this depiction, see also Webb, *Good Eating*, 78–81.

59   Southgate, *Groaning*, 121.

60   See Michael Pollan, *The Omnivore's Dilemma* (London: Bloomsbury, 2006), 304–33.

61   Karl Barth, *Church Dogmatics III.4: The Doctrine of Creation*, trans. A. T. Mackay et al. (Edinburgh: T&T Clark, 1961), 355.

62   Pollan, *Omnivore's Dilemma*, 333.

63   Southgate, *Groaning*, 95.

64   Moltmann, *Way of Jesus Christ*, 296–97.

65   Holmes Rolston III, *Environmental Ethics: Duties to and Values in the Natural World* (Philadelphia: Temple University Press, 1988), 154.

66   J. Louis Martyn, "Epistemology at the Turn of the Ages," in *Theological Issues in the Letters of Paul* (Edinburgh: T&T Clark, 1997), 95.

67   Thomas Berry, *The Dream of the Earth* (San Francisco: Sierra Club, 1988), 9; quoted in Sean McDonagh, *The Death of Life: The Horror of Extinction* (Blackrock, Colo.: Columba, 2004), 85.

68   Jenkins, *Ecologies of Grace*, 230.

69   Cf. further Martin, *Corinthian Body*, 94–96; Horrell, *Solidarity*, 121–24.

70   Anne Primavesi, *Gaia's Gift: Earth, Ourselves, and God after Copernicus* (New York: Routledge, 2003).

71   Here we are necessarily thinking primarily of relationships involving humans—predator and prey of course establish relationships of mutual dependence, but not ones characterized by reconciliation, at least as we normally understand it.

72   Sigurd Bergmann, "Atmospheres of Synergy: Towards an Eco-theological

Aesth/Ethics," *Ecotheology* 11 (2006): 326–56, and references to his earlier work therein.

73 For an example of this type of understanding see, e.g., the work of Alexander Schmemann, such as *The World as Sacrament* (1965; repr., London: Darton, Longman, & Todd, 1966).

74 "A thing is right where it tends to preserve the integrity, stability and beauty of a biotic community. It is wrong when it tends otherwise" (Aldo Leopold, *A Sand County Almanac: With Essays on Conservation from Round River* [1949; repr., Oxford: Oxford University Press, 1966], 262).

75 Celia Deane-Drummond, *The Ethics of Nature* (Oxford: Blackwell, 2004), 32–34.

76 Cf. Tom Regan, *The Case for Animal Rights* (London: Routledge, 1988). For an analysis and critique of Regan, see Lisa Kemmerer, *In Search of Consistency: Ethics and Animals* (Leiden: Brill, 2006), 59–102.

77 Lovelock, *Ages of Gaia*, 143–45.

78 Cf. Primavesi, *Gaia's Gift*. It is this kind of conviction that underpins the Earth Bible's ecojustice principle of "mutual custodianship," an alternative to the more unidirectional and arguably patronizing notion of "stewardship." See above §§1.3, 2.1.

79 What follows is closely based on the argument in Christopher Southgate, "The New Days of Noah? Assisted Migration as an Ethical Imperative in an Era of Climate Change," in *Creaturely Theology*, ed. Celia Deane-Drummond and David Clough (London: SCM Press, 2009), 249–65; see also Christopher Southgate, Cherryl Hunt, and David G. Horrell, "Ascesis and Assisted Migration: Responses to the Effects of Climate Change on Animal Species," *Eur J Sci Theol* 4.2 (2008): 99–111.

80 See Horrell, *Solidarity*, 231–41.

81 On this commitment to the poor as a "centripetal" force in earliest Christianity, rooted in the ministry of Jesus and in the Jewish Torah, see Fern K. T. Clarke, "God's Concern for the Poor in the New Testament: A Discussion of the Role of the Poor in the Foundation of Christian Belief (Early to Mid First Century C.E.)," Ph.D. dissertation, University of Exeter, 2000.

82 Lev 19; Deut 10:17-18, 14:28-29, 24:14-22; 2 Sam 22:28; Job 5:15; Pss 9:12, 10:12, 34:6, 107:41, 132:15; Isa 25:4, 49:13; Amos 2:6, 4:1, etc.

83 Though material deprivation does seem to have been Paul's central concern in respect of the Jerusalem collection.

84 Particularly important in the Christian tradition is Matthew 25:34-46 where the hungry, the thirsty, the stranger, the naked, and those in prison are all those who are close to Christ in their need. See Bruce J. Malina, *The New Testament World: Insights from Cultural Anthropology, Third Edition*,

Revised and Expanded (Louisville, Ky.: Westminster John Knox, 2001), 99–100.

85 Southgate, Hunt, and Horrell, "Ascesis"; cf. also Southgate, "New Days."

86 Cf. Northcott, *Moral Climate*, 81–119.

87 E.g., Pacific islands such as Kiribati.

88 For ecotheologians invoking the Earth as "the new poor," see Fox, *Cosmic Christ*, 147; McFague, *Body of God*, 165. See also Northcott, *Moral Climate*, 42, advocating an "option for the poor," and Neil Messer's ethical criterion, "Is [a project] good news for the poor?" (Messer, *Selfish Genes*, 229–30).

89 Anthony J. McMichael, *Planetary Overload: Global Environmental Change and the Health of the Human Species* (Cambridge: Cambridge University Press, 1995), 307–9; also Herman E. Daly and John B. Cobb Jr., *For the Common Good* (1989; repr., Boston: Beacon, 1994).

90 Jason S. McLachlan, Jessica J. Hellmann, and Mark W. Schwartz, "A Framework for Debate of Assisted Migration in an Era of Climate Change," *Conserv Biol* 21 (2007): 297.

91 Pacala and Socolow suggest a series of "wedges" to be driven in to stabilize climate and halt the crisis, increasing combinations of which will have increasing effects (S. Pacala and R. Socolow, "Stabilization Wedges — Solving the Climate Problem for the Next 50 Years Using Current Technologies," *Science* 305 [2004]: 968–72; and comment in Mark Lynas, *Six Degrees: Our Future on a Hotter Planet* [London: Fourth Estate, 2007], 293–98).

92 Don E. Marietta Jr., *For People and the Planet: Holism and Humanism in Environmental Ethics* (Philadelphia: Temple University Press, 1994).

BIBLIOGRAPHY

Abbott-Smith, G. *A Manual Greek Lexicon of the New Testament.* Edinburgh: T&T Clark, 1936.

Adams, Edward. *Constructing the World: A Study in Paul's Cosmological Language.* Edinburgh: T&T Clark, 2000.

— — —. "Paul's Story of God and Creation." In Longenecker, *Narrative Dynamics in Paul,* 19–43.

— — —. "Retrieving the Earth from the Conflagration: 2 Peter 3.5-13 and the Environment." In Horrell, Hunt, Southgate, and Stavrakopoulou, *Ecological Hermeneutics,* 108–20.

— — —. *The Stars Will Fall From Heaven: Cosmic Catastrophe in the New Testament and its World.* Library of New Testament Studies 347. London: T&T Clark, 2007.

Alter, Robert. *The Art of Biblical Poetry.* New York: Basic Books, 1985.

Amery, Carl. *Das Ende der Vorsehung: Die Gnadenlosen Folgen des Christentums.* Hamburg: Rowohlt, 1972.

Ancil, Ralph E. "Environmental Problems: A Creationist Perspective Our Biblical Heritage [*sic*]." *Creation Social Science and Humanities Society Quarterly Journal* 6, no. 4 (1983): 5–9. http://www.creationism.org/csshs/v06n4p05 .htm (accessed May 14, 2006).

— — —. "Man and His Environment: The Creationist Perspective." *Creation Social Science and Humanities Society Quarterly Journal* 12, no. 4 (1989): 19–22. http://www.creationism.org/csshs/v12n4p19.htm (accessed August 5, 2009).

Anderson, Bernhard W. "Creation and Ecology." In *Creation in the Old Testament*, edited by Bernhard W. Anderson, 152–71. Philadelphia: Fortress, 1984.

————. *From Creation to New Creation: Old Testament Perspectives*. Minneapolis: Fortress, 1994.

Balabanski, Vicky. "Critiquing Anthropocentric Cosmology: Retrieving a Stoic 'Permeation Cosmology' in Colossians 1:15-20." In Habel and Trudinger, *Exploring Ecological Hermeneutics*, 151–59.

————. "Hellenistic Cosmology and the Letter to the Colossians: Towards an Ecological Hermeneutic." In Horrell, Hunt, Southgate, and Stavrakopoulou, *Ecological Hermeneutics*, 94–107.

Balz, Horst R. *Heilsvertrauen und Welterfahrung: Strukturen der paulinischen Eschatologie nach Römer 8, 18-39*. Beiträge zur evangelischen Theologie. Theologische Abhandlungen 59. Munich: Kaiser, 1971.

Baranzke, Heike, and Hedwig Lamberty-Zielinski. "Lynn White und das Dominium Terrae (Gen 1,28b). Ein Beitrag zu Einer Doppelten Wirkungsgeschichte." *Biblische Notizen* 76 (1995): 32–61.

Barbour, Ian. *Religion and Science: Historical and Contemporary Issues*. London: SCM Press, 1997.

Barclay, John M. G. *Colossians and Philemon*. New Testament Guides. Sheffield: Sheffield Academic Press, 1997.

————. "Paul's Story." In Longenecker, *Narrative Dynamics in Paul*, 133–56.

————. "Thessalonica and Corinth: Social Contrasts in Pauline Christianity." *Journal for the Study of the New Testament* 47 (1992): 49–74.

Barker, Margaret. *The Great High Priest: The Temple Roots of Christian Liturgy*. New York: T&T Clark, 2003.

Barr, James. "Man and Nature — The Ecological Controversy and the Old Testament." *Bulletin of the John Rylands University Library, Manchester* 55 (1972): 9–32.

Barrett, C. K. *A Commentary on the Epistle to the Romans*. Black's New Testament Commentaries. 1957. Revised edition, London: A&C Black, 1971.

————. *A Commentary on the First Epistle to the Corinthians*. Black's New Testament Commentaries. 1968. 2nd ed., London: A&C Black, 1971.

————. *A Commentary on the Second Epistle to the Corinthians*. Black's New Testament Commentaries. London: A&C Black, 1973.

————. *Essays on Paul*. London: SPCK, 1982.

————. *From First Adam to Last*. London: A&C Black, 1962.

Barth, Karl. *Church Dogmatics I.1: The Doctrine of the Word of God*. 2nd ed. Translated by G. W. Bromiley. Edinburgh: T&T Clark, 1975.

————. *Church Dogmatics III.3: The Doctrine of Creation*. 2nd ed. Translated by G. W. Bromiley and R. J. Ehrlich. Edinburgh: T&T Clark, 1960.

————. *Church Dogmatics III.4: The Doctrine of Creation*. 2nd ed. Translated by A. T. Mackay, T. H. L. Parker, H. Knight, H. A. Kennedy, and J. Marks. Edinburgh: T&T Clark, 1961.

— — —. *Church Dogmatics IV.2: The Doctrine of Reconciliation*, vol. 2. Translated by G. W. Bromiley. Edinburgh: T&T Clark, 1958.

Barth, Markus. "Christ and All Things." In *Paul and Paulinism: Essays in Honour of C. K. Barrett*, edited by M. D. Hooker and S. G. Wilson, 160–72. London: SPCK, 1982.

Barth, Markus, and Helmut Blanke. *Colossians: A New Translation with Introduction and Commentary*. Anchor Bible 34B. Translated by Astrid B. Beck. New York: Doubleday, 1994.

Barton, Stephen C. "New Testament Eschatology and the Ecological Crisis in Theological and Ecclesial Perspective." In Horrell, Hunt, Southgate, and Stavrakopoulou, *Ecological Hermeneutics*, 266–82.

Bassler, Jouette M., ed. *Pauline Theology*. Vol. 1, *Thessalonians, Philippians, Galatians, Philemon*. Minneapolis: Fortress, 1991.

— — —. "A Response to Jeffrey Bingham and Susan Graham: Networks and Noah's Sons." In *Early Patristic Readings of Romans*, edited by Kathy L. Gaca and L. L. Welborn, 133–51. Romans through History and Culture Series. New York: T&T Clark, 2005.

Bauckham, Richard. *Beyond Stewardship: The Bible and the Community of Creation*. 2006 Sarum Lectures. London: Darton, Longman, & Todd, forthcoming.

— — —. *God and the Crisis of Freedom: Biblical and Contemporary Perspectives*. Louisville, Ky.: Westminster John Knox, 2002.

— — —. "Joining Creation's Praise of God." *Ecotheology* 7 (2002): 45–59.

— — —. "Reading the Synoptic Gospels Ecologically." In Horrell, Hunt, Southgate, and Stavrakopoulou, *Ecological Hermeneutics*, 70–82.

— — —. "Where is Wisdom to be Found? Colossians 1.15-20 (2)." In *Reading Texts, Seeking Wisdom*, edited by David F. Ford and Graham Stanton, 129–38. London: SCM Press, 2003.

Beal Jr., R. S. "Can A Premillennialist Consistently Entertain a Concern for the Environment? A Rejoinder to Al Truesdale." *Perspectives on Science and Christian Faith* 46 (1994): 172–77.

Beasley-Murray, Paul. "Colossians 1:15-20: An Early Christian Hymn Celebrating the Lordship of Christ." In *Pauline Studies: Essays Presented to Professor F. F. Bruce on His 70th Birthday*, edited by Donald A. Hagner and Murray J. Harris, 169–83. Grand Rapids: Eerdmans, 1980.

Beisner, E. Calvin. *Where Garden Meets Wilderness: Evangelical Entry into the Environmental Debate*. Grand Rapids: Eerdmans, 1997.

Beker, J. Christiaan. *Heirs of Paul: Paul's Legacy in the New Testament and in the Church Today*. Edinburgh: T&T Clark, 1992.

— — —. *Paul the Apostle: The Triumph of God in Life and Thought*. Edinburgh: T&T Clark, 1980.

Bell, Richard H. "Rom 5.18-19 and Universal Salvation." *New Testament Studies* 48 (2002): 417–32.

Bennett, Gaymon, Martinez J. Hewlett, Ted Peters, and Robert J. Russell, eds. The Evolution of Evil. Göttingen: Vandenhoeck & Ruprecht, 2008.

Bergmann, Sigurd. "Atmospheres of Synergy: Towards an Eco-theological Aesth/Ethics." Ecotheology 11 (2006): 326–56.

Berry, R. J., ed. The Care of Creation. Leicester: InterVarsity, 2000.

— — —. Ecology & Ethics. London: InterVarsity, 1972.

— — —. God's Book of Works. The Nature and Theology of Nature. New York: T&T Clark, 2003.

Berry, Thomas. The Dream of the Earth. San Francisco: Sierra Club, 1988.

Best, E. One Body in Christ: A Study in the Relationship of the Church to Christ in the Epistles of the Apostle Paul. London: SPCK, 1955.

Bieringer, Reimund. "2 Kor 5,19a und die Versöhnung der Welt." Ephemerides Theologicae Lovanienses 63 (1987): 295–326.

Bindemann, Walther. Die Hoffnung der Schöpfung: Römer 8,18-27 und die Frage einer Theologie der Befreiung von Mensch und Natur. Neukirchen-Vluyn: Neukirchener Verlag, 1983.

Blackburn, Simon. The Oxford Dictionary of Philosophy. New York: Oxford University Press, 1994.

Blass, Friedrich Wilhelm, A. Debrunner, and Robert W. Funk. A Greek Grammar of the New Testament and Other Early Christian Literature. Chicago: University of Chicago Press, 1961.

Bockmuehl, Markus N. A. The Epistle to the Philippians. Black's New Testament Commentaries. London: A&C Black, 1998.

— — —. Jewish Law in Gentile Churches. Edinburgh: T&T Clark, 2000.

Bolt, John. "The Relation between Creation and Redemption in Romans 8:18-27." Calvin Theological Journal 30 (1995): 34–51.

Bonaventure. "The Tree of Life." In Bonaventure: The Soul's Journey into God; The Tree of Life; The Life of St. Francis, translated by Ewert Cousins, 117–75. London: SPCK, 1978.

Bonhoeffer, Dietrich. Ethics. Edited by Eberhard Bethge. Translated by Neville Horton Smith. London: Collins, 1964.

Booker, Christopher. Why We Tell Stories. New York: Continuum, 2004.

Bouma-Prediger, Steven. For the Beauty of the Earth: A Christian Vision for Creation Care. Grand Rapids: Baker Academic, 2001.

Bowker, John. The Targums and Rabbinic Literature: An Introduction to Jewish Interpretations of Scripture. Cambridge: Cambridge University Press, 1969.

Boyarin, Daniel. A Radical Jew: Paul and the Politics of Identity. Berkeley: University of California Press, 1994.

Boyer, Paul. When Time Shall Be No More: Prophecy Belief in Modern American Culture. Cambridge, Mass.: Belknap, 1992.

Braaten, Laurie J. "All Creation Groans: Romans 8:22 in Light of the Biblical Sources." Horizons in Biblical Theology 28 (2006): 131–59.

Bradley, Ian. *God Is Green: Christianity and the Environment.* London: Darton, Longman, & Todd, 1990.

Breytenbach, Cilliers. *Versöhnung: eine Studie zur paulinischen Soteriologie.* Wissenschaftliche Monographien zum Alten und Neuen Testament 60. Neukirchen-Vluyn: Neukirchener, 1989.

Brown, William P. *The Ethos of the Cosmos: The Genesis of Moral Imagination in the Bible.* Grand Rapids: Eerdmans, 1999.

Bruce, F. F. *The Epistles to the Colossians, to Philemon, and to the Ephesians.* Grand Rapids: Eerdmans, 1984.

Brueggemann, Walter. *Reverberations of Faith: A Theological Handbook of Old Testament Themes.* Louisville, Ky.: Westminster John Knox, 2002.

Budiansky, Stephen. *The Covenant of the Wild: Why Animals Chose Domestication.* London: Phoenix, 1997.

Bultmann, Rudolf. "New Testament and Mythology: The Problem of Demythologizing the New Testament Proclamation [1941]." In *New Testament and Mythology and Other Basic Writings,* edited by Schubert M. Ogden, 1–43. London: SCM Press, 1985.

— — —. "Das Problem der Ethik bei Paulus." *Zeitschrift für die neutestamentliche Wissenschaft* 23 (1924): 123–40.

— — —. "The Problem of Ethics in Paul." In *Understanding Paul's Ethics: Twentieth-Century Approaches,* edited by Brian S. Rosner, 195–216. Grand Rapids: Eerdmans, 1995.

— — —. *Theology of the New Testament,* vol. 1. Translated by Kendrick Grobel. London: SCM Press, 1952.

Burggraeve, Roger. "Responsibility for a 'New Heaven and a New Earth.'" *Concilium* 4 (1991): 107–18.

Burney, C. F. "Christ as the ΑΡΧΗ of Creation." *Journal of Theological Studies* 27 (1926): 160–77.

Burridge, Richard A. *Imitating Jesus: An Inclusive Approach to New Testament Ethics.* Grand Rapids: Eerdmans, 2007.

Byrne, Brendan. "Creation Groaning: An Earth Bible Reading of Romans 8.18-22." In Habel, *Readings,* 193–203.

— — —. "An Ecological Reading of Rom 8.19-22: Possibilities and Hesitations." In Horrell, Hunt, Southgate, and Stavrakopoulou, *Ecological Hermeneutics,* 83–93.

— — —. *Romans.* Sacra Pagina 6. Collegeville, Minn.: Liturgical Press, 1996.

Calvert, Samantha Jane. "'Ours Is the Food That Eden Knew': Themes in the Theology and Practice of Modern Christian Vegetarians." In *Eating and Believing: Interdisciplinary Perspectives on Vegetarianism and Theology,* edited by Rachel Muers and David Grumett, 123–34. New York: T&T Clark, 2008.

Campbell, Douglas A. *The Deliverance of God: An Apocalyptic Rereading of Justification in Paul.* Grand Rapids: Eerdmans, 2009.

————. *The Quest for Paul's Gospel: A Suggested Strategy.* Journal for the Study of the New Testament Supplement 274. New York: T&T Clark, 2005.

————. *The Rhetoric of Righteousness in Romans 3.21-26.* Journal for the Study of the New Testament Supplement 65. Sheffield: JSOT Press, 1992.

————. "Romans 1:17—A *Crux Interpretum* for the ΠΙΣΤΙΣ ΧΡΙΣΤΟΥ Debate." *Journal of Biblical Literature* 113 (1994): 265–86.

————. "The Story of Jesus in Romans and Galatians." In Longenecker, *Narrative Dynamics in Paul*, 97–124.

————. "Unravelling Colossians 3.11b." *New Testament Studies* 42 (1996): 120–32.

Campolo, Tony. *How to Rescue the Earth without Worshipping Nature: A Christian's Call to Save Creation.* Milton Keynes: Word, 1992.

Carley, Keith. "Psalm 8: An Apology for Domination." In Habel, *Readings*, 111–24.

Case, Shirley Jackson. *The Millennial Hope: A Phase of War-time Thinking.* Chicago: University of Chicago Press, 1918.

Chang, Hae-Kyung. *Die Knechtschaft und Befreiung der Schöpfung. Eine exegetische Untersuchung zu Römer 8,19-22.* Bibelwissenschaftliche Monographien 7. Wuppertal: Brockhaus, 2000.

Cheney, Jim. "Naturalizing the Problem of Evil." *Environmental Ethics* 19 (1997): 299–313.

Christoffersson, Olle. *The Earnest Expectation of the Creature: The Flood-Tradition as Matrix of Romans 8:18-27.* Stockholm: Almqvist & Wiksell, 1990.

Chryssavgis, John, ed. *Cosmic Grace, Humble Prayer: The Ecological Vision of the Green Patriarch Bartholomew I.* Grand Rapids: Eerdmans, 2003.

Clark, Stephen R. L. *How to Think about the Earth.* London: Mowbray, 1993.

Clarke, Fern K. T. "God's Concern for the Poor in the New Testament: A Discussion of the Role of the Poor in the Foundation of Christian Belief (Early to Mid First Century C.E.)." Ph.D. diss., University of Exeter, 2000.

Clifford, Paula. *"All Creation Groaning": A Theological Approach to Climate Change and Development.* London: Christian Aid, 2007.

Clough, David. *On Animals: Theology.* New York: T&T Clark, forthcoming.

Clouse, Robert G., ed. *The Meaning of the Millennium: Four Views.* Downers Grove, Ill.: InterVarsity, 1979.

Coakley, Sarah. "Theological Meanings and Gender Connotations." In *The Work of Love: Creation as Kenosis*, edited by John Polkinghorne, 192–210. Grand Rapids: Eerdmans, 2001.

Common Declaration on Environmental Ethics: Common Declaration of John Paul II and the Ecumenical Patriarch His Holiness Bartholomew I. (2002). http://www.vatican .va/holy_father/john_paul_ii/speeches/2002/june/documents/hf_jp-ii_sp e_20020610_venice-declaration_en.html (accessed August 4, 2009).

Conradie, Ernst M. *An Ecological Christian Anthropology: At Home on Earth?* Aldershot, Vt.: Ashgate, 2005.

— — —. "Interpreting the Bible amidst Ecological Degradation." *Theology* 112 (2009): 199–207.

— — —. "The Redemption of the Earth: In Search of Appropriate Soteriological Concepts in an Age of Ecological Destruction." Unpublished paper, Yale Divinity School, 2008.

— — —. "The Road towards an Ecological Biblical and Theological Hermeneutics." *Scriptura* 93 (2006): 305–14.

— — —. "Towards an Ecological Biblical Hermeneutics: A Review Essay on the Earth Bible Project." *Scriptura* 85 (2004): 123–35.

— — —. "What on Earth is an Ecological Hermeneutics? Some Broad Parameters." In Horrell, Hunt, Southgate, and Stavrakopoulou, *Ecological Hermeneutics*, 295–313.

Cooper, Tim. *Green Christianity: Caring for the Whole Creation.* London: Spire, 1990.

Corley, Kathleen E. "1 Peter." In *Searching the Scriptures*. Vol. 2, *A Feminist Commentary*, edited by Elisabeth Schüssler Fiorenza, 349–60. London: SCM Press, 1995.

Cranfield, Charles E. B. *A Critical and Exegetical Commentary on the Epistle to the Romans.* Vol. 1, *Romans I–VIII*. The International Critical Commentary. Edinburgh: T&T Clark, 1975.

— — —. "Some Observations on Romans 8:19-21." In *Reconciliation and Hope: New Testament Essays on Atonement and Eschatology presented to L. L. Morris on his 60th Birthday*, edited by Robert Banks, 224–30. Exeter: Paternoster, 1974.

Cumbey, Constance E. *The Hidden Dangers of the Rainbow: The New Age Movement and Our Coming Age of Barbarism.* Shreveport: Huntington House, 1983.

— — —. *A Planned Deception: The Staging of a New Age "Messiah."* East Detroit, Mich.: Pointe Publishers, 1985.

Daly, Herman E. and John B. Cobb Jr. *For the Common Good.* 1989. Reprint, Boston, Mass.: Beacon, 1994.

Daly, Mary. *Beyond God the Father: Toward a Philosophy of Women's Liberation.* London: Women's Press, 1986.

Davies, W. D. *Paul and Rabbinic Judaism: Some Rabbinic Elements in Pauline Theology.* 1948. 2nd edition, London: SPCK, 1955.

Deane-Drummond, Celia E. *Creation Through Wisdom.* Edinburgh: T&T Clark, 2000.

— — —. *The Ethics of Nature.* Oxford: Blackwell, 2004.

— — —. "Shadow Sophia in Christological Perspective: The Evolution of Sin and the Redemption of Nature." *Theology and Science* 6 (2008): 13–32.

Deissmann, Adolf. *Paul. A Study in Social and Religious History.* Translated by William E. Wilson. London: Hodder & Stoughton, 1926.

Deming, Will. *Paul on Marriage and Celibacy: The Hellenistic Background of 1 Corinthians*

7. Society for New Testament Studies Monograph 83. Cambridge: Cambridge University Press, 1995.

Devlin, Christopher, ed. *The Sermons and Devotional Writings of Gerard Manley Hopkins.* London: Oxford University Press, 1959.

Dodd, C. H. *The Epistle of Paul to the Romans.* Moffatt's New Testament Commentary. London: Houghton, 1932.

Domning, Daryl P. and Monika K. Hellwig. *Original Selfishness: Original Sin in the Light of Evolution.* Aldershot, Vt.: Ashgate, 2006.

Donelson, Lewis R. *Colossians, Ephesians, 1 and 2 Timothy, and Titus.* Westminster Bible Companion. Louisville, Ky.: Westminster John Knox, 1996.

Donfried, Karl P. *The Romans Debate.* Rev. ed. Edinburgh: T&T Clark, 1991.

Downing, F. Gerald. *Cynics, Paul and the Pauline Churches.* New York: Routledge, 1998.

———. "Review of Habel, Norman C. and Balabanski, Vicky (eds.), *The Earth Story in the New Testament.* The Earth Bible 5. London: Sheffield Academic Press, 2002." *Biblical Interpretation* 12 (2004): 311–13.

Drane, John W. *Paul: Libertine or Legalist? A Study in the Theology of the Major Pauline Epistles.* London: SPCK, 1975.

Dunn, James D. G. *Christology in the Making.* London: SCM Press, 1980.

———. *The Epistles to the Colossians and to Philemon.* New International Greek Testament Commentary. Grand Rapids: Eerdmans, 1996.

———. *The New Perspective on Paul: Collected Essays.* Wissenschaftliche Untersuchungen zum Neuen Testament 185. Tübingen: Mohr Siebeck, 2005.

———. "Once More, ΠΙΣΤΙΣ ΧΡΙΣΤΟΥ." In *Pauline Theology.* Vol. 4, *Looking Back, Pressing On,* edited by E. Elizabeth Johnson and David M. Hay, 61–81. Minneapolis: Fortress, 1997.

———. *Romans 1–8.* Word Biblical Commentary 38A. Dallas, Tex.: Word Books, 1988.

———. *Romans 9–16.* Word Biblical Commentary 38B. Dallas, Tex.: Word Books, 1988.

———. *The Theology of Paul the Apostle.* Edinburgh: T&T Clark, 1998.

Dyer, Keith D. "When Is the End Not the End? The Fate of Earth in Biblical Eschatology (Mark 13)." In Habel and Balabanski, *The Earth Story in the New Testament,* 44–56.

Dyrness, William. "Stewardship of the Earth in the Old Testament." In *Tending the Garden,* edited by Wesley Granberg-Michaelson, 50–65. Grand Rapids: Eerdmans, 1987.

Earth Bible Team, The. "Conversations with Gene Tucker and Other Writers." In Habel and Wurst, *The Earth Story in Genesis,* 21–33.

———. "Ecojustice Hermeneutics: Reflections and Challenges." In Habel and Balabanski, *The Earth Story in the New Testament,* 1–14.

———. "Guiding Ecojustice Principles." In Habel, *Readings,* 38–53.

Echlin, Edward P. *The Cosmic Circle: Jesus and Ecology*. Blackrock, Colo.: Columba, 2004.

Eckberg, Douglas Lee, and T. Jean Blocker. "Christianity, Environmentalism, and the Theoretical Problem of Fundamentalism." *Journal for the Scientific Study of Religion* 35 (1996): 343–55.

Edwards, Denis. "Every Sparrow that Falls to the Ground: The Cost of Evolution and the Christ-Event." *Ecotheology* 11 (2006): 103–23.

— — —. *The God of Evolution: A Trinitarian Theology*. Mahwah, N.J.: Paulist Press, 1999.

Edwards, Michael. *Towards a Christian Poetics*. London: Macmillan, 1984.

Elsdon, Ron. "Eschatology and Hope." In Berry, *Care*, 161–66.

Engberg-Pedersen, Troels. *Paul and the Stoics*. Edinburgh: T&T Clark, 2000.

Esler, Philip F. *Galatians*. New York: Routledge, 1998.

Fee, Gordon D. *The First Epistle to the Corinthians*. New International Commentary on the New Testament. Grand Rapids: Eerdmans, 1987.

— — —. *Pauline Christology: An Exegetical-Theological Study*. Peabody, Mass.: Hendrickson, 2007.

Ferretter, Luke. *Towards a Christian Literary Theory*. Basingstoke: Palgrave Macmillan, 2003.

Fiddes, Paul S. *Freedom and Limit: A Dialogue between Literature and Christian Doctrine*. Macon, Ga.: Mercer University Press, 1999.

Finger, Thomas. *Evangelicals, Eschatology, and the Environment*. The Scholars Circle 2. Wynnewood, Pa.: Evangelical Environmental Network, 1998.

Finsterbusch, Karin. *Die Thora als Lebensweisung für Heidenchristen*. Studien zur Umwelt des Neuen Testaments 20. Göttingen: Vandenhoeck & Ruprecht, 1996.

Fiorenza, Elisabeth Schüssler. *In Memory of Her*. London: SCM Press, 1983.

— — —. "Missionaries, Apostles, Co-workers: Romans 16 and the Reconstruction of Women's Early Christian History." *Word and World* 6 (1986): 420–33.

— — —. "The Will to Choose or to Reject: Continuing Our Critical Work." In *Feminist Interpretation of the Bible*, edited by Letty M. Russell, 125–36. Philadelphia: Westminster, 1985.

Fitzmyer, Joseph A. *Romans: A New Translation with Introduction and Commentary*. Anchor Bible 33. New York: Doubleday, 1993.

Flor, Elmer. "The Cosmic Christ and Ecojustice in the New Cosmos." In Habel and Balabanski, *The Earth Story in the New Testament*, 137–47.

Fowl, Stephen E. "Christology and Ethics in Philippians 2:5-11." In *Where Christology Began: Essays on Philippians 2*, edited by R. P. Martin and B. J. Dodd, 140–53. Louisville, Ky.: Westminster John Knox, 1998.

— — —. *The Story of Christ in the Ethics of Paul: An Analysis of the Function of the Hymnic Material in the Pauline Corpus*. Journal for the Study of the New Testament Supplement 36. Sheffield: Sheffield Academic Press, 1990.

Fox, Matthew. *The Coming of the Cosmic Christ*. San Francisco: Harper & Row, 1988.

——. *Original Blessing*. Santa Fe: Bear, 1983.

Frye, Northrop. *Anatomy of Criticism*. 1957. Reprint, Princeton: Princeton University Press, 2000.

Furnish, Victor Paul. *II Corinthians*. Anchor Bible 32A. New York: Doubleday, 1984.

——. *Jesus According to Paul*. Cambridge: Cambridge University Press, 1993.

——. *Theology and Ethics in Paul*. Nashville: Abingdon, 1968.

——. "Uncommon Love and the Common Good: Christians as Citizens in the Letters of Paul." In *In Search of the Common Good*, edited by Dennis P. McCann and Patrick D. Miller, 58–87. New York: T&T Clark, 2005.

Gager Jr., John G. "Functional Diversity in Paul's Use of End-Time Language." *Journal of Biblical Literature* 89 (1970): 325–37.

Galloway, Allan D. *The Cosmic Christ*. London: Nisbet, 1951.

Gibbs, John G. *Creation and Redemption: A Study in Pauline Theology*. Novum Testamentum Supplement 26. Leiden: Brill, 1971.

——. "Pauline Cosmic Christology and Ecological Crisis." *Journal of Biblical Literature* 90 (1971): 466–79.

Gorday, Peter, ed. *Ancient Christian Commentary on Scripture: Colossians, 1–2 Thessalonians, 1–2 Timothy, Titus, Philemon*. Ancient Christian Commentary on Scripture New Testament 11. Chicago: Fitzroy Dearborn, 2000.

Gordley, Matthew E. *The Colossian Hymn in Context: An Exegesis in Light of Jewish and Greco-Roman Hymnic and Epistolary Conventions*. Wissenschaftliche Untersuchungen zum Neuen Testament 2.228. Tübingen: Mohr Siebeck, 2007.

Gorman, Michael J. *Cruciformity: Paul's Narrative Spirituality of the Cross*. Grand Rapids: Eerdmans, 2001.

——. *Inhabiting the Cruciform God: Kenosis, Justification, and Theosis in Paul's Narrative Soteriology*. Grand Rapids: Eerdmans, 2009.

Granberg-Michaelson, Wesley. "Introduction: Identification or Mastery?" In *Tending the Garden*, edited by Wesley Granberg-Michaelson, 1–5. Grand Rapids: Eerdmans, 1987.

Green, R. P. H., ed. and trans. *Saint Augustine: On Christian Teaching*. Oxford World's Classics. Oxford: Oxford University Press, 1997.

The Green Bible. London: HarperCollins, 2008.

Gregorios, Paulos Mar. "New Testament Foundations for Understanding the Creation." In *Tending the Garden*, edited by Wesley Granberg-Michaelson, 83–92. Grand Rapids: Eerdmans, 1987.

Gribben, Crawford. "Rapture Fictions and the Changing Evangelical Condition." *Literature and Theology* 18 (2004): 77–94.

Grudem, Wayne. *Systematic Theology: An Introduction to Biblical Doctrine.* Leicester: InterVarsity, 1994.

Gunther, John J. *St. Paul's Opponents and Their Background: A Study of Apocalyptic and Jewish Sectarian Teachings.* Novum Testamentum Supplement 35. Leiden: Brill, 1973.

Gunton, Colin. "Atonement and the Project of Creation: An Interpretation of Colossians 1:15-23." *Dialog* 35 (1996): 35–41.

Habel, Norman C. "Geophany: The Earth Story in Genesis 1." In Habel and Wurst, *The Earth Story in Genesis,* 34–48.

Habel, Norman C., ed. *The Earth Bible.* Vol. 1, *Readings from the Perspective of Earth.* Cleveland, Ohio: Pilgrim, 2000.

— — —, ed. *The Earth Bible.* Vol. 4, *The Earth Story in Psalms and Prophets.* Cleveland, Ohio: Pilgrim, 2001.

— — —. "An Ecojustice Challenge: Is Earth Valued in John 1?" In Habel and Balabanski, *The Earth Story in the New Testament,* 76–82.

— — —. "Introducing Ecological Hermeneutics." In Habel and Trudinger, *Exploring Ecological Hermeneutics,* 1–8.

— — —. "Introducing the Earth Bible." In Habel, *Readings,* 25–37.

Habel, Norman C., and Peter Trudinger, eds. *Exploring Ecological Hermeneutics.* Society of Biblical Literature Symposium 46. Atlanta: Society of Biblical Literature, 2008.

Habel, Norman C., and Shirley Wurst, eds. *The Earth Bible.* Vol. 2, *The Earth Story in Genesis.* Cleveland, Ohio: Pilgrim, 2000.

— — —, eds. *The Earth Bible.* Vol. 3, *The Earth Story in Wisdom Traditions.* Cleveland, Ohio: Pilgrim, 2001.

Habel, Norman C., and Vicky Balabanski, eds. *The Earth Bible.* Vol. 5, *The Earth Story in the New Testament.* Cleveland, Ohio: Pilgrim, 2002.

Hahm, David E. *The Origins of Stoic Cosmology.* Columbus: Ohio State University Press, 1977.

Hahne, Harry Alan. *The Corruption and Redemption of Creation: Nature in Romans 8.19-22 and Jewish Apocalyptic Literature.* Library of New Testament Studies 336. New York: T&T Clark, 2006.

Hall, Douglas John. *The Steward: A Biblical Symbol Come of Age.* 1982. Revised edition, Grand Rapids: Eerdmans, 1990.

Halter, Hans, and Wilfried Lochbühler, eds. *Ökologische Theologie und Ethik.* 2 vols. Graz: Styria, 1999.

Hampson, Daphne. *After Christianity.* London: SCM Press, 1996.

— — —. *Theology and Feminism.* Oxford: Basil Blackwell, 1990.

Hanson, Stig. *The Unity of the Church in the New Testament: Colossians and Ephesians.* Uppsala: Almqvist & Wiksells, 1946.

Harrison, J. R. "Paul, Eschatology, and the Augustan Age of Grace." *Tyndale Bulletin* 50 (1999): 79–91.

Harrison, Peter. "Subduing the Earth: Genesis 1, Early Modern Science, and the Exploitation of Nature." *Journal of Religion* 79 (1999): 86–109.

Harrisville, Roy A., and Walter Sundberg. *The Bible in Modern Culture: Theology and Historical-Critical Method from Spinoza to Käsemann.* Grand Rapids: Eerdmans, 1995.

Hartman, Lars. "Universal Reconciliation (Col 1,20)." *Studien zum Neuen Testament und seiner Umwelt* 10 (1985): 109–21.

Hauerwas, Stanley. *A Community of Character: Toward a Constructive Christian Social Ethic.* Notre Dame, Ind.: University of Notre Dame Press, 1981.

Hauerwas, Stanley, and David Burrell. "From System to Story: An Alternative Pattern for Rationality in Ethics." In *Why Narrative?*, edited by Stanley Hauerwas and L. Gregory Jones, 158–90. Grand Rapids: Eerdmans, 1989.

Haught, John F. *God After Darwin: A Theology of Evolution.* Boulder, Colo.: Westview, 2000.

Hauke, Manfred. *Women in the Priesthood? A Systematic Analysis in the Light of the Order of Creation and Redemption.* Translated by David Kipp. San Francisco: Ignatius, 1988.

Hay, David M., ed. *Pauline Theology.* Vol. 2, *1 and 2 Corinthians.* Minneapolis: Fortress, 1993.

Hay, David M., and E. Elizabeth Johnson, eds. *Pauline Theology.* Vol. 3, *Romans.* Minneapolis: Fortress, 1995.

Hayes, Katherine M. *"The Earth Mourns": Prophetic Metaphor and Oral Aesthetic.* Academia Biblica 8. Atlanta: Society of Biblical Literature, 2002.

Hays, Richard B. *The Faith of Jesus Christ: The Narrative Substructure of Galatians 3:1–4:11.* 1983. Revised edition, Grand Rapids: Eerdmans, 1997.

———. *First Corinthians.* Interpretation: A Bible Commentary for Teaching and Preaching. Louisville, Ky.: John Knox, 1997.

———. "Is Paul's Gospel Narratable?" *Journal for the Study of the New Testament* 27 (2004): 217–39.

———. *The Moral Vision of the New Testament.* Edinburgh: T&T Clark, 1997.

Hayter, Mary. *The New Eve in Christ.* Grand Rapids: Eerdmans, 1987.

Heap, Brian, and Flavio Comin. "Consumption and Happiness: Christian Values and an Approach towards Sustainability." In *When Enough Is Enough: A Christian Framework for Environmental Sustainability*, edited by R. J. Berry, 79–98. Nottingham: Apollos, 2007.

Hengel, Martin, and Anna Maria Schwemer. *Paul between Damascus and Antioch: The Unknown Years.* London: SCM Press, 1997.

Hill, Brennan R. *Christian Faith and the Environment: Making Vital Connections.* Maryknoll, N.Y.: Orbis, 1998.

Hillert, Sven. *Limited and Universal Salvation: A Text-Oriented and Hermeneutical Study of Two Perspectives in Paul.* Coniectanea Biblica New Testament Series 31. Stockholm: Almqvist & Wiksell, 1999.

Hinderaker, John. "Bill Moyers Smears a Better Man than Himself." http://power lineblog.com/archives/2005/02/009377.php (accessed July 31, 2009).

Hooker, Morna D. "Authority on Her Head: An Examination of I Cor. XI.10." *New Testament Studies* 10 (1964): 110–16.

— — —. *From Adam to Christ: Essays on Paul.* Cambridge: Cambridge University Press, 1990.

— — —. "Were There False Teachers in Colossae?" In *Christ and Spirit in the New Testament*, edited by Barnabas Lindars and Stephen S. Smalley, 315–31. Cambridge: Cambridge University Press, 1973.

Hopewell, James F. *Congregation: Stories and Structures.* Philadelphia: Fortress, 1987.

Horrell, David G. *The Bible and the Environment: Towards a Critical Ecological Biblical Theology.* Biblical Challenges in the Contemporary World. Oakville, Conn.: Equinox, 2010.

— — —. "Biblical Vegetarianism? A Critical and Constructive Assessment." In *Eating and Believing: Interdisciplinary Perspectives on Vegetarianism and Theology*, edited by Rachel Muers and David Grumett, 44–59. New York: T&T Clark, 2008.

— — —. "Ecojustice in the Bible? Pauline Contributions to an Ecological Theology." In *Bible and Justice: Ancients Texts, Modern Challenges*, edited by Matthew J. M. Coomber. Oakville, Conn.: Equinox, forthcoming.

— — —. "*The Green Bible*: A Timely Idea Deeply Flawed." *Expository Times* 121 (2010): 180–85.

— — —. *An Introduction to the Study of Paul.* 2nd ed. New York: T&T Clark, 2006.

— — —. "Particular Identity and Common Ethics: Reflections on the Foundations and Content of Pauline Ethics in 1 Corinthians 5." In *Jenseits von Indikativ und Imperativ: Kontexte und Normen neutestamentlicher Ethik/Contexts and Norms of New Testament Ethics*, edited by Friedrich Wilhelm Horn and Ruben Zimmermann, 197–212. Wissenschaftliche Untersuchungen zum Neuen Testament 2.238. Tübingen: Mohr Siebeck, 2009.

— — —. "Paul's Narratives or Narrative Substructure? The Significance of 'Paul's Story.'" In Longenecker, *Narrative Dynamics in Paul*, 157–71.

— — —. *Solidarity and Difference: A Contemporary Reading of Paul's Ethics.* New York: T&T Clark, 2005.

— — —. "Theological Principle or Christological Praxis? Pauline Ethics in 1 Cor 8.1–11.1." *Journal for the Study of the New Testament* 67 (1997): 83–114.

Horrell, David G., Cherryl Hunt, Christopher Southgate, and Francesca Stavrakopoulou, eds. *Ecological Hermeneutics: Biblical, Historical and Theological Perspectives.* New York: T&T Clark, 2010.

Hubbard, Moyer V. *New Creation in Paul's Letters and Thought.* Society for New Testament Studies Monograph Series 119. Cambridge: Cambridge University Press, 2002.

Hübner, Hans. "Paulusforschung seit 1945. Ein kritischer Literaturbericht." *Aufstieg und Niedergang der römischen Welt* II.25 (1987): 2649–2840.

Hultgren, Arland J. "The Pastoral Epistles." In *The Cambridge Companion to St Paul*, edited by James D. G. Dunn, 141–55. Cambridge: Cambridge University Press, 2003.

Hunt, Cherryl. "Beyond Anthropocentrism: Towards a Re-reading of Pauline Ethics." *Theology* 112 (2009): 190–98.

Hunt, Dave. *Peace, Prosperity, and the Coming Holocaust: The New Age Movement in Prophecy*. Eugene, Ore.: Harvest House, 1983.

Interfaith Council for Environmental Stewardship. "The Cornwall Declaration on Environmental Stewardship" (2000). http://www.cornwallalliance .org/docs/the-cornwall-declaration-on-environmental-stewardship.pdf (accessed July 31, 2009).

Intergovernmental Panel on Climate Change (2009). http://www.ipcc.ch/index .htm (accessed August 4, 2009).

International Theological Commission. "Communion and Stewardship: Human Persons Created in the Image of God" (2004). http://www.vatican.va/roman _curia/congregations/cfaith/cti_documents/rc_con_cfaith_doc_20040723 _communion-stewardship_en.html (accessed August 5, 2009).

Jackson, Tony Ryan. "The Historical and Social Setting of New Creation in Paul's Letters." Ph.D. diss., University of Cambridge, 2009.

Jackson, Wes. *Becoming Native to This Place*. New York: Counterpoint, 1994.

Jenkins, Willis. *Ecologies of Grace: Environmental Ethics and Christian Theology*. New York: Oxford University Press, 2008.

Jewett, Robert. "The Corruption and Redemption of Creation: Reading Rom 8:18-23 within the Imperial Context." In *Paul and the Roman Imperial Order*, edited by Richard A. Horsley, 25–46. Harrisburg: Trinity Press International, 2004.

— — —. *Paul's Anthropological Terms: A Study of Their Use in Conflict Settings*. Leiden: Brill, 1971.

— — —. *Romans*. Hermeneia. Minneapolis: Fortress, 2007.

John Paul II. "Apostolic Letter *Mulieris Dignitatem*." Libreria Editrice Vaticana (1988). http://www.vatican.va/holy_father/john_paul_ii/letters/documents/ hf_jp-ii_let_29061995_women_en.html (accessed January 8, 2007).

— — —. "Letter to Women." Libreria Editrice Vaticana (1995). http://www .vatican.va/holy_father/john_paul_ii/letters/documents/hf_jp-ii_let _29061995_women_en.html (accessed January 8, 2007).

John Ray Initiative, The. http://www.jri.org.uk (accessed August 26, 2009).

Johnson, E. Elizabeth, and David M. Hay, eds. *Pauline Theology*. Vol. 4, *Looking Back, Pressing On*. Minneapolis: Fortress, 1997.

Jones, James. *Jesus and the Earth*. London: SPCK, 2003.

Käsemann, Ernst. *Commentary on Romans.* Translated by G. W. Bromiley. Grand Rapids: Eerdmans, 1980.

— — —. "Justification and Salvation History in the Epistle to the Romans." In *Perspectives on Paul,* 60–78. New Testament Library. London: SCM Press, 1971.

— — —. "A Primitive Christian Baptismal Liturgy." In *Essays on New Testament Themes,* 149–68. Studies in Biblical Theology 41. London: SCM Press, 1964. Original essay was published in 1949.

Keesmaat, Sylvia C. "Echoes, Ethics and Empire in Colossians." Paper presented at the annual meeting of the Society of Biblical Literature, Washington, D.C., November 2006.

— — —. *Paul and his Story: (Re)Interpreting the Exodus Tradition.* Journal for the Study of the New Testament Supplement 181. Sheffield: Sheffield Academic Press, 1999.

Kemmerer, Lisa. *In Search of Consistency: Ethics and Animals.* Leiden: Brill, 2006.

Kern, Otto. *Orphicorum Fragmenta.* 1922. Reprint, Berlin: Weidmann, 1963.

Kidd, Reggie M. *Wealth and Beneficence in the Pastoral Epistles: A "Bourgeois" Form of Early Christianity?* Society of Biblical Literature Dissertation Series 122. Atlanta: Scholars Press, 1990.

Kittel, Gerhard, ed. *Theological Dictionary of the New Testament.* Translated by G. W. Bromiley. 10 vols. Grand Rapids: Eerdmans, 1964–1976.

Krolzik, Udo. *Umweltkrise, Folge des Christentums?* Stuttgart: Kreuz, 1979.

Kropf, Richard W. *Evil and Evolution: A Theodicy.* 1984. Reprint, Eugene, Ore.: Wipf & Stock, 2004.

LaHaye, Tim, and Jerry B. Jenkins. *Left Behind.* Wheaton, Ill.: Tyndale House, 1995.

Lakes, Greg. "Headwaters News: James Watt." Center for the Rocky Mountain West at the University of Montana, 2004. http://www.headwatersnews .org/p.watt.html (accessed February 20, 2007).

Lampe, G. W. H. "The New Testament Doctrine of *KTISIS.*" *Scottish Journal of Theology* 17 (1964): 449–62.

Lapidge, Michael. "Stoic Cosmology." In *The Stoics,* edited by John M. Rist, 161–85. Berkeley: University of California Press, 1978.

— — —. "Stoic Cosmology and Roman Literature, First to Third Centuries A.D." *Aufstieg und Niedergang der Römischen Welt* II.36.3 (1989): 1379–1429.

Leenhardt, Franz J. *The Epistle to the Romans: A Commentary.* London: Lutterworth, 1961.

Leopold, Aldo. *A Sand County Almanac: With Essays on Conservation from Round River.* 1949. Reprint, Oxford: Oxford University Press, 1966.

Leske, Adrian M. "Matthew 6.25-34: Human Anxiety and the Natural World." In Habel and Balabanski, *The Earth Story in the New Testament,* 15–27.

Liedke, Gerhard. *Im Bauch des Fisches: Ökologische Theologie.* Stuttgart: Kreuz, 1979.

Lightfoot, J. B. *Saint Paul's Epistles to the Colossians and to Philemon: A Revised Text with Introductions, Notes and Dissertations.* New York: Macmillan, 1886.

Lincoln, Andrew T. "The Household Code and Wisdom Mode of Colossians." *Journal for the Study of the New Testament* 74 (1999): 93–112.

———. "The Letter to the Colossians." In *The New Interpreter's Bible,* Vol. 11, edited by Leander E. Keck, 551–669. Nashville: Abingdon, 2000.

Lincoln, Andrew T., and A. J. M. Wedderburn. *The Theology of the Later Pauline Letters.* Cambridge: Cambridge University Press, 1993.

Lindsey, Hal. *The Late Great Planet Earth.* London: Lakeland, 1971.

Linzey, Andrew. *Animal Theology.* London: SCM Press, 1994.

Lipton, Diana. "Remembering Amalek: A Positive Biblical Model for Dealing with Negative Scriptural Types." In *Reading Texts, Seeking Wisdom,* edited by David F. Ford and Graham Stanton, 139–53. London: SCM Press, 2003.

Lloyd, Michael. "Are Animals Fallen?" In *Animals on the Agenda,* edited by Andrew Linzey and Dorothy Yamamoto, 147–60. London: SCM Press, 1998.

Lochbühler, Wilfried. *Christliche Umweltethik: Schöpfungstheologische Grundlagen, Philosophisch-ethische Ansätze, Ökologische Marktwirtschaft.* Forum Interdisziplinäre Ethik 13. Frankfurt am Main: Peter Lang, 1996.

Lohfink, Norbert. *Theology of the Pentateuch: Themes of the Priestly Narrative and Deuteronomy.* Translated by Linda M. Maloney. Edinburgh: T&T Clark, 1994.

Lohmeyer, Ernst. *Die Briefe an die Philipper, an die Kolosser und an Philemon.* 11th ed. Kritisch-exegetischer Kommentar uber das Neue Testament (Meyer-Kommentar) 10A. Göttingen: Meyers, 1956.

Lohse, Eduard. *Colossians and Philemon.* Translated by William R. Poehlmann and Robert J. Karris. Hermeneia. Philadelphia: Fortress, 1971.

Long, A. A., and D. N. Sedley, eds. *The Hellenistic Philosophers.* 2 vols. Cambridge: Cambridge University Press, 1987.

Longenecker, Bruce W. "The Narrative Approach to Paul: An Early Retrospective." *Currents in Biblical Research* 1 (2002): 88–111.

———, ed. *Narrative Dynamics in Paul: A Critical Assessment.* Louisville, Ky.: Westminster John Knox, 2002.

———. "Narrative Interest in the Study of Paul." In Longenecker, *Narrative Dynamics in Paul,* 3–16.

Loughlin, Gerard. *Telling God's Story: Bible, Church, and Narrative Theology.* Cambridge: Cambridge University Press, 1996.

Lovelock, James. *The Ages of Gaia: A Biography of Our Living Earth.* Oxford: Oxford University Press, 1989.

Lucas, Ernest. "The New Testament Teaching on the Environment." *Transformation* 16.3 (1999): 93–99.

Ludlow, Morwenna. "Power and Dominion: Patristic Interpretations of

Genesis 1." In Horrell, Hunt, Southgate, and Stavrakopoulou, *Ecological Hermeneutics*, 140–53.

Lull, David J. "Salvation History: Theology in 1 Thessalonians, Philemon, Philippians, and Galatians: A Response to N. T. Wright, R. B. Hays, and R. Scroggs." In Bassler, *Pauline Theology*, 1:247–65.

Lutz, Charles P. "Loving All My Creaturely Neighbors." *Trinity Seminary Review* 25 (2004): 97–105.

Lynas, Mark. *Six Degrees: Our Future on a Hotter Planet*. London: Fourth Estate, 2007.

Lyonnet, S. "L'hymne christologique de l'épitre aux Colossiens et la fête juive du nouvel an (S. Paul, *Col.*, 1,20 et Philon, *De spec.leg.*, 192.)." *Recherches de Science Religieuse* 48 (1960): 93–100.

MacDonald, Margaret Y. *Colossians and Ephesians*. Sacra Pagina 17. Collegeville, Minn.: Liturgical Press, 2000.

— — —. *The Pauline Churches: A Socio-historical Study of Institutionalization in the Pauline and Deutero-Pauline Writings*. Society for New Testament Studies Monograph Series 60. Cambridge: Cambridge University Press, 1988.

MacIntyre, Alasdair. *After Virtue: A Study in Moral Theory*. London: Duckworth, 1981.

Maier, Harry O. "Barbarians, Scythians and Imperial Iconography in the Epistle to the Colossians." In *Picturing the New Testament: Studies in Ancient Visual Images*, edited by Annette Weissenrieder, Friederike Wendt, and Petra von Gemünden, 385–406. Wissenschaftliche Untersuchungen zum Neuen Testament 2.193. Tübingen: Mohr Siebeck, 2005.

— — —. "Green Millennialism: American Evangelicals, Environmentalism, and the Book of Revelation." In Horrell, Hunt, Southgate, and Stavrakopoulou, *Ecological Hermeneutics*, 246–65.

— — —. "A Sly Civility: Colossians and Empire." *Journal for the Study of the New Testament* 27 (2005): 323–49.

Malherbe, Abraham J. *Paul and the Thessalonians: The Philosophic Tradition of Pastoral Care*. Philadelphia: Fortress, 1987.

Malina, Bruce J. *The New Testament World: Insights from Cultural Anthropology*. Third Edition, Revised and Expanded. Louisville, Ky.: Westminster John Knox, 2001.

Marietta Jr., Don E. *For People and the Planet: Holism and Humanism in Environmental Ethics*. Philadelphia: Temple University Press, 1994.

Marshall, I. Howard. "The Meaning of 'Reconciliation.'" In *Unity and Diversity in New Testament Theology: Essays in Honor of George E. Ladd*, edited by Robert A. Guelich, 117–32. Grand Rapids: Eerdmans, 1978.

Martin, Dale B. *The Corinthian Body*. New Haven, Conn.: Yale University Press, 1995.

— — —. *Sex and the Single Savior*. Louisville, Ky.: Westminster John Knox, 2006.

Martin, Ralph P. *Ephesians, Colossians, and Philemon.* Interpretation: A Bible Commentary for Teaching and Preaching. Atlanta: John Knox, 1991.

— — —. *Reconciliation: A Study of Paul's Theology.* Atlanta: John Knox Press, 1981.

— — —. "Reconciliation and Forgiveness in the Letter to the Colossians." In *Reconciliation and Hope: New Testament Essays on Atonement and Eschatology presented to L. L. Morris on his 60th Birthday,* edited by Robert Banks, 104–24. Exeter: Paternoster, 1974.

Martyn, J. Louis. "Epistemology at the Turn of the Ages." In *Theological Issues in the Letters of Paul,* 89–110. Edinburgh: T&T Clark, 1997.

— — —. "Events in Galatia: Modified Covenantal Nomism versus God's Invasion of the Cosmos in the Singular Gospel: A Response to J. D. G. Dunn and B. R. Gaventa." In Bassler, *Pauline Theology,* 1:160–79.

— — —. *Galatians.* Anchor Bible 33A. New York: Doubleday, 1997.

Maslin, Mark. *Global Warming: A Very Short Introduction.* Oxford: Oxford University Press, 2004.

Matlock, R. Barry. "Detheologizing the ΠΙΣΤΙΣ ΧΡΙΣΤΟΥ Debate: Cautionary Remarks from a Lexical Semantic Perspective." *Novum Testamentum* 42 (2000): 1–23.

McAfee, Gene. "Chosen People in a Chosen Land: Theology and Ecology in the Story of Israel's Origins." In Habel and Wurst, *The Earth Story in Genesis,* 158–74.

McDaniel, Jay B. *Of God and Pelicans: A Theology of Reverence for Life.* Louisville, Ky.: Westminster John Knox, 1989.

McDonagh, Sean. *The Death of Life: The Horror of Extinction.* Blackrock, Colo.: Columba, 2004.

— — —. *The Greening of the Church.* Maryknoll, N.Y.: Orbis, 1990.

— — —. *Passion for the Earth.* London: Geoffrey Chapman, 1994.

McFague, Sallie. *The Body of God: An Ecological Theology.* London: SCM Press, 1993.

McGrath, Alister E. "The Stewardship of the Creation: An Evangelical Affirmation." In Berry, *Care,* 86–89.

McKibben, Bill. *The Comforting Whirlwind: God, Job, and the Scale of Creation.* Grand Rapids: Eerdmans, 1994.

McLachlan, Jason S., Jessica J. Hellmann, and Mark W. Schwartz. "A Framework for Debate of Assisted Migration in an Era of Climate Change." *Conservation Biology* 21 (2007): 297–302.

McMenamin, Mark A. S. "Gaia and Glaciation: Lipalian (Vendian) Environmental Crisis." In *Scientists Debate Gaia,* edited by Stephen H. Schneider, James R. Miller, Eileen Crist, and Penelope J. Boston, 115–27. Cambridge, Mass.: MIT Press, 2004.

McMichael, Anthony J. *Planetary Overload: Global Environmental Change and the Health of the Human Species.* Cambridge: Cambridge University Press, 1995.

McNeill, John T., ed. *Calvin: Institutes of the Christian Religion.* Vol. 1, Books I.i to III.xix. Library of Christian Classics 20. London: SCM Press, 1960.

———, ed. *Calvin: Institutes of the Christian Religion.* Vol. 2, Books III.xx to IV.xx. LIbrary of Christian Classics 21. London: SCM Press, 1960.

Meeks, Wayne A. "The Image of the Androgyne: Some Uses of a Symbol in Earliest Christianity." *History of Religions* 13 (1974): 165–208.

———. "The Man from Heaven in Paul's Letter to the Philippians." In *The Future of Early Christianity: Essays in Honor of Helmut Koester*, edited by B. A. Pearson, 329–36. Minneapolis: Fortress, 1991.

Mell, Ulrich. *Neue Schöpfung: Eine traditionsgeschichtliche und exegetische Studie zu einem soteriologischen Grundsatz paulinischer Theologie.* Beihefte zur Zeitschrift für die neutestamentliche Wissenschaft 56. Berlin: Walter de Gruyter, 1989.

Merz, Annette. *Die fiktive Selbstauslegung des Paulus: Intertextuelle Studien zur Intention und Rezeption der Pastoralbriefe.* Novum Testamentum et Orbis Antiquus 52. Göttingen: Vandenhoeck & Ruprecht, 2004.

Messer, Neil. *Selfish Genes and Christian Ethics: Theological and Ethical Reflections on Evolutionary Biology.* London: SCM Press, 2007.

———. "Natural Evil after Darwin." In *Theology after Darwin*, edited by R. J. Berry and Michael Northcott, 138–54. Carlisle: Paternoster, 2010.

Metzger, Bruce M. *A Textual Commentary on the Greek New Testament.* 2nd ed. New York: United Bible Societies, 1994.

Michaels, J. Ramsey. "The Redemption of Our Body: The Riddle of Romans 8:19-22." In *Romans and the People of God*, edited by Sven K. Soderlund and N. T. Wright, 92–114. Grand Rapids: Eerdmans, 1999.

Milbank, John. *Theology and Social Theory: Beyond Secular Reason.* Oxford: Blackwell, 1990.

Mitchell, Margaret M. "Corrective Composition, Corrective Exegesis: The Teaching on Prayer in 1 Tim 2,1-15." In *Colloquium Oecumenicum Paulinum.* Vol. 18, *1 Timothy Reconsidered*, edited by Karl P. Donfried, 41–62. Leuven: Peeters, 2008.

———. *Paul and the Rhetoric of Reconciliation.* Louisville, Ky.: Westminster John Knox, 1991.

Moltmann, Jürgen. *The Way of Jesus Christ: Christology in Messianic Dimensions.* Translated by Margaret Kohl. London: SCM Press, 1990.

Moo, Douglas J. *The Epistle to the Romans.* New International Biblical Commentary on the New Testament. Grand Rapids: Eerdmans, 1996.

———. *The Letters to the Colossians and to Philemon.* The Pillar New Testament Commentary. Grand Rapids: Eerdmans, 2008.

— — —. "Nature in the New Creation: New Testament Eschatology and the Environment." *Journal of the Evangelical Theological Society* 49 (2006): 449–88.

Moule, C. F. D. *The Epistles to the Colossians and to Philemon.* The Cambridge Greek New Testament Commentary. Cambridge: Cambridge University Press, 1962.

Murphy-O'Connor, Jerome. "I Cor. VIII,6: Cosmology or Soteriology?" *Revue Biblique* 85 (1978): 253–67.

— — —. "Pauline Studies." *Revue Biblique* 98 (1991): 145–51.

Murray, John. *The Epistle to the Romans.* New International Commentary on the New Testament. Grand Rapids: Eerdmans, 1968.

Naess, Arne. "The Shallow and the Deep, Long-Range Ecology Movement. A Summary." *Inquiry* 16 (1972): 95–100.

Nash, James A. *Loving Nature: Ecological Integrity and Christian Responsibility.* Nashville: Abingdon, 1991.

Newman, Carey C. *Paul's Glory-Christology: Tradition and Rhetoric.* Novum Testamentum Supplement 69. Leiden: Brill, 1992.

Northcott, Michael S. *An Angel Directs the Storm: Apocalyptic Religion and American Empire.* New York: I. B. Tauris, 2004.

— — —. *The Environment and Christian Ethics.* New Studies in Christian Ethics. Cambridge: Cambridge University Press, 1996.

— — —. *A Moral Climate: The Ethics of Global Warming.* London: Darton, Longman, & Todd, 2007.

O'Brien, Peter T. *Colossians, Philemon.* Word Biblical Commentary 44. Dallas, Tex.: Word Books, 1982.

O'Donovan, Oliver. *Resurrection and Moral Order: An Outline for Evangelical Ethics.* 2nd ed. Grand Rapids: Eerdmans, 1994.

Orr, David W. "Armageddon versus Extinction." *Conservation Biology* 19 (2005): 290–92.

Osborn, Lawrence. *Guardians of Creation: Nature in Theology and the Christian Life.* Leicester: Apollos, 1993.

Pacala, S., and R. Socolow. "Stabilization Wedges—Solving the Climate Problem for the Next 50 Years Using Current Technologies." *Science* 305 (2004): 968–72.

Palmer, Clare. "Stewardship: A Case Study in Environmental Ethics." In *The Earth Beneath: A Critical Guide to Green Theology.* Ian Ball, Margaret Goodall, Clare Palmer, and John Reader, 67–86. London: SPCK, 1992.

Pauck, Wilhelm, ed. and trans. *Luther: Lectures on Romans,* edited by John Baillie, John T. McNeill, and Henry P. Van Dusen. Library of Christian Classics 15. London: SCM Press, 1961.

Paulsen, H. "Einheit und Freiheit der Söhne Gottes—Gal 3.26-29." *Zeitschrift für die neutestamentliche Wissenschaft* 71 (1980): 74–95.

Pelikan, Jaroslav, ed. *Luther's Works*. Vol. 26, *Lectures on Galatians 1535, Chapters 1-4*. St. Louis, Mo.: Concordia, 1963.

Peters, Ted. *Playing God: Genetic Determinism and Human Freedom*. New York: Routledge, 1997.

Peters, Ted, and Martinez J. Hewlett. *Evolution from Creation to New Creation*. Nashville: Abingdon, 2003.

Pizzuto, Vincent A. *A Cosmic Leap of Faith: An Authorial, Structural, and Theological Investigation of the Cosmic Christology in Col. 1:15-20*. Biblical Exegesis and Theology 41. Leuven: Peeters, 2006.

Pokorný, Petr. *Colossians: A Commentary*. Translated by Siegfried S. Schatzmann. Peabody, Mass.: Hendrickson, 1991. German original published in 1987.

Polkinghorne, John. "Pelican Heaven." *Times Literary Supplement*, April 3, 2009.

Pollan, Michael. *The Omnivore's Dilemma*. London: Bloomsbury, 2006.

Porter, Stanley E. "Is There a Center to Paul's Theology? An Introduction to the Study of Paul and His Theology." In *Paul and His Theology*, edited by Stanley E. Porter, 1–19. Leiden: Brill, 2006.

———. Καταλλάσσω *in Ancient Greek Literature, with Reference to the Pauline Writings*. Estudios de Filología Neotestamentaría 5. Cordoba: Ediciones El Almendro, 1994.

Powell, Mark Allen. *What Is Narrative Criticism? A New Approach to the Bible*. London: SPCK, 1993.

Primavesi, Anne. *Gaia's Gift: Earth, Ourselves, and God after Copernicus*. New York: Routledge, 2003.

Prokurat, Michael. "Orthodox Perspectives on Creation." *St. Vladimir's Theological Quarterly* 33 (1989): 331–49.

Pyatt, B., G. Gilmore, J. Grattan, C. Hunt, and S. McLaren. "An Imperial Legacy? An Exploration of the Environmental Impact of Ancient Metal Mining and Smelting in Southern Jordan." *Journal of Archaeological Science* 27 (2000): 771–78.

Räisänen, Heikki. *Paul and the Law*. Wissenschaftliche Untersuchungen zum Neuen Testament 29. Tübingen: Mohr Siebeck, 1983.

Regan, Tom. *The Case for Animal Rights*. London: Routledge, 1988.

Rehman, Luzia Sutter. "To Turn the Groaning into Labor: Romans 8.22-23." In *A Feminist Companion to Paul*, edited by Amy-Jill Levine and Marianne Bickenstaff, 74–83. Cleveland, Ohio: Pilgrim, 2004.

Resch, Alfred. *Der Paulinismus und die Logia Jesu in ihrem gegenseitigen Verhältnis*. Texte und Untersuchungen 12. Leipzig: Hinrichs, 1904.

Reumann, John. *Philippians: A New Translation with Introduction and Commentary*. Anchor Bible 33B. New Haven, Conn.: Yale University Press, 2008.

———. *Stewardship and the Economy of God*. Grand Rapids: Eerdmans, 1992.

Rogerson, J. W. "The Creation Stories: Their Ecological Potential and

Problems." In Horrell, Hunt, Southgate, and Stavrakopoulou, *Ecological Hermeneutics*, 21–31.

Rolston III, Holmes. "Disvalues in Nature." *The Monist* 75 (1992): 250–78.

— — —. *Environmental Ethics: Duties to and Values in the Natural World*. Philadelphia: Temple University Press, 1988.

— — —. "Naturalizing and Systematizing Evil." In *Is Nature Ever Evil?* edited by Willem B. Drees, 67–86. New York: Routledge, 2003.

— — —. *Science and Religion: A Critical Survey*. 1987. Reprint, Philadelphia: Templeton Foundation, 2006.

Roose, Hanna. "Die Hierarchisierung der Leib-Metapher im Kolosser- und Epheserbrief als 'Paulinisierung': Ein Beitrag zur Rezeption Paulinischer Tradition in Pseudo-paulinischen Briefen" *Novum Testamentum* 47 (2005): 117–41.

Rosner, Brian S. *Greed as Idolatry: The Origin and Meaning of a Pauline Metaphor*. Grand Rapids: Eerdmans, 2007.

— — —. *Paul, Scripture, and Ethics: A Study of 1 Corinthians 5-7*. Leiden: Brill, 1994.

Ruether, Rosemary Radford. *Gaia and God: An Ecofeminist Theology of Earth Healing*. London: SCM Press, 1992.

— — —. *Sexism and God-Talk: Towards a Feminist Theology*. London: SCM Press, 1983.

Runia, David T. *Philo in Early Christian Literature: A Survey*. Compendia Rerum Iudiacarum ad Novum Testamentum. Section III: Jewish Traditions in Early Christian Literature 3. Minneapolis: Fortress, 1993.

Russell, Colin A. *The Earth, Humanity, and God*. London: University College London, 1994.

Russell, David M. *The "New Heavens and New Earth." Hope for the Creation in Jewish Apocalyptic and the New Testament*. Studies in Biblical Apocalyptic Literature 1. Philadelphia: Visionary, 1996.

Russell, Robert J. *Cosmology: From Alpha to Omega*. Minneapolis: Fortress, 2008.

— — —. "Entropy and Evil." *Zygon* 18 (1984): 449–68.

Sampley, J. Paul. *Walking between the Times: Paul's Moral Reasoning*. Minneapolis: Fortress, 1991.

Sanday, William, and Arthur C. Headlam. *A Critical and Exegetical Commentary on the Epistle to the Romans*. 5th ed. The International Critical Commentary. Edinburgh: T&T Clark, 1905.

Sanders, E. P. *Jesus and Judaism*. London: SCM Press, 1985.

— — —. *Paul*. Oxford: Oxford University Press, 1991.

— — —. *Paul and Palestinian Judaism: A Comparison of Patterns of Religion*. London: SCM Press, 1977.

Sanders, Jack T. *The New Testament Christological Hymns*. Society for New Testament Studies Monograph Series 15. Cambridge: Cambridge University Press, 1971.

Santmire, H. Paul. *Nature Reborn. The Ecological and Cosmic Promise of Christian Theology.* Minneapolis: Fortress, 2000.

Schillebeeckx, Edward. *Christ: The Christian Experience in the Modern World.* Translated by John Bowden. 1977. Reprint, London: SCM Press, 1988.

Schmemann, Alexander. *The World as Sacrament.* 1965. Reprint, London: Darton, Longman, & Todd, 1966.

Schnelle, Udo. *Apostle Paul: His Life and Theology.* Translated by M. Eugene Boring. 2003. English version, Grand Rapids: Baker Academic, 2005.

Schrage, Wolfgang. "Bibelarbeit über Röm 8,19-23." In *Versöhnung mit der Natur,* edited by Jürgen Moltmann, 150–66. Munich: Kaiser, 1986.

— — —. *The Ethics of the New Testament.* Translated by David E. Green. Edinburgh: T&T Clark, 1988.

Schreiner, Thomas R. *Romans.* Baker Academic Commentary on the New Testament. Grand Rapids: Baker Academic, 1998.

Schweitzer, Albert. *The Mysticism of Paul the Apostle.* 2nd ed. 1931. Reprint, London: A&C Black, 1953.

— — —. *The Quest of the Historical Jesus.* 1913. New ed., edited by John Bowden. London: SCM Press, 2000.

Schweizer, Eduard. *The Letter to the Colossians.* Translated by Andrew Chester. 1976, Reprint, London: SPCK, 1982.

Scott, Alan. *Origen and the Life of the Stars.* 1991. Reprint, Oxford: Oxford University Press, 1994.

Scott, Martin. *Sophia and the Johannine Jesus.* Journal for the Study of the New Testament Supplement 71. Sheffield: Sheffield Academic Press, 1992.

Scott, R. B. Y. "Wisdom in Creation: The 'āmôn of Proverbs VIII 30." *Vetus Testamentum* 10 (1960): 213–23.

Scroggs, Robin. "Paul and the Eschatological Woman." *Journal of the American Academy of Religion* 40 (1972): 283–303.

— — —. "Salvation History: The Theological Structure of Paul's Thought (1 Thessalonians, Philippians, and Galatians)." In Bassler, *Pauline Theology,* 1:212–26.

Segovia, Fernando F., and Mary Ann Tolbert. *Reading from This Place.* 2 vols. Minneapolis: Fortress, 1995.

Şenocak, Nesliha. "The Franciscan Order and Natural Philosophy in the Thirteenth Century: A Relationship Redefined." *Ecotheology* 7 (2003): 113–25.

Seymour, John, and Herbert Girardet. *Far from Paradise: The Story of Human Impact on the Environment.* London: Green Planet, 1990.

Shuster, Marguerite. "The Redemption of the Created Order: Sermons on Romans 8:18-25." In *The Redemption,* edited by Stephen T. David, Daniel

Kendall, and Gerald O'Collins, 321–42. New York: Oxford University Press, 2004.

Sibley, Andrew. *Restoring the Ethics of Creation: Challenging the Ethical Implications of Evolution.* Camberley: Anno Mundi Books, 2005.

Sideris, Lisa. "Writing Straight with Crooked Lines: Holmes Rolston's Ecological Theology and Theodicy." In *Nature, Value, Duty: Life on Earth with Holmes Rolston, III,* edited by Christopher J. Preston and Wayne Ouderkirk, 77–101. Dordrecht: Springer, 2007.

Sittler, Joseph. "Called to Unity." In *Evocations of Grace: The Writings of Joseph Sittler on Ecology, Theology, and Ethics,* edited by Steven Bouma-Prediger and Peter Bakken, 38–50. Grand Rapids: Eerdmans, 2000. Essay was originally published in 1962.

― ― ―. *Essays on Nature and Grace.* Philadelphia: Fortress, 1972.

― ― ―. "A Theology for Earth." In *Evocations of Grace: The Writings of Joseph Sittler on Ecology, Theology, and Ethics,* edited by Steven Bouma-Prediger and Peter Bakken, 20–31. Grand Rapids: Eerdmans, 2000. Essay was originally published in 1954.

Smith, Ian K. *Heavenly Perspective: A Study of the Apostle Paul's Response to a Jewish Mystical Movement at Colossae.* Library of New Testament Studies 326. New York: T&T Clark, 2006.

Sobosan, Jeffrey G. *Romancing the Universe: Theology, Science and Cosmology.* Grand Rapids: Eerdmans, 1999.

Southgate, Christopher. "Environmental Ethics and the Science-Religion Debate: A British Perspective on Barbour." In *Fifty Years in Science and Religion: Ian G. Barbour and His Legacy,* edited by Robert J. Russell, 239–48. Aldershot: Ashgate, 2004.

― ― ―, ed. *God, Humanity, and the Cosmos: A Companion to the Science-Religion Debate.* Rev. ed. New York: T&T Clark, 2005.

― ― ―. *The Groaning of Creation: God, Evolution, and the Problem of Evil.* Louisville, Ky.: Westminster John Knox, 2008.

― ― ―. "The New Days of Noah? Assisted Migration as an Ethical Imperative in an Era of Climate Change." In *Creaturely Theology,* edited by Celia Deane-Drummond and David Clough, 249–65. London: SCM Press, 2009.

― ― ―. "Protological and Eschatological Vegetarianism." In *Eating and Believing: Interdisciplinary Perspectives on Vegetarianism and Theology,* edited by Rachel Muers and David Grumett, 247–65. New York: T&T Clark, 2008.

― ― ―. "Re-reading Genesis, John, and Job: A Christian's Response to Darwinism." Paper presented at the 4th meeting of the International Society for Science and Religion. Robinson College, Cambridge, 2009. To be published in *Zygon: Journal of Religion and Science* (December 2010).

― ― ―. "Stewardship and its Competitors: A Spectrum of Relationships between Humans and the Non-Human Creation." In *Environmental Stewardship: Critical*

Perspectives, Past and Present, edited by R. J. Berry, 185–95. New York: T&T Clark, 2006.

Southgate, Christopher, and Andrew Robinson. "Varieties of Theodicy: An Exploration of Responses to the Problem of Evil Based on a Typology of Good-Harm Analyses." In *Physics and Cosmology: Scientific Perspectives on the Problem of Evil in Nature*, edited by Nancey Murphy, Robert J. Russell, and William Stoeger SJ, 69–90. Berkeley: CTNS, 2007.

Southgate, Christopher, Cherryl Hunt, and David G. Horrell. "Ascesis and Assisted Migration: Responses to the Effects of Climate Change on Animal Species." *European Journal of Science and Theology* 4.2 (2008): 99–111.

Steck, Odil Hannes. *Welt und Umwelt*. Biblische Konfrontationen. Stuttgart: Kohlhammer, 1978.

Stendahl, Krister. "The Apostle Paul and the Introspective Conscience of the West." *Harvard Theological Review* 56 (1963): 199–221. Reprinted in Stendahl, *Paul among Jews and Gentiles*.

— — —. *Paul among Jews and Gentiles*. Philadelphia: Fortress, 1976.

Stettler, Christian. *Der Kolosserhymnus: Untersuchungen zu Form, traditionsgeschichtlichem Hintergrund und Aussage von Kol 1, 15-20*. Wissenschaftliche Untersuchungen zum Neuen Testament 2.131. Tübingen: Mohr Siebeck, 2000.

Still, Todd D. "Eschatology in Colossians: How Realized Is It?" *New Testament Studies* 50 (2004): 125–38.

Stowers, Stanley K. *A Rereading of Romans: Justice, Jews, and Gentiles*. New Haven, Conn.: Yale University Press, 1994.

Strandberg, Todd. "Bible Prophecy and Environmentalism." http://www.raptureready.com/rr-environmental.html (accessed December 18, 2007).

Strickland, Spencer. "Beware of Global Warming! (2 Peter 3:6-7)." http://jeremiahdanielmccarver.wordpress.com/2008/08/07/beware-of-global-warming-2-peter-36-7 (accessed April 2, 2009).

Stroup, George W. *The Promise of Narrative Theology*. 1981. Reprint, London: SCM Press, 1984.

Swartley, Willard M. *Covenant of Peace: The Missing Peace in New Testament Theology and Ethics*. Grand Rapids: Eerdmans, 2006.

Tanner, Kathryn. "Eschatology and Ethics." In *The Oxford Companion to Theological Ethics*, edited by Gilbert Meilaender and William Werpehowski, 41–56. Oxford: Oxford University Press, 2007.

— — —. "Eschatology without a Future?" In *The End of the World and the Ends of God*, edited by John Polkinghorne and Michael Welker, 222–37. Harrisburg: Trinity, 2000.

Thielicke, Helmut. *Theological Ethics*. Vol. 1, *Foundations*. Abridged and translated ed. Translated by William H. Lazareth. Grand Rapids: Eerdmans, 1966.

Thiselton, Anthony C. *New Horizons in Hermeneutics: The Theory and Practice of Transforming Biblical Reading*. Grand Rapids: Zondervan, 1992.

Thompson, G. H. P. *The Letters of Paul to the Ephesians, to the Colossians, and to Philemon*. Cambridge Bible Commentary. Cambridge: Cambridge University Press, 1967.

Thompson, John B. *Studies in the Theory of Ideology*. Cambridge: Polity, 1984.

Thompson, Marianne Meye. *Colossians & Philemon*. Two Horizons New Testament Commentary. Grand Rapids: Eerdmans, 2005.

Thrall, Margaret E. *A Critical and Exegetical Commentary on the Second Epistle to the Corinthians I–VII*. Vol. 1. International Critical Commentary. Edinburgh: T&T Clark, 1994.

Tomson, Peter J. *Paul and the Jewish Law: Halakha in the Letters of the Apostle to the Gentiles*. Minneapolis: Fortress, 1990.

Tonstad, Sigve. "Creation Groaning in Labor Pains." In Habel and Trudinger, *Exploring Ecological Hermeneutics*, 141–49.

Toolan, Michael J. *Narrative: A Critical Linguistic Introduction*. 2nd ed. New York: Routledge, 2001.

Torrance, Thomas F. *Divine and Contingent Order*. Oxford: Oxford University Press, 1981.

Towner, W. Sibley. "The Future of Nature." *Interpretation* 50 (1996): 27–35.

Tracy, Mark. "The Ronald Reagan Years — The Real Reagan Record: Environment." http://www.geocities.com/thereaganyears/environment.htm (accessed January 2007).

Trebilco, Paul. "The Goodness and Holiness of the Earth and the Whole Creation (I Timothy 4.1-5)." In Habel, *Readings*, 204–20.

Trible, Phyllis. *God and the Rhetoric of Sexuality*. London: SCM Press, 1978.

— — —. *Texts of Terror: Literary-Feminist Readings of Biblical Narratives*. Philadelphia: Fortress, 1984.

Tucker, Gene M. "Rain on a Land Where No One Lives: The Hebrew Bible on the Environment." *Journal of Biblical Literature* 116 (1997): 3–17.

Turner, Marie. "God's Design: The Death of Creation? An Ecojustice Reading of Romans 8.18-30 in the Light of Wisdom 1–2." In Habel and Wurst, *Wisdom Traditions*, 168–78.

Tyrrell, George. *Christianity at the Crossroads*. London: Longmans, Green & Co., 1910.

Vaage, Leif E., and Vincent L. Wimbush, eds. *Asceticism and the New Testament*. New York: Routledge, 1999.

van Kooten, George H. *Cosmic Christology in Paul and the Pauline School: Colossians and Ephesians in the Context of Graeco-Roman Cosmology with a New Synopsis of the Greek Texts*. Wissenschaftliche Untersuchungen zum Neuen Testament 2.171. Tübingen: Mohr Siebeck, 2003.

Verhey, Allen. *The Great Reversal: Ethics and the New Testament*. Grand Rapids: Eerdmans, 1984.

Vischer, Lukas. "Listening to Creation Groaning: A Survey of Main Themes of Creation Theology." In *Listening to Creation Groaning: Report and Papers from a Consultation on Creation Theology Organised by the European Christian Environmental Network at the John Knox International Reformed Center from March 28 to April 1st 2004*, edited by Lukas Vischer, 11–31. Geneva: Centre international réformé John Knox, 2004.

Vögtle, Anton. "Röm 8,19-22: Eine Schöpfungstheologische oder anthropologisch-soteriologische Aussage?" In *Mélanges bibliques en hommage au R. P. Béda Rigaux*, edited by Albert Descamps and André de Halleux, 351–66. Gembloux, Belgium: Duculot, 1970.

Volf, Miroslav. *Exclusion and Embrace: A Theological Exploration of Identity, Otherness, and Reconciliation*. Nashville: Abingdon, 1996.

von Balthasar, Hans Urs. *The Glory of the Lord: A Theological Aesthetics*. Vol. 6, *Theology: The Old Covenant*. Edited by John Riches. Translated by Brian McNeil and Erasmo Merikakis. Edinburgh: T&T Clark, 1991.

— — —. *The Glory of the Lord: A Theological Aesthetics*. Vol. 7, *Theology: The New Covenant*. Edited by John Riches. Translated by Brian McNeil. San Francisco: Ignatius Press, 1989.

Waaler, Erik. *The Shema and the First Commandment in First Corinthians: An Intertextual Approach to Paul's Re-reading of Deuteronomy*. Wissenschaftliche Untersuchungen zum Neuen Testament 2.253. Tübingen: Mohr Siebeck, 2008.

Wainwright, Elaine. "Which Intertext? A Response to 'An Ecojustice Challenge: Is Earth Valued in John 1?'" In Habel and Balabanski, *The Earth Story in the New Testament*, 83–88.

Wallace, Howard N. "Rest for the Earth? Another Look at Genesis 2.1-3." In Habel and Wurst, *The Earth Story in Genesis*, 49–59.

Walsh, Brian J., and Sylvia C. Keesmaat. *Colossians Remixed: Subverting the Empire*. 2004. UK edition, Milton Keynes: Paternoster, 2005.

Walter, Nikolaus. "Gottes Zorn und das 'Harren der Kreatur.' Zur Korrespondenz zwischen Römer 1,18-32 und 8,19-22." In *Christus Bezeugen. Festschrift für Wolfgang Trilling zum 65. Geburtstag*, edited by Karl Kertelge, Traugott Holtz, and Claus-Peter März, 218–26. Leipzig: St. Benno, 1989.

Ward, Keith. "Cosmos and Kenosis." In *The Work of Love: Creation as Kenosis*, edited by John Polkinghorne, 152–66. Grand Rapids: Eerdmans, 2001.

Watson, Francis. "Hermeneutics and the Doctrine of Scripture: Why They Need Each Other." Paper presented at the meeting of the Australian Theological Forum in Canberra, 2008. Publication forthcoming.

— — —. "Is There a Story in These Texts?" In Longenecker, *Narrative Dynamics in Paul*, 231–39.

— — —. *Paul and the Hermeneutics of Faith*. New York: T&T Clark, 2004.

— — —. "Strategies of Recovery and Resistance: Hermeneutical Reflections on Genesis 1–3 and its Pauline Reception." *Journal for the Study of the New Testament* 45 (1992): 79–103.

— — —. Text, Church, and World: Biblical Interpretation in Theological Perspective. Edinburgh: T&T Clark, 1994.

Webb, Stephen H. Good Eating. Grand Rapids: Brazos, 2001.

Weisman, Alan. The World without Us. London: Virgin Books, 2007.

Wenham, David. Paul: Follower of Jesus or Founder of Christianity? Grand Rapids: Eerdmans, 1995.

Wesley, John. The Works of the Rev. John Wesley, A. M. 3rd ed. Vol. 6. London: John Mason, 1829.

Westerholm, Stephen. Perspectives Old and New on Paul: The "Lutheran" Paul and His Critics. Grand Rapids: Eerdmans, 2004.

White Jr., Lynn. "The Historical Roots of our Ecologic Crisis." Science 155 (1967): 1203–7.

Wildman, Wesley J. "Incongruous Goodness, Perilous Beauty, Disconcerting Truth: Ultimate Reality and Suffering in Nature." In Physics and Cosmology: Scientific Perspectives on the Problem of Evil in Nature, edited by Nancey Murphy, Robert J. Russell, and William Stoeger SJ, 267–94. Berkeley: Center for Theology and Natural Science, 2007.

Wilkinson, Loren. "New Age, New Consciousness, and the New Creation." In Tending the Garden, edited by Wesley Granberg-Michaelson, 6–29. Grand Rapids: Eerdmans, 1987.

Wilkinson, Loren, Peter DeVos, Calvin B. DeWitt, Eugene Dykema, Vernon Ehlers, Derk Pereboom, and Aileen Van Beilen. Earthkeeping: Christian Stewardship of Natural Resources. Grand Rapids: Eerdmans, 1980.

Wilkinson, Loren, Peter De Vos, Calvin B. DeWitt, Eugene Dykema, and Vernon Ehlers. Earthkeeping in the Nineties: Stewardship of Creation. Rev. ed. Grand Rapids: Eerdmans, 1991.

Wilson, R. McL. A Critical and Exegetical Commentary on Colossians and Philemon. The International Critical Commentary. New York: T&T Clark, 2005.

Wilson, Walter T. The Hope of Glory: Education and Exhortation in the Epistle to the Colossians. Novum Testamentum Supplement 88. Leiden: Brill, 1997.

Wink, Walter. Engaging the Powers. Minneapolis: Fortress, 1992.

Witherington III, Ben. Paul's Narrative Thought World: The Tapestry of Tragedy and Triumph. Louisville, Ky.: Westminster John Knox, 1994.

— — —. Women and the Genesis of Christianity. Cambridge: Cambridge University Press, 1990.

— — —. Women in the Earliest Churches. Society for New Testament Studies Monograph Series 59. Cambridge: Cambridge University Press, 1988.

Wrede, W. Paul. Translated by Edward Lumin. London: Philip Green, 1907.

Wright, N. T. The Climax of the Covenant. Edinburgh: T&T Clark, 1991.

— — —. The Epistles of Paul to the Colossians and to Philemon. Tyndale New Testament Commentaries. Leicester: InterVarsity, 1986.

— — —. Evil and the Justice of God. Downers Grove, Ill.: InterVarsity, 2006.

————. *Jesus and the Victory of God.* London: SPCK, 1996.

————. "Jesus Is Coming—Plant a Tree." In *The Green Bible,* I-72–I-85.

————. "The Letter to the Romans." In *The New Interpreter's Bible, Vol. 10,* edited by Leander E. Keck, 393–770. Nashville: Abingdon, 2002.

————. *New Heavens, New Earth: The Biblical Picture of Christian Hope.* Cambridge: Grove, 1999.

————. *The New Testament and the People of God.* London: SPCK, 1992.

————. *The Resurrection of the Son of God.* London: SPCK, 2003.

Yates, Roy. *The Epistle to the Colossians.* Epworth Commentaries. London: Epworth, 1993.

Young, Frances. *The Art of Performance: Towards a Theology of Holy Scripture.* London: Darton, Longman, & Todd, 1990.

Young, Frances, and David F. Ford. *Meaning and Truth in 2 Corinthians.* London: SPCK, 1987.

Young, Richard Alan. *Is God a Vegetarian? Christianity, Vegetarianism, and Animal Rights.* Chicago: Open Court, 1999.

Ziesler, John. *Paul's Letter to the Romans.* London: SCM Press, 1989.

Zimmermann, Ruben. "Jenseits von Indikativ und Imperativ. Entwurf einer 'impliziten Ethik' des Paulus am Beispiel des 1. Korintherbriefes." *Theologische Literaturzeitung* 132 (2007): 259–84.

INDEX OF BIBLICAL REFERENCES

INDEX OF AUTHORS

INDEX OF SUBJECTS

DATE DUE

261.8

Horrell & others

AUTHOR

Greening Paul

TITLE

DATE DUE	BORROWER'S NAME